Imagination and Realities

Nepal Between Past and Present

Imagination and Realities

Nepal Between Past and Present

Gérard Toffin

ADROIT

Adroit Publishers

New Delhi

ISBN : 978-81-87393-30-6

First Published in 2016

Published by
ADROIT PUBLISHERS
4675/21, Ganpati Bhawan, Ansari Road,
Daryaganj, New Delhi-110 002
Phone : 011-23266030

Distributors
AKHIL BOOK DISTRIBUTORS
email: akhilbooks@yahoo.com
akhilbks@gmail.com

Typesetting - Gaurav Graphics, New Delhi, INDIA
Printed at: Milan Graphics, New Delhi, INDIA

Preface

Life often hangs by a thin thread. This book was written before, during and in the aftermath of the two earthquakes (7.8 and 7.3 on the Richter scale) that devastated Nepal in April and May 2015. All of a sudden, on 25 April, just before noon, in the space of about thirty seconds, what had been feared by a large number of well-informed persons and scientists actually happened. A terrifying earthquake, not as strong as the one in January 1934 however, shook the country. A second quake, less violent, hit Nepal on the 12 May 2015. Tremors were felt on the subcontinent all the way to Chennai. Almost 9,000 persons died in Nepal and about 20,000 were wounded. There was massive devastation in the hills and middle mountains, from Gorkha in the west to Dolakha and Solukhumbu districts in the east, and in some old Newar settlements of the Kathmandu Valley. Monuments were reduced to rubble in a large part of central Nepal. The earthquakes wreaked damage in 14 of the country's 75 districts. About a fifth of Nepal's 28 million people were affected. Although most high-rise buildings in the Kathmandu Valley resisted, a number of them underwent such a serious structural damage that they were declared dangerous and are no longer habitable. Thousands of survivors were made homeless and forced to camp, day and night, for weeks under makeshift tents and tarpaulins, in open spaces for fear of aftershocks. People tried to consolidate their fissured homes by bracing the front and back with wooden beams.

Earthquakes, *bhūkampa*, are unfortunately a constituent part of Nepali history. Local chronicles testify to these unpredictable tectonic calamities over the ages. Nepali people commonly assert that a major *bhūkampa* occurs every century. Seismologists were expecting an even worst one, much stronger, making a far greater number of victims. And they do not exclude the fact that this might happen in the next few decades. Each earthquake brings its cohort of distress, sorrow, death and despair. The catastrophic event in 2015 was no exception. It caused enormous loss in terms of housing and infrastructures in the country. It also greatly affected people's morale: the Nepali population suffered serious psychological trauma during the weeks after 25 April. The earth shook nearly everyday for more than a month. The large number of Nepalis living abroad and the small foreign *bideshi* community with affective links to the Himalayan country watched with consternation, shock, and deep concern the tragic photographs and videos posted on Facebook, the Internet and other media. I myself was in Nepal a few weeks before the event and went back to Kathmandu Valley in July 2015. It is difficult to say where I wished I had been on 25 April.

The national disaster in 2015 will have considerable consequences, economically, socially and politically, in matters of tourism, schooling, people's livelihood, etc. over the years to come. At the moment, it is difficult to foresee the impact. Evaluating the consequences of past earthquakes in the course of history, even simply in political terms, is problematical.[1] According to the government, the overall damage is estimated at about $10 billion, nearly half of its gross domestic product (GDP) which amounts to $19.2. New national building regulations were promulgated in the aftermath, setting a height limit for new buildings.

At any rate, there will be a before and an after *bahattar sāl* (2072 BS in the local Vikram Sambat calendar), just as there was a before and an after for the last great earthquake in January 1934 (*nabbe sāl*, i.e; 1990 Vikram Sambat), of magnitude 8.2 on the Richter scale, at a time when Nepal was a secluded kingdom, forbidden to outsiders. In matters of construction, what was left of traditional dwellings before 2015 will no doubt disappear at a rapid pace with the growing use of cement and the adoption of modern architectural designs. In the hills, unsightly corrugated roofs are likely to totally replace traditional roofing materials (wood, slate, grass and tiles).

This tragedy has hastened the writing of the long-awaited constitution. On 8 June 2015, less than two months after the earthquake, the four main political parties (Nepali Congress, UML Communist, Madhesh Forum and UCPN Maoists) signed a 16-point agreement to draft a Constitution. They agreed to federate the country into eight provinces but they left the issue of the names of these federal provinces and of their boundaries to a later decision. On 30 June 2015, after a long and rather obscure process, a first draft of the constitution was tabled on the Constituent Assembly. The total absence of transparency in the deliberations has left the average Nepali fearing that "the constitution writing has been hijacked by a cabal of political leaders" (Kanak Dixit).[2] In the following weeks, this draft was submitted to the general public for discussion. It was subsequently amended in August 2015.

Backed by a coalition of three dominant parties (Nepali Congress, Communist Party of Nepal (UML), and Maoist (UCPN)), the constitution (*sambidhān*), was endorsed by the Constituent Assembly with an overwhelming majority, far above the required two-thirds majority, including a large number of Dalits (former untouchables), Ādivāsī/Janajāti ('indigenous' ethnic groups), Muslims and Madhesī (from Tarai plains), all of them members of three above-mentioned parties. Yet most Tarai political organizations (especially Loktantrik Madhesi Morcha) and Tharus (the so-called 'indigenous group' of these flatlands) expressed their dissents about the new federal mapping and other measures concerning citizenship. They did not sign the document. The Tharus in particular did not agree to their territory being split into two.

Finally, after much unrest and violent opposition in the southern flatlands (over 40 people died in clashes, among both protesters and security forces), the constitution was promulgated on 20 September 2015. The text consolidates democracy, the republic, and introduces a number of inclusive provisions. It consecrates the power of parliament and abandons the presidential system advocated by Maoists. The number of provinces, *pradesh*, is reduced to seven, the Tarai plains being split into five different units.

The state of Nepal is defined as "indivisible, sovereign, secular, inclusive, socialism-oriented". However some points are fuzzy or conservative. Women's demands concerning the transmission of Nepali citizenship to their children in case they married a foreigner for instance have not been fully satisfied. The foreign husband first has to take Nepali citizenship. And a single mother will have difficulty passing on her citizenship to her child. Similarly, a number of issues raised by Ādivāsī/Janajāti (about the right to land and to natural resources for instance) have been omitted altogether. According to Article 7.2, in the provinces, only the language spoken "by the majority" other than Nepali may be used as an official language. This is a restrictive clause towards other minority languages. Social rights and claims to equality are recognized but there is a lack of hierarchy among the large group of marginalised people listed in the bill (Article 18.3).[3]

Secularism is proclaimed, but it is ambiguously associated with the protection of *sanātana dharma*, a Hindu concept designating the righteous eternal religion, and sometimes used as an alternative term for Hinduism. This association is a major concession to those upper-caste Hindus who are in favour of a Hindu state, *hindu rāshtra*. The possibility of changing its religion from Hinduism to Christianity or Islam is therefore limited (article 31, 3), as was the case in previous constitutions. Restoring an ancient notion prevalent in Nepal during Rana and Shah rule reveals the continuity of the national politico-cultural repertoire, despite political changes. In addition, the cow (sacred for Hindus) is made, as before, the national animal. For a majority of Nepalis, the country's fundamental identity was at stake here.

In the matters of territorial reorganization, the federalizing process finally led to a revised and updated form of decentralisation linking the hills to the southern plains. It is more a lifting of the pre-existent mapping than a structural change. The provinces, *pradesh*, for instance, will have less powers than originally envisaged: their autonomy in matters of law, banking and foreign aid will be limited. Again in this field, the durability of ancient centralized structures has prevailed. The authors of the constitution obviously intend to counter the centrifugal forces within the country and to impose a more or less unitary framework that goes beyond ethnic and geographical identities. Chapter 1 and 2 of the present book will help to understand the politics that lie behind this new mapping.

Two comments need to be made right away. First, despite mass protests and acts of violence across the Tarai, the political elite from the hills has clearly dictated the enforced territorial reorganization to the inhabitants of the plains. Power has not been redistributed among the country's leading groups. The constitution remains hill-centric in its orientation. It reveals a mark of defiance vis-à-vis the Tarai, and, indirectly, towards India. Second, by approving the whole process, the Maoists will be regarded as blatant traitors by their former followers: Māobādī leaders have totally abandoned the defence of ethnic group territories (as well as the redistribution of land from large landholders to the landless). All in all, this federalization will dissatisfy a large number of Nepalis, in the Tarai as well as among Ādivāsī/Janajāti, even if adjustments are conceded after the promulgation. It is likely that the provinces' boundaries will remain a major issue at the heart of the state's political arena and, most probably, a source of lasting conflict.

There is nothing uncommon in this uncertain situation. All states, even democracy, are based on a balance of power. They express the domination of some groups, or the coalition of some groups over the rest of the population at a given moment in the course of history. The notion of social harmony is a myth.

Whatever happens in the future, these two events,—the earthquake and the proclamation of the constitution—will have far-reaching consequences on the lives and on the representations that Nepali people construct about themselves and their country. They will not only affect the realities of the nation, its economy, its political or demographic condition, but will also have a large bearing on people's imagination, their ideas through which they consider the state of the nation and its population—the narrative of Nepali people through the ages.

Postscript

The promulgation of the long-awaited constitution in September 2015 has engendered a severe crisis in Nepali-Indian relations and in the economy of the Himalayan country. Narendra Modi's government has decided to back Madhesīs groups in the Tarai plains who reject the new constitution and demand that state borders be redefined. Delhi has subsequently blocked the entry of goods into Nepal along its border (even if it denies this and argues that its truck drivers and freight forwarders have voiced worries about the deteriorating situation across the border). This embargo (Nepali: *nākābandī*) brings to mind the 15-month blockade that India imposed in 1989-1990 after the decision by Nepali authorities to buy sophisticated weapons from China. Just as 25 years ago, this hindrance has triggered a nationwide shortage of fuel, kerosene and gas.

The present crisis has jeopardised the livelihood of ordinary Nepali citizens, especially those living in urban centres. People were not able to go home to see their families during the Dasain (Dasherā) festival and they have now to rely on firewood for cooking instead of gas. Both sides of the border are now ruled by black-marketeers who smuggle feel with high profit margins. All over Nepal the prices of manufactured goods and basic foodstuffs have skyrocketed. The impact on the economy is such that experts are suggesting a possibility of negative fiscal year for 2015. Tourism and agriculture are particularly badly affected. The crisis, for instance, resulted in a shortage of chemical fertilizers and pesticides, and has disrupted market access to farm produces (Nepal Economic Forum).

These events clearly go to show Nepal's persisting dependency on its powerful southern neighbour as far as vital goods are concerned. In addition, the ongoing blockade has put a stop to the emergency reconstruction efforts in the wake of the April-May 2015 devastating earthquakes. So far demands by members of Nepali civil society and by governments in the European community to lift the embargo have gone unheard. In retaliation, cable TV operators in Nepal have blocked 42 Indian channels. As I prepare to send this manuscript to the editor, the situation is volatile in the Nepali Tarai plains and very tense between the two countries.

Endnotes

1 The history of earthquakes in Nepal is no longer simply traced using archives and *vamshāvalī* chronicles. Seismologists and geologists now use paleo-seismological logging of river-cut cliffs and trench walls to precisely date past earthquakes and to evaluate their intensity. See S. N. Sapkota, L. Bollinger, Y. Klinger, P. Tapponnier, Y. Gaudemer and D. Tiwari, "Primary surface ruptures of the great Himalayan earthquakes in 1934 and 1255", *Nature Geoscience* **6**, 71–76 (2013).

2 Kanak Dixit, "Feeling for Province Two", *The Kathmandu Post*, 14 August 2015.

3 Mukta Lama Tamang, "Forgotten promises", *The Kathmandu Post,* 21 September 2015.

Paris, 11 November 2015, Laxmī pūjā day

(25 Kārtik, 2072 Bikram Sambat).

Acknowledgments

I would first of all like to express my deep gratitude to Bernadette Sellers, CNRS Villejuif, who has revised all the papers brought together in this book. She has very often done more than simply improve my English. By pointing to some awkward expressions, she has prompted me to clarify my arguments. The form is never independent from the main arguments of a text.

In Nepal, I have received an enormous amount of help from friends and colleagues. Foremost among them are Shova Shakya, Anuj Rimal, Prasant Shresta and Raju Shakya. They have helped to collect and check a large corpus of information. They have also provided me with invaluable contacts in Kathmandu, Patan, which, all together, has broadened my mind and enabled me to follow new lines of research. My sincere thanks go to Nirmal Tuladhar, whose network and kindness are invaluable, to Mahesh Raj Pant, a former colleague at CNRS, now based in Samshodhana Mandala, and to Pranaya Shumsher J.B. Rana, who has read and commented some parts of the manuscript. I am indebted also to Dipak Gyawali, Pramod Raj Sedhain, Deepak Thapa, Rajendra Pradhan, Bihari Krishna Shrestha, Kamal Prakash Malla, Ashmina Ranjit, Komal Citrakar, Kurchi Dasgupta, Sita Rana Magar, Manju Tuladhar, Maheshraj Maharjan, Prof. Ganesh Man Gurung, Sujeev Shakya, Shristi Timilsina, Padma Ratna Tuladhar, Madhab Lal Maharjan, Monalisa Maharjan, Prof. Om Gurung, Riddhi Baba Pradhan, late Min Bahadur Shakya, Kanako Nakagawa, Anita

Maharjan, Sulochana Chwaju, Niraj Lawoju, Mrigrendra Bahadur Karki and Narmadeswar Pradhan. They all provided me with assistance in one or several aspects of my research. Some of them have suggested some clarifications and have supplied information on one or several topics. Prasant Shrestha has kindly given me permission to reproduce a photograph of an image of Indra he took in Panauti. Satya Mohan Joshi has been a remarkable guide in matters of Newar theatre and performances. In Hyderabad, India, Dr Kamal K. Misra kindly commented a first draft of one the articles published here.

Within CNRS, Villejuif, I am much obliged to Philippe Ramirez, Olivia Aubriot, Tristan Buslé, Joelle Smadja and Daniela Berti, who occasionally read some drafts. They rightly suggested some modifications or pointed out some parallels in other parts of the Himalayas.

I would also like to mention the warm welcome that my articles received at *The Kathmandu Post*, where most of the pieces published here first appeared. A particular mention must go to Akhilesh Upadhya, Gyanu Adhikari, and Pranaya J.B. Rana.

Last but not least, I am greatly indebted to Davender Sharma, Akhil Sharma and all the team at Adroit Publishers in Delhi for the preparation and the finalisation of this book.

Contents

Introduction: Nepal Revisited

Ideas and Realities

This book, *Imagination and Realities,* aims to paint a comprehensive portrait of contemporary Nepal through various geographical, social and cultural aspects, whether real or imagined, pragmatic or ideal, all of which plays a fundamental role in the manifold national fabric. The study basically combines culture, politics and society in a broad comparative perspective. I wish to go beyond academic boundaries and to open new perspectives.

The realities of the country are multi-faceted. They include first and foremost the Himalayan summits which foreign high-budget expeditions and semi-professional Sherpas climb every year. They also concern the low plains in the south, which are poorly integrated into the rest of the country, and so close to India that the prospect of a much-needed international airport in this area is problematical for security and political reasons. In between, they encompass the steep rural middle hills that have given birth over the ages to an original, distinctive multi-ethnic and multi-caste culture. Moreover, let us not forget in this depiction the densely populated (about 3.5 million inhabitants) and the polluted Kathmandu Valley that was the home of a brilliant urban civilisation in the Middle Ages and is still replete with elegant temples and historic monuments.

This does not make up the whole picture however. Various

clichés are commonly associated with Nepal. A smiling honest people, who readily refer to you as "brother" or "sister"; hard-working peasants fond of public gatherings, feasts and festivals, and, to mention just one of their typical cultural features in central and western regions, their *dohorī* alternate songs sung by men and women; a lost Eden of religious pluralism and tolerance; the realm of Shiva and his ascetics; a paradise for trekkers, botanists, bird-watchers and linguists in search of languages that are spoken only by a minority; a failed state, abandoned by an increasing number of migrants who look for asylum abroad; corrupt bureaucrats and narrow-minded self-centred politicians; one of the poorest countries in the world where the collective sum of remittances from thousands of migrants in the Gulf and Malaysia is slowly exceeding the income from the traditional rural economy and from agricultural produce; and last but not least, one of the last strongholds of communist ideology. Are these statements stereotypes or realities? What is the role of imagination in the most familiar perceptions of Nepal?

Beyond these various representations, the most striking and blatant reality of Nepal is the huge divide that exists between rural zones and urban centres [**83**]. The contrast is even more marked in remote mountainous regions that are difficult to access. The dissimilarities between these two worlds extend to nearly almost all aspects of social and cultural life. Even if they have become increasingly "urban" in their traditional milieu, peasants (81.8 per cent of the total population) mostly live according to an ancient natural rhythm that is fixed by the seasons and the agricultural calendar. By contrast, urbanites (18.2 per cent) have developed a modern style of living, housing, transport, and occupation. Urban dwellers are dressed differently and are consumers of imported commodities that epitomize modern life. This all-important rift is mentioned several times in the book and each time its sociological consequences are discussed. Obviously, the situation of women differs in these two contrasted universes: it is much more circumscribed and determined by ancient laws in villages. Similarly, city enclaves are much less entrenched than rural areas in the segregationist caste system.

Despite its exceptional biological and human diversity, its high tourism potential, the economic and political realities are bleak. What does the future hold for a country so poorly endowed with economic resources, so heavily dependent on foreign aid and so tightly sandwiched between two mammoth rather expansionist states? *Imagination and Realities* is my attempt to bring all these issues into focus and to answer these questions by means of a long-term historical perspective. Nepal certainly has happy, delightful, brilliant, insouciant aspects but also a dark, shady, often hidden side (conspiracy, assassination, hideous crimes, all-pervading corruption, poor governance, and dependency links), which from time to time has led the country to disaster.

Nepal and South Asia

With its history and populations, its culture and religion (mainly Hinduism and Buddhism), this Himalayan state belongs resolutely to South Asia. People, commodities, ideas, religions have always circulated between the southern plains and the northern Himalayan mountains. There is still intense movement back and forth today. Indeed, Nepal cannot be dissociated from the culture and the history of India. With the latter it shares the classical Sanskrit tradition—which is both Hindu and Buddhist—as well as the extreme diversity of the subcontinent's socio-cultural context which is sometimes far removed from ancient sacred texts. The two countries have close links. What happens in India is likely to have immediate repercussions in Nepal.

One particular feature of Nepal is sometimes mentioned: the fact that this country has never been colonized. Admittedly, the Himalayan kingdom maintained its independence from the East India Company in the eighteenth and nineteenth centuries and was never subjected to British colonial rule. However, this statement requires further discussion. Following the Sugauli Treaty (1816), Kathmandu agreed to the presence of a British residency in the capital and adopted a relentless pro-British policy allowing, among many other things, the recruitment of Gorkha soldiers into the British colonial army. Moreover, Rana rulers accepted a subservient status to the British Crown, and in 1857, during the Sepoy Revolt, they rushed to the help of the colonial rulers in India. By and large, this situation of dependence was not that different from the indirect rule enforced by the British Rāj in India. Thus, Nepal definitely has its place in nineteenth-century South-Asian colonial history. This book aims to reconsider the country in the light of this common past.

There is one difference, however: Nepal did not witness the emergence of a powerful nationalist movement to counter a foreign colonialist force occupying the country, as was the case in India. The question of nationalism in India is a contentious and delicate subject. It has been said that the anti-colonial fight was mainly the politics of the urban educated anglicised elite that presumed to speak on behalf of the country's rural population.[1] Yet nationalist ideas have been defended by charismatic leaders and have rapidly become part of the nation's political memory (with variations depending on the region). On the other hand, in Nepal, oppositional political forces rallied against the autocratic and oligarchic Rana system, which was finally overthrown in 1951. India became more or less successfully united through its nationalist movement and its legendary leaders, whereas its Himalayan neighbour fought an internal war exclusively within its political elite. This contrast needs to be borne in mind when studying Nepal's present difficulties and its incapacity to unite its people towards a common political goal.

This book furthermore sets out to situate this Himalayan country not only in relation to its Asian neighbours—mainly India—but more generally to today's increasingly interconnected world. And indeed a parallel is constantly drawn with the Western world. I have long been convinced that a state like Nepal cannot be fully understood without resorting to a broader evaluation which is not restricted exclusively to the countries concerned but is open to those separated in geographical space and time.

Social Change

This book stems from the need for clarification in the study of social change. It complements my previous work on the subject.[2] I seek to understand the recent tumultuous changes taking place in the country, as well as the shift from a traditional monarchy to a republic, which represents a turnaround in local history [Ch. **11**]. More generally speaking, I discuss the gradual opening of the country since the fall of the Rana oligarchy in 1951—which in Nepali is called *sāt sāl*, i.e. 2007 in the country's official Vikram Sambat calendar—and the subsequent internal changes it brought about. This process has considerably broadened mindscapes and lived geographies. It has broken a number of boundaries, even if it has also triggered new socio-political closures and barriers.

Since Nepal opened its borders to the outside world, it has been undergoing a transitional period, shifting from an old traditional pre-modern socio-cultural order to the present globalized, internationalized modern world. A large part of the country still lives according to old traditions but another part—the younger generation, the middle class, urban areas—has already set a foot in the modern world. People face unstable and fractured societal realities; in cities they challenge new trends that influence urban life. Moreover, the nation-state is experimenting with a process of democratization and is instituting new federal units. At the same time, it has to tackle the rise of new collective identities and a surge in social movements that are emerging on the margins of society, such as among the Dalit community. It is also facing the ever-growing process of globalization and the thousands of people out-migrating in search of employment. The number of those who have left the country for this reason over the last two decades amounts to 3.45 million.[3] These Nepali expatriates have, over time, developed intense nostalgia for the world they have left behind.

By and large, reflecting on change, on its parameters and processes lies at the very heart of my work here. My aim is to comprehend the phenomena of resilience and

structural transformations within some specific and well-circumscribed contexts. The strength of religion, its importance in social and private life, for instance, persists in spite of secularizing forces. Religious representations still shape people's minds. However, a wind of change is now blowing, especially in urban areas [28]. A number of new organizations are emerging. They focus on the self and on happiness to the detriment of former rituals and godly images. As far as values and codes of conduct are concerned, any analysis therefore has to take into account both the constant changes and innovations, and the routinized practices and beliefs that have so far shaped a great variety of Nepali trajectories. Throughout the book I argue that the changes that are blatantly noticeable in urban centres have met with remarkable resistance at family and caste level.

To explore the subject, I have relied empirically on my numerous years of fieldwork (from 1970 to today) in rural and urban areas of the Kathmandu Valley, in the districts of Nuwakot and Dhading, Gulmi and Argha Khanchi, and my trips to many other parts of Nepal, including the eastern Tarai for my research among Pranāmīs. My whole array of experiences provides for comparisons and proposals regarding more general issues. However the bulk of the documentation under consideration here was collected over the last six years, from 2009 to 2015, among various families that belong to the Kathmandu Valley urban middle class, especially Newars but also Parbatiyās. I worked mostly in Patan but I also followed some families in Panauti, Bhaktapur and Kathmandu. The data on which this study is based are therefore, for the most part, hitherto unpublished.

Closed and Open Society

Theoretically, they are many ways of analysing the transitional period which Nepal is currently undergoing, between the pre-1951 Rana age and today's modern era. I would like to suggest one possible reading frame in terms of *closed/open society*. These two concepts, which were especially formulated by Karl Popper, the British philosopher of science, in his book *The Open Society and its Enemies* (1945), belong more to the field of philosophy and sociology than to ethnography. Yet they have proved appropriate in understanding the process of change that occurs in a number of developing countries, including contemporary Nepal, which is still rooted in pre-modern patterns of life. These concepts, which at first sight may appear to be old-fashioned, seem to me to be much more useful than the common dichotomy of tradition (a disputable word) versus modernity.

A particularly relevant illustration of the concept of closed society, [or social closure], within Nepal is the periodical claustration of a number of rural communities for ritual purposes at certain fixed times of the year. Ethnographers have described the centrality of this phenomenon among various ethnic groups in Nepal, such as the Tharus, the Gurungs, the Magars.[4] Even today, in some Newar Jyāpu villages of the Kathmandu Valley, not far from the urban centres, some localities are closed to outsiders (even Nepalis) on some ritual occasions, especially at night-time. This is the case of Pyangaon village (Lalitpur District), for instance, on the eleventh day of the month of Bhādau (August-September), during the bright fortnight. This day marks the start of the local annual festival. Villagers who, over the past year, have mourned the death of a child of less than three months old have to distribute curd to all the households in the village.[5] Extreme purity, *pavitra*, is necessary in the locality during that particular evening and night. This occasional seclusion from the outside world is commonplace in many tribal zones of South East Asia.[6] It serves to reinforce social links within the community as well as between the villagers and the local tutelary deities. During the ritual period of closure, evils spirits are supposed to be driven away from the village.

Geographical mobility across the borders, especially between India and Nepal, or the northern Nepali enclaves and Tibet, is an age-old phenomenon in these Himalayan regions and dates back at least to the eighteenth century. People were forced to travel and to emigrate temporarily (or permanently) to sustain their livelihoods and to complement a rather limited production from a mountain agro-system. Dirk Kolff, in his study *Naukar, Rajput, and Sepoy* (1990), describes a military labour market that existed throughout the subcontinent from the fifteenth through to the nineteenth century. Poverty-stricken dwellers of the Himalayan foothills would leave their villages to seek employment and to enrol in the army of a regional *rāja*. Gurkha mercenary recruits who enrolled in the British army from the beginning of the nineteenth century onwards are to be seen in the same light. In all these cases, crossing the border, especially between India (Muglān) and Nepal, was synonymous with suffering, treachery (*dhokhā*) and despair. Journeys to the south sometimes called for long rituals of purification on return [**25**]. Countries outside Nepal were still conceived as being a major source of impurity (*apavitratā*).[7]

In the same way, as C. Fürer-Haimendorf has clearly shown, trans-Himalayan trade back and forth between the north and south, dates back a long time.[8] Mountain communities have been closely involved in these economic movements which ultimately set the pace of their annual cycle of life. As a matter of fact, the closure of Nepal during the Rana period was mainly political and directed at Westerners. It did not prevent the population from moving around inside the country, except towards the capital, the centre of power, and its immediate surrounding area. In former periods, the Kathmandu Valley boasted a highly cosmopolitan civilization that welcomed travellers and migrants from the north as well as the south. In many aspects, it was already an open society.

What happened from the mid-twentieth century onwards represents a change of scale, of destination and of the volume of mobility. Geographical mobility became widespread and benefited from the expanding road network and the development of aeronautics in the country. Over the last decades, migrations to the Gulf and to Malaysia, and to many other destinations all over the planet, have been a constantly growing phenomenon. The archipelagos of interlinked Nepalese diasporas across the world play a bigger role in social events. New forms of cosmopolitanism undermine the social closures and the semi-hermetic social boundaries of the past. What is more, these flows of population are accompanied by other forms of openness. The number of inter-caste marriages for instance is on the rise. Nepal is increasingly becoming an open society—with its promise of a brilliant future, but also its uncertainties—in the modern sense of the term.

This flux and these forms of hybridity testify to the ongoing radical changes in the social fabric as well as in mindscapes. They have introduced flexibility in former codes, new ideas in mentalities and they are slowly transforming social relationships. The opening of the country's market to new products and the Westernisation of lifestyles are also engendering profound changes. The celebration of mobility and of trans-border networks tends to erase former closed links and self-centred groups.[9] Social introversion does of course subsist in many places—not only in remote rural regions (with their strongly identifiable neighbourhoods, even traditional Newar towns constitute pockets of resistance)—and the process of development sometimes induces a reaction in the form of isolationism. However, the main trend is indeed towards more openness.

Admittedly, the concept of "open society" may be contested or relativized in some ways. Isis (Dahesh), the Islamic State, is thus socially speaking a closed society, virtually a clandestine group when it acts outside its own territory in Syria and Irak. However, the Internet and other modern media enable its members to broaden their influence worldwide. In modern society, the boundaries between "open" and "closed" are much more blurred than in the past. This is an indisputable fact. And yet, when the social and economic situation is viewed from an historical perspective, the analytical potential of the dichotomy under discussion remains strong, at least as an ideal-type conceptualisation.

What is more, the opposition between closed and open society goes well beyond any spatial connotations. It exceeds issues of boundaries, ghettoization, increasing circulation of people all over the world and cross-border connectivity. In Karl Popper's view, the notion heightens major sociological transformations. The passage from a closed to an open society particularly implies the shift from organic, tribal communities in which human beings are subject to strict collective social rules, to societies in which individuals are confronted with personal decisions and where freedom of thought is encouraged. Politically, the British philosopher saw in this change a necessary passage from authoritarian or dictatorial systems to democracy and, from a religious viewpoint, to more pluralist outlooks. An open society is oriented towards depersonalized relationships with no face-to-face encounters (such as those experienced on Facebook or in techniques of artificial insemination which leads to more abstraction in social relations). More often than not, the result is isolation and anxiety. That is the reason why lost unity is never forgotten and from time to time conservationist ideologies call for a return to the primeval organic social state. Reactionary forces in particular are frequently disconcerted by the instability and rapid social change that an open society unleashes.

This model applies relatively well to Nepal. The Himalayan country has experienced not only a change of political system but also major transformations in the social structure, lending more flexibility to social relations. Contemporary (*samasāmayik*) Nepali culture and society can be regarded as being torn between closed, communitarian forces and a more open, democratic pull. The social fabric is changing and old social bonds are often broken. Such an approach is akin to Louis Dumont's opposition between the holistic traditional world and modern individualist society, yet it has the advantage of not overly stressing the prevalence of hierarchy in holistic societies. In fact, in matters of hierarchy and egalitarianism, huge differences exist between the caste system and segmentary tribal societies. These two types of "closed society" cannot be considered as hierarchical in the same way or to the same extent. The conflation of them into one category is a disputable aspect of Dumont's theory. In addition, the notion of open society is better suited to analysing the current process of the globalization of ideas and goods, and the accelerated movement of persons worldwide.

One point, however, needs to be underlined. From a socio-political viewpoint, democratic society is the most achieved form of open society. This political regime creates the most favourable conditions for the largest circulation of goods, news and people within its territory. In striking contrast, authoritarian, dictatorial regimes, both past and present, tend to curb the free transmission not only of news but also sometimes of goods and exchanges between individuals in the country. As rightly pointed out by Louis Dumont,[10] these anti-democratic regimes can be seen as holistic reinforcements against local autonomous bodies and the rise of individualism. This is particularly the case of communist countries which impose a top-down control of social bonds, destroying any opportunity for popular protests. The tension between local aspirations and the dictatorial communist structure is especially striking in China. In Nepal, the 1990 democratic turn has positively resolved the internal contradiction between the post-Rana opening of the country and the holistic anti-democratic panchayat structure.

The Rise of the Individual

A concurrent issue linked to this social metamorphosis runs through a number of chapters in this book. Here I refer to the rise of the individual in the currently transformed and increasingly open Nepali society. Modernization and the rapid pace of globalisation have released the self from old social bonds.[11] Ties to caste, family and other basic ascribed organisations have been weakened by new social groupings, hybridity and newly achieved status based on merit and personal initiative. There is a growing need for individual freedom in art, business, science, and many other areas as well. Individuals now strive more and more to be free to think and to revise their failed plans and impressions in the light of experiences and more critical thought. These transformations create new forms of initiative and liminality in social actions, especially among urban middle-class people and the younger generation. It is worth noting in this concern that transnational contexts play an increasingly important role in shaping social identities among young people.

Despite this, Nepal is still made up, for the most part, of traditional forms of belonging. Collective identities play a salient role in all circumstances. On the whole, values revolve around the group, whereas Western cultures globally promote autonomy, regardless of the huge variations observed from one country to another. This opposition does not have to be reified but neither should it be ignored. The dialectics between the self and the community is therefore a vital process which needs to be thoroughly examined. Such tension traverses the whole book and provides the study with a broader perspective.

The Work of Imagination

The first topic of this book is therefore change and resilience. A second theme runs through this volume. It focuses on the work of imagination, the *imaginary*, in Nepali society and its historical development. What does this notion encompass and what project do I have in mind? For the study at hand, the usual definition of the term "imagination" as found in dictionaries: "The ability to imagine things that are not real (or which are not present to the senses)" is not quite precise enough. Broadly speaking, this aptitude designates the cognitive capacity to form a sort of mental representation of a particular thing. It is therefore closely linked to consciousness and intellectual activity. As understood here, the concept is very far from the error-prone faculty sometimes attributed to imagination, to the exclusion of all other connotations. The creations of the imagination do not automatically annihilate, destroy, or disavow reality by creating a kind of fantastic non-reality. They also help to decipher the empirical world. They are a condition for all thought and part of reality.

Yet a certain vagueness subsists in the terms. A large number of works in the field of philosophy of the mind and psychology have tried, for instance, to differentiate between this concept and related notions of perceiving, conceiving, desiring and believing. Cognitive and experimental sciences have clarified some determining points but without covering the manifold realities of this human faculty. The varieties of imagination are almost infinite and discourage all clear-cut taxonomies. This is obviously a slippery concept.[12]

I will leave these cognitive issues aside. In the present undertaking, imagination/imagery will be considered mostly in its relation to contemporaneous realities and socio-cultural backgrounds. What interests me here is developing a socio-anthropological perspective on social imagination; and more notably its role and function in daily life, in cultural patterns and in social action. In actual fact, the realm of imagination covers very different aspects and forms. For the sake of clarity, I will take the word in its broader sense that encompasses four other concepts to which it is closely related. 1°) *The representation of reality*, i.e. the mental image of a perceived external reality. To imagine something is to form a particular sort of mental representation of that thing. As such, representations are intrinsically linked to the general process of abstraction and play a role in the production of knowledge. This is the basic elementary level in all mental imagery. 2°) *The symbolic* or *symbolic function*, which refers to any acknowledged system of values and significations, is the basis of most religions throughout the world. Codes give an object its proper meaning. 3°) *Fiction*, which mostly pertains to the world of literature, theatre and cinema. It includes the lavish world of man-made images, both in the folk and literate world, and the way it has evolved through the ages. 4°) *The ideological*, that is the investment of political or religious purposes for a specific type of imaginary, such as eschatological or revolutionary. This instrumentalisation alters and perverts the real and carries political meaning.

One of my basic points therefore is that the symbolic function (which gives meaning to words and concrete realities) may be considered as being encompassed by the notion of imagination. For the simple reason that everything thought has first to be imagined. With this functional quadripartite architecture now in place, let me reveal the core ideas I wish to develop. By and large, imagination is one of the organizing principles of human action. It is deeply entrenched in social practices and productive of them in a number of cases. As Cornelius Castoriadis claimed, every society institutes itself through the creation of "social imaginary constructions".[13] Fiction and other fabrications of the mind belong both to the infrastructure and to the superstructure of societies.[14]

I contend that Nepal is both intrinsically real and imaginatively produced. It is imaginatively produced primarily on the basis of South Asian indigenous concepts but also by Western utopia and fancies (e.g. Marxism). Rather than conveying real past events, the fictive and the imaginary have played a vital role for instance in social unrest and in political stakes. Myths based on revolution and on supposedly necessary violence to erase an old political system are powerful motors of change. This has been the case in Nepal just as in other countries. Maoist guerrillas were moved by a feeling (that indeed corresponded to the truth) of being blatantly ignored by the State, as well as by the glorious imagery about people's revolution and its heroes.

As a rule, mental images are all-important in the daily praxis of individuals and groups, even in situations of absolute material necessity. Gender studies in Nepal and India, for instance, have furthered the role of constructed ideas and stereotypes of mainly a religious nature, therefore perpetuating women's subordinate position. In addition, all artefacts and routine objects have a symbolic dimension that bestows meaning on them. Religion and other representations guide individuals and provide them with grounds to act upon. They are supposed to protect individuals against unseen dangerous forces. These forms of social imagination constitute the cement of society, uniting people who belong to the same culture around common ideals and shared ideas. They have a real bearing on social practices.

The quadripartite scheme proposed above has to be viewed from an historical perspective. Imagination does not operate in quite the same way when different historical eras and periods are taken into consideration. In his *Theory of the Novel* (1916), the literary theorist and influential philosopher György Lukács (1885-1971) showed, for instance, how fiction which is specific to the modern novel is linked to the gradual emergence of modern times that are characterised both by the fragmentation of the social order and the isolation of the individual. Well before Karl Popper, he opposed this fragmented society to the "closed" organic society of the past where the individual is embedded in a homogenous social and cultural order. In closed traditional society, the sets of elements are meaningfully interrelated in such a way that the essence of each element can only be understood in relation to the others'.

Here there is a strong link to the first theme in our book: social change and modernity. Lukács further demonstrated that Cervantes's *Don Quixote* (first published in Spanish in 1605) reflects this strategic shift with his ambiguous and lonesome hero, which is a far cry from traditional models of integrated societies and traditional epic texts. In this case, as in others, societal disintegration triggers a dichotomy between individual emotions and objective facts. Such a disjunction gives rise to heroic forms of denial of social reality. The novel—an important component of imagination in its fictive form—is an attempt at dealing with the absence of this relationship between life and essence within a totality. As we will see, it is possible to see the emergence of a new Nepali literature (as in the case of many other countries) in the light of this opposition [**39**].

Later, the French philosopher Michel Foucault validated this view and elaborated on it. He sees *Don Quixote,* the picaresque Spanish novel, a monument of world literature, as the result of a fracture, a separation between words and things (*The Order of Things: An Archaeology of the Human Sciences*, New York, 1973). This historical perspective is crucial. A few pages on from here I provide another diachronic example in opposing symbolic thought and ideology. Obviously, modernity is characterised by a loss of totality.

Self-Perception and Social Science

The vision that people have of their lives, of the place where they reside and of the current transformations they are undergoing is a particularly interesting topic, directly linked to the study of imagery constructions. It definitively plays a role in the changes themselves, whether these ideas induce innovations or whether they slow them down. Anthropologists have stressed the importance of self-perceptions of changes among local groups.[15]

However, as I show in the following chapters, these visions themselves are very often plural. They vary according to sex, class, caste and other parameters that define the person concerned. In other terms, they reflect more basic social phenomena of which they are the manifestations. Nepali people, for instance, have many different ideas about China and the Chinese, about the West and Americans, or, to return to our privileged theme, about changes, *parivartan*. Most members of upper-Hindu castes are likely to lay emphasis on the general decline of moral values during the Kali Yuga era of decay, peasants would lament the deterioration of their conditions and the decline in agriculture due to modernity, the young middle urban class would mention the multiple benefits they have derived from change, whereas their parents would grieve over the loss of traditions (though this concern has also been observed among younger generations).

And what about the poorest migrants and the pitiful conditions they face in order to sustain their impoverished families? *Dukha*, suffering, physically and mentally, is both a cultural perception, which covers many other realms in the Nepali imagination, and a description of a harsh reality. Mallika Shakya recently recalled how important this notion is in classical Nepali literature, especially in the *Munā-Madan* epic penned by Laxmi Prasad Devkota (1936)[16] as well as in contemporary Nepali novels.[17] In these literary works, *dukha* imagery is associated with Nepali life abroad and with the relatives left behind at home. This concept is indeed a constituent part of the Nepali identity, both past and present.

How does one cope with all these divergent views and self-perceptions? Social science actually starts when these more or less imaginary conceptions and conceptual representations are confronted with empirical realities and with socio-cultural backgrounds. Otherwise, they remain anecdotal, superficial, or wholly idealistic just as most cognitivist propositions may, unfortunately, be regarded. Anthropology is not psychology. It is a confrontation between imaginary productions and realities.

Manifold Realities and the Imaginary

Most of the manifold realities that Nepali and other Himalayan people deal with are therefore impregnated with images, symbols and religious representations, i.e. imaginary productions. The mental is never separate from the material. This is particularly the case of concepts of time and space to which I have devoted a number of studies over the years. I have thus demonstrated how, in Nepal (as in India), the traditional idea of town, *nagar* or *purī*, is permeated with cosmological ideas and with political devices which try to promote the status of royal settlements.[18] In the same vein, I have shown how the forest in most Nepali cultures is infused with supernatural entities and submerged with images of wilderness. Woodland areas and the "jungle" are regarded with fear, yet at the same time with a certain appeal and passion.[19] They are invested with a combination of material realities and imagination. These sacred geographies have a considerable bearing on daily life and on religious practices.

Here, I address a new topic in my research; it focuses on traditional and modern theatre. In Nepal, just as in India, theatre, *nātak*, and dance play a particularly important role in social and religious life. It is in fact a realm where the two opposed worlds of truth and fiction are precariously balanced. Stage performances and acting are fully relevant to our discussion which addresses the interplay between imagination and certainties.

In short, one conclusion to my current research is that, by and large, the role of imagination is at least just as important in modern life and in present styles of performance as in pre-modern times. It can even be considered that the role of fictionalized narratives and artificial realities is greater in modern, open types of societies. From a social perspective, the texture of relationships between individuals is no longer woven out of face-to-face encounters but out of much broader relationships (belonging to the national community, for instance) which can only be conceptualized by the imagination. In the same way, indigenous movements in the quest for an ethnic sense of unity are founded on imagined constructions that extend well beyond the village viewpoint or circumscribed valley, to include transnational communities living in different corners of the world. They are grounded on global and territorialized fictive bonds. As Arjun Appadurai claimed: "The imagination is now central to all forms of agency, is itself a social fact, and is the key component of the new social order" (1996: 31).[20]

I will, however, go a step further than Appadurai. It seems to me than in close, self-contained societies, the imagination belongs more to the realm of the *symbolic*: it is enclosed within a fixed set of images and conceptions. In our present modern, often transnational social outlook, the imagination extends well beyond fixed boundaries; it navigates in an open-ended universe. It belongs more to the realm of purely *fictionalized constructions* or to the *ideological*; it is more susceptible to alterations and sudden change than in the past. Moreover, in most cases, imagery portraying the nation, democracy, republicanism and class conflict takes on new significance, challenging mythological and spiritual allegories. It moves and fills people with more enthusiasm than religions of the past, save religious fundamentalisms. Despite their flexibility and reversibility, the reverberations of these narratives may be far-reaching and all-important.

Similarly, our lives are increasingly linked to fictive representations, including films, novels and performances. As far as modern media (especially the Internet) are concerned, they shape new representations and engender new relationships between fancy and reality. We will come back to these issues in the epilogue.

Imagination and Memory

By the same token, my interest lies in the impact of reconstructed pasts and imagined recollections. Let me take a more general view of these issues. Memory often proceeds by way of imagery: remembering, for instance, is closely related to imagining. People's memories rarely constitute a veridical record of past personal experiences. Despite this, they play a crucial role in the construction of the self and in personal histories. From a broader perspective, the issue here pertains to relentless dialectics between failing to remember real facts and consecutive fictional conceptions that lie at the juncture between objectivity and subjectivity. When realities prove misleading and political objectives fail to be met, there is a need to rely increasingly on the imagination and to make new plans which more often than not take the form of a return to the past. Traditions are often reinvented for a new purpose.

I intend to decipher the current Nepali situation in the light of these restructurings of the past and of intermittent memory. Although they are an integral part of reality, imagined horizons are often underestimated in social analysis. This book intends to compensate for this shortcoming and to focus on the repertoire of imagination and visions of the past. To quote the French medieval historian Jacques Le Goff who, in his work, expresses a marked interest in anthropology: "A history without imagination is a mutilated and disincarnated history".[20] "The history of imaginary seeks to understand what motives people to think, to act and to feel. It deals with history of mentalities and sensitivities".[21] To paraphrase him, I would assert that analysing society and culture without scrutinizing the creative imaginative forces at work lacks, both sociologically and anthropologically, substance and merely appertains to rules, regulations and normative aspects. I have broadened the scope here by taking into account the frequent manipulations of social objectives by politicians, activists and minority groups. In this respect, the field of contentious memories, which is crucial in contemporary Nepal, is particularly fertile.

Unity and Diversity

Nepal is not only made up of Hindus—the great majority of the population—but also of Buddhists, Christians, Muslims, and of various followers of tribal cults. One can go from an almost capitalist caste of traders and investors to a rural community of orthodox Brahmans or to a hard-to-reach self-contained inwardlooking ethnic group, and then to almost illiterate "untouchables" or peasants, with highland herders some way in between. The country is extremely diverse and its internal fragmentation partly due to the compartmentalized local topography has few equivalents in the world. There is therefore a real danger when speaking about Nepal "as a whole".

I am convinced, however, that general laws are at work throughout the country, obviously not with the same momentum from one group to another or from one region to another, but for the most part in the same direction. Sociologically speaking, Nepal is not a world of singularities. The official discourse glorifying diversity hides a powerful underground process of general standardization. Endangered minority languages which are now spoken by fewer and fewer people are an example worth mentioning in this respect.

Theoretical Orientation and Methodology

The hundred or so short pieces compiled here are all documented and scholarly constructed. They are organized into thirteen comprehensive interrelated chapters focusing on culture, society, politics, and the environment. These chapters explore various socio-cultural phenomena through the lens of sociology, social anthropology and history. Religious practices, pilgrimages, sacred epic texts, urban spaces, theatre, politics (especially democracy and revolutionary issues), ethnicity, museums, politics of memory, and many other topics on which I have personally carried out research, have in turn been thoroughly investigated. As far as the methodology is concerned, I constantly switch back and forth from theory to empirical studies. The whole book aims at portraying contemporaneous Nepal somewhere between the past and present, between a closed and open globalized world. It is hoped that the book will help to reflect on this country in a more comprehensive manner than before.

Instead of seeking a vain and delusive elementary structure of human cognitive abilities to explain the cultural diversity of human beings, my perspective privileges social and cultural analysis. It would be a serious mistake to study social processes from an ahistorical and dogmatic viewpoint. The infinite socio-cultural diversity of the world cannot be simply reduced to preordained, ill-defined ideal or exclusively logical categories. This universalizing, so-called "ontological" method, developed by Philippe Descola[23] and others, such as Eduardo Viveiros de Castro, relies excessively on Eurocentric paradigms. The term "ontology" itself is inappropriate for most Eastern philosophies (Indian, Chinese, etc.), which deal much more with cosmologies than with beings.

A rigid framework is therefore inappropriate. Such a scheme cannot apply to the diversity of the ethnographic situation throughout the world. It is dangerous to de-territorialize culture and to reason independently from any contextually informed situation. When restricted to cognitivist capacities, the power of abstraction is better suited to mathematics and philosophy than to anthropology and social sciences. That is why, in the following chapters, I substantiate a series of dialectics between the real and the imaginary, taking concrete examples and giving priority to a sociological understanding of situations. My approach is context-dependent.

Some readers will perhaps object to or regret the fragmentary form of the book. My response is that each essay is the result of years of research and constant elaboration. Each was worked and reworked several times before the finishing touches were made. Some pages of this book have been reformulated more than ten times. Altogether, the viewpoint adopted here, that is putting each theme historically and culturally into perspective is, in my opinion, an original undertaking in the present state of research. The reader will discover in this constellation of texts valuable material and relevant concepts to fully analyse Nepal's current political, cultural and economic upheavals. In addition, the organization of the volume allows the reader to navigate freely through the book. They can start reading anywhere and then skip a few chapters before coming back to an earlier point at their guise.

From a methodological viewpoint, I consider myself at the crossroads between anthropology, sociology and history. In this respect, *Imagination and Realities* fully illustrates my present approach, which is basically multidisciplinary. I consider that the present changes occurring in South Asia cannot be understood through the prism of anthropology alone. Data from the past must also be taken into account and a broader perspective on the evolution of society must be introduced. A mono-disciplinary standpoint is therefore inadequate, especially when the researcher pleads the specificity of their anthropological perspective to exempt them from the exigencies of other social sciences. I must admit that my views have evolved considerably over the decades, especially since my first monographic study on Pyangaon village which was published in 1977. These changes have been nurtured by my more recent global studies in an urban context, especially among the middle class and occasionally among remarkable anglicized members of the upper class. The course of my research since my first years in Nepal has in fact been characterized by a constant broadening of the scope of my interests and methodological procedures. Nowadays, I try to take into account, as far as I can, interactions between the global and the local. As a matter of fact, it is almost impossible to situate a village event or a local observation without connecting it to the more all-encompassing forces and without considering its relation to the state.

However, I remain faithful and dedicated to the anthropologist's specific vision which has the unique privilege of considering social facts and the values from the point of view of the very persons studied, not only from the outside. Some of the pieces here are simply reformulations in anthropological terms of a sentence heard from a Nepali friend and substantiated by observations. My personal aim is to search for micro details and micro events that may reveal significant phenomena or totalities. Ethnographic observations provide invaluable insight into the actual functioning of a society and offer glimpses of the way modernity is experienced in contemporary urban and rural settings. This is what I have tried to do throughout this book.

At the same time my analysis embraces a self-distanced perspective that introduces a comparative angle. In anthropological jargon, these two different approaches are respectively termed *emic* (internal views to a culture) and *etic* (outside view). The interaction between indigenous and Western modes of thinking is a key element in the present undertaking. It is hoped that this innovative combinative approach will broaden the readership and lead to far-reaching results in matters of cultural and political studies.

Methodologically, I distinguish three different levels, from observation to the final formulation, in any conventional socio-cultural analysis. 1) A strict empirical level, in which the researcher immerses himself in his fieldwork and absorbs everything around him like a sponge. This level implies full-time observation, a compilation of visual and written documents with as few pre-conceived ideas as possible, and dedicated participation in the local community. 2) The contextual and perspective standpoint, in which each fact is related, linked to others and inserted into a chain. The angle may be linguistic, historical, sociological, anthropological, or, even better, all four combined. 3) The third step is the socio-anthropological analysis which represents efforts to theorize —such as the notion of "open society" or "social imagination" developed in the present book. This three-tiered exercise, shifting back and forth to each level of the analysis, optimizes a full comprehension of socio-cultural research themes.

Some of the texts were published over the last three years in the leading Nepali newspaper *The Kathmandu Post*. They have been slightly revised here and in some cases expanded. Two [**27** and **82**] have been written in collaboration with another author (Shova Shakya and Joëlle Smadja respectively). Both authors have kindly given their permission to reproduce the jointly written texts here. Most of the present pieces, however, have never been published before. My reflections have gradually matured in the course of writing these articles. The relatively short format of each piece has prompted me to synthesize my views in a readable and concise way for the reader. A last word of caution is necessary: the books and articles referred to in each section do not claim to cover all the relevant bibliography on that subject.

Notes

1 Sunil Khilnani, *The Idea of India*. New York: Farrar Strauss Giroux, 1997, Chapter 1.

2 Gérard Toffin, *From Monarchy to Republic. Essays on Changing Nepal*. Kathmandu: Vajra Books, 2013.

3 This figure corresponds to flows, not to stock of migrants, the number of which is difficult to evaluate. Qatar, Malaysia, Saudi Arabia, the UAE, and Kuwait, are the top five destinations for finding work and have the highest number of Nepali migrant workers. As far as India is concerned, it probably now has more than two million Nepali migrant workers (Sondra Hausner & Jeevan Sharma, "On the way to India. Nepali rituals of border-crossing", in D. Gellner (ed.) *Borderland and Lives in Northern South Asia*, Durham & London: Duke University Press, 2013, p. 97).

4 Cf. Anne de Sales, "Notes sur la claustration villageoise au Népal", in S. Karmay and P. Sagant (eds), *Les habitants du Toit du Monde*, Nanterre : Université de Paris X, and Gisèle Krauskopff, "Naissance d'un village tharu : à propos des rites

de claustration villageoise", *L'Ethnographie*, 1987, LXXXIII, 1-2 (100-101), pp. 131-157.

5 G. Toffin, *Societé et Religion chez les Néwar du Népal*. Paris: Éditions du CNRS, 1984, p. 93.

6 See A.W Macdonald, "Notes on the cloistering of villages in South-East Asia", in A.W. Macdonald, *Essays on the Ethnology of Nepal and South Asia*, Kathmandu: Ratna Pustak Bhandar, 1983, vol.1, pp. 81-102.

7 On these migrations and the Nepali diaspora of that time, see, for instance, Michael Hutt, "Being Nepali without Nepal: Reflections on a South Asian Diaspora", in D. Gellner, J. Pfaff-Czarnecka and J. Whelpton (eds.), *Nationalism and Ethnicity in a Hindu Kingdom. The Politics of Culture in Contemporary Nepal*. Amsterdam: Harwood Academic Publications, 1997, pp. 101-144.

8 C. von Fürer-Haimendorf. *Himalayan Traders. Life in Highland Nepal.* London: John Murray, 1975.

9 Yet sociologists and geographers have highlighted how the increasing flow of people across national boundaries has engendered various forms of securitization of Western societies, including the building of walls, camps, and strict controls over migrants and refugees. Nation states frequently close their borders and defend their territorial sovereignty against what they see as a threat to their identity, security and stability. De-territorialisation processes have to be apprehended in conjunction with these opposite forms of re-territorialisation (Cf. Turner, Bryan S. "The Enclave Society. Towards a Sociology of Immobility", *European Journal of Social Theory*, 2013, 10 (2): 287-303).

10 Louis Dumont, *Homo aequalis (volume 2). German Ideology. From France to Germany and back.* Chicago: Chicago University Press, 1996.

11 On the process of globalization, see Gérard Toffin & Joanna Pfaff-Czarnecka, *Facing Globalization in the Himalayas. Belonging and the Politics of the Self.* Delhi: Sage, 2014.

12 Some authors have made a clear distinction between imagination and imagery. For André Malraux, for instance, the French novelist and art theorist, the first term embraces the "realm of dreams", whereas the second specifically designates the "domain of forms" (*L'Homme précaire et la littérature*, Paris: Gallimard, 1977, p. 179). However, in most cases, the two words cannot be totally separated. In English, "imagery" commonly has the meaning of "products of imagination", "mental images", or "pictures produced by an imagining system". In actual fact, imagery is a way of using our imagination. In the present book, these two concepts will be considered jointly.

13 Cornelius Castoriadis, *The Imaginary Institution of Society.* Cambridge: MIT Press, 1987, p. 184.

14 A growing corpus of social science literature, especially in the field of anthropology, deals with the theme of imagination and imagery. See for instance Tine M. Gammeltoft, "Toward an Anthropology of the Imagery: Specters of Disability in Vietnam", *Ethos,* 42 (2), pp. 153-174. Close examination of imagery constructions of society obviously opens up new perspectives in the sociological and anthropological study of society See also Maurice Godelier, *L'imaginé, l'imaginaire et le symbolique.* Paris: CNRS Editions, 2015.

15 For instance: Anne de Sales, "Time, Identity and Hisorical Change in the Hills of Nepal", in *The European Bulletin of Himalayan Research*, 39, 2011, pp. 106-126.

16 This epic narration is based on an old Newari (Nepā Bhāshā) song.

17 Mallika Shakya, "Nation and Border in the Twentieth-Century Nepali Novels: Parijat and B.P. Koirala". Paper presented at the 4th International Conference on Nepal and the Himalayas, (Social Science Baha), Kathmandu, 2015.

18 Gérard Toffin, 1982. "La notion de ville dans une société asiatique traditionnelle; le cas de la vallée de Kathmandou", *L'Homme*, XXII (4), pp. 101-117.

19 Gérard Toffin, 1985. "La forêt dans l'imaginaire religieux des populations de l'Himalaya népalais », *Revue de l'histoire des religions*, 2005, 222 (2), pp. 177-207.

20 Arjun Appadurai, *Modernity at Large. Cultural Dimensions of Globalization.* Minneapolis: University of Minnesota Press, 1996.

21 Jacques Le Goff, 1985. *L'imaginaire médiéval. Essais.* Paris: Gallimard (Bibliothèque des Histoires), p. VII. Translated into English by Arthur Goldhammer under the title *The Medieval Imagination.* Chicago/London: University of Chicago Press, 1988.

22 Interview with Jacques Le Goff, *Lire,* 2005, 1 May.

23 Philippe Descola, 2013. *Beyond Nature and Culture.* Chicago: Chicago University Press (with a foreword by Marshall Sahlins). The book was brilliantly reviewed by Bruce. Kapferer, 2014. "Back to the future. Descola's neostructuralism", *Hau, Journal of Ethnographic Theory,* 4 (3), pp. 389-400, and Stephan Feuchtwang, 2014. "Too ontological, too rigid, too ahistorical but magnificent", *Hau, Journal of Ethnographic Theory,* 4 (3); pp. 383-387.

CHAPTER

1

The Idea of Nepal

Nepal is characterized both by its geographical diversity, the wide range of its ecological milieux, from north to south and from east to west, and by its mosaic of populations, an amazing patchwork of castes and ethnic groups speaking different languages (about ninety still spoken today) and dialects scattered across the country. Over the centuries, these small societies with their own specific culture have been caught between two opposite forces: an inward-orientated trend leading towards compartmentalization, and a force driven by centuries of interaction, which tends to unify the country, often forcefully, and to homogenize it. These contradictory forces are still active today. It is difficult to find a district or sub-district occupied by a single caste or ethnic group. The difficulties in restructuring the federal state are rooted in this situation. Even the Tarai plains, where the Madhesī population are demanding more autonomy, are made up of multiple ethnicities.

There are widespread preconceived ideas and misconceptions about Nepal. For instance, lots of people do not realize how globalized this country already is as they dream about lost valleys in the mountains preserving unscathed, ancient cultural features. Stereotypes associated with various groups are also an enduring feature of social life. They are based mostly on derogative metaphors reducing persons to supposed traits of people as a group. Janajāti ethnic groups are thus commonly labelled as quarrelsome drunkards by high Hindu castes. And Madhesī people (inhabiting the southern flatlands) are referred to in a depreciatory way by Hill people as *dhoti* due to the men's Indian dress.[1] Deep suspicion is rife in the country among the myriad of ethnic groups and contrasted geographical regions. Moreover, I have often observed a remarkable lack of knowledge and of curiosity among communities regarding their closest neighbours. Customs practised in the next valley or in an adjacent village are often totally unknown.

The following texts aim to explore these opposing forces and to bring together a broad reflection on Nepal. They address the complexities and ethnicities of present-day Nepal from a new perspective afforded by the combined analysis of recent and past events. The texts also try to situate Nepal in relation to India and China, the two fastest growing global powers in this region and, more broadly speaking, within South Asia and the Himalayas. One question, among many others, arise again and again in this first part and in the remainder of the book: to what extent does the republican idea of a federalist democracy established in 2008 correspond to the concrete realities of the country?

1. Situating Nepal

When looking at a map of the Himalayas, Nepal appears as a small land-locked country, with no access to the sea. It is hemmed in between two mammoth states, India and China, which play a prominent role in the global game of economics and politics. King Prithivi Narayan is reported to have depicted this peripheral situation more than two centuries ago in his *Divya Upadesh* [*Divine Instruction*], describing Nepal as a yam (*tarul*) stuck between two boulders.[2] Since then, Nepal has strived to maintain a fine balance between the two powerful giants it has for neighbours. This role of buffer state between the two rival superior powers is a long-standing feature of Nepalese foreign policy. It is thanks to this that the country has preserved its independence since the eighteenth century. Nepal remained neutral during the short Sino-Indian War of 1962, though the conflict prompted Kathmandu to improve its relations momentarily with Delhi.

The situation has varied somewhat depending on the period in question. During the Panchayat years (the palace was the source of all authority), for instance, the Shah monarchy cultivated a close relationship with China to counter India's influence (India was conceived as a threat because of its close relations with democratic forces in Nepal). However, links between Nepal and India are extremely strong, much more so than between Nepal and China. Economically, Nepal is highly dependent on India but very little on its northern neighbour.

Flows of migrants have long travelled from India to Nepal, and more recently in the opposite direction. This has never been the case between Nepal and China, save for Tibetan people who migrated (on a much lesser scale) southwards. China may well help Nepal to depend less heavily on India, but it cannot replace the latter. Indeed, from an Indian point of view, Nepal is part of its strategic "sphere of influence" and is a major concern for its security. China, for its part, views its small southern neighbour with anxiety, particularly with regards the Tibetan minorities who have settled in Nepal and who are forever protesting against its much-contested policy in Tibet.

These geopolitical aspects are of vital importance. However, other associated parameters have to be taken into account to situate Nepal more accurately. In fact, this country oscillates between two regional ensembles. According to the first one, Nepal is part of the Hindu Kush Himalayan belt, a geographical entity encompassing eight countries, including China, Pakistan, India, Bhutan, and Burma. Some international centres (International Centre for Integrative Mountain Development, ICIMOD, for instance, which has its headquarters in Nepal) adhere to this definition which has received international support. A number of research centres worldwide, in Europe and in the United States, also recognise this classification. This geographical definition has the advantage of emphasising a number of shared mountain constraints and its overall peripheral situation. It also stresses the historical links that have been forged through the ages between these mountainous countries on both sides of the range. Yet there is a certain lack of congruence: for instance, in Nepal, the low plains of the Tarai, a zone of major economic and political import, do not quite fall within this ensemble.

"South Asia", the alternative concept, links Nepal to its southern partners, i.e. a block of eight countries, including India, Pakistan, and Sri Lanka. This concept, which ignores China to the north, is relatively recent. It was established in the wake of studies that the United States launched in the area and is largely inherited, with a few exceptions, from the administrative boundaries of the British Raj. It is also somewhat linked to the concept of the Indian subcontinent.[3] The notion of South Asia has been criticised by various persons for being a concept that is exogenous to the region and for its fluctuating boundaries. The regional body for the area is the South Asian Association for Regional Cooperation, SAARC, an organisation specialised in economic cooperation created in 1985. Some Nepali intellectuals, such as those involved in the Himal Association, have popularised this South Asia idea in Nepal. Their journal *Himal* became *Himal Southasian* in 1996 to introduce a cross-border perspective. Kanak Mani Dixit, the director, has suggested that "South Asia", to which without a doubt Nepal firmly belongs, is more a question of sensibility than of geographical region. *Himal Southasian* has established close contact with the elite of the respective member countries of this ensemble.

In fact, culturally and linguistically, Nepal is closely associated with India. For Hindus, who make up the majority of the population in Nepal and India, the two countries are one. A common mythology, a number of shared heroes and divinities, numerous pilgrimage networks and sacred rivers link them together. The influence of Sanskrit Hindu culture is deeply entrenched in Nepal, and Nepalis feel much more at home in this country than in China—which is sometimes regarded as a land of ogres, *rākshasa* (the Chinese, it is said, eat everything)—even if they sometimes blame Indians for treating them in a colonialist and paternalist way. Indians and Nepalis belong to the same cultural and historical entity. What's more, the two countries have overlapping ethnicities. This common background plays a major role in the mental representation of the country. "Himalaya" after all is an Indian notion, which goes back to classical India, although these northern regions have always been situated on the margins of the main Indian centres of civilisation.

Since the fall of the Shah monarchy in 2008, China has obtained the effective support of successive Nepalese governments to obviate and curb rebellious activity by Tibetans in Nepal in protest against the Han occupation of Tibet. In exchange they have repeatedly pledged military assistance to its small southern neighbour. When the Maoists were in power, China used its ideological commonalities to quell the Free Tibet movement. Tibetans living in Nepal are now closely monitored by the police. They can practise their religion freely but they cannot engage in anti-Chinese activities.

However, China has now raised its objectives and has implemented a whole range of initiatives in South-East Asia and South Asia. Comforted by its enormous potential, its ever-increasing economic strength and its emerging status as an economic superpower, it looks towards its southern borders and the Indian Ocean (a major route for China's oil imports from the Gulf) with greedy eyes. In 2013 it launched major corridor-extension projects. According to the official version, this is to revive the Silk Road which historically linked China to Central Asia and Europe, and to develop political ties. India is opposed to this project for obvious reasons, but Nepal, pragmatically, expects to reap the benefits of it and to develop its economy and its means of communication. Let us not forget, as far as this is concerned, that over the last centuries Nepal has derived great benefit from the Transhimalayan trade routes that crisscross its territory. Kathmandu could reduce its economic dependency on India by joining the Promethean programme.

In December 2014 Kathmandu signed a four-point document endorsing the Silk Road project. The agreement stipulates that Nepal will be connected to the Chinese railway line in Tibet which recently went as afar as Shigatse. The plan is to extend the network to several sites in Nepal, including the capital Kathmandu. China would also like to build the railway line as far as Lumbini, the birthplace of Buddha, near the Nepal-India border in south-western Nepal. This project would clearly improve connectivity between neighbouring countries but it would also have political overtones. In addition, together with other counties in SAARC, Nepal has received the support of various Chinese banks. In matters of tourism, several flights at present connect Kunming to Kathmandu and the number of Chinese visitors to Nepal is already increasing exponentially.

The geopolitical landscape and economic relations between Nepal and its two neighbours are therefore changing at a rapid pace. A broader Asian perspective needs to be adopted here. Let us consider the situation in Laos where, unhindered by the local government, China is gradually taking possession of the north of the country after building roads and railways. A comparison with the proliferation of Chinese projects in the Himalayas raises serious questions. The integration of these former peripheral areas into China's zone of influence is clearly under way.

Would it be possible for Nepal to maintain its sovereignty and to benefit from the competition between its two giant neighbours without becoming involved in a possible conflict? This is a key issue because areas of friction between China and India are not limited to boundary demarcations. Competition over control of the huge strategic hydroelectric resources of the Himalayan region, for instance, is pivotal. Both neighbours have proposed building huge dams in Nepal. One might predict that Nepal will increasingly become a zone of competition between India and China and that an equidistance policy will be more and more difficult to maintain in the future.

2. *Living Together*

In the second half of the eighteenth century, Prithivi Narayan Shah conquered and unified Nepal. Born in Gorkha, this king defined nearly all the country's present boundaries. He achieved this by creating a war machine, a warmongering state where most resources and efforts were channelled into the military. On proving to be a master of warfare and a skilled strategist, he annexed large tracts of land, some of which were given to his military chiefs. The conquest ended with the treaty of Sugauli which was ratified in 1816. Prithivi Narayan and his successors did not unfortunately conquer the hearts of all the people living in the conquered territories. The institution of the Shah monarchy and its associated conservative Brahmanism succeeded in keeping the country united for two centuries. However, a prevailing feeling of bitterness persisted among those who had been vanquished, especially among Tibeto-Burman speaking groups. Though reunited, the different communities retained radically divergent memories of the past.

The compartmentalized geography of the country, the shifting boundaries of the Tarai and the cultural differences between this plain region and the hills of Nepal have prevented the total unification of the country. These combined factors (heightened by the Rana dynasty) have increased the degree of compartmentalization and fragmentation. Ethnic revolts have occurred from time to time over the last two centuries, especially after the collapse of the clan-based Rana oligarchy in 1951 and the first successive attempts at creating a democratic state. The inner division and politics of subordination have left their mark on a number of official documents including Jang Bahahur Ain (Code) dated 1854. Any valid history of the country has to take into account these long-term conflicts.

Nepal's unification does not therefore only mean the creation of a new nation state. It also symbolizes the subjugation of a number of subjects with the use of arms. Prithivi Narayan absorbed small Hindu kingdoms in the hills to the west and in the central part of the country as well. However, here, the process took place between entities belonging to the same sociocultural background, and who, what is more, exchanged wives. Prithivi Narayan Shah himself married the daughter of the Sen King of Makwanpur and his mother was the daughter of the king of Palpa. In striking contrast, there was no intermarriage with Tibeto-Burman speaking communities, save with Magars who had long been living in small Hindu Parbatiyā kingdoms, in the same geographical region, and had in many ways supported Prithivi Narayan's conquest. Ranas and Shahs accepted Newar women as concubines but not as queens or princesses.

The democratic movement and the fall of the monarchy have created a new context. Old resentment, which has been heightened by years of endured censorship and autocracy, has re-emerged. Divisions and fragmentation have increased considerably to the point of threatening the unity of the country. I am inclined to think that the Maoist insurgency of 1996-2006 needs to be seen in this light. It was backed by a number of Janajāti groups who were seeking a higher level of public recognition and who were (among other things) eager to avenge their former conquerors. In the new democratic landscape, the quest for identity has gradually become one of the major sources of inner tension and dispute, even going as far as to overshadow class conflicts.

In addition, Madhesīs living in the Tarai plain, who share a common culture and language with people across the border in India, complain of having been treated as second-class citizens by the Pahārī Nepalis from the hills for the last 240 years or so. They argue that the Tarai has been administrated like a colony over the years by central government in Kathmandu and has not been granted enough independence. They set up a political organisation: the Madhesī Janadhikār Forum (MJF), which was registered in 2008 with the Election Commission, with a cross-party platform. This organization ensured them some dignity and audience that former political parties have failed to provide. But it later split into several opposed factions. Madhesīs are presently striving for proportional representation in all state bodies. They are also demanding more autonomy on a continuous, unbroken territory covering the whole Tarai (or divided in two parts). This claim is the most contentious issue in the present debate. Despite persisting blatant discriminations, in 2008, the first-ever President of Nepal (Yadav) and his Vice-President (Jha), two prestigious positions, were chosen from among Madhesīs. And during the 2008-2013 period, Madhesī politicians were the swinging force in parliamentary arithmetic.

The situation in the Tarai is even more complex if the Tharus, the main "indigenous", Ādivāsī, ethnic group in the region, are to be considered. As the tragic events of 25 August 2015 — about 25 people killed in a riot started in Kailali by Tharu activists — recall, this ethnic group (1.7 million people in 2011) has a distinct identity and does not want to be confounded with the Madhesī people. Tharus are demanding a Tharuhat province made up of areas where they have sizeable populations. Indeed, Kailali is regarded as one of their main native lands in the Tarai. So far, in this district, 40 per cent of the local population belong to this indigenous group.

The question today is about finding a balance between the necessary unity of the country and the obligation to recognize its huge diversity in matters of culture, language and religion. If one sacrifices unity for diversity, society will inevitably fall apart. If one sacrifices diversity for unity, homogeneity will forever remain an abstraction and there will be never-ending conflicts. This is a complex issue as the delay in writing a new constitution has demonstrated. The persistence of corporate groups with a common language, a link to a specific territory, and a strong sense of distinctiveness, precludes any simple solution. These elementary social bonds have to find their place within a broader social space that is shared equally with others groups on the basis of reciprocity. In other words, the impersonal abstract individual, which is traditionally the cornerstone of democracy in the West, cannot be the basis of the state today in a country like Nepal.

The solution lies within a negotiated democratic framework that seeks to reconcile unity and diversity, liberty and integration. The adopted principles must simultaneously reject the centralistic spirit that condemns the diversity of private beliefs, loyalties and memories, and the obsession with identity that confines everyone within a community and paves the way for segregation and holy war. The November 2013 elections, which were shared by all Nepalis whatever their place of residence, have proved an important step forward. They have contributed to a great extent to creating a shared feeling of belonging. It has fused people around the same practices and values, irrespective of their ethnic group, lineage, caste and region.

One of the current difficulties, in my opinion, is the widening gap between the segregationist stances rooted in ethnic groups'/castes' rhetoric and the more hybrid, multiethnic, multicaste society that is slowly emerging in Nepal. These new trends, which cannot be contested, contradict in many ways hardliners who still rely exclusively on strong communitarian ethnic, geographical (*tarāī/pahār*) or caste links. The number of inter-ethnic and inter-caste marriages, for instance, is constantly on the rise. This creates new interrelations and new forms of sociability, which undermine formerly isolated communities. Similarly, newly established groups made up of past or present members of a class of schoolchildren or of a sports club, or of any other activities, build more and more bridges and transversal links, which transcend ancient boundaries. These new networks that have undergone exponential growth testify to major social changes.

I would like to end this all too short analysis by addressing the issue of migration. Communities of the Nepali diaspora are also organised on more outward-looking lines than within traditional Nepali society. Even if homeland bashing (seen as corrupt, ineffective, underdeveloped, nepotistic, etc.) is common among them, these *Prabāsī* (as they are called in Nepali) expatriates are in the process of developing new forms of "Nepaliness" that go beyond internal cleavages.

Remodelled social structures and new figures of patriotism are therefore slowly emerging inside and outside the country. "New Nepal", *Nayā Nepāl*, will most probably evolve through these profound structural changes from below rather than because of any political decision taken at the top.

3. Cult of Heroes

Every country worships its heroes: its national founding fathers, poets, writers, warriors, political leaders who have, amongst other things, served the interests of their country. These heroic figures strengthen nationalist feelings and nurture the national memory. Interestingly, the choice of heroes can be a source of conflict between different visions. To assert their ideas, political parties sometimes pit various well-known figures against each other. Indian Congress heroes are not the same as those for the Bhāratīya Janatā Party (BJP), save for a handful they have in common.

I argue that Nepal's recent political history reveals a major shift in the selection of the nation's heroes over the last decades. The return to democracy in 1990 and the introduction of a multicultural policy have been a major step in this respect. The main (though not exclusive) body involved in these matters is the Nepal Academy, *Nepāl Rājakiya Pragyā Pratisthān*.

For a long time since its creation in 1957, this institution chose official national heroes, *rāshtriya vibhūtiharū* —from the Sanskrit word *vibhūti*, "strength, energy, divinely inspired power, sacred ash" —, among Hindu or Buddhist legendary or historical figures who are associated in some way with the country. Among them, mention can be made of King Janak, Sitā, Gautam Buddha, Bhrikuti. The Nepal Academy has also granted this coveted title to some of the country's eminent royal figures, and in particular to three members of the Shah royal house: Rama Shah (the founder of the dynasty) Prihivi Narayan and King Tribhuvan. Some military heroes, commanders (Amar Singh Thapa, Balbhadra Kunwar) and Bhimsen Thapa have been added, as well as famous writers (Bhanubhakta Acharya and Motiram Bhatta) who played a role in developing the national language.

Most of these nominations form an unequivocal narrative, which is dedicated to the glory of the Shah Hindu nation and is enshrined in school textbooks. There is nothing unusual about this if we consider that the chairperson of the Academy used to be the king himself. This was at the time of panchayat party-less royal rule. However, in 1999, the government declared Sankhadhar Sakhwa, the alleged founder of the Nepāl Sambat calendar and a member of the Newar community, a national hero. A commemorative postage stamp carrying his portrait was issued in 2003. A memorial statue was erected in Tansen in January 2012 and another one in Damak (Jhapa) in 2014. This marked the success of the Newar indigenous movement after a long campaign (launched in the 1920s by Dharmaditya Dharmacharya) and the recognition of the prominent role played by this group in the fight for democracy.

Interestingly enough, Sankhadhar Sakhwa was a merchant from Kantipur (Kathmandu) supposedly from a Shūdra caste. Etymologically, his name is linked to a Sanskrit/Prākrit word meaning "trade, credit, storeroom".[4] According to a legend recounted in local chronicles, this merchant played a trick on King Ananda Malla, the ruler of Bhaktapur at the time. He suggested that if sand was taken from the river Lakhu Tirtha situated at the junction between Bhatikhu and Vishnumati at a specific time of the year, it would turn into gold. The king ordered sand to be brought from this place at the given time but Sankhadhar Sakhwa prevailed on the king's porters to carry to his own house the loads of sand they had just dug up from the river. And indeed the sand turned into gold. Having obtained so much wealth in this way, Sakhwa paid off all the country's outstanding debts. To commemorate this event, it was decided to introduce a new era in Nepal called Nepāl Sambat which started on 20 October AD 879. Though the tale may not necessarily be true, this era took on such importance for dating events that it became an integral part of the Newars' cultural heritage and a means of giving prominence to their specificity compared to the Vikram Sambat calendar later chosen by the Shah dynasty.

Some years later, in 2002, Pasang Lhamu Sherpa (1961-1993), the first Nepalese woman to climb Everest, on 22 April 1993 at the age of thirty-two, was declared *rāshtriya vibhūti*. She was the mother of three children. She now stands as the second woman among all *vibhūtiharū* just behind Sītā. By choosing her, the Academy recognized the importance of Sherpas in the mountaineering conquest of the Himalayan summits.

More recently, in 2066 B.S. (2009-2010 A.D.), Mahaguru Phalgunanda (1885-1949), a pre-eminent religious figure among Kirants, especially Limbus, was attributed the title by the government itself. This mystic, known for his miracles, funded the Satya Hangma religion, which is heavily influenced by the Vaishnava creed and directly linked to the Josmanī sect, a reformist Sant movement. Phalgunanda banned animal sacrifices despite the prevalence of this practice in Kirant traditional culture.[5] Interestingly, these syncretistic beliefs and practices were the object of a revival in eastern Nepal towards the end of the Panchayat era. Most followers dressed in white are Limbus and Rais. Although they follow the Hindu creed, this religious system has become part of the Kirant culture.

Recent nominations reveal a shift over the last decades from previous Gorkhali mono-cultural nationalism to a more pluralistic paradigm. Yet there is some ongoing resistance. Interestingly enough, no Ranas yet figure on the official list of national heroes. The time has not yet come. Similarly, the rebel Lakhan Thapa, whose statue can be seen in the streets of Pokhara and who is worshiped as a hero by Magars, is still too controversial a figure in the eyes of many people. It also seems that there is some difficulty in recognizing as an ethnic hero Yalambara (or Yellung), whom Kirant groups cherish. According to fictional history reported by local chronicles, Yalambara was the first Kirant king.

He is also the legendary founder of the city of Patan in the Kathmandu Valley.

Conflicts between local and national narratives obviously underlie these matters. Idealized ethnic heroes serve to pave the way for indigenous causes, which sometimes run counter to mainstream politics. What is at stake here is of the utmost importance since worshipping as heroes political martyrs (*shahid*) of the democratic movement and of the People's War shapes people's memories and the country's past. They are not only myths; they gradually become part of meaningful realities.

4. A Nation-State in the Making

When discussing nationalism and state-building in Nepal, it is worthwhile recalling that the word *Nepāl* originally applied to a very small part of the country. It is a well-known fact that for a very long time this term first designated only the Kathmandu Valley. Today still, Newars (whose ancestral land is the Kathmandu Valley) and Tamangs use the word *Nepāl* colloquially in this restricted sense. The meaning of the term only extended to cover the whole territory of the state, as we know it today, at the end of the eighteenth century, after the conquest of Prithivi Narayan Shah, the king of Gorkha.

This does not mean that the different geo-cultural areas did not have any contact prior to that period. Social groups maintained long-lasting mutual links, though on a relatively small scale. Khasas from far western Nepal raided the Kathmandu Valley several times in the thirteenth and fourteenth centuries, and upper Parbatiyā castes started to settle in the central region from the sixteenth century onwards. Yet these different areas were not administered by only one government organization.

In fact, in the past, the country was divided into several small Hindu kingdoms and chieftainships. Even within these structures, the concept of state was rather different from what has prevailed in the West since the beginning of the Middle Ages. Villages and local communities were loosely linked to the overall state structure. The concept of ceremonial or theatre state (Geertz[6]) seems more relevant in the definition of these ensembles which were more interested in showcasing their power than, for instance, in supervising their subjects. As far as tribal areas were concerned, lineage headmanship, which was often based on dominant clan precedence, predominated.

The nation state started to mature in Nepal at the turn of the nineteenth century. The Sugauli treaty in 1816, which put an end to the Nepal-British war, was vital in this respect. It drew more or less fixed boundaries (one of the most emblematic and visible symbols of a nation state) in the country, save in the Tarai plains where changes occurred in 1860 when the British retroceded most of this area to Nepal. Later, Shahs and Ranas provided this emerging state with more robust administrative structures.

Has this process been achieved today? If we consider the well-known definition of a nation developed by Renan, the French historian, according to which a nation is neither natural nor indeed shaped by ethnicity and geography, but is based on "elective affinities" ("A nation is a soul, a spiritual principle..."), the answer is clearly no.[7] Nepal is still made up primarily of distinct ethnic caste groups and regional units, whose identities still hinder or at least make difficult the emergence of a real shared sense of citizenship. The texture of the population is far from being homogeneous. Just like India, Nepal is an amazing conglomerate of faiths, subcultures and languages.

A particularly stark contrast still exists between Nepal's middle mountains and the southern lowlands of the Tarai. The Tarai population (Madhesī or Tarāībāsī) sometimes has more in common with India's Uttar Pradesh and Bihar than with the Nepalese hill people (Pahāriyā or Pahārī, "people of the hills"). Madhesīs regularly cross over and marry on the other side of the Nepalese-Indian border. Their culture differs considerably from the one found in the hills. They speak Hindi, Bhojpuri, Awadhi, Maithili, in contrast to Nepali and the Tibeto-Burman languages spoken in the hills and mountain areas. Madhesīs and Pahāriyā cannot consequently share a common sense of "Nepaleseness", *nepālipan*. Each ethno-geographical group views its relations with India differently. They have different attachments.

Some thirty years ago (1975), Frederik H. Gaige showed how the Tarai was loosely integrated into the nation state.[8] In the nineteenth century and the first part of the twentieth century, the Shahs and Ranas relied mainly on hill-centric conceptions to build the nation. Parbatiyā castes, and more generally Pahāriyā still dominate the state apparatus, though the Tarai plains play a major role in the national economy and house more than half of the country's population. Nowadays, the situation has slightly improved but the contrast between the two groups is still striking. For instance, recruitment of Madhesīs into the Nepali army is extremely low due to the reluctance of the central state and of persisting stereotypes. A particularly contentious issue concerns the difficulties Madhesīs face when applying for Nepali citizenship. Some of them are in fact suspected of being Indians or, at least, of not being full-blooded Nepalis. Indeed, the ruling class in the hill areas is obsessed by a fear of being invaded by its southern neighbour. Madhesīs are often described as the New Delhi fifth column.

However, most Nepalis endure a similar, difficult situation. Nearly all of them feel a sense of belonging to a poor country coveted by its two powerful neighbours, a fragile land regularly hit by earthquakes and affected by several other natural disasters, such as floods and landslides. They all have a dubious opinion of their politicians. They regard them as being more preoccupied by their own personal interests than by their citizens' welfare or by the development of remote regions. In other words, Nepalis share more difficulties and privations than any remotely accessible benefits. A recent enquiry revealed, for instance, the large proportion of Nepalis among those who sell their kidneys for thousands of rupees in India. What better indicator of their unfortunate condition? In my opinion, the current process of globalization and the migration of poorer sections of the population to the Gulf or to Malaysia have developed this sense of wider belonging based on hardships, *dukha*.

The current rescaling of the national territory runs the risk of hampering the nascent sense of common citizenship. This is obviously a complex issue that cannot be addressed in the space of a few sentences. As a matter of fact, the conundrum of Nepal's unity raises a variety of contradictory responses. It must be recalled in connection with this that the Seven Party Alliance's historic agreement which was signed during Janāndolan II promised to restructure the state in a way that would reflect social, cultural, geographical, ethnic, and linguistics diversities. The objective was to make representative democracy more inclusive and participatory. The disappointment among those who still support this ideal is easy to understand when some parties—notably Congress but also CPN-UML, (Communist Party of Nepal, Unified Marxist-Leninist) to some extent—lend more importance at present to economic parameters and to the link between the hills and plains than to pluri-ethnicity. These activists feel betrayed by the country's traditional elite.

Nevertheless, the danger of fissiparous tendencies triggered by ethno-linguistic divisive and almost separatist statements must not be undermined. Restoring regions reminiscent of the pre-Gorkali conquest period would seem anachronistic today. Similarly, the risk of further separating the hills and the plains must not be taken too lightly. Negotiated solutions need to be found between the two camps—the centralists and the federalists. The main problem in overcoming these conflicting orientations is the strong defiance towards political leaders. Today, in a context where governments of all stripes fail to rule in the public's interest, there is an almost generalised feeling of antipathy towards the state—which, admittedly, is absent in most sectors of public life.

5. *Enforced Boundaries*

The statement: "Nepal is India in the making", written by the famous French Indologist Sylvain Lévi in his historical study of Nepal, published in 1905-1908, is still often quoted by various social scientists. Sylvain Lévi was a Sanskritist and an eminent scholar of Indian and Nepalese studies. He gained the respect of the Brahman and Buddhist pandits he met and worked with during his three sojourns in Nepal between 1898 and 1928. By this forceful expression, Lévi meant that Nepal has repeated most of the steps taken by India in the past, from the Maurya to the Gupta dynasties. According to him, the ancient pre-Aryan populations of Nepal have gradually been Indianised culturally and linguistically over the ages. They were first influenced by Indian Buddhism and subsequently almost absorbed by Brahmanical culture. In all these respects, Nepal has, on the whole, steadily reproduced India's course of history. It has repeated the genesis of the subcontinent.

Despite its accuracy regarding ancient and medieval history, Lévi's statement is less true of the more recent period of Nepal's history. Indeed, since the unification of the country and during the domination of the Shah dynasty over the former kingdom, Nepal's policy has been running counter to its southern neighbour's, politically and even culturally. Prithivi Narayan and his successors regarded India as being corrupted by Islamic penetration and British rule. Both of these invaders, of very low rank within the Hindu caste system, were considered to have altered India's ancient Hindu heritage. The Nepalese authorities referred to the Indian subcontinent as Muglān, from the word Moghol, that is the country of the Moghols (Muslims), with a negative meaning. It is a well-known fact that one of the pillars of Nepal's Shah royal policy was the preservation of a genuine Indian Hindu culture, *asal hindustān*, within the Himalayan kingdom. Hindu values, in danger of being lost in India, were seen as cementing the Nepali identity and as encompassing the ethnic and linguistic diversity of the Himalayan kingdom.

Notwithstanding (and thanks to) its determined assistance to the Raj, Nepal was never colonized. The British even retroceded a large part of the Tarai to the Rana authorities to express their gratitude for their help during World War I. Over the years, the border between the two countries has been just as much political as cultural. After the Independence of India in 1947, the Shah/Rana regime found itself in an awkward situation. The shift by India towards republicanism, federalism, secularism was felt in Kathmandu to be an even greater danger than the British presence. After a ten-year transition period, the Shahs invented the autocratic panchayat system. It was a way of resisting India's influence and of offering an alternative to the Indian republican model. Viewed from an international perspective, Nepal was no longer "India in the making", for the country was building a regime to counter the Indian model and its subsequent influence. The ideological content was more in keeping with the conceptual imagery of *Bhārat* than *India*, to mention an opposition that the Hindu nationalist wing in India often put forward.

Since 2008, the situation has once again been reversed. The abolition of royalty in Nepal and the proclamation of a secular federal republic correspond to a move almost similar to the one initiated sixty years ago by the government of India. Today, Nepal is more in line with modern Indian history and is facing a series of shared problems. Similar solutions to various contentious issues are being adopted or are under consideration. However, the Nepali Maoist movement has resuscitated a nationalist, anti-Indian ideology that sometimes evokes the Shah's ancient chauvinistic policy. India is suspected of ulterior imperialistic motives and of plotting against Nepali sovereignty. Its ultimate aim would be to 'eat', that is to swallow up the independent Himalayan state. Maoists often accuse other mainstream political parties of 'selling' Nepal to India.

For a fuller understanding of Sylvain Lévi's expression, it must also be said that Nepal and India are not uniform, homogeneous countries. They are both characterised primarily by their diversity. The two countries include large areas, not only in the peripheries but also in their heartland, that are situated outside the pale of mainstream Hinduism. Their history cannot be limited to a history of the Sanskritization process. Other religions, such as Islam, Buddhism and Christianity, have large minorities and play an important role. What's more, Nepal, like India, is divided by internal boundaries, such as the one between the *pahār* (*pahād*) and the *tarāī*, which are of crucial significance and cannot be ignored. Sylvain Lévi was a great scholar, more in phase with the ancient legacy of India than with modern, post-Malla Nepali history. He was more concerned with the Kathmandu Valley and the former petty Caubīsī (twenty-four) Hindu kingdoms of central Nepal than with the rest of the Himalayan country. How would he have judged the process of de-Hinduization that has been taking place within some ethnic groups for the last two decades?

6. *Imagining Nepal*

As curious at it may seem today, Nepal has long been seen in the West as a peaceful, enchanting, almost mystical Shangri-La lying amidst the snow-capped Himalayan Mountains and green sloping hills. For a long time, foreigners mistook it for Tibet. They fancifully associated it with highland Buddhist monasteries occupied by monks endowed with supernatural powers. In fact, Nepal was commonly perceived as a mountainous Buddhist country cut off from everything, populated by placid habitants living their lives away from the trivial preoccupations of the outside world, totally given over to their "superstitions". Among the numerous books inspired by these enduring images, *Tintin in Tibet* by Hergé is one of the most famous. Nepal and Tibet were uncharted countries to be explored.

These fanciful ideas still attract a number of foreigners travelling to Nepal to do a trek or sightseeing, or in search of an ashram or meditation centre, or simply to play out their fantasies. Local people have even been totally seduced by some of these ideas; they have, for instance, appropriated them for business purposes. On the whole, Tibetan monasteries still receive more visits than Hindu temples. Behind these mythicized representations lie unseen realities: the old martial tradition of upper Parbatiyā castes (the country's largest population), the bloody plots and murders among ruling families through the ages, the long-lasting contrast between rural huts and the neoclassical Rana palaces of the elite in the Kathmandu Valley, the wretched status of the so-called untouchables, the large majority of Hindu followers among the population, etc. All these aspects have often been either overlooked or neglected.

The first and second wave of foreign anthropologists who worked in Nepal contributed more or less to these dominant distorted ideas. They settled in villages in the north or in the middle-mountain region, inhabited mostly by Tibetans or ethnic groups speaking Tibeto-Burman languages. Sustained by friendly family lifestyles, these researchers spent months in their hosts' houses. From this fieldwork they brought back a wealth of information mainly about the local way of life, the regulating forces, and the cultural patterns. They provided an invaluable view from the inside. But these data were often disconnected from the actual history of the country. Links with the state and political aspects were largely underestimated. Very few researchers focused on the relationships, whether peaceful or otherwise, between different groups.

In the worst cases, wild fabrications paint local life (for instance in the eastern regions) through a Westernized lens as a permanent conflict between individuals, thus undermining the more positive links that bind people together. Some anthropologists, keen to contrast indigenous societies with the Western capitalist world, have also denied headmen, *thulo mānche*, any coercive power and have portrayed the middle hills as being deprived of real hierarchical structures. Even the Maoist revolution has been exoticised by Western scholarship and has been portrayed as creating a totally new social world. Furthermore, towns in the Kathmandu Valley have been regarded as cosmograms replete with enlightened semiotics, almost totally ignoring their human realities and individual trajectories.

The focus has mainly been on family life, kinship and, most of all, shamanism and possession, two mutually related phenomena that have exerted unrestrained fascination on Western anthropologists, a fascination that is unparalleled in Nepal itself. Shamans—their apprenticeship, their beliefs, their paraphernalia and their shamanic ecstatic séances—have captivated researchers from faraway countries, especially from the U.S.A., the U.K., France and Germany. All these studies have contributed to the understanding of shamanic practices and theology. Yet they stress, either directly or indirectly, the "otherness" of Nepal and of Nepali people. At the very heart of this enterprise lies an attempt to portray Nepalis as "different".

Nepal has become the land of the "last": the last shamans, the last transhumant shepherds, the last Hindu kingdom, the last example of Indian Buddhism in the world, etc. By the same token, the contemporary, more global situation and economic realities have hardly been investigated, save some exceptions. The Tarai plains used to be an unknown land and historical links with India were underestimated.

Nearly sixty years after Nepal opened its borders, these chimeras have come to a brutal end. The People's War led by the Māobādīs has dampened such enchanted and exotic visions. The success of the Maoist ideology in a country like Nepal and its victory in the April 2008 election surprised everybody, including anthropologists and the different foreign embassies in Kathmandu. In the space of a few years, guerrillas professing an ideology inspired by the worst forms of Stalinism and anti-democratic principles paralysed the country and took control of a large part of Nepal, apparently with the consent—if not the support—of part of the population. Nepali people have seemingly chosen another dream, the opposite of what Westerners and the Nepali political elite had imagined for them. What is more, this unforeseen revolutionary uprising came, paradoxically, after the mighty Soviet Union was broken up into 15 nations and after the failure of the communist ideology in most parts of the world. To many observers, the Nepali case comes across as quite incongruous. Experts are used to explaining this situation by the extreme backwardness of rural areas and by the resentment of ethnic groups towards high Hindu castes who seized their territories in the eighteenth and nineteenth centuries.

The exodus of Nepali workers to the Gulf for a life of hard labour has also contributed to portraying a blacker picture. The sight of these workers, badly dressed, anxious, with inadequate luggage, unable to find their own seat on board a plane, and most of whom are travelling by air for the first time in their lives, has amazed Westerners. Idealist views of Nepal have been thoroughly transformed: suddenly the stark reality cannot be denied. Migration towards India goes back a very long time in the history of the Nepali population. But new destinations and the considerable rise in the number of departures over recent years have lent this phenomenon a new, dramatic dimension. It reminds me, personally, of the Air France flights arriving from Bangkok and Saigon in the early 1980s, full of Vietnamese refugees in the back of the plane after the communist takeover in 1975. The motives may differ, but the uprooting experience is practically the same.

With its recurrent *bandha,* national strikes, paralysing the country, its government's instability, its persisting areas of poverty, its entrenched forms of caste hierarchy, its corrupt bureaucrats, their short-sighted policies, their incapacities, the enchanted images of Shangri-La and other rosy, fanciful images are now a thing of the past. Nepal has become better known today for its extreme forms of bounded work, its inhuman discriminations against menstruating women and its child labour, its political anarchy, *manparitantra* or *arājakatā*. Tourists soon discover the polluted realities in the streets of the large cities and riparian slums in many places. Most of the genuine architectural heritage of the Kathmandu Valley, — extremely fragile as the April 2015 earthquake that hit Nepal has reminded us—, is being replaced by so-called "modern" buildings, every one identical in style and materials all the way from Cap Cormorin to Kathmandu and from Calcutta to Gujarat. The exoticising attraction of a chimerical Nepal is on the wane. It is high time for us to venture beyond the romantic veil covering Nepal and to demythologize previous ideas.

7. *Living High*

The central Himalayas—where Nepal lies—is generally seen as a hybrid region, an interface where Indo-Aryan and Tibeto-Burman languages and cultures dovetail and overlap. Most social scientists consider that this vast range straddles the border of two of the world's major cultural areas: South Asia and Central Asia. The upland peripheries of Indic and Tibetan cultural forms meet, combine and collide in these valleys. In 1978 James Fisher claimed that: "the Himalayas are not so much a boundary, border, or buffer, as a zipper which stitched together these two densely textured cultural fabrics".[9] Whatever the case may be, over the years, this "Indo-Tibetan interface" model has shed light on a number of cultural complexities of the Himalayan region.

A decade ago, a new paradigm known as *Zomia* (a term for "highlander" in a number of Tibet-Burman languages spoken in Burma, India and Bangladesh) made its first appearance in Himalayan research. This exotic-sounding name was coined in 2002 by the Dutch social scientist Willem van Schendel in an article published in a geographical journal.[10] He proposed that the highlands of Asia, from the western Himalayan range through the Tibetan plateau to the lower end of the peninsular Southeast Asian highlands be considered a political and historical entity significantly distinct from the usual geographical divisions of Asia: Central, South, East, and Southeast. "Zomia" constitutes, he argued, a neglected transnational area, which overlaps segments of all four sub-regions without truly belonging to any of them. According to him, it is an area marked by a sparse population, historical isolation, political domination by powerful surrounding states, marginality of all kinds, and huge linguistic and religious diversity. In 2007, van Schendel opted to extend Zomia further westward and northward, to include southern Qinghai and Xinjiang within China, as well as a fair portion of central Asia, encompassing the highlands of Pakistan, Afghanistan, Tajikistan, and Kyrgyzstan.

The rationale behind the geographically dominated notion of Zomia (altitude, remoteness, fringe) is the focus on the highland borderlands of Asia and their diverse ethnicities, which amount to between 120 and 150 million people. According to van Schendel, this inland region would be inhabited by populations deprived of independent states and situated on the margins of official borders. The idea is certainly interesting, especially in matters of cross-boundaries studies. Such a transnational approach does have considerable potential for generating cross-disciplinary dialogue, notably among global historians, geographers and anthropologists.

In a book published in 2009, James C. Scott makes use of this Zomia concept to stress the self-governability of Himalayan people on the fringes and their state avoidance over the last centuries.[11] Scott stresses some other alleged aspects of these groups such as their relatively egalitarian structure, oral religious tradition and high level of mobility. Admittedly, most of the time, these hinterlands escaped exogenous political interference. Up to the present day, the history of Nepal shows traces of resistance in many ethnic groups and a real sense of autonomy. It is also true that those faced with conflict or oppression in the southern plains or in the northern kingdoms have over the years taken refuge in these highland, forested areas. Nepal has been populated in this way.

There are many other positive aspects to these viewpoints. Any anthropologist specialized in Nepalese studies and who has travelled through northern and eastern Burma, and northern Thailand or Laos, would rapidly reach the conclusion that a number of features are common to the ethnic groups located in central and eastern Nepal, and not only in terms of their mountainous landscape or linguistics. However, a number of theoretical assumptions underlying this concept of Zomia are difficult to accept. My aim here is to point out some of these difficulties and to test the proposals against Nepali realities. I will limit myself to three major aspects.

Firstly, the assumption that Zomia is made up of ethnicities living some distance from the seat of regional and global power and often out of reach of the main urban centres is only partially true. I argue that the central Himalayas were not totally isolated in the past and that they were not inaccessible, as is asserted. Its present population is the result of historical migrations stretching over centuries. After settling in separate regions, these people never ceased to establish mutual relationships with each other or with cultures to the north, in Tibet, and to the south, in India. Zomian ethnic groups were never totally cut-off from their surroundings. Moreover, this area has always been traversed by highly frequented trans-Himalayan trade routes linking the two regions. These trade routes have had many ramifications throughout the highlands.

Secondly, the diversity of situations in this interstitial zone needs to be taken into account. Having worked for more than four decades on one of the main state-centres of the central Himalayas—the Malla city kingdoms of the Kathmandu Valley—I am, understandably, inherently reluctant to accept this idea of an ungoverned non-state region. Petty kingdoms and chiefdoms were a feature of pre-modern Nepali Himalayan populations; Magars and Tamangs keep alive the memory of former kings. State structures were for the most part embryonic, but they did exist.

Thirdly, Zomian peripheries are not the only region in Asia to be characterized by such marginalities. The same model can be applied to a number of fringe regions situated on the Indian subcontinent itself, starting with tribal zones in forested areas. Until recently these zones were not totally included in the kingship political systems of the surrounding caste people. Moreover, their populations are characterized by more or less egalitarian features (despite local chiefdoms and, occasionally, small kingdoms).

Altogether, this Zomia concept seems to me to be a contentious notion, based on dubious assumptions and full of abstract unreliable generalisations. Too much ink has already been spilt on these nebulous theories and wild speculations. Scholars would be better resuming their in-depth, basic studies using primary sources and working from the ground up. Local historiographies as well as studies on inter-dynamic groups and non-caste forms of hierarchy will probably teach us more about the gradual process of how these diverse regions integrated the encompassing states.

Notes

1. In Newari, Madhesī are often called Marshya, which is a derogative term.
2. Ludwig F. Stiller, *Prithivi Narayan Shah in the light of Dibya Upadesh*, Ranchi: Catholic Press, 1968.
3. Cf. the special issue of the online journal *Samaj*, 10 (2014), *Ideas of South Asia*, published by the *Centre d'études de l'Inde et de l'Asie du Sud*, Paris.
4. Kamal. P. Malla, *From Literature to Culture. Selected Writings on Nepalese studies, 1980-2010*. Kathmandu: Himal books, 2015, p. 273.
5. Cf. Martin Gaenszle, "The Power of Script: Phālugunanda's Role in the Formation of Kiranti Ethnicity", in V. Arora & N. Jayaram (eds.), *Routeing Democracy in the Himalayas*. Delhi: Routledge, 2013, pp. 50-73. Phalgunanda is believed to have discovered the Kiranti script in a cave. Satya Hangma religion is a mix of both tribal and Hindu elements.
6. Clifford Geertz, *Negara: The Theatre State in Nineteenth Century Bali*. Princeton: Princeton University Press, 1980.
7. Ernest Renan, *What is a Nation?* (conference 1882). Internet Archive, Wayback Machine, 2011.
8. Frederick H. Gaige, *Regionalism and Nationalism Unity in Nepal*. Berkeley: University of California, 1975.
9. James F. Fisher (ed.), *Himalayan Anthropology. The Indo-Tibetan Interface*. The Hague: Mouton, 1978.
10. Willem van Schendel, 2002, "Geographies of knowing, geographies of ignorance: jumping scale in Southeast Asia" *Environment and Planning: Society and Space* 20(6), pp. 647 – 68.
11. James C. Scott, *The Art of not being Governed: An Anarchist History of Upland Southeast Asia*. Yale: Yale University Press, 2009.

CHAPTER

2

Facets of Identity

The rise of claims to an identity — the term comes from the Latin word *idem* — is a major phenomenon throughout the globe in this beginning of the twenty-first century, and a source of recurring conflicts. Its manifestations can be broken up into a number of different facets: religious, ethnic, political, which are not automatically interlinked. The feelings on which they are based are mainly reactions against ongoing globalization (which creates a hybridity of cultures and languages), and anxious responses towards the ever-growing modernizing forces. They express a fear of deracination, a search for roots, a quest to bond and belong. In some cases, these sentiments provoke social movements in defiance of the capitalist expansion that is seeping further and further into societies.

These dynamics generally lead to the creation of self-contained groups, jealous of each other's culture and prerogatives, consolidating their own interests in corporate associations, curled up around their individual specificities. They may even engender physical and mental ghettos. "Substantialization of caste" is an example of such reinforcement and introversion of social groups to the detriment of cooperation. In Nepal, the fear of the loss of traditions, culture and land has nurtured major conflicts that have bearings on political life. The Maoists cynically exploited such a sense of ethnic separateness and long-standing hostility towards Hindu castes. The litigious issue of federalism, which galvanizes Tibeto-Burman language-speaking ethnic groups as well as Hindu upper castes in contemporary Nepal, is a plain illustration of how an identity issue is turned into a political issue [**2**, **9** and **11**].

It is particularly perilous, politically and scientifically, to deal with these ethnic and other forms of identity. At first, one is tempted to reject the old-fashioned ideas defended by ethnic activists and to drive them back to nineteenth-century prehistory of anthropology. I myself have written a series of critical articles opposing the proliferation of ethnic identity-based claims.[1] Ethnicity (*jātīyatā*) movements frequently rely on inappropriate notions of discrete small-scale cultures without any contact with their neighbours. In addition, divisiveness in the name of identity, whether ethnic or regional, constitutes a real danger for the integrity of the nation. Yet, on second thoughts, any researcher, at one moment or another in the course of their work, comes to ponder the extraordinary myriad of ethnic and linguistic communities that constitutes Nepal. This diversity is a treasure that needs to be preserved. To oppose or to undermine this mosaic will only lead to more violence than Nepal has already endured and to undemocratic ways of resolving problems. The issue of contestation against centralized government and its bureaucracy therefore needs to be addressed and the dynamics of contention have to be carefully examined.

Identity also plays a role at a larger, national level. The nationalist signs and postures that heighten the Nepali identity versus Nepal's powerful neighbours cannot be underestimated. The *daurā-suruwāl* (and *topī*), men's official national dress, showcased on all government occasions, has, for instance, become an ostensible symbol of Nepali identity, though one may rightly questions the representativeness of this uniform (reminiscent of the one-dress Panachayat era) in terms of social and ethnic diversity.

8. The Romance of Ethnicity

How will "new Nepal" conciliate equality and identity? The two concepts differ in a number of aspects. They even have contradictory and competing meanings. Equality is a universalistic concept based on the individual. Its best and earliest expression is the 1789 French *Declaration of the Rights of Man and of the Citizen* which declares that all men are born and remain (free and) equal in rights. In this declaration, the word "man" encompasses genders, races, cultures, religions, and other specificities. This equality is supposed to be valid at all times and in all places.

The concept of identity (*asmitā, pahicān*) has a more particularistic connotation. It relates to the individuality of a particular person or to the sameness of a definable group, its members' common sense of belonging and self. In the latter collective sense, which is the one most used today in Nepal, the notion refers to the dignity of their members, their rights as a community. It may designate a gender group (women, for instance), an ethnic or religious community or whatever other social category, and can be divided ad infinitum by intersecting the parameters. The UNESCO charter lends much more importance to collective types of identity than the 1789 individualistic French declaration.

Ethnicity is, of course, one of the most important manifestations of (and claims to) identity in present-day Nepal. The Nepal Federation of Indigenous Nationalities (NEFIN) has succeeded in unifying the action of 56 ethnic groups from Nepal, each with its own identity, particularities, within a wide organisation claiming a joint sense of belonging. The label Ādivāsī/Janajāti clearly distinguishes its constituent members from other groups in Nepal. The rejection of the caste system and its internal hierarchy (except for Newars), the fact that most of them speak or used to speak non Indo-European languages (with the exception of the Tharus and some others), their subjugated position since the eighteenth century are shared common features.

This ethnic current has proved to be extremely powerful in terms of mobilising the public and organising *bandha*. Each of these groups presently lays claim to its own customs (for instance, in books written in Nepali by local authors chosen by Ādivāsī Janajāti Utthān Pratishthān, a pan-Nepali ethnic organization which has been officially recognized by the authorities), their own festivals, costumes, and so forth. Interestingly enough, such a sense of community has not gone beyond the associative level. NEFIN has often even expressed its disagreement with the mainstream four-party decisions. In spite of efforts by some activists, it has not become a united political party. In fact, this is one of its weaknesses.

Another problem is that many other forms of ethnicity or collective assertive movement are emerging in the country. One may quote Chetri Samāj which contests the Janajātis' exclusive claim to indigeneity. Chetris contend that they are just as *ādivāsī* as Gurungs, Magars, or other groups, which in some parts of Nepal (in the west) is actually true. They also associate their sense of identity with the history of Nepal and with the process of its unification. In other words, they do not want to be called immigrants in what they claim to be their homeland.

Among other collective identity movements, mention may be made of feminist groups with their own specific demands which are diametrically opposed to male-dominated society. A number of *mahilā* (women) associations exist, divided between Janajāti *mahilā* and Parbatiyā *mahilā*, and possibly between Buddhist, Hindu and Muslim *mahilā* groups.

Dalits are, of course, also fighting for their own identity, in a more difficult manner due to their former subservient status in the caste system. Yet their actions are sometimes impeded by the logic of ethnicity itself: Newars, for instance, ban or try to ban their former untouchables from joining Dalit associations. They stress the solidarity among all Newars, whatever their caste may be, on the basis of their ethnic identity. What about Hindu and minority religious associations? And regional entities, especially the Tarai? All these movements are organised and defend their own identity. These opposing forces perturb the political landscape, overtly as well as in an underground manner, often running counter to the parties' political game. And the media is inundated with identity politics.

How can a common sense of Nepali citizenship emerge under these conditions? How can a democracy be maintained when faced with so many divisive forces? How can a person, for instance, be at the same time a Dalit, a Newar, a women and a Nepali? These multiple forms of belonging have to be recognised and hierarchised in a way that is acceptable to everybody. Exclusive claims always engender counter-claims, some of which are reasonable. And ethnophobia is a logical result of excessive identity demands and preferential rights. Since the 1990s, the various governments' policies have tended to reinforce collective links more than to guarantee the emancipation of individuals. Affirmative action measures have been taken here and there. Nepal follows the Indian model in these matters, between positive discrimination and federalism, granting much more importance to collective identities than in Euro-American countries, with the risk of limiting free individual competition and impoverishing the debate.

To put it bluntly, fighting exclusively for a Schedule Tribe (ST), a Schedule Caste (SC) or OBC status, as is often the case in India, is not a satisfactory political model. In India, in fact, democracy has not put a stop to caste distinctions, although ritual roles governing food transactions are becoming obsolete due to modern living conditions.[2] Whatever the case may be, such turmoil is what makes the Nepali situation so appealing and interesting at the present time. Beyond its inchoate situation, this new Himalayan republic is one of the most innovative multicultural laboratories in South Asia in matters of social change.

9. Imagined Territories

After eight years of deliberations, numerous *bandhas* and mass demonstrations, the Constitution has finally been proclaimed in 2015. During this exceedingly long process, the proposed federal options varied considerably from one party or political organization to another. Some emphasised the ethnic and linguistic factors, others geographical regions, while others suggested a combination of different elements.

Nepali Congress and Communist CPN-UML, the two dominant parties in Constituent Assembly II elected in 2013, were known among commentators as reluctant federalists. They opted for an enlarged decentralised architecture. As I write this piece, the names of the seven newly established provinces and the power to be delegated to these local entities have not yet been decided. More protests, *bandhas* and riots are predictable.

Regionalization and federalization had their supporters in each camp. How can the extreme ethnic, cultural and ecological diversity of the country be reflected without jeopardising the country's unity and harmony? How to avoid a balkanisation of Nepal, a process that can lead to economic impoverishment, external intervention and ruin of the country's integrity? Only a combination of multiple factors negotiated between readily willing political parties is a reasonable option. The present government has adopted such a viewpoint and refused regional provinces based on ethnic identity. In the following lines I hope to contribute to the discussion and provide, when possible, some clarifications.

Federalist and autonomous claims based on ethnicity are supported by some solid justifications. Up until the second part of the eighteenth century, what is now Nepal was compartmentalized into numerous autonomous kingdoms and chiefdoms mostly on an ethno-cultural basis. The conquest by Prithivi Narayan Shah and his followers was achieved to the detriment of these previously independent or semi-autonomous political entities. Over the centuries, various forms of resistance against the new centralized Hindu State have periodically expressed their discontent. The Maoist war itself, during the period 1996-2006, can be seen, at least partly, as an upsurge against the Hindu upper-caste establishment, which has ruled the country for centuries. Today still, some VDCs are for the most part inhabited by a dominant ethnic group that considers its territory to be its own rightful property. These ancestral homelands are highly charged with religious values and governed by strong forms of belonging. They are strengthened every year by rituals that highlight the direct link between ancestors and local guardian/patron deities.

However, it is doubtful that whole mono-ethnic regions existed in the past. Magars have long cohabitated with Khas people in Magrant. In the course of their history Gurungs and Western Tamangs have assimilated local Ghale groups. The situation has been slightly different in the east, a region that was the last to submit to forced integration by the Gorkhas. Yet, even in these areas, we cannot ignore the impact of Hindu kingdoms (such as Chaudandi or Vijayapur) located in the southern plains.

In the past, the Newars assimilated a number of immigrants from India, and the former Valley of Nepal has indeed become a melting pot of different cultures. Throughout Nepal local ethnic groups have always welcomed newcomers and have assimilated them. The peopling process has taken place in interaction with several groups. The quest for the pure origins of such and such a group is a matter of internal politics rather than a scientific undertaking. The timely book recently edited by Joëlle Smadja on territorial changes in the Himalayas,[3] with contributions by three Nepali scholars (Dahal, Hacchethu and Khanal), shows that territories (and among them ethnic territories) have never remained static. They have, on the contrary, always undergone changes in the past and are forever being rebuilt.

Moreover, the cartography of social spaces has radically changed over the last decades. Admittedly, the present map of the population of Nepal highlights some persisting homogenised ethnic homelands here and there. Yet, it more often shows a considerable hybridization of populations and an increasingly marked interethnic and inter-caste mosaic. In some of their ancestral homelands, *ādivāsī/janajātis* are now the minority among the waves of migration (Gurungs, Magars, Newars, for instance). In other words, the current names of suggested provinces based on a mono-ethnic group may be linguistically grounded but, socially and culturally speaking, they have largely been imagined.

It may even be asserted that the force of the post-1990 ethnic rising is inversely proportional to the realities of local ties and to the persistence of local languages. The old social order upon which these bonds were founded is clearly on the decline. The present period is more and more the time for ethnic diasporas dotted over the world, in Europe, the Gulf countries, Australia or the U.S.A., rather than for closed introverted territories in the Nepalese hills and in the Tarai. In other words, Nepali *ādivāsī/janajāti* must prevent political parties from exploiting their culture for the sole purpose of gaining power at their expense. They must decide for themselves the sort of non-confrontational future they wish to secure in a basically diverse country, while respecting everyone's cultural rights.[4] Nepal needs better communication, good roads, development, not autonomous ethnic enclaves.

In this respect, the case of North-East India and particularly of Assam, where a number of Nepali expatriates live, must be borne in mind by activists. The setting up of new ethnic boundaries and ethnicized territories in this part of the world has created perennial inner conflicts, the displacement of populations, hatred and violence.[5] These federal territories have not given the local groups concerned more freedom than before, but have led to lasting military intervention by the central state and total closure of the newly created states. Nepal deserves something better.

10. Museums of Ethnic Culture

During my first years at CNRS, I was posted not to a university but to the former *Musée de l'Homme*, Paris's erstwhile ethnographic museum. This famous institution housed important collections of artefacts that had been brought back from Nepal (and from many other countries) between 1960 and 1970 by various French experts, most of whom were anthropologists. I myself donated to this museum various items illustrating the material culture of the Jyāpu Newars and of the Western Tamangs of Ankhu Khola (Dhading district) among whom I carried out my first fieldwork in Nepal. At that time, the study of material culture and objects used in daily life was an important part of any university course in anthropology and a significant field of research in this discipline, especially in its non-structuralist current. I remember that, up until 1968, one of the final examinations in the degree course in ethnology at the Sorbonne University included the study of one or two material items selected from this Museum. This was phased out long ago from French university courses in anthropology, and in 2006 the ethnographic collections of the *Musée de l'Homme* were transferred to what is now the *Musée du Quai Branly*, in Paris, a museum that focuses mainly on the artistic qualities of non-Western ethnographic items, and largely overlooks the former cultural contextual study of artefacts.

Ethnographic museums have prevailed in the West since the nineteenth century but their existence in the South and in the East is more recent. It dates back mostly to the contemporary post-colonial period. In fact, the proliferation of such museums in non-Western countries only became a global trend in the 1990s and at the beginning of the twentieth-first century. This phenomenon is linked to the rise of ethnic identities and the recognizance of the rights of indigenous cultures by the United Nations. It is a particularly exciting process to explore since it lies at the crossroads between ethnicity and the politics of culture. As a rule, these ethnographic museums echo the on-going ethnicisiation of culture.[6]

In Nepal, the movement was amplified by the post-panchayat political paradigm in favour of multiculturalism. Today these museum institutions play an active role in ethnogenesis and in the negotiation of collective identities. They provide ethnic groups with visibility and illustrate their quest for lost cultures. Since the 1990s, an ethnic museum is a way of asserting one's identity throughout the country and a manner of revitalizing one's cultural heritage in a multicultural political context. It is also a mark of modernity. For an ethnic group, not having a museum today is to admit that a minimum level of civilisation does not apply to it!

The main national project, the Nepal National Ethnographic Museum (*Nepāl Rāshtrīya Jātīya Sãngrahālaya*), is a government-run programme. Its purpose is to illustrate the cultural patchwork of Nepal in terms of both ethnic groups and castes. The concept of this museum (NMEN) was launched in 1995 by Professor Ganeshman Gurung from Tribhuvan University with the help of a Norwegian anthropologist, Harald Skar, who has now retired. The building, situated in Kirtipur municipality, on the way to Champadevi Mountain, has still not been completed for financial reasons. However, the committee in charge of it has opened an exhibition hall on the first floor of the Central Tourism Board, in Bhrikutimandap, Kathmandu. It displays a series of artefacts that have been categorised on an ethnic and caste basis. Only thirteen outstanding ethnic groups have been chosen. A second room contains other showcases devoted to lesser-known communities. Here museology makes use of male and female dummies in ethnic attire, showing the diversity of each group's specific clothing and jewellery. The collections are rich but the museum is under-equipped in terms of its library, documentation and electronic devices. The final Champadevi project is aimed at representing the culture of 103 Nepalese groups.

The small Regional Museum of Pokaraha (Nayabazar), which was built in 1985, is another state-funded museum. It has an archaeological section, a good collection of musical instruments, and a number of items belonging to Gurung, Tharu, Darai, Thakali ethnic groups, and to Kāmī, Damāī, Gandharva castes. At least two other national ethnographic museums, or at least museums possessing an ethnographic section, have already opened across the country, in Dhankuta and Surkhet. The building of another government museum, devoted to the Tharu culture, is scheduled for Nawalparasi District (Western Nepal), which is far from any tourist route. These museums come under the Ministry of Culture, Tourism and Civil Aviation.

Ethnic museums (*jātīya sañgrahālaya*) that are set up at community level and managed by specific communities on an associative basis are an alternative to these official government undertakings. The best example is the Jyāpu Samaj Ethnographic Museum in Lalitpur (opened in 2012). Its showcases not only Jyāpu culture but by and large, the Newars' whole rich ethnic fabric. It is a well-known fact that Jyāpu peasants claim to be the indigenous stratum among Newars and the depositary of their more ancient culture. The museum is located both on the ground floor and in the basement of the imposing red-brick Malla-styled Jyāpu Academy building (Bhola Ganesh) [**15**]. The large room is divided into three main sections, featuring various tools and cooking utensils, musical instruments and traditional clothes, as well as religious items used during festivals and ceremonies. An interesting exhibit shows miniature clay figurines drawing Rāto Matsyendranāth cart. Large numbers of items are crammed together on tables draped in red velvet cloth. They have been sourced from discarded objects and from donations from the community.[7]

Another example is the Tharu Cultural Museum, *Tharu sānskritik sañgrahālaya*, in Chitwan (Bachhauli), which opened in 2006. It illustrates various Tharu festivals, in particular Phaguwā (Holī), and displays a wide range of fishing artefacts, one of the Tharus' main economic activities. Like other museums of its kind, dummies represent Tharu men and women going about their traditional activities. Similar projects, but much more modest in terms of their size and ambition, have sprung up all over the country. In Pokhara and in Lamjung, as far as the Gurungs are concerned, in Kathmandu for the Rais, etc.

The International Mountain Museum, designed by John Sanday, also deserves a mention. The Nepal Mountaineering Association (NMA), a non-government and non-political organization, opened this museum in February 2004 thanks to substantial Japanese funding. The museological content has greatly benefited from the ICIMOD's (International Centre for Integrated Mountain Development) knowledge of mountains in Nepal and around the world. The museum (floor area of 3,110 square metres) brings together items from various cultural groups living in the Annapurna region (Gurung, Thakali), but also belonging to more distant regions, such as the Limbus, Rais and so on. It makes use of dummies to valorise the exhibits. Another feature is a Tibetan prayer room that has been faithfully reconstituted. The coherent intellectual framework based on the relationship between Man and his environment is the hallmark of the exhibition.

And lastly, there are more or less private initiatives, backed by foreign or international institutions. The Changu Narayan Living Traditions Museum (LTM), which has been set up in the *sattals* (wood-covered shelter) surrounding Vishnu's religious complex, and is curated by Judith Chase, an American citizen, is perhaps the most noteworthy of them. It opened in March 2012 and consists of four sections illustrating the four major geographical regions of Nepal: the Tarai, the middle hills, the Kathmandu Valley and the high mountains of the Himalayas. Chase's own collection of artefacts includes tools, cooking utensils, clothing and religious objects. The intricate ceremonial wall murals from Mithila are particularly impressive. Excellent photographs accompany the exhibits. Unfortunately, the museum was partly destroyed by the earthquake in 2015.[8]

The marked boom in ethnographic museums over the last two decades in the country epitomizes a process of the *museification of culture*. This does not mean that the items showcased are no longer used in daily and ritual life. It simply means that today there is a growing need to display them. Ethnic objects are no longer restricted to their traditional practical usage. They have acquired a representational role; they have become a tool for ethnic assertion. From a sociological standpoint, the shift from being functional cultural items to being exhibited in glass cases is a major issue. These objects have become a public expression of a culture and are dissociated from their normal use in everyday life.

The growing number of these museums also comes at a pivotal moment when ethnic material cultures are on the decline or have totally disappeared. As a matter of fact, traditional artefacts are gradually being replaced in daily life by modern items. The local knowledge required to make them is dying out [**79**]. Patan's Jyāpu Ethnographic Museum shows some musical instruments that no one knows how to play any more. Similarly, the knowledge of the environment and of its natural resources upon which these objects are based is rapidly dying out, especially among the young generation.

The artefacts presented in these museums safeguard material and symbolic cultures that are under threat. However, the rather inadequate means to stage the collections tend to mummify the items. The generalised use of dummies, like those to be found in clothes shops in bazaars, accentuates the outmoded presentation. Moreover, films or videos rarely accompany items. There are no multimedia facilities, no interactive programmes, no audio recordings. Furthermore, the everyday objects on display are rarely contextualised in terms of the present day, and the aesthetic dimension of the artefacts is simply absent. The exhibits keep the memory of the ethnic group alive but tend to portray a necrology of the past and a frozen-in-time image of the culture. In other words, the objects are presented in a somewhat fossilized manner, without underlying the dynamic and transformational aspects of local cultures. Understandably, most of these museums suffer from a lack of visitors.

11. Ethnocidal State

Broadly speaking, the debate concerning the federalization of the country opposes two lines of thought: those who merely want to reinforce existing forms of decentralisation dating back to panchayat times and those who propose that a wide range of powers be transferred to new federal subunits. The first emphasises the need for a strong state and the danger of splitting the country. The second, deeply hostile to the central state apparatus, maps out a new Nepal grounded on cultural differences and calls for a radical restructuring of the nation. This fundamental opposition between centralists and federalists, which is firmly rooted in Nepali politics, will linger long after the promulgation of a new constitution. The genealogies of the second movement, so prominent in present-day Nepal, are worthwhile tracing back, at least in part.

The anti-state school of thinking goes back a long way. In South Asia, one of the best illustrations is Mohandas Gandhi. Gandhi was extremely defiant towards state power. He was much more acquiescent towards culture, the individual and small self-ruled communities. The Mahatma saw in the state apparatus "violence in a concentrated and organized form". He asserted that the state can never be weaned off violence to which it owes its very existence. He often claimed that: "man has a soul whereas the state is a soulless machine". His model was therefore based on self-rule and autonomy, *svarāj*, self-governance. According to his view, power must lie directly in the hands of the people. Gandhi therefore strongly opposed the state, which he saw as amoral and incompatible with freedom.[9] He advocated for a minimal level of state intervention and was totally opposed, in connection with this, to Indian Congress. Nehru in particular was convinced of the legitimacy of the state's role and its crucial importance in economic and social fields. The Gandhian *antistatism* vision still has its followers in India among a number of social movements that oppose repressive local and central government.

In the nineteenth and twentieth centuries, most European political thinkers, especially socialist theorists, defended the need for a strong state, notably to reduce inequalities. By contrast, liberal economists and politicians mostly support an anti-statist mode of thinking. Anarchists, like Bakounine (1814-1876), provided this stream of thought with its most radical expressions. In matters of ethnic rights, an important concept, *ethnocide,* emerged in the West at the end of the 1960s and in the 1970s. It was mainly formulated by a French anthropologist, Pierre Clastres, who died accidentally in 1977 at the age of forty-four.[10] Ethnocide can be defined as the systematic destruction of the lifestyle and the way of thinking of people who differ from mainstream society.[11] It does not necessary imply the physical extermination of people (genocide). Genocide kills people while ethnocide kills their spirit. Ethnocide, so Clastres said, is the negation of differences. It is characteristic of colonial rule or other situations where coercion is applied.[12] The *ādivāsī/janajāti* groups of Nepal can be seen as an endogenous South-Asian expression of anti-statist thought. This movement is opposed to centralized bureaucracy and is fighting for an alternative federal state model. Members of NEFIN, their main pan-ethnic indigenous organisation, rely on the organizing capacity of ethnic groups to build their policies.

The intellectual lineage of antistatism is therefore diverse and comes from different corners of the world, in an apparently uncoordinated way. Gandhi was an extremely religious person whereas anarchists are by definition atheist. Western liberal thinkers, for their part, insist on keeping private religion separate from politics and collective issues. In Nepal, the *ādivāsī/janajāti* movement is mainly divorced from Hinduism and relies partly on non-Hindu cults. On some occasions, its members shift to Buddhism. The remark has often been made that the development of monistic states conceals a transfer of sacrality from the declining forms of religion to more appealing and apparently "secular" political concepts.

According to Clastres, Western civilisation is ethnocidal in itself. The Europeans who invaded the Americas from 1492 onwards practised systematic ethnocide towards indigenous peoples, seeking over time to abolish their religions, communities and languages. They did the same thing a few centuries later in North America with indigenous Indians. Full of their own superiority, they looked down on all other cultures as being inferior. The history of Western expansion in the nineteenth century is punctuated by the methodological massacre of autochthonous peoples. Yet this destruction is not the exclusivity of European and North American modern civilisation. The same process took place in pre-modern times in Asia and in Africa. In fact, this is to be found in all conquering states, even pre-modern ones. In an article published in 1990, Harka Gurung, the great Nepali geographer, explicitly compared the Gorkha conquest in the eighteenth and nineteenth centuries to the invasion of the Americas by Europeans.[13] He called Parbatiyās "conquistadors" and lay emphasis on the process of expropriating land that accompanied the conquest of the centre and east middle mountains of Nepal. Ethnic minorities in Nepal were coerced into abandoning their languages and cultures.

Clastres also applied this concept of ethnocide to the destruction by centralist Jacobin revolutionaries of ancient pre-revolutionary French autonomous provinces and their habitually different languages/customs. According to him and other anti-statist thinkers, the state is basically opposed to a diversity of cultures. It dictates terms to minorities. It also invents dubious notions, such as "serving the state" and disseminates them among the elite to reinforce its ever-growing powers. "Every state organization is ethnocidal. Ethnocide is the State's normal mode of existence", so this French author claimed. Totalitarian states, such as Stalinist and fascist states, merely developed these monolithic leanings into frantic political pathologies.

In Nepal, *ādivāsī/janajāti* groups are more or less inspired by anti-statist ideas. They defend minority cultures against intervention by the state, which is conceived as a foreign coercive force. The state, they say, merely uses the concept of development to achieve its leaders' political ends. The same line of thought is defended by the Anglo-American *Survival International* organization. The defence of ethnic identities is the motto of all these groups.

The globalization of cultures and economies throughout the planet has hastened the impact of these destructives forces. Actually, the eradication of minority cultures has been achieved at a rapid pace. Despite frequent uprisings, deterritorialization and mass deportations are deliberately undertaken. Throughout the twentieth century, capitalist and communist states bulldozed minority cultures. "Something is rotten in the state of the state", so Ashih Nandy asserts.[14]

The concept of ethnocide has been deservedly criticized.

As I have showed above, it covers a much larger process than the one originally conceived by Clastres. It involves Western as well as non-Western states. Islamic civilization, for instance, has done no better than European states in these matters. Moreover, the eradication of a minority culture by invading superior forces leaves pending the question of the voluntary submission of a wide array of cultures to a civilisation that provides its members with improved agricultural techniques, new seeds, and new tools. Throughout Nepal, ethnic groups have greatly benefited from the introduction of rice cultivation and terraced agriculture on slopes by hill-dwelling upper-Hindu castes. Finally, the concept of ethnicity is grounded in a major separation between stateless and state societies that contradicts ethnographic realities. A small pre-modern lineage society can in the same manner engender totalitarian social forces. I myself have experienced such confined settings and oppressive structures in rural Nepal. Abusive simplifications therefore seriously question the validity of the concept.

Despite these conceptual reservations, cultures are increasingly refusing to sing their swansongs and to enter history books. They fight against state bureaucracies that constantly jeopardise their survival and their way of life in the name of so-called modernity and economic viability. Is it really possible to oppose these pluralist views? The defence of placed-based cultures against globalizing forces and state centralistic tendencies is clearly a requirement of the day. The modern nation-state is obviously a serious threat to the diversity of cultures.

12. Concealed Identities

Sociologists and social anthropologists often conceptualize social identity as a rigid social phenomenon that produces fixed boundaries and marked feelings of difference. In South Asia for instance, discussions about identity focus mainly on the sense of belonging to several primeval social groups and on the rise of collective identity movements in recent years. How is the membership of these groups determined?

What are their characteristic attributes? What claim do they make? What are the socio-historical determinants?

Regrettably, the numerous cases where reverse situations occurred at a particular moment in history are often forgotten. By that I mean periods and situations during which a person's identity is hidden from the authorities or simply from their neighbours, which is the opposite of the process of ethnicity. Here the onus is on escape from the firm, fixed lines of ethnic or religious identity. More oblique, shifting and flexible selfhood comes to the fore. If we believe, like the philosopher Michel de Certeau (1925-1986), that an ethnic group exists only when it runs the risk of existing, what about groups or individuals who do not want to exist openly for what they are but for what they pretend to be?

In the Western world, this concealment has particularly been used among religious and ethnic minorities. A number of Jews changed their names during or after World War II to avoid persecution, segregation and the horror of war camps in Germany or in Poland during the period 1941-1944. They adopted standard Christian names, hiding any indication of their ethnic-religious surname. The principal motive was their fear of anti-Semitism. During the Middle Ages, Jews from Spain and Portugal were even forced to convert to Christianity by the religious and political authorities. Despite changing their official creed, they continued to practise their original Hebraic religion in secret.

Similarly, a number of Armenians converted to Islam to escape the deportations and death marches undertaken by the Turks in 1915. Yet they continued to live in hiding as Armenians, marrying among their own community and, in some cases, clandestinely reverting to Christianity. They are known as Crypto-Armenians or Hidden Armenians. This status has been handed down through generations.

Such extreme cases are not totally unheard of in the Himalayas, a region that is renowned for its rich ethnic mosaic. It is a well-known fact, for instance, that in ancient times Buddhists in the Kathmandu Valley were forced to convert to Hinduism. In the nineteenth century, Pranāmī followers were pursued and forced by orthodox Brahmans to burn their holy books. Despite this, they continued to practise their religion secretly. Similarly, after the Gurkhalis came to power at the end of the eighteenth century, Christian converts were under the obligation either to flee to Northern India or to practise their faith clandestinely. During my fieldwork in upper Ankhu Khola (Dhading District) in the 1980s, I discovered that some Tamang villages had wholly or partially converted to Christianity since the early twentieth century. Yet this religious affiliation was kept hidden.

There are plenty of stories in the Himalayan regions where people voluntarily hide their identity and claim to have another one. Whole Tamang villages located on the periphery of the Ankhu Khola watershed decided long ago to call themselves Gurung in order to enrol in the Gorkha battalions. Tamangs living in the neighbouring districts east and west of the Kathmandu Valley were in fact banned from enlisting. Similarly, in the Kathmandu Valley itself, Newar peasants who were eager to be recruited among Gorkha mercenaries call themselves Nagarkoti (another name for members of the Pahari micro-ethnic group) because Newars were not allowed into the army until 1951. Enlisting among martial castes could thereby lead to a shift in one's identity.

Today, there is still a strong contrast between the self-assertion of Janajāti groups in claiming their ethnic identity and the shame felt by most Dalits in disclosing their family name to outsiders. Members of these so-called former "untouchable castes" still suffer from low self-esteem due to persisting bans that are enforced by high- and middle-caste groups. How can one actually enjoy belonging to a group which is denied all its rights? Admittedly, caste associations such as the Nepā Khadgī Sewā Samiti (Khadgī Samāj) are slowly helping to change this mindscape and today proudly wear their ceremonial white dress as a mark of their caste. But, by and large, low-caste people try as far as possible to hide their real identity. They are eager to be addressed by more honorific names.

Frequent changes in caste membership must also be

mentioned in this respect. Certain castes have the possibility of climbing the social ladder by consigning their original family name to oblivion and by adopting the caste name of a group ranked a little higher in the hierarchy. Thus, members of the Newar peasant caste became Shresthas not only by migrating towards the hills but also by moving within the Kathmandu Valley [**53**, **54**]. In my book *Society and Religion among the Newars*,[15] I also mention several cases of non-Newar families who have successfully become Shresthas through inter-ethic marriage with Newars. In all these situations, a social identity is gradually forgotten and a new one adopted. This shift is based on a self-re-evaluation process.

Masked identities reveal an oppressive society where the stigmatization of minority groups prevails. Caste mobility on the other hand demonstrates that an individual is never stuck within a specific identity. Whatever the case, identity appears to be contingent on specific dialectics of events. It is a constructed process that needs to be contextualised and put into an historical perspective. It would be interesting to explore in more detail how these dual selves, the veiled and the asserted, coexist within the same person and the inner tension that this creates.

13. To Whom Does Lumbini Belong?

Lumbini, the birthplace of the historic Lord Buddha, is a fascinating place to investigate how an archaeological site takes on an international dimension.[16] In the course of a recent visit, I was able to watch groups of people of different nationalities, each under the guidance of a priest or a master, performing religious functions in the Sacred Garden near the Maya Devi temple. Some were Burmese, others Thai. A white American Buddhist group was also present. Most of them were there to worship Buddha and to chant religious hymns while others circumambulated the Ashoka pillar and the Bodhi tree. Some were listening to a talk given by their teacher. Offerings consisted of flags, coins, butter and oil lamps, incense and candles, perfumed water. From an archaeological site discovered in 1896, Lumbini has slowly been transformed into a major sacred pilgrimage site. It has been totally reshaped and reinterpreted. It must not be forgotten, however, that the use of the place as a pilgrimage site dates back to Mauryan times.

Religious life is also intense in the Monastic Zone that extends to the North. This zone, which has been divided into 42 plots, is occupied by several temples and monasteries. German and French Buddhist buildings have been put up next to Nepalese, Bhutanese, Tibetan or Sikkimese religious centres, some of which are imposing structures. It all makes for an international Buddhist hub. A central canal, about two kilometres in length, separates the zone into two enclaves: one in the east for Theravāda monasteries, and the other in the west for Mahāyāna. A Japanese architect, Professor Kenjo Tange, who was in charge of the Lumbini Development Master Plan between 1972 and 1978, designed the whole area, including the Sacred Garden, in a well-defined geometrical fashion based on a grid-pattern.

According to the Lumbini Development Trust, which is the organisation in charge of the site's maintenance and administration, 1.19 million pilgrims visited Lumbini in 2014. Of these, 901,621 were Nepalese visitors. Among the foreign visitors, 154,216 were from India, 37,600 from Sri Lanka, 24,733 from Thailand and 20,718 from China. These figures are up by 40 percent compared to the previous year.[17]

The internationalisation of the site went a step further when Lumbini's central area measuring 130 by 150 metres was inscribed on the World Heritage List in 1997. The core zone became a "world heritage property". UNESCO's involvement was followed rapidly by that of Japan, which invested massively in the holy area and built a World Peace Pagoda (Shanti Stupa) nearby. Today, South Korea has become heavily involved as well. In 2012, a South-Korean urban planner, Kwaak Young Hoon, proposed a lotus-shaped design for the 5x5-square-mile area. The project is based on the Lumbini Vishva Shanti Nagar (World Peace City) concept and highlights the message of peace and humanity in

Buddhism. The estimated cost is US $ 762 million. Today, Lumbini is a popular place for international conferences and seminars. The locality hosts different schools of Buddhism from every corner of the world.

Despite the globalization of the site, the Lumbini Development Trust is a hundred per cent Nepalese. The area is the property of the Government of Nepal. No private properties have been granted to any foreign national religious organizations. Yet, there are numerous financial, political and ideological encroachments. Lumbini is in fact a major source of competition between Nepal's two largest neighbours: India and China.

India is very near, only 20 km away, and has an eye on this archaeological and religious site. For a time, it did not recognize Lumbini as the native place of Lord Buddha and Tilaurakot as the ancient Kapilvastu. India's scientific authorities stress that today's state borders did not exist at the time of Buddha's birth and that India was the cradle of Buddhism. On the sub-continent, the idea prevails that although Buddha's *janmabhūmi* (birthplace) is perhaps in Nepal, his *karmabhūmi* (work place) is in India. As a matter of fact, Lumbini is one of four famous major Buddhist pilgrimages on the Indian subcontinent (with Sarnath, Bodhgaya and Kushinagara).

Furthermore, in spite of Lumbini being an official UNESCO World Heritage site, some Indian experts claim that the original capital of Kapilavastu was situated in Piprahwa, in Siddharthnagar district in the Indian state of Uttar Pradesh, not far from the Nepali border. An old stūpa built at the time of Ashoka has been discovered in this village. It is said to contain some of the ashes of Shakyamuni Buddha's bones. It is therefore understandable that, in August 2014, when Narendra Modi, the fifteenth prime minister of India, mentioned on the occasion of his first visit to Nepal, that Lumbini is the birthplace of Buddha, the whole Nepalese nation was delighted. However, no Indian Prime Minister had ever visited Lumbini.

As for Beijing, it shows a voracious appetite for affairs concerning Lumbini. This is partly for religious reasons; over the years China has become more religiously tolerant and portrays itself as the supreme protector of Buddhism, boasting that it is the biggest country in the world in terms of the number of Buddhist followers. Chinese officials and politicians recall the ancient historical relations that their country has forged with Nepal, as well as the journey Chinese pilgrims made to Lumbini between the second and the seventh centuries AD.

Yet the Chinese people's growing involvement in Lumbini is mainly for economic and financial reasons. Among many other things, Beijing supports the Hong-Kong-based foundation "The Asia Pacific Exchange and Cooperation Foundation" (APECF) headed by Xia Wunan, a Chinese citizen and former economist and banker. The APECF project, which was launched in 2011, aims to invest US $3 billion to develop Lumbini.. The situation has become strongly politicized with the direct involvement of the Maoist leader and former Prime Minister of Nepal, Pushpa Dahal. Dahal accepted a key position in the APECF Chinese endeavour. He was nevertheless obliged to resign from his position as coordinator of the "Lumbini Development National Steering Committee" (set up in October 2011) because of the controversy that it caused in Nepal.

A number of Buddhists in South Asia and in South-East Asia are opposed to the Chinese project. They are afraid that Lumbini will be turned into a commercial "Buddhaland" bazaar, a mega shopping area. The Korea International Cooperation Agency (KOICA), which is backing Kwaak Young Hoon's project (US $762 dollars), and is supported by the UN, is a serious rival. For the time being, the replacement of Maoist-led governments by a Congress-ULM coalition in 2013 has positively changed the situation. Yet the conflict opposing Nepal's two powerful neighbours is further heightened by the ambitions of China in matters of railway communications. Beijing would like to extend its Xinjiang-Tibet Railway to Kathmandu, and possibly to Lumbini by

2020. Five Chinese companies are also vying for the one-billion-US-dollar contract for the development of Gautam Buddha Airport (with a 3,000-metre runway) planned in Lumbini/Bhairava.

India, which is also involved in building this international airport, is extremely preoccupied and remains suspicious of China's intentions. Competition over the renowned pilgrimage site is turning into a rat race between the two superpowers. Lumbini's territory is therefore under pressure. In the light of these foreign ambitions and the billions dollars involved, Nepal's independence seems rather limited, somewhat nominal even.

At the same time, the Tharu indigenous population living in the Lumbini area is observing the strategic manoeuvres with the greatest concern. Powerless, they are being increasingly dispossessed of their original territory and they are being left by the wayside. This is probably why, today, Tharus claim to be the descendants of Buddha [17]. In this manner they are asking for a share in the territory's ownership.

I would like to make one final remark. Contrary to the Pāshupati Development Trust—the organisation in charge of *Pashupāti kshetra*, the area belonging to the prominent Hindu god Pashupāti in the Kathmandu Valley—, the notion of an eminent divine ownership of Buddha does not exist. Landownership here is purely secular. This is one significant difference between Hinduism and Buddhism.

14. Religious Radicalism

Religion engenders a specific sense of identity among followers. In South Asia, where a person's religion is recorded during decennial censuses, this facet of identity is well grounded and plays a pivotal role in defining a person's selfhood and community links. The memories of Partition in 1947 are still vivid in everybody's mind. In what follows, I argue that the more these forms of identity converge with politics and foster xenophobic feelings towards other religions, the greater their propensity to develop radicalism. The sentiment of being attacked, threatened, is sometimes enough to engender religious extremism and can eventually lead to violence. In these ideological constructions, religious affiliation is privileged to the detriment of all other determinants.

Over the centuries, every religion has nurtured the development of fundamentalist or extreme groups. Christianity gave birth, for instance, to the Ku Klux Klan, which advocates white supremacy, and to Jehovah's Witnesses, who are very influential today in Nepal and whose beliefs are based on a deviant interpretation of the Bible. Many of these groups are categorized in Europe as dangerous sectarian religious organizations. In South Asia, the establishment of a true Islamic state based on holy law and the inculcation of religious values throughout society is one of the more visible illustrations of religious radicalism, causing war and violence. The propagation of Wahhabism on the subcontinent has obviously precipitated this Islamic radicalism. Similarly, as far as India and Nepal are concerned, the Hindutva saffron ideology has prompted a strong nationalist Hindu movement over the last decades, which has influenced domestic politics and has triggered widespread Islamophobia. Old commitment to religious pluralism has turned into strident religious chauvinism. Even Buddhism, a religion known for its tolerance, sometimes turns xenophobic (notably against Islam), as in some regions of Burma, under the leadership of certain monks.

By and large, these movements are situated at the crossroads between religion and politics. They do not limit religion to the private sphere but expand it to all socio-political issues. Radicalism may sometimes take the form of a return to an allegedly pure, fundamental, unaltered form of religion. An unbridled imagination, confusion between this world and the Other world are characteristic features. In fact, the dogma of followers is anchored in extreme forms of believing.

Most religious extremists therefore have a fanatical sense of righteousness. They usually think they alone know the truth and that no one else does. Moreover, these persons dehumanize whoever does not fit into their point of view and they idealize historic figures associated with the defence of their ideas. The Other is demonized. To sum up, religious radicalism is a perversion, a pathological aberration of identity, rooted in false dichotomies. It strengthens the use of antagonistic categories such as "we" and "you". It has pernicious effects on the general vision a person has of human beings.

One burning issue in matters of religious affiliation is conversion. From a Hindu extremist point of view, conversion to another religion is a form of rapt, a theft of one's primordial identity by an alien group. In India, Hindutva-affiliated groups and Rāshtrīya Swayamsewak Sangh (RSS) activists consider conversion as a lethal threat to the Hindu community, that is—in their vocabulary—to Mother India. For them, all Indians are "naturally" and originally Hindus. A drop in the number of Hindu followers and a simultaneous rise in the number of Muslims and Christians recorded at the decennial censuses are met with fear and anxiety.

Hindutva faith-groups have developed campaigns aimed at encouraging converts (to Christianity or to Islam) to convert back to Hinduism. Such reconversion programmes, *ghar wāpsī* (or *dharma jāgran,* "religious awakening"), are staged publically in Hindu temples during Hindu festivals. Organizers view these reconversions as a return to old religious roots. In fact, they fuel communalism and are often accompanied by confrontations with the police. They are far-removed from the *sāmājik samarasatā* ("social harmony") concept advocated by RSS and the *Sangh Parivār*.

In India, there is total freedom to profess, to practise and to propagate one's faith providing that one does not disrupt public order and one does not attempt to influence other people's morality. By contrast, in Nepal, the right to convert another person has not yet been recognized. Proselyting is still illegal despite the increasing number of Christians in the country. It is commonly believed that conversion (*dharma parivartan*) to Christianity is achieved by offering sums of money, various financial advantages and a means of transport (such as a motorbike) to people with a low income. These assumptions, which in many cases happen to be true, provoke outrage not only among Hindu radicals but also among left-wing politicians. In 2015, Pushpa Dahal Prachanda raised concern about the growing number of Christians in Nepal. He said it poses a threat to Nepal and neighbouring India and China (*The Himalayan Times*, 20 July 2015). Nonetheless, conversion to Christianity of Nepal's most popular star-cum-singer-cum-actress Anju Panta runs counter to these common ideas. It has prompted emotion throughout the country where 80 per cent of the population are of Hindu faith.

The return to royalty in Nepal as advocated today by Hindu radical activists is another closely related issue. Hindu militant extremists see the current secularization process as a danger to the country's integrity. For this reason, they propose that the monarchy be restored. For them, Nepal (like India) is a sacred land, *dhārmika* (or *pavitra*) *bhūmi*. The king is seen primarily as a defender of Hindus. In sum, the Nepali national identity is supposed to be embodied in the Hindu culture. For these activists, Nepal has become religiously diverse not through immigration but through conversion. The radical ideas they stand for are closely related to the ones RSS defends in India.

Does this mean that RSS and Kamal Thapa's Nepali conservative political party, Rāshtrīya Prajātantra Party, are "fascist", as leftist groups here and there claim? Not by any means. This comparison with German Nationalist Socialist ideology is a total misconception. Hindutva and its satellite organisations are mainly religious and express a form of religious radicalism. In stark contrast, National Socialism was anti-religious from the very start.

Notes

1 Cf. for instance: G. Toffin, "The Adivasi/Janajāti Movement in Nepal: Myths and Realities of Indigeneity", in Vibha Arora and N. Jayaram, eds, *Routeing Democracy in the Himalayas*, 2013, Delhi: Routledge, pp. 29-49.

2 André Béteille, "India's Destiny not Cast in Stone", *The Hindu*, 21 February 2012.

3 Joëlle Smadja, (ed.), *Territorial changes and territorial restructurings in the Himalayas*. Delhi: Adroit, 2013.

4 The idea of including prior rights, *agrādhikār*, for selected ethnic groups in the new provinces was defended by most *Janajāti* groups. But it was finally given up.

5 Sanjib Barua, *Durable Disorder. Understanding the Politics of Northeast India*, Delhi: Oxford University Press, 2007.

6 A more detailed version of this paper was presented in July 2015 during the Fourth Annual Social Science Baha Conference on Nepal and the Himalayas which was held in Kathmandu.

7 Among the Newars, mention can also be made of the ethnographic museum specifically devoted to the Udāy Buddhist community which is to be found in Asan Tol, Kathmandu. It is run by Udāy Samāj, a caste organization.

8 The Folk Music Museum, in Tripureshwar (Kathmandu), belongs to this category of museum. It was registered with the Government of Nepal in 1997 and it opened to visitors in 2002. It was badly damaged by the earthquake in April 2015 (see *The Himalayan Times*, 26 July 2015). It houses 600 different types of traditional Nepali musical instruments.

9 Bidyut Chakrabarty, *Social and Political Thought of Mahatma Gandhi*. Abingdon: Routledge, 2006.

10 Pierre Clastres, "De l'ethnocide", *L'Homme*, 14 (3-4), 1974, pp. 101-110. See also Robert Jaulin, *La paix blanche. Introduction à l'ethnocide*, Paris: Seuil, 1970.

11. According to some French scholars, the term "ethnicity" was first introduced by Georges Condominas (1921-2011), a prominent French anthropologist who worked in the hills of Central Vietnam (Mnong People).

12. At practically the same time, Michel Foucault (1926-1984), in his teachings at *Collège de France*, established a link between the eighteenth-century Enlightenment movement, the strengthening of the state, and the emergence of new forms of domination. In Foucault's critique of modernity, progress, the development of reason and rationality become sources of constructs of domination, saturating everyday life with control over the individual. The French philosopher focused his analysis on these forms of policing, surveillance and disciplinary apparatus (*The Birth of the Clinic* and *The Archaeology of Knowledge*). According

to him, the modern state and rationality are coercive forces that dominate the individual through social institutions.

13. Harka Gurung, "State and Society in Nepal", in Gellner, D., J. Pfaff-Czarnecka & J. Whelpton, *Nationalism and Ethnicity in a Hindu Kingdom. The Politics of Culture in Contemporary Nepal.* Amsterdam: Harwood Academic Publishers, 1997, pp. 495-532.
14. Ashish Nandy, *The Romance of the State and the Fate of Dissent in the Tropics.* Delhi: Oxford India Paperbacks, 2007, p. 14.
15. Gérard Toffin, *Société et religion chez les Néwar du Népal.* Paris: Éditions du CNRS, 1984.
16. *The Sacred Garden of Lumbini. Perceptions of Buddha's birthplace.* Paris/Kathmandu: UNESCO, 2013.
17. wwwlumbinitrust.org

CHAPTER

3

The Architecture of Memory

By and large, memory can be analysed from three main standpoints. The concept is first linked to identity, whether personal and collective. The two notions logically presuppose one another. Remembering and forgetting are fundamental to the creation of identities and to our negotiations with the surrounding world. Our identities are the result of the networks to which we belong (family, work, nation). But they are also constructed out of reminiscences from the past. We select, rework, and highlight these recollections throughout our lives. In the collective realm, one example of this necessary relationship between memory and identity is the frequent use of so-called "sites of memory", architectural or purely imaginary, to sustain the cohesiveness of a group [**20**]. This makes heritage a contested issue and often a realm of tension or violent confrontation.

Secondly, memory is linked to history even though the two concepts are not synonymous. Memory is by its very nature selective and subjective. It is an ongoing process which is highly susceptible to manipulation. Admittedly, some historians have stressed that even in their discipline the past is constructed and reconstructed in keeping with present needs. Yet, since it is recollected in textbooks, history is normally based on irrefutable documents. The course of historical events established by professional academics has a touch of truth about it, whereas memory is always subject to mistakes and omissions. Today, conflicting and contentious memories about Nepal oscillate between attested facts and distorted recollections. The appropriation of the past by actors in the present is subjected to multiple political dynamics.

Thirdly, memory must be regarded as a group phenomenon and be studied as a social fact. As demonstrated by Maurice Halbwachs, a student of Durkheim, the French sociologist, memory is not possible outside group membership.[1] Although memories may seem purely personal, they are social because of the greater complexity which is required for these recollections. The debate must therefore be shifted beyond the frame of personal and individual aspects. Memory is a changing process which is influenced by class, ethnicity, religion, gender, and other distinguishing marks. In complex societies like Nepal, collective memories are always plural.

The texts below illustrate these three aspects.

15. Visions of the Past

Representations of the past play an all-important role in the construction of any nation's repertoire of belonging. It is worthwhile, in this respect, considering a few museums that opened in Nepal within recent years: they not only "stage" the past in specific ways, but they also constitute a collective memory. To be more precise, they are indicative of the relationship people have with their national heritage. Interestingly, the objects and imagery exhibited differ greatly from one case to another. Let us look at some examples and review the situation.

Narayan Hiti Palace Museum, in the centre of the Nepali capital, is housed in the Shah dynasty's former royal palace. It is of great symbolic value. To convert the former residence of the dethroned king into a museum expresses first and foremost a determination to transform a secluded place, a seat of power, into a public space which can be accessed by all Nepali citizens. It is a way of turning the page on the monarchy for ever, as many other European countries have done. However, a visit to this museum is rather puzzling. Anybody who has already visited the palaces of Indian princes with whom the Shah family was and still is in close contact and sometimes even married to (in Rajasthan in particular) cannot fail to be disappointed. Firstly, the modernist, gloomy building built by the American architect Polk at the end of the 1960s cannot be compared with the grandiose neo-classical palaces of India, which have also been turned into either museums or luxury hotels. They cannot even be compared, in terms of their quality, to the best-preserved Rana palaces in Nepal. The furniture, the rooms, the decorative elements, as well as the paintings lack grandeur and glory. In fact, the museum portrays a rather pitiful image of the Shah monarchy. As for the slaughter committed on 1 June 2001, the low building where it took place has been demolished, leaving visitors rather bewildered. All in all, the visit is disappointing. The museum looks more like a proclamation of death than anything else.

Patan Museum, which opened in 1997, is also housed in a former, historical palace. It belonged to the Mallas who reigned over this royal town from the thirteenth to the eighteenth century. It is an exceptional museum that illustrates the sophisticated Newar medieval civilisation in a most splendid manner. Set up in Patan's magnificent Durbar Square in a building recently restored with the assistance of the Austrian government, it is a perfect site for the exquisite collection of divine images, wooden artefacts, gilded repoussé work, ritual objects and paintings permeated with hidden transcendent presences. This museum is devoted to religious art, particularly to aristocratic Malla-sponsored art. It has become a museum of international renown and competes with Asia's foremost art museums. Even more importantly, this museum has become a living site for Nepali artists thanks to temporary modern art and photography exhibitions. It is even used as a venue for cultural events. As such, it not only focuses on the past but it is also orientated towards the present.

The third museum I would like to talk about only opened its doors in 2012. It is also situated in Patan, in the southeastern part of the city, and it follows the new fashion of ethnic "indigenous" museums [**10**]. It was entirely created by this Newar city's Jyāpu Samāj and has been set up in a new building that includes some elements of the traditional architectural style. It displays an astonishing collection of secular (for instance, agricultural and cooking implements) and religious objects, which are unique in the Kathmandu Valley. The artefacts are exhibited in a standard ethnographic manner. In some cases, puppets help to visualize the living culture; for instance, the festival of Rāto Matsyendranāth. The collection fully portrays the rich Newar popular culture and is therefore worthwhile seeing as a follow up to a visit to the Patan Museum.

Any anthropologist visiting this memory-laden museum would be thrilled to see such a large collection of objects. Yet, at the same time, one cannot help noticing that this fascinating exhibition introduces a certain distance between the present and the original Newar living culture. By and large, this ethnic museum trend not only represents a revival of local *ādivāsī-janajāti* cultures but it is also a sign that these traditional cultures and old life-styles are slowly dying out due to modernisation and globalisation. Jyāpu culture, for instance, is nowadays less and less based on agriculture owing to the urbanisation frenzy and the concomitant deruralization of the Kathmandu Valley. Museums seem to be specifically needed when culture is in danger.

These three memory sites, among many others in Nepal, transport the past into the present and represent various forms of loss in the face of change. In fact, they each portray a different facet of Nepali cultural and historical heritage. In my opinion, Narayan Hiti Palace museum expresses a persisting difficulty in addressing the monarchical past, a memory permeated with harrowing political events. The other cases exemplify two sides of a specific culture, which—at least in the Kathmandu Valley—has become part of the national heritage. Patan Museum fully embraces the modern world and universalistic aesthetic values. As such, it receives visits from a large number of foreign tourists. The third museum which is devoted to Jyāpu (and Newar) culture and still lies outside the normal tourist circuit has so far received very few visitors. This rather parochial edifice was built by the Newars themselves and is dedicated to the glory of their culture. Unfortunately, living elements are turned into inanimate patrimonial artefacts, disconnected from daily activities and rituals [**10**]. How is life to be infused into them?

16. Memories of Civil War

Every country across the world has a hidden past. Memories are often too traumatic to be consciously brought to the surface. Japan and Germany, the two defeated nations held responsible for starting World War II, have, for instance, recurrent difficulties in recognizing their responsibility for the millions of deaths and the devastation over those five years of global conflict. The recent financial demands made by the radical left-wing Syriza Greek government about the damage caused by the hardship its country suffered under German occupation (one of the worst in Europe) between 1941 and 1945 is one reminder of this. In France, the internal conflict between French resistance fighters and followers of Maréchal Pétain in the years 1940-44 during the same war is still a traumatic memory. Nearly seventy years on, it still has a direct bearing on French political life.

Likewise, the 1996-2006 internal conflict between the Maoists and the security forces of the erstwhile royal Nepal government (over 17,000 people were killed) has not totally blown over. The national rhetoric of reconciliation adopted by the seven anti-royalist party alliance in 2006 has not soothed all the wounds. Burying the hatchet is easy, but recognizing crimes of murder, torture, abduction and rape that were committed during the civil war in the name of the revolution or in order to defend the state against so-called terrorists proves to be much more problematical. The United Nations Office of the High Commissioner for Human Rights (UNOHCHR) reports at least 9,000 cases of violations of international laws during the prolonged conflict, even though, to date, no one has been prosecuted. The state has already provided the victims with some compensation. But many other families are still waiting for reparation and for justice to be done. The wounds of these wartime crimes have yet to heal.

Numerous atrocities were committed on both sides. The bombing of a civilian bus in 2005 by Maoists, which killed 36 passengers, was one of the most tragic visible events. But the list of civilians who were killed because they refused to donate 25 per cent of their salaries to the revolutionary cause or did not attend functions organised by the rebels has yet to be drawn up. In fact, thousands of Nepalis fled their villages when the Māobādīs threatened to kill them and to seize their property if they refused to make "donations" to the People's Army.

Similarly, the army is responsible for a number of massacres of unarmed people and civilians who were suspected of supporting the rebellion, and of committing acts of torture in order to obtain information about the enemy's movements. According to the records of the International Committee of the Red Cross (ICRC), a large proportion of the 1,347 who "disappeared" are presumed to have been killed while in state custody. Most of these disappearances have not been resolved.

It is difficult to identify the atrocities committed by Maoists since the Māobādīs constructed a collective imagery of martyrs, which has been widely disseminated through tributes, ceremonies and poems. In Maoist rhetoric, these martyrs are models for the future and guides in subsequent struggles. Likewise, the police and the army, pillars of the modern Nepali state, are reluctant for obvious reasons to recognize their responsibility. Many of the suspects still serve in the police and the army and some of them have even been promoted. The state is always reluctant to recognize its black sheep, except when identification serves its own interests.

It has taken a long time for the government to address these issues. Under pressure from the international community, the criminalisation of enforced disappearances was finally established in 2009. In April 2014, the government of Nepal set up two separate transitional justice commissions: the Truth and Reconciliation Commission (TRC) and the Commission on Investigation of Enforced Disappeared Persons (CIEDP). The Act (TRC Act) was passed under article 33 of the 2007 Interim Constitution to provide relief to the families of the victims and to reconcile the country. These commissions were charged with investigating all types of inhuman acts committed against victims in violation of international laws and other crimes against humanity in the course of the Maoist-launched People's War: torture, looting, rape, abduction, forceful eviction from homes or off land, kidnapping, etc.

The setting up of these structures has sparked a number of reactions. International human rights groups, such as Amnesty International and Human Rights Watch, have joined local activists and Nepali legal professionals in voicing grave concern. They have denounced collusion between the political parties, the army, the police and the Māobādīs to hush up these criminal cases. They have expressed reservations about the members of these commissions who have been appointed by political parties. Many people accuse the commissioners of being party loyalists with neither political independence nor the relevant expertise.

Moreover, the discretionary power of the politically appointed Attorney General in these affairs to decide whether to file a case against those accused of serious crimes has been questioned. Other procedures and blatant shortcomings (regarding delays, for instance, or the confidentiality of those testifying) have also been criticised. International experts have called for more transparency and have pointed to a number of flawed provisions which do not comply with international legal obligations and standards. For purely diametrically opposing reasons, a breakaway Maoist faction has openly refused to acknowledge this process of transitional justice. In the field, those seeking justice stage protests and hunger strikes. Some of these persons have died.

Associations of victims—the National Victims Alliance, amongst others—, have also criticised all the attention that has focused on prosecutions and not enough on the victims' basic needs. The victims demand financial and social rights such as the right to education or to a pension. They ask for an effective policy of reparation to cover economic, social, educational, health and psychosocial aspects. They complain that they have never been consulted on any of these matters.

But the greatest fear is blanket amnesty. Since the very beginning, political leaders have introduced into the legislation provisions for amnesty. The international community and representatives of civil society have criticized the specifications that have so far been drafted. The Supreme Court has played a very positive role in this respect. It has ruled against granting amnesty to those who have committed serious human rights violations and/or abuses. It has repeatedly ordained that these provisions are unlawful.

How to escape from these dynamics of resentment? The lack of any effective prosecution of war criminals is a major injustice to victims. Impunity for perpetrators will be a disaster for the young fragile Nepali democracy and will worsen existing socio-political tensions. No exemption is admissible. Impunity, *dandahīnatā*, is one of the worst sins of democracy. Such violations of human rights need to be addressed and brought into the public sphere according to democratic rules. Reluctance to subject the war-time past to scrutiny could also damage Nepal's image globally or jeopardise much-needed international aid and assistance. Considerable efforts are still required to establish the legitimacy of the aforementioned Commissions and to win the trust of the survivors of Nepal's civil conflict. Doubts will only dissipate after these requirements have been met.

There are two major problems here. Firstly, the persons who currently run Nepal and are responsible for the relevant files are, for the most part, the same as those who fought against each other during the civil war. As a result, the perpetrators who are close to the authorities reject any process that would lead to their conviction. Secondly, the political polarisation of the all-state apparatus and of the public administration has tainted the independence of the appointed officials. These two combined constraints may prove to be an obstacle and to generate a grotesque masquerade. By and large, the purely human-rights approach has not yet been totally accepted by high officials.

The accountability for war crimes must also take into account ethnicity-and caste-related realities. It is no coincidence that Dalits and Ādivāsī-Janajāti have the highest proportion of victims that suffered state violence during the conflict. For instance, in Bardiya District, indigenous Tharus constitute the majority of those still missing. Civil and political rights do not exist in isolation from social and economic rights. Among many other things, these evidences have direct implications on the social makeup of legal institutions and Human Rights NGOs, which are mainly made up of members of upper-caste hill groups.

Disjunction between the country's official recollections on the one hand, and individual memory on the other hand is a clear sign of disharmony between state institutions and individual people. In Nepal, the two are worlds apart, and this gulf increases day by day. Any credibility in the process of reconciliation will thereby require new procedures, public hearings and the active participation of various associations. All state structures, without exception, must be forced into listening to the voices of the people.

17. Invented Memories

Over the last decades, modern Western literature has made considerable use of the theme of memory loss. Marguerite Duras (1914-1996), a prominent French author, devoted whole books to lapses of memory among persons struggling to retrieve fragments of their past from a few indelible details imprinted on their minds. In many cases, what can be called "creative memory" paints over "real" facts from the past. "The memory is cursed with what hasn't happened" (*Blue Eyes, Black Hair*). For Duras, "When the past is recaptured by the imagination, breath is put back into life". She believed that forgetfulness is the real memory and in her texts she continually fictionalized her personal history and the past. These ghosts of memories lie at the crossroads between recollection and imagination.

The reconstruction of the past has also become a major topic in the field of social science, particularly in history and anthropology. The book edited by E. J. Hobsbawm and T.O. Ranger, *The Invention of Tradition* (1983), is a milestone in this direction. In their introduction, the authors critically assert that many apparently or supposedly ancient traditions often have relatively recent origins and have sometimes even been invented. The phenomenon is particularly clear in the development of nations and of nationalism. Soon after this, Benedict Anderson created the associated concept of *imagined communities* (1983), in which he posits that nations and nationalisms are the product of modernity and have been created as a means to a political and economic end.[2] These questions are currently central issues towards understanding the patterns of historical and anthropological research.

Nations are not the only entities concerned. The rewriting of the past is also a major process at work in a number of ethnic groups throughout the world. I would like to illustrate this idea by taking some examples from two Janajāti groups in Nepal, the Tharus and the Gurungs. Tharus are known to anthropologists and other observers as an ethnic group that formerly practised a semi-nomadic lifestyle in or on the edge of the Tarai tropical forest. They have settled in different parts of the Nepali and Indian Tarai and display diverse cultural features depending on the place where they live. There are major differences between Rana Tharus in western Nepal, Dangauras Tharus (from Dang), and those living in Sunsari and Jhapa districts. Interestingly, activists belonging to this group have recently developed the idea of an original Buddhist connection. Their ancestors, so they claim, were followers of Buddha and adopted this religion (Chiara Letizia)[3] very early on. They ultimately assimilated Hindu cultural practices due to the prevalence of the surrounding Hindu chiefdoms and small kingdoms. Historians have found little proof of such a postulated origin. It would seem that Tharus used this imagined construction as a way of developing an alternative and a supposedly more noble identity than Hindu (Buddhism is seen as a religion of peace) to compensate for their historically subordinate status.

In a similar vein, Susan Hangen, an American anthropologist, has shown how a Gurung association, Mongol National Organization (MNO), defends the idea of this ethnic group's Mongol origin.[4] According to these theories, Gurungs are of different racial stock from Hindus. This reconstruction of the past aims at bestowing a common faith on members of the group and at crediting them with explicitly "prestigious" origins. Yet the invention of a Mongol race is a poorly documented concept and an obvious distortion of the facts. It makes use of a dangerous old-fashioned racial concept that has been rejected by scientists.

Many other examples could be quoted. A number of Nepali ethnic groups are currently engaged, via their intellectuals, in a quest for a great tradition that people could boast about. This quest aims at setting themselves aside from high Sanskritic Hindu castes that are regarded as former "conquistadores" of their territories—to use a word favoured by the late Harka Gurung [**11**]. Literary and local folk groups are often guided by ideas of this kind. They try to distance themselves from the all-encompassing process of Nepalization that started in the course of the eighteenth and nineteenth centuries. Such an impassioned vision of the past, backed by the indigenous NEFIN movement, provides a collective means of shaping a common ethnic identity that is distinct from the Nepali Hindu mainstream. The subaltern status to which most of these groups were relegated during pre-modern times in Nepal therefore lays the ground for reparation.

By and large, views on cultural identity are heavily entrenched in political concerns. In a number of cases, selected remnants of the past are retained to the detriment of others. They serve to construct an inaccurate image of the national heritage. The nationalist, non-governmental RSS (Rāshtrīya Swayamsevak Sangh) organization set up in India in 1925 during the colonial period, has thus constructed an imaginary, puritanical, exclusivistic form of Hinduism which is far from the findings that scholars have documented. In matters of sexuality and female freedom, such a device leads to reactionary practices. Today, despite some weekly magazines, *India Today* for instance, backed by a middle class claiming more sexual freedom, there is a tendency in many parts of the subcontinent to maintain a paternalistic, characteristically chauvinistic attitude towards women. RSS is campaigning against sexual education in schools and stresses “family values” (*kutumb prabodhan*). The organization has also launched a vehement attack on the valuable book by Wendy Doniger O’Flaherty about Shiva (*Shiva, The Erotic Ascetic*, 1973) which describes this deity not only as an ascetic but also as a lover obsessed with eroticism. The magnificent erotic sculptures on the outer walls of Khajuraho, Eklingi, Konarak, Bhubaneshwar temples, and of so many other Hindu religious sites, simply seem to have been forgotten.

18. Urban Palimpsests

City-dwellers in the Kathmandu Valley are gradually being cut off from their old traditional urban roots that have been passed down practically discontinuously through the generations. They have adopted new lifestyles and have moved their residence from one place to another, generally from the centre to the periphery, to more spacious bungalows and villas. At the same time, colonies and settlements have been set up and multi-storey apartment blocks have being built for the upper-middle class. In addition, the proportion of the exogenous population, i.e. non-Newars, is on the rise. A new urban landscape, together with new landmarks and buildings, has emerged amidst traffic jams and thick clouds of exhaust fumes. Similar changes have been observed throughout the world. In Europe, historical towns are slowly being turned into museums, dissociated from the old socio-religious bonds shared by the population. In the Kathmandu Valley, like anywhere else, the vital bond people have maintained with the city's different historical layers is gradually shrinking.

As a matter of fact, the three main cities, Kathmandu, Lalitpur and Bhaktapur, as well as other smaller urban settlements like Kirtipur, Panauti, Banepa, are legacies of an ancient urban civilisation that developed over the years. Most of these cities' matrixes date back to the first centuries A.D., long after the second wave of urbanization which took place in the Gangetic plain and the Indus valley. In the course of the Licchavi, Thakuri, Malla and the more recent Rana-Shah periods, these settlements became a crucible of a highly original civilization. The geographical location of its kingdoms between the trans-Himalayan trade routes to Tibet and India favoured this development.

The monumental sites in these Nepalese cities have long attracted pilgrims, experts, and archaeologists from all over the world. Crowds of tourists visit them today. However, attention must also be drawn to the more hidden social and religious history of these cities that was forged during the early Thakuri and Malla eras. Among other things, I refer of course to the exceptional network of Buddhist *vihāra*s (monasteries). These *bāhāhs*, as they are called today, are unique in the Asian world and still function as socio-religious entities despite the poor state of their architecture and environment. Each *bāhāh* is an art treasury and more often than not contains old written documents. This also calls to mind the old Maharjan *tol* neighbourhoods on which the three former Malla capital cities were built, and which lend so much importance to religious music and cultic practices.

Bāhāh and *tol*s still play a crucial role in mapping these old cities and represent remote layers of history that need to be preserved. They are part of the old urban fabric and the basis of underlying social bonds. These sites, hidden out of sight of external visitors and almost uncharted socio-religious units, also belong to Nepal's intangible heritage.

Interestingly enough, rituals performed over the years have preserved the memory of these different layers upon which cities have been built. During Dasain in Lalitpur, for instance, Māneshvarī, an old Thakuri deity associated with the royal palace, is honoured in Mul Chok's Durbar Square in the same way as Taleju and Dvimāiju goddesses who pertain to the subsequent Malla period. Similarly, during the Rāto Mastyendranāth festival, which is celebrated every year in Lalitpur, the descendants of Thakujuju Malla royals from Bhaktapur, dressed in their ancient costumes and waving a *tarvār* sword, have to be present before the start of certain rituals [cf. book cover]. Such communal rituals constitute a living memory of the past and of the ancient links between cities. They have preserved polyphonic histories that have been mixed and hybridized in time and space.

Each city in the Kathmandu Valley can in fact be compared to a palimpsest, with a series of layers that have left their mark and are a vestige of specific epochs. For the first time in history, however, the present era, with its stamp of modernity, is in the process of absorbing and destroying these traces. We are witnessing a rapid shift from traditional agro-cities (*rus in urbe*, country in the towns) based on their rural quarters as well on their craft and trade activities, imbued with religion and sacred sites, to modern cosmopolitan metropolises dominated by money and mercantile ends. A new urban geography based on income and money flows is replacing the old preordained spatial division into castes. The corollary to this is that the traditional fusion between gods and men has been substituted by a wider separation between profane and sacred activities. To use a Weberian expression, cities are becoming "disenchanted" worlds.

Despite recent attempts by the authorities and local initiatives to render cities more attractive and the air safer, this superposition of various historical periods is in great danger. Conservationist measures, the *safa tempo* policy banning the use of diesel and many other campaigns have had little effect on the chaos that prevails today. They have not succeeded in curbing the prevalent anarchy in matters of building regulations. Laws voted by the government and municipalities to preserve historic sites are often bypassed. And the countless master plans prepared by international organizations to preserve these cultural ensembles have dismally failed.

So far, demolition and eviction seem to be the only answers from the government and municipalities. The on-going frenetic urbanisation (*saharīkaran* in Nepali) of the Valley clearly threatens the rich, living, immaterial urban heritage as well as UNESCO World Heritage Sites [**86**]. If Nepalis are not careful, the Kathmandu Valley is likely to lose its links with the past and its inimitable charm. Its cities will increasingly resemble any other overcrowded South Asian metropolis.

19. Cities without Addresses

Navigating in Kathmandu or in any other city of Nepal, both in and outside the Kathmandu Valley, and trying to locate a friend's house is an unforgettable experience. Contrary to most urban conurbations in the West, but like many other Asian countries (such as Japan), no address as such exists for any of the houses. The latter do have a postal address, a number written on the side facing the street, but this is used mainly for postal and tax purposes. This is a mark for Census or cadastral registration purposes rather than a means of finding your bearings within the city. A friend you are visiting would never give you this information to find his house. Instead, he would provide you with the name of the neighbourhood. Similarly, in new extensions, most of the streets have no names, or, if they do, these names have mostly never been heard of.

To find somebody's house, especially in densely populated areas, you have to play detective and to be patient. The best solution, of course, is to be able to contact your friend by mobile phone so that they can guide you step by step. They can also communicate in this way with your taxi driver, supposing that you have one. After various attempts and hesitations, you will finally reach your destination. The search is particularly difficult because over the last decades anarchic urban development has created a multitude of unnamed lanes and alleyways that are difficult to recognize if you yourself do not live in the neighbourhood. Furthermore, a street map, if you are lucky to get one, will be of no real help. The difficulties get worse, of course, at night-time when there are no visual landmarks, especially if you disturb some innocent dogs resting in the street that seemingly rule over the territory, hotly defending it against all sorts of unknown visitors.

Your task will no doubt be less difficult in old historic centres. Despite the complicated structure of buildings surrounding a series of inner courtyards, *cok,* linked together by dark narrow passages, there are well-known landmarks to locate your position and your friend's house. Some lanes may even have names (in Nepā Bhāshā) derived from their straight or curved form or other physical appearances. The old pre-modern streetscape is replete with Ganesha and Devī temples, which are there to guide you. Moreover, in old networks of houses, each neighbourhood (and in most cases each courtyard) has a specific name. Besides, once you find yourself in the right neighbourhood, you will be more likely to find somebody who recognizes the name of your friend and who can direct you to their house. Local orientation schemes can tell us much of the ways in which urbanites think urban space.

After all, it is a well-known fact that these old historic cities in the Kathmandu Valley are structured like a *mandala*, i.e. a miniature cosmogram aligned with the cardinal directions and providing a bridge between the macrocosm and the microcosm. The space is theoretically arranged (or at least is thought to be arranged) according to this type of cosmological model. Most researchers have convincingly demonstrated that cities such as Lalitpur, Kathmandu,

Bhaktapur are structured according to geometric devices and to the location of temples, like a mirror of the whole cosmos to which the city is supposedly related. In some cases, the main lanes are arranged according to an orthogonal layout with recurrent right angles. This street pattern helps to locate houses much more easily than curved lines and winding streets.

Suburban areas have an entirely different morphology. In these recently built neighbourhoods, you have to make your way through an unstructured no man's land with few landmarks to help you track down a house. Schools (which do have names), shops, trees (if they have not been cut down) or bridges serve as landmarks. Yet the suburbs lack the unity that characterizes the urban space in the heart of cities, even if at first sight the latter seems secret and hidden away. Suburban communities are surprisingly less closely knit. People know less about each other and therefore cannot help you—indeed they are likely to get you even more lost.

Many years ago, while working alongside three French architects, I studied how, at the intersection of transport axes, a city (Panauti) had extended beyond the gates of its old town (*dhokā*) and former boundaries. The ensuing monograph demonstrated that in these new areas the ancient organic unity of the spatial system and the wall-to-wall corridor structure of traditional dwellings rapidly disappear.[5] Space is disorganised and life's economic necessities are disconnected from socio-religious functions. The symbolic meaning of the old dwelling, which was structured according to common religious practices, has almost vanished. The purely economic logic (the ability to buy an expensive piece of land in order to build a house) has engendered a chaotic ensemble that remains outside a pre-ordained traditional social space. Some well-off residential areas with houses (often bearing a name) surrounded by a garden are an exception.

The absence of a proper address for houses in pre-modern towns is understandable. In these areas, the quality of space was traditionally subordinated to social units and the various functions of a dwelling —religious, economic and social— merged. As a matter of fact, people living in these *tol*s do not feel the need to give every street a name. They have a clear mental map of the area and a good network of nearby relatives and neighbours, which compensates for the lack of names for roads or lanes. Such a situation parallels many other former pre-industrial towns throughout the world. Nevertheless, the lack of a proper address is more surprising and—to put it plainly—irritating in the suburbs where ancient spatial features have been lost and where old landmarks have disappeared.

The marked absence of a standard visible system of labelling streets points to two interrelated features. On the one hand, it reveals the persistence of traditional dwellings and native/indigenous modes of space conceptualization to guide people in their daily lives. Strikingly, in old city centres urbanites have their own particular perception of the city and their own winding itineraries along narrow snaking paths/alleys beyond the main axes. On the other hand, this dearth reveals the weakness (and the lack of interest) on the part of the state and municipalities in establishing a set nomenclature: at local level, a stateless appropriation of living space still prevails.

20. Sites of Memory in Ruins

The deadly 7.8 magnitude earthquake on 25 April 2015, together with its numerous aftershocks, has devastated the Kathmandu Valley's cultural heritage. In all, across central Nepal, 721 monuments over 20 districts have been damaged: 133 totally destroyed, 229 slightly damaged and 40 of them are in a state of demolition.[6] Beyond the loss of human lives and the priority given to looking for and rescuing survivors, it is a terrible tragedy for the whole of Nepal. The damaged buildings were the heart and soul of the country's identity. They sustained a sense of pride among all Nepalis. This destruction has been a particular blow to the Newars, whose architectural achievements and historic monuments have greatly suffered. In addition, these monuments were a major tourist attraction for international travellers and largely contributed to the country's overall economy. Their loss will trigger considerable financial, political and cultural consequences.

Among the seven groups of monuments and buildings in the region, which are on the list of UNESCO World Heritage Sites, three (the royal palace squares in the three ancient Malla capitals), including the nine-storey Basantapur tower in Kathmandu, have been almost totally destroyed and two others (Svayambhunath, the double-roofed temple at Changu Narayan, dedicated to Vishnu), have been partly damaged. In fact, Changu Narayan needs to be rebuilt. In Patan Darbar Square, the temples of Shanker Narayan, Char Narayan (also called Jagannarayan) and Uma Maheshvar (made of stone) have totally collapsed.

Yet many other temples, former monasteries and various key buildings have been hit. The iconic, 60-metre high, white Dharahara tower built in 1832, which was one of Kathmandu's most visible monuments, has been razed to the ground. Kasthamandap, the temple that gave the capital city its name, and Kalomochan temple built in the Mughal style by Jang Bahadur along the Bagmati have been reduced to pieces of wood and rubble. More than ten neighbourhood temples in Patan have been flattened. In Bungamati, the Rāto Mastyendranāth temple was destroyed during the festive performance dedicated to the god. The damage caused to the structure of Rana palaces and mansions still needs to be assessed but the nineteenth- and twentieth-century parts of Hanuman Dhoka, the Kaiser Library of Kaiser Mahal, Durbar High School, Lalitkalā College, parts of Singha Durbar, and the Nepal Association of Fine Arts (NAFA) Naxal building are now in a state of ruin. Outside the Kathmandu Valley, the palaces in Gorkha and Nuwakot, and the temple of Manakamana have also been seriously hit.

In fact, the Kathmandu Valley is a concentration of an exceptional number of historic monuments, both secular and religious. These buildings were erected between the twelfth century and the beginning of the twentieth century, if we include the exceptional Rana palace architectural heritage. Some *caityas* are even older and date back as far as the fifth century A.D. Their maintenance is ensured by local bodies or by private individuals. Other sites come directly under the Ministry of Culture.

These temples and monuments altogether represent a unique testimony to Nepali culture, with the major part belonging to the ancient civilisation of the Kathmandu Valley, which is one of the most vibrant in the Himalayas. Despite successive mega earthquakes over the ages (1833, 1934, for instance), and the current unrestrained wave of urbanisation, these temples and monuments have for the most part survived and are visited and used for various functions (both secular and religious). They are part of the recognized urbanscape; they are living places shared by all. When destroyed in the past, they were (save some exceptions) rebuilt over the centuries. Yet, during the process of reconstruction, many temples were altered in shape, size and style. Domes replaced multi tiers and many were plastered with a white wash concealing the original work of the Newari style of temple architecture. Despite these changes, the Kathmandu Valley is an exceptional living museum of bygone ages, representing successive superposed historical layers.

Some monuments have resisted more than others. Pashupatināth's main temple has seemingly not been affected. The situation varies enormously from one place to another. Surprisingly, the five-tiered Nyatapol, the Dattatreya, and Bhairavanāth temples in Bhaktapur have more or less resisted, sustaining only minor damage. Similarly, Patan's stone Krishna Mandir has not collapsed. Just as in 1934, the stone pavement, locally referred to as Bhairava, on which the city of Panauti is built, has safeguarded its main local historic monuments. But the second earthquake, of magnitude 7;3, two weeks later on the 12 May, affected more buildings such as the Kumbheshvar temple in Patan, which lost its last tier, and worsened the damage already caused to Bodnath and Svayambhu stūpas.

The vulnerability to earthquakes of each historical site varies according to its individual location, shape, and construction. Unfortunately, after the 1934 earthquake, some temple repairs were hastily made, using cheap, flimsy materials (like mud and mortar). Walls held together by strong metal sheets, such as in temples at Pashupatināth, or those used in the renovation of Patan Darbar Square (Patan Museum), have proved to be more solid. The number of recent renovations, the underground structure, and the height of a building are also of great import in these matters. Whatever the case, most of the buildings have been greatly weakened.

Historical monuments play a crucial role in the symbolic imagination and are closely linked to the identity of human groups. Temples and other outstanding buildings are vital historic landmarks. They are living sites of memory. I vividly remember, in June 1973, the hopelessness of many Nepali residents of Kathmandu when the Singha Durbar Rana palace was in flames and fell to the ground. Such a desperate reaction reveals a deep attachment to the monuments of the past. In fact, monumental buildings memorialise the nation's intermingled eras from the past. They are symbolically charged sites.

UNESCO has announced an in-depth expertise of the damage "based thereon to advise and provide support to the Nepalese authorities and local communities on its protection and conservation". Emphasis should be laid on the restoration techniques to be used, given that the 2015 earthquake has shown the extreme fragility of these monuments. Yet it is difficult to imagine fully quake-resistant temples in this country which is so often affected by seismic activity. This structural weakness is apparent even in day-to-day life. In the 1980s, I myself saw the roofs of Vishvanāth temple in Patan Durbar Square fall down all of a sudden during the rainy season, quite independent of any earthquake.

Past experiences attest to the fact that the UN's cultural organisation will hardly be able to undertake the preliminary archiving work and the subsequent rebuilding task on its own. Other forms of cooperation with individual countries will be required. At any rate, the reconstruction will take many years, perhaps even decades.

21. Remembered Past

During the second half of the twentieth century, the notion of cultural heritage took on increasing importance. Today, it is the focus of international concern. It pervades official and local discourses, whether in Nepal, India or any other country. The same can be said of the original French term *patrimonialisation*, which is now also occasionally used in English. The word designates the process of "making" something a "heritage", the necessity of preserving elements, both material and immaterial, which have been recognized as being of cultural significance. In this process, components belonging to the past are attributed a value that is to be handed down to future generations. In the following, I wish to stress the link between these concepts and the realm of memory —social memory in particular.

To start with, let us make some definitional remarks. The very notion of 'heritage' needs to be thoroughly examined from an anthropological and economic viewpoint. The concept initially referred to properties in the legal sense of the term: something that is inherited and passed down from previous generations as an asset and which is legally registered. There is, however, a major difference as far as the common acceptance of the word is concerned. "Cultural heritage" refers to joint property that belongs to a group, to a nation, or to the whole of humanity. This communalization of property has the remarkable consequence of withdrawing the monument or site from market forces. Thus, the thing that is valued and preserved escapes ipso facto the world of trade as well as that of the gift and counter-gift. On being officially recognised, a building acquires an immaterial value, which cannot be reduced to mere economic worth.

Two other notional aspects need to be specified. By applying the concept of heritage to cultural domains (buildings, values, traditions), UNESCO and most national states have stressed the transmission of culture from the past to the present, and from the present to the future. Thus, in a very positive manner, they have given a dynamic and trans-generational meaning to the somewhat ahistorical concept of culture. On the other hand, the internationalisation of the concept has enhanced cultural diversity. It has introduced into the field of heritage the question of minority cultures, sometimes to the detriment of well-known Western literate civilizations of classical antiquity, the Roman, Hellenist and Byzantine legacies.

The concept of heritage is directly linked to memory and identity. In Nepal, as in other parts of the world, it represents a glorious past that is liable to evoke positive identification. Not only are we shaped by the past but we ourselves also shape the past. A classified monument materializes or, to put it even better, embodies social memory. A number of social issues, which have sometimes been overlooked by UNESCO's definitions, should be taken into account here. Oblivion, rupture and invention may intervene in the transmission of a tradition from one generation to another. These transformations are of crucial import in the functioning of society. Social groups do not hand down everything from one generation to another. They operate a selection. Structural amnesia is commonplace in this field. One notorious example is the difficulty Turkey's government has in recognizing the Armenian genocide of 1915-23. What is important at a particular moment in their history may be negligible at other times; the reason being that, by the very act of remembering, the group asserts its identity, its political rights, its dominance over other groups. In fact, claiming a culture and claiming traditions are still important ways of expressing national and local identities.

Oblivion and hiding are crucial in constructing social memory. Temporal discontinuities especially have to be considered. Some sites can be forgotten for long periods of time and then be reinvented by social communities. Lumbini for instance, the birthplace of Lord Buddha, practically fell into oblivion for centuries before suddenly, owing to contingent factors, being re-discovered in the nineteenth century by General Khadga Shamsher Rana and the German archaeologist, Anton Führer, upon unearthing an Ashokan pillar. Over the last decades the archaeological site has been transformed into a cultic area, a living Buddhist place associated with the historic Gautama Buddha [**13**].

In most cases, collectivisation of the above-mentioned monument/custom leads to its founder's name fading into oblivion. Who knows which Khmer king built the Bayon, the Baphuon, Bantheay Samre, and other similar buildings in Cambodia? Who knows (save a few persons concerned) who erected the temple of Krishna Mandir in Patan or the Kumārī's palace in Kathmandu? The visibility of the building and its environment predominate. Likewise, the exact process of rebuilding monumental sites subsequent to a major earthquake in the Kathmandu Valley (how were they rebuilt? By whom? With what money? Which ones were not rebuilt? Has there been any change in usage?) has often been forgotten.

Conflicting memories must also be acknowledged. Let me take the example of the festival of Indra Jātrā (festivals are recognized by UNESCO as part of the world's immaterial heritage), an important pageant in the Kathmandu Valley, which is celebrated every year at the end of the month of August or in September. The festival is mainly a Newar celebration, but it combines different post-Gorkhali-conquest elements that were added after 1768. Two distinct collective living heritages belonging to the Newars and to the Parbatiyās respectively therefore coexist. Historically, the first represents the vanquished people, the second the conquering people. Interestingly enough, the festival is performed on the very day Kathmandu was captured by Prithivi Narayan's army. The problem is therefore inescapable: who actually celebrates what during this festival? As I showed in a recent book on the subject, a detailed analysis beyond the actual unanimous festival celebrations reveals persisting dividing lines between these two groups.[7] The divide between them is still present in memories despite the iconic all-Nepal participation of the living goddess Kumārī.

A clear conclusion can therefore be drawn: cultural heritage is always bound up in power relations. It always has to be seen from a relational perspective. Historic monuments can served hegemonic ends and can be utilised by groups to politically assert their identity to the detriment of other communities. These sites are class- and ethnic-related. In fact, in the ethnic and caste mosaic that makes up Nepal, cultural heritage cannot be reduced to national patrimony. Each group has its own culture and occasionally has to fight against the state and other groups to defend its heritage. Past culture legitimises the present. Unfortunately, all too often UNESCO's conceptualisation overlooks such conflicts, disagreements and tensions. More complexities and sociological perspectives need to be introduced.

Notes

1 Maurice Halbwachs, *On Collective Memory*. Chicago: The University of Chicago Press, 1992.

2 Benedict Anderson, *Imagined Communities: Reflections on the Origins and Spread of Nationalism*. New York/ London: Verso Books, revised edition, 2006.

3 Chiara Letizia, "Buddhism Activism, New Sanghas, and the Politics of Belonging among some Tharu and Magar communities from Southern Nepal", in G. Toffin & J. Pfaff-Czarnecka, *Facing Gobalization in the Himalayas. Belonging and the Politics of the Self.* Delhi: Sage, 2014, pp. 289-325.

4 Susan Hangen, "Race and the Politics of Identity in Nepal", *Ethnology*, 44, 1, 2005, pp. 49-64.

5 Vincent Barré, Patrick Berger, Laurence Feveile, Gérard Toffin. *Panauti, une ville au Népal*. Paris: Berger-Levrault, 1981.

6 According to Ram Kunwar, senior archaeologist, Department of Archaeology, in *ECS Nepal*, July-August 2015, p. 61.

7 Gérard Toffin, *La fête-spectacle. Théâtre et rite au Népal*. Paris: Éd. de la Maison des Sciences de l'Homme, 2010.

CHAPTER

4

The Locus of Religion

It is practically impossible to understand anything about present-day Nepal without taking into consideration the religiosity of people and the basic religious/moral values to which they are committed. An exclusively political account of the country misses many points. We in France live in a country where there is a legally instituted separation between religion and society. What is more, our churches are almost empty, expect on Sunday morning during the weekly morning mass, and we are obliged to import priests from Africa to face the alarming decline of religious vocations for priesthood. In Nepal, religion continues to be a constituent element of society and of the cultural heritage, even within the new republican secularized framework. Nepalis are able to adopt a somewhat distanced (and rather fatalistic) view of their religion, but ritual activities and beliefs play a vital part in their daily existences. Whether Hindu and Buddhist, they live in a world where religion provides a significant backcloth for meaningful social action. Relationships with deities are fundamental, even at the most subaltern level of the social hierarchy.

The question therefore arises: is it possible to construct a secular state in these conditions? Seen from a Tamang, a Magar or a Chetri peasant village, located at two or three days walk from Kathmandu, and engaged in performing a death ritual, a shamanic séance or any other collective ceremony, the current debate about secularism seems surrealistic, beyond comprehension. The political elite based in the capital has confiscated the discussions on these subjects without really taking into consideration the will and the considerations of the people. In reality, most villagers have a poor understanding of this notion of secularism.

My perspective has more general implications. In contrast to Marxist theories, I argue that in most societies throughout the world, religion is not merely a surface phenomenon. It constructs and reconstructs social organization at a deep-rooted level. Such a theoretical proposition contradicts the Marxist view, according to which: "The mode of production of material life determines the process of social, political and intellectual life" (Marx, *A Contribution to the Critics of Political Economy,* 1859). My assumption applies particularly to pre-industrial, pre-modern worlds where religion is a crucial part of society and a determinant element of the codes of conduct. For a non-believer and an entirely rational spirit, religion belongs to imagination, superstition and fancies. For social scientists, these beliefs and practices ultimately have two aspects: a representational and a pragmatic one. Religion must in any case be understood both as an imaginative creation of the mind, i.e. a system of representations of the world, and as a driving force behind the whole social process. Creeds are believed and put into action; this is the key issue.

Nepal is a fertile ground for studying these processes. In contrast to Western Europe, which is based on a culture of loss, of downfall (of god, religion, culture, political ideals, empire, prosperity), Nepal is still anchored in a meaningful world, replete with living values and resilient social links which do not need a strong state to exist. In the following pages, I offer seven reflections on the subject, starting with more general issues and subsequently moving on to empirical ones. As I will show, the field of religion is not unified. It is divided into different poles: caste-based religion/asceticism, possession/standard ritual practices, etc. The last text deals with current changes which open new avenues for more private individual spiritual activities, centred on the body and the self. I will come back to the relationships between religion and politics later [chapter 10].

22. *Tenacity of Religion*

Contrary to the theory of secularization, which was in vogue not long ago, religion re-emerged in the late twentieth century and at the beginning of the twenty-first century as a matter of crucial importance. In a number of countries, it has even become a contentious issue both at regional and national level. The rise of religious fundamentalism in particular is one of the most remarkable phenomena of the last decades, and not only in Muslim countries. The success of Bhāratīya Janatā Party, BJP, and of the Hindutva movement in India is an excellent example of the increasing relevance of religion in political affairs. The proclamation at the beginning of the twentieth century by the German philosopher Friedrich Nietzsche: "God is dead", has therefore proved to be totally erroneous. With the notable exception of Europe, which is undergoing a remarkable "unchurching" process, modernity has not in fact prompted a decline in religion. Forms of religiosity may have changed but the centrality of faith is visible nearly everywhere. As stated by Peter Berger, our world is as "furiously religious as it ever was".[1] This phenomenon has taken most observers by surprise.

In Nepal, and more generally in South Asia, religion has so far not been totally severed from daily life and the encompassing social order. A deeply Hindu (and Buddhist) culture continues to prevail throughout the country. Holy sites attract an increasing number of pilgrims, temples are visited daily or weekly, and the rites of passages, from birth to death, are still carried out ceremonially by all communities. Hinduism, Buddhism, Islam and Christianity, all religions are extremely alive. Up to now they have played a crucial role in establishing social cohesion and in constituting personal identity. Spiritual achievements and itineraries are highly praised and recognised by a majority of people. It must be admitted that Sanskrit, the traditional Hindu religious language, is on the decline, but this is no new feature and it has no real effect on the degree of popular religiosity. In fact, Nepal still counts as one of the most religious countries in the world.

The monarchy has been overthrown but the experiences of the last years have proved that democratic regimes can coexist in this part of the world with vibrant faith and persisting religious practices. As a matter of fact, the proclamation of Nepal as a secular (in Nepali: *dharmanirapeksha*) country does not mean much in a country where religion is diffused all over the country in a ramified and non-authoritarian way. Noticeably, a single religious body does not embody ecclesial authority, as is the case in Christian Europe. The separation of the state and the church, like the one that occurred in France in 1905 with its far-reaching consequences, is therefore unimaginable in Nepal.

Let me refer to my own personal experience while contemplating the future of religion in Nepal. I have the feeling that in many cases modernization (including higher education) provokes a reaction that strengthens existing religion or carves out new religious niches. Here I refer to various forms of militant piety, religious activism and revivalism, emphasis on conversion and doctrinal fundamentalism. These new forms concern all religions in Nepal. The success of Protestant sects among deprived groups is a particularly illustrative example. Similarly, Muslims are tempted by more extremist and radical religious issues. Religion has often become increasingly entangled in questions of identity. The success of yoga and meditation practices among a large part of the population is also a noteworthy phenomenon [**28**].

From my own study of reformist Hindu movements in the contemporary setting, such as the Pranāmī, Kabīr Panthī or more traditional ones such as the Vaishnava schools, I have also learnt how intense social bonds can be among followers of a specific *sampradāya*. These groups have developed peculiar spiritual traditions, they have divinized their founders and they worship their own texts (written in *prākrit* languages among reformist groups). Their adherents altogether constitute an impassioned community, strengthened by a number of religious ceremonies. The importance of these groups in the present Hindu religious landscape, in both rural and urban areas, must not be underestimated.

It is difficult to grasp the relationship between politics and religion in these religious organizations. Any clear-cut conclusions are practically impossible. It is obvious that politics interfere in the sacred sphere, sometimes in a vicarious way. But it would be a mistake to reduce all religious activities and beliefs to non-religious instrumentalist motives. Adherents of *sampradāyas* fail to understand social scientists (more often atheists with secular beliefs) who accuse them of being the religious arm of Sangh Parivār (Hindu right-wing political movement). They insist on the differences in language and emphasise their personal, genuinely spiritual motivations. Thinking politics is not always significant.

All in all, the concept of secularization needs to be seriously reconsidered. It emerged in nineteenth-century Europe, a part of the world where the rise of individualism and the growing dominance of a scientific mindset have undermined the communal basis of religious beliefs and behaviour. Simultaneously, in the aftermath of the French Revolution, the development of republican ideas and of a democratic landscape ruined the former prevalence of Christian official churches and other religious bodies in matters of politics and mundane affairs. In these countries, the 'desinstitutionalization' of religion has entailed a gradual internalisation of religious practises and faith, which are dissociated from the social order.

Nepal and India are presently working out their own conception of secularism, which is more respectful of religion than in Europe. The trajectories are different and are based on home-grown traditions. Democracy in South Asia entails a pluralization of religion rather than a decline of religiosity. It recognizes more readily the multiplicity of faiths within one state. Nonetheless, the fact cannot be ignored that, for a growing number of young middle-class Nepalis, religion—like so many things—has entered the world of optional beliefs and preferences. In many cases, tradition is no longer a sacred legacy to be transmitted faithfully from generation to generation, but a cultural heritage on which people draw selectively at their own discretion. The reality of Nepal is therefore twofold: mores are still encoded in religious patterns, but they are gradually evolving towards more individualist ways and personal autonomy.

23. The Language of Possession

Possession is a prevailing aspect of daily life in the whole of Nepal. The country's economic development, the extension of the road network and the gradual introduction of Western medical treatment in rural areas have not generated any profound changes. On the contrary, the post-1990 period of turmoil has seen a surge in cases of female possession in some parts of the country (Pustak Ghimire).[2] One cannot stay in a village for long without either being told tales of possession or witnessing a healing session associated with ecstatic practices. From North to South and from East to West of the country, it is commonly accepted that supernatural beings can take possession of people and create an altered state of awareness. When taken all together, these beliefs and practices constitute a pervasive pole of religious life, often hidden behind colourful festive celebrations and standard ritualistic procedures. They are also typical of India: possession prevails from Rajasthan to Bengal, to Andhra Pradesh to Himachal Pradesh and Uttarakhand. In all these regions, it is a more or less institutionalized cultic element, especially (but not exclusively) in relation to goddesses.

There is, of course, a whole range of disparities between these divine embodiments and the spiritual techniques concerned. For instance the symptoms of possession vary. The embodied person sometimes shivers and shakes. In other cases, he or she just dances without trembling. Music and prolonged chanting sometimes take place whereas in other cases they are conspicuously absent. Here, spirits and deities speak through the mouth of the entranced person, transforming the séance into an oracular one; elsewhere, the individual remains silent, merely expressing his/her possessed or trance-like state through unrestrained behaviour. Here and there, the séance takes the form of an organised collective event performed at a fixed time in the calendar and possession is induced through the constant beating of a drum or the use of *gānjā* (marijuana). The person possessed may even belong to a sort of sacred "college" of practitioners. Elsewhere, one may witness involuntary individual possession, the body of the person being raped, so to speak, sometimes savagely by a malevolent spirit or a witch, creating a state of despair and suffering. In some places, the entranced person drinks the blood of sacrificed animals; elsewhere they refrain from ingesting anything. Indeed, trance can come in the form of auspicious possession by a deity or the terrifying capture of the body by an evil being.

What is more, shamanism and shamanic séances, which are all-important in Nepal, constitute a specialized religious field. In this case, the intercessor possesses a special costume, a headdress. They travel towards the spirits according to their own rules. More importantly, shamanism is characterized by the notion of a journey outside the body, which does not exist in other cases of possession. The shaman (*jhānkri* / *dhāmī*) remains aware and expresses their mastery over the spirits. They use a secret chanted language. The world with which they communicate is mainly a world of spirits, unlike the Hindu realm of gods and goddesses. Moreover, shamanism implies associated tutelary deities and a master-disciple relationship.

Yet in most cases the language of possession shows strong similarities. By and large, trance provokes an altered state of consciousness, a dispossession of the self, which is marked by fainting, collapsing, convulsions, shrieking, violent movements, emotional outbursts, rolling eyes, and the like. The person has no memory of what happened during this ecstatic experience after regaining awareness. The human body in fact "dies" symbolically to allow supernatural agents to enter it. A person's external senses and self-control cease to exist during these experiences; the body becomes engulfed in or is seized by unseen forces. Possession implies a change in personality, an alteration of the person's consciousness, the loss of any rational behaviour. In the Western world, such dispossession of the self is interpreted in psychiatric terms, such as hysteria, epilepsy, and other psychoses. For a psychiatrist, believing in witches is not a far cry from mental illness and hallucinations. In Nepal, as in India, the divine and supernatural lexicon prevails. These alterations to a person's consciousness are understood either as a recognized means of communication between the world of the spirits and humans or as a disorder induced by a spirit/goddess.

A word of caution is in order here. One might be tempted to see in these dissociative states a distinctive feature of popular or folk religion as opposed to more elaborate written religious traditions. According to this point of view, shamanism and possession would come exclusively under oral tradition. This dichotomy is misleading. Indologists and Sanskritists, like Madeleine Biardeau, have shown the multiple interconnections between possession and Shāstric conceptions associated with prestigious divinities such as Vishnu.[3] In fact, the possessed person is frequently seen as a *vāhana* of the god/goddess and a parallel is drawn between them and the notion of *avatār*, i.e. the descent of the god. Interestingly, the entranced person is called *ghorā*, horse,[4] in various Himalayan regions, as if he was used by deities as a mount. In Nepal, just as in India, popular religion is in fact rooted in very elaborate conceptions that are found in mythologies and sacred scriptures. Priests (Brahmans) cannot unequivocally be opposed to healers; a great deal of interdependence exists between the two. Both provide their clients with services and use similar protective and curative mantras. Similarly, possession, *āvesha*, is recognized in Tantric texts and is understood as identification with powerful deities. A common vocabulary prevails as if the two levels —possession and strict standardized ritual activities— belong to a common overall system.

Both men and women can be possessed. *Jhānkri*s and *dhāmī*s are overwhelmingly men, though some are women.

However, in Nepal as in India, women are much more frequently affected by possession. Young wives in particular are recurrently attacked and suffer from self-dispossession that necessitates ritual exorcism. Few of them become divinely possessed practitioners and go on to cure other persons. Hence, a gender issue is at stake here. The prevalence of women in matters of possession is undoubtedly related to their peripheral and subjugated position in society. Ecstatic states provide them with a vehicle to resist or to evade the harsh reality. They sometimes show signs of the alteration to their body by rolling their eyes, sticking out their tongue (allusion to Kālī), and with their long dishevelled hair.[5]

More often than not, possession or the treatment of such an affliction takes on a spectacular aspect not dissimilar from a theatrical performance. Shamanistic séances and other charismatic techniques of treating possessed persons evoke a religious drama, with an assumed script, specific rules and some form of acting/playing. Indeed, possession is a performance in itself, a public enactment, a spectacle for everyone to watch, acted out privately within the family or collectively at village level. Family or group participation in the proceedings is obviously an actual part of the therapy and a way to restore "normal" behaviour in the persons affected. Reciprocally, it has often been noted that Western opera and some modern dance music also have a possession dimension equivalent to non-Western possession ceremonies. Anthropologists have been intrigued by such similarities.

Whatever the case may be, these temporary losses of identity need to be understood as culturally constructed symbolic systems, within which individuals are encapsulated. The person is conceived as regularly possessed by external agents. Such proximity with spirits and deities denotes a close relationship between the profane and the sacred and a lack of boundaries between humans and otherworld agencies. This is one of the main sociological lessons with which we will be repeatedly confronted in this book. The self in Nepal and South Asia is vulnerable and is dependent on external spiritual forces that are superior to a person's own will.

The dark side of the human psyche can submerge the person at any moment. Subjectivities oscillate permanently between autonomy and externally induced agency. The whole world is made up of uncertainties and instabilities. However, when dispossessed of himself, the possessed person is not rejected from the community and placed in a specialized medical institution, as in Western countries, but healed and gradually reintegrated into the group. What a significant difference!

24. Labelling and Living Realities

Decennial censuses provide information of considerable value for social science research. In this respect, the religious landscape portrayed by the 2011 Central Bureau of Statistics first of all shows a remarkable stability in the number of Hindu followers, or to be more exact, of persons claiming to be Hindu. The figure rose from 80.6 per cent to 81.3 per cent (after a drop of nearly ten per cent over the previous decade 1991-2001) during the period 2001-11. By and large, the bulk of the Nepali population remains faithful to Hinduism. Such stability is indeed meaningful if we consider the sustained fight against Brahmanical hierarchical values by different sections of society over the same period, as well as the abolishment of the Hindu monarchy in 2008. Secondly, the number of people who regard themselves as Christians has more than tripled over the last ten years, reaching the still low number of 1.4 per cent. The other results do not reveal any major changes. The surprising slight decrease in the Buddhist category (9 per cent in 2011 instead of 10.7 in 2001) and the slow increase in Islam (4.4 per cent in 2011 instead of 4.2 in 2001) are to be noted.

As soon as these results were published, they were contested by several groups. The Federation of National Christian-Nepal claims that the number of Nepali people who have converted to Christianity is largely underestimated. The Federation (FNCN) estimates the number of Christians at more than 2.5 million. In a similar though opposing way, the powerful Nepal Federation of Indigenous Nationalites (NEFIN) burnt copies edited by the Central Bureau Statistics, asserting that the figure of 81.3 per cent of Hindus is overestimated and does not correspond to the reality. Janajātis were probably expecting a higher percentage of Buddhists, *prakriti* (nature worshippers), or perhaps shamanic followers. Complaints have been made about the forms the questions took as well as enumerator biases.

Even if Nepal is officially a secular country today, i.e. recognizing theoretically the plurality of religion and respecting all faiths equally, such disputes are understandable. This recalls how crucial religion is in matters of identity in South Asia and the important issues the enumeration of religions raises at national level. The results of the census buttress identity politics and extremists' religious chauvinism. The breakdown of the population into the different ethnic groups and castes in the census provoked similar grievances. As a matter of fact, the record of religious belonging is one of the more subjective data collected from the census questionnaires. After all, neither Hindus nor Buddhists are or were registered in Nepal by Hindu or Buddhist authorities at district level, as happened in medieval times in Western European ecclesiastic catholic parishes. Contrary to data pertaining to residence, marriage, even *jāti* and *thar*, answers related to religion are only subject to self-appreciation.

Census data are contested not only because they picture a balance of religious forces within the general population. They also have a considerable bearing on public discourse about stratification and inequality. They may serve, among many other things, to implement an affirmative action policy. As far as religion is concerned, for instance, FNCN is already claiming new job opportunities for Christians by allocating specific reservation quotas and allotting a certain share of the national budget to the community. Similarly, the claims made by Muslim representatives to have their own separate familial laws may also be reinforced by these figures.

Statistics are indeed important. Nevertheless, the country's religious reality differs greatly from the clear-cut classification and categories given in the census. Tamangs are followers of Tibetan Buddhism as well as local cults attached to the territory and *jhānkrism* (shamanic religion). They also celebrate their own version of Tihār and Dasain Hindu festivals. Newar Buddhists, for their part, worship a number of divinities they share with Hindus. Magars and Gurungs follow a mixture of Hindu, autochthonous and shamanic cults. And what about the divisions between Mahāyāna and Theravāda Buddhism, between the different Shaiva or Vaishnava sects among Hindus, or between Catholics and Protestants? What about the new syncretistic cults centred on yoga, meditation and Āyurveda backed by a growing proportion of the urban middle class? Furthermore, what about the different practices of Western Hills Hindus compared to those of Madhes Tarai Hindus. One may wonder whether these groups practise the same religion, which is uniformly labelled Hindu. These variations beyond the lines of the mainstream religions are of utmost significance and may entail different attitudes and behaviour. Statistical data therefore fail to provide an accurate picture of religious realities. They tend to freeze and essentialize religious identities beyond a specific context.

Two further elements deserve a mention in this discussion. Firstly, the quasi-absence of any questionnaires that were returned marked "no-religion". Atheism, for those who are *nāstik*s [atheist], is still almost a derogative word as far as moral values are concerned in Nepal, even if a number of urban upper-middle class individuals distance themselves more and more from religion, and no longer worship gods in temples. Secondly, the perennial refusal of political authorities to recognise and to legally admit *dharma parivartan*, i.e. conversion to another religion, seems to be an increasingly delicate issue.[6] In a country where one is allowed to choose one's own political representatives during elections or to read a newspaper of one's choice, the ban on converting to another religion will be more and more difficult to maintain, or put it in another way, to defend.

25. The Divine Marathon

The greatest public mobilization in the Kathmandu Valley

in the run-up to the 19 November 2013 election was not a call for a political rally, but a religious mass event. This happened on 18 October (and very early the next day), during the full moon, in the area surrounding Lalitpur and Kathmandu on the occasion of the Dipankhā Yātrā. According to most press reports, this procession in honour of the Dipankara deities of the Newar Buddhist pantheon brought together between half a *lākh* and one *lākh* (i.e. 50,000-100,000) of people. Some claims one *lākh* and a half. Participants circumambulated 131 religious sites, starting from Nag Bahal in Lalitpur and ending at Mahālakshmī temple, Lagan, Lalitpur. The route covered 66 kilometres (according to organizers), which can be travelled in a little more than 24 hours. The full circuit went through Bungamati, Khokana, Chobar, Svayambhu, Ichangu, then back to its starting point through Pasupatinath. Based on my own calculations, I estimated that there were more than 50,000 participants. When a religious gathering attracts such large numbers, the event is more than just sacred. It calls for some sociological and even political comment.

Dipankhā Yātrā is a procession that is organized periodically by Nag Bahal, the most affluent ancient Buddhist monastery in Lalitpur. It is not celebrated on a fixed date but during an auspicious conjunction of planets. It has been performed since at least the Middle Ages on the initiative of Newar Buddhists. Six such events have been celebrated over the last hundred years. The last one was eight years ago, in October 2005. A book written in Nepā Bhāshā (Newari) containing religious and historical data concerning the procession was published on the last two occasions. An aetiological legend speaks of an incarnation of Buddha in the form of a blue-horned bull. A statue of the sacred animal now stands in the courtyard of Nag Bahal. A person who intends to take part in the pilgrimage must offer a small cup (*kisli*) of rice and *paisā* [coin] to this bull the day before the *yātrā*. Contrary to Samyak and Pañcadāna—two other major Buddhist celebratory events—no Dipankara icons are exhibited on this occasion.

Participants are made up mainly of Newars. The members of this ethnic group account for approximately 96 per cent of the procession and include not only Buddhists but also a number of Hindus. The Dipankhā Yātrā event therefore presents a strong communal dimension and asserts the cohesion of Newar ethnicity as a whole. Admittedly, each participant has their own motivations and joins the procession individually, of their own accord. In many ways it is a journey of the self. Yet as a collective event, the procession goes beyond any internal religious division and enhances ethnic identity. The rest of the serpentine cortege is made up of Parbatiyā community members, for the most part religiously inclined Bāhuns. Interestingly, those taking part in such a pilgrimage do not undertake it for pragmatic purposes, to fulfil a vow in exchange for some expected boon for instance, but for more transcendental and altruistic purposes: peace in the world, prosperity for their country and so forth. Gaining personal merit (*punya*) is also a strong motivation.

The throng of pilgrims displays modern trends. To complete such a long distance, the walkers don special dress. Men and women carry bags on their backs for their food, water and other necessary utensils. They all wear caps and a light shawl to protect their head and arms from the sun. Some of them even walk with ski sticks as if they were on a trek in the hills or mountains. Such attire lends a characteristic sporty touch to the pilgrimage. Participants are expected to draw the maximum benefit from the walk if the full distance is covered. These marathon men and women are indeed allowed to rest here and there, and even to take a nap at set places along the route. Charities associated with temples provide them with first aid for their sore feet and other physical ailments. Toilets and refreshments are also available along the way. The number of teenagers of both sexes is surprisingly high for this kind of traditional religious event. It contradicts the standard discourse about the loss of tradition among the young.

Such types of religious procession are common in Nepal. They are organised not only in the Kathmandu Valley, with great panache during Newar pageants, but also throughout the hills among *ādivāsī/janajāti* ethnic groups. At festive times or on special dates in the lunar calendar, people belonging to specific local groups gather to circumambulate the boundaries of their settlements, to climb a holy mountain or to travel to a high-altitude lake. These collective marches are based on a sacred conception of small bounded territories and they assert the ownership of one group over its social space. They renew a vital link dating back to their ancestors. These closed territories protected by divinities strongly influence the conceptualization of space and border. They play a great role in the current ethnic demands that are sweeping the country from West to East.

It is important to bear in mind the importance and persistence of these inner spatial zones over the centuries at a time when restructuring the state is at work. Interestingly, such territories have a deep-rooted ethnic character but they are much smaller than the provinces suggested by some Janajāti political leaders. Yet, in September 2015, Nepal finally chose to go beyond these local boundaries and to demarcate territories on other grounds than according to ethnicity.

26. Local Festivals as Social Facts

The various festivals staged throughout the country provide exceptional insight into Nepalese society and culture. These events not only reveal the religious leanings and the spirit of joy that animates the population. They also impart knowledge of local communities and of their social structure. For instance, my understanding of Nepali culture has been greatly facilitated by my attending the Dasain festival in Musikot (Gulmi District) in the early 1990s. The hierarchical aspect of the caste system, the high-ranking Thakuris, the duties that are required of low castes towards the rest of society, as well as the close relationship between Magars and high Hindu Parbatiyā castes, cannot be fully understood without attending such a ceremonial event. Festivals are the nexus of religion and society.

In the Kathmandu Valley and in the surrounding area, the celebration of festivals highlights the importance of the territorial dimension in the Newar cultural heritage. Each city, each village has its own festival, celebrated at different times in the lunar calendar (in some cases, for instance for Bhaktapur's Bisket Jātrā, it is determined according to the solar calendar). These festivals are called *jātrā*, a term that means "procession", *yātrā*, in old Indic languages. They constitute the acme of social life.

For each settlement, the communal festival generates an intensification of social interactions, and the exchange of food and ceremonial services between groups. The divisive aspects of caste are momentarily forgotten, ushering in a sense of oneness among the territorial community. The sense of obligation that links respective hierarchical groups is a dominant feature of these events.

Jyā Punhi (the full moon of the month of Jesṭha, May-June), also called Palanti Punhi, is the most important festival in Panauti (or Palanti, as it is called colloquially), the small historic Newar city located at the junction between the rivers Punyamati and Rosi, in the Banepa valley, where I carried out fieldwork in the late 1970s. Over a period of almost ten days, the inhabitants of Panauti (95 per cent Newar) celebrate and pay homage to their main protecting deities: Indreshvar Mahādev, Bhadrakālī, Unmatta Bhairava and Brahmāyanī. The idols are taken out of their temples, placed in their respective palanquins or ceremonial chariots and carried or pulled through the different quarters of the city according to a prescribed route. It is a time for merriment, family gatherings, feasts, and visits to friends. A number of animal sacrifices are offered to blood-drinking deities (goddesses and Bhairava in particular). People play music, eat meat and drink alcohol. Jyā Punhi also corresponds to a seasonal change, announcing the coming of the nourishing monsoon rains.

Jyā Punhi is the "festival of the territorial community", *desh jātrā*, of Panauti. It is specific to this city and cannot be found in any other Newar town or village. People from Banepa, Bhaktapur, and sometimes even from Nala, come to attend. The pageant portrays the unity of the locality and its distinctiveness. It strengthens the social bonds between inhabitants. All the Newar castes living in the city work together to fulfil the various ceremonial functions. As priests of Indreshvar Mahādev, the major deity and temple in the city, Jangams play a particularly important ritual role, even though they are not Newars. They belong to a Hindu Lingāyat group which originally came from India during the Middle Ages at the invitation of the Malla kings. Tantric rituals are performed at night by Karmācārya Newar priests in various Mātrikā temples, especially in the elegant two-tiered Brahamānayī Mandir situated just outside the city, near the confluence of the two local rivers.

Lower castes also have specific functions to fulfil. Pode fishermen and sweepers, for instance, are responsible for the intestines of a buffalo that is sacrificed to Thampa Bhairava (Thampa comes from Sanskrit *stambha*: sacrificial post). They offer some of this offal to Indreshvar Mahādev on the eve of the full moon within the precincts of the temple of this Shaivaite deity, and they carry the leftovers to other parts of the city. This fascinating ritual is called *lā pulegu*, "to pull meat". It commemorates the death of a past usurper (who goes by the name of Bhāju Kasa) and the final victory of Bhupatindra Malla, a famous Bhaktapur king, over this trickster. Such symbolic victory of rightful principles over evil forces, demons and cannibalistic beings, is a major theme in all these religious festivals, whether local or pan-Nepali.

One of my Nepali students, Maheshraj Maharjan, discussed in his MA the importance of the concept of *jātrā svo vanegu*, "to go and see the festival", during these events so characteristic of Newar culture and society.[7] This expression is used by Newars to designate the act of coming to attend such festivals. Those concerned are primarily daughters who have married into different settlements from their own, various other relatives, and close friends. All are invited to celebrate the *jātrā* and they are given meat and alcohol. The concept underlines the social bonds that link a specific locality to the outside world.

This Nepā Bhāshā concept also stresses the theatrical dimension of *jātrās*. As I have demonstrated elsewhere, these festivals are first of all performed to pay homage to the gods. They are said to pacify and to conciliate them. Yet they are also showcased to provide the Newars and onlookers with an enjoyable spectacle. People sit on the tiered bases of temples or stand at the window of their houses to watch the procession. Having a good view of the deities and of the members of the retinue, with their attire and their musical instruments, is vital. A sense of aesthetic pleasure permeates the religious concept of *darshan* (vision of the god).

In some cases, local pageants become events that have national resonance. This is the case of the Kathmandu's Indra Jātrā and of Patan's Rāto Matsyendranāth Jātrā. These two festivals, which are staged in the two largest cities of the Kathmandu Valley, attract spectators and pious persons from very far away. In the past, the participation of the king (Malla Newar, then Shah and Rana) was required. Today, the President of Nepal has to attend those two festive ceremonies, ensuring—in the eyes of the population—a link between the past and the present.

27. Bewitched

Anthropology endeavours to understand irrational phenomena in a rational, scientific manner. Behind popular practices and forms of belief, it seeks to elucidate a coordinated and interconnected system of ideas. It stresses the social and symbolic logic sustaining what at first sight seems to be fanciful and false conceptions. From this perspective, witchcraft is mainly a way of explaining the occurrence of otherwise inexplicable misfortunes. It is also a means of accusing a supposedly particularly malevolent person of harming a relative or neighbour by magical means. Such is, for instance, the position upheld by Jang Bahadur's 1854 Nepali *Muluki Ain* code which, in its special section about *boksi* [or *boksī*] (witches), not only asserts that sorceresses deserve punishment but also, and perhaps mainly, addresses the issue of the reliability of accusing somebody of being a witch or wizard. If the allegation is erroneous, the persecutor is fined.[8]

Witches and wizards are transcultural figures who are found throughout the world. However, they are mainly associated with remote areas, a low literacy rate and a peasant mode of life. In Nepal, cases of witchcraft are reported all over the country, in Himāl, Pahād and the Tarāī. Anthropologists have explored the wide range of concepts associated with it and its links with possession, traditional medical aetiology, healing and exorcizing therapies. In Nepal, *boksi* are especially related to *dhāmī, jhānkri* shamans and exorcists, *tunā-munā* charms (use of mantra-tantra), *dākinī* beings, etc. The patterns of accusation are mostly grounded in restricted social spaces, close networks of persons belonging to the same village or the same *tol* neighbourhood. The process generally expresses inner social conflict and can be described as a way of relieving stress using a scapegoat that is singled out for unmerited treatment. Rumour (*hallākhallā* in nepali) is pre-eminent in these affairs. More importantly, the bewitched person generally needs a mediator, a witch-doctor (*baidya* or *dhāmī*), to designate the evil person responsible and to deviate the spell. This diviner is part of the realm of sorcery.

In Nepal, as in many other countries, witchcraft has a strong gender dimension. Witchcraft is mainly associated with women (*boksi/boksini*), even though wizards (*bokso*) also exist. More often than not, widows who are isolated from their family circle and have no conjugal bonds, or any other single women, are suspected of using evil supernatural powers. *Boksi* are even said to sacrifice their husbands to become a witch. As a matter of fact, in men's imaginations, witchcraft characterises the darker side of womanhood, the one supposedly linked to demons, seduction, danger, sexuality, and so on. For his part, the renowned French historian, Michelet, who painted a very sympathetic picture of witches in his 1862 book on the topic, sees sorceresses as a manifestation of women's rebellion against oppression by priests and the aristocracy.[9]

Belief in witches is still widespread in present-day Nepal. Children are terrified of suspected witches and do not dare to come out of their houses when *boksi* are said to gather in certain temples or forests at night. In Kathmandu, this happens on Ghantakarna day (in the month of Sāun, July-August) at Mhaipi. The following case, observed in 2006, is typical of an accusation made against a woman for being a sorceress. This took place in Saptari, in a non-formal education centre. One of the female participants was refused access to the class. She was blamed for being a *boksi* because one of the members' children had fallen ill. Rumour was that she had used witchcraft against another family. The whole village shared these suspicions and refused to allow her to attend the training course. It was very hard to convince them that the accusation was groundless and that children can fall ill at any time.

Interestingly enough, witchcraft exists not only in rural areas but also in cities. A few months ago in Patan city, an 80-year-old Newar widow was considered by her own younger son to be a witch and was driven out of her own house. The reason was that her daughter-in-law had become ill. The educated grandchildren consulted a witch doctor who apparently blamed the mother. The son's wife and her children gradually stopped having anything to do with her. The old woman could not understand the reason for this rejection. Finally, everybody stopped talking to her and prevented her from going into other people's rooms, even into the kitchen to fetch drinking water. The old woman suffered tremendous anguish. In the end, the family consulted another witch doctor to find out whether she was really a *boksi* or not. The *būrhi* [old woman] was subsequently confirmed to be a witch and definitively expelled from her own house that had been built by her husband. She is staying at present with her elder son and his family, but has fallen into a state of deep depression. She says: "I gave my jewellery, money and house to them, but my own son accused me of being a *boksi* and threw me out."[10]

Such cases are exceedingly common. They appear in the media in poignant situations only, when recourse is made to torture or killing (the accused person can be burnt alive). Each year, cases of violence (*himsā*) against alleged *boksi* are reported in different places. These unfortunate accused women are beaten, driven out of the village, forcefully fed human excrement, excluded from the village's social activities, and often undergo other savage forms of harassment. What is more, a sudden explosion in the number of bewitched women (*boksi lagyo*) or of accusations against so-called witches frequently occurs here and there with, more often than not, a tragic ending. Instead of seeking harmful agents in the outside world, the witchcraft system denounces a human being, generally a weak person who cannot defend oneself. In the present-day context of a democracy in the making, the silence surrounding these facts is getting louder. There is obviously a real danger in holding such beliefs. Will Nepal ever be a witch-free society?

28. Religion on the Move

When carefully considered, the motto "Let us be happy" seems rather appropriate in the current Nepali situation. Political failure, disillusionment with politics, power cuts, a shortage of so many basic necessities, an economic crisis, the exodus of the population to foreign countries, severe environmental degradation, repeated *bandhas*, the list of the acute problems faced by the Nepali people is long. Issues pertaining to happiness and pain-relief that have been raised by so many new religious therapists and practitioners of contemporary Nepal, including Vikashananda, the guru of Godavari Gurukul hermitage in the southern part of the Kathmandu Valley, are thereby particularly relevant to these troubled times. Can these difficulties explain the success of these spiritual figures in Nepali cities? My answer to this question is definitely yes.

The proliferation of new religious groups, mostly derived from India, is a striking phenomenon in Nepal's contemporary urban landscape. Brahmā Kumārī, Kripālu, The Art of Living, Sathya Sāi Bābā, Rām Dev Yog Pīth, etc., most of these faith-based organizations have emerged in Nepal since the 1990s, sometimes even before then. Vipassanā Buddhist meditation, which has its own characteristics, also needs to be associated with these developments. For a number of Nepali people belonging to the middle and upper class, these organizations play an increasing role in religious and social life. The phenomenon not only concerns the Kathmandu Valley but also the main towns in the Tarai and in the hills.

What do these movements teach? The resolution of personal conflicts, mental equilibrium, relaxation, better daily hygiene, and health — *svāsthya*. They propose a philosophy of pain and offer relief from sorrow and grief. Some focus on yoga (remember Rām Dev *shivir* in Tundikhel in 2010), others on meditation and Āyurveda medicine. The Self instead of the Community — that is the message of the hermit of Godavari, as well as of other gurus and mahārājs in the current Nepali Hindu context. In fact, the success of these groups in the country reveals an individualization of religion. "Let us be happy!" Not in the disappointing contentious public sphere, but privately, within the inner circle of friends and relatives.

In many ways, this religious discourse belongs to the ancient Hindu and Buddhist culture of Nepal. Yet it runs counter to dominant conventional mainstream religion. The almost total rejection of the caste system, of luxurious temples and of lavish divine imagery, and the importance some of them lend to women (Brahmā Kumārī), represent a radical break with former traditions. In addition, these movements welcome followers of other religions, Christians and Muslims, for instance, and people of any caste and ethnic group. They have a universalistic dimension which appeals to the rising middle class more than old local values, and they are better suited to the increasing sense of equality among the people.

Admittedly, a parallel runs between the success of these movements in Nepal and their propagation in India over the last decades. All in all, these transformations reveal a broader crisis of values: the growing divide between a public and the family self (*bhitra/bāhira*), the conflict between tradition and modernity in all aspects of daily life, growing uncertainties in the economic and political realms, more open competition between individuals, and the loosening of traditional rules. They also express the impact of globalization and internationalization. Religion here becomes disconnected (though not totally) from former caste-kin bound practices and beliefs, which were taken for granted. Individual options, if not conversions, are more highly valued. Young urban Nepalis see in these new spiritual figures and their techniques a modern, progressive way of practising religion.

These groups should not be seen as an expression of the Hindu Right. They have received support or encouragement from the Nepali all-party republican authorities. In some ways, they are more disconnected from the old royal cults, more adapted to the secularized programme advocated by most political bodies. Prachanda, the Maoist leader, himself expressed his interest in some of these groups and called for a synthesis between Maoism and spirituality. One reason could be the investment of these organizations in charitable works and welfare activities –the building of hospitals, health centres, orphanages, visits to prisons to help criminals to become useful members of society, humanitarian relief action in the event of natural disasters (flooding, for instance), and so forth.

These religious transformations are highly significant at a deeper level than daily political intrigues. The rise of Christianity and Theravāda Buddhism, the changes within the Nepali Muslim community, the rejection of massive blood sacrifices within some sections of the population [**29**], and, as I have shown here, emphasis on happiness and *svāsthya* among townspeople, all these reveal massive transformations in a country where religion is still intimately linked to daily life. To take one example, the spirit of ecumenism and transnationalism propagated by these religious groups directly challenge the ethnic nationalist discourse, prevalent in the Nepali political ideological landscape. In stark contrast, they correspond to a more inclusive pan-Nepali form of citizenship, beyond any internal divisions. Revolution with guns is devalued; revolution of mind (*manokrānti*) is more highly valued. Changing forms of religion are therefore an excellent indicator of the current transformations in a country like Nepal in this globalizing world.

Notes

1 Peter L. Berger (ed.), *The Desecularisation of the World: Resurgent Religion and World Politics.* Grand Rapids: Eerdmans, 1999.

2 Pustak Ghimire, "Living Goddesses Everywhere? On the Possession of Women by the Goddess Bhagavati in Some Mountain Villages of Eastern Nepal", in D.N. Gellner, S.L. Hausner, C. Letizia, (eds.), *Religion, Secularism and Ethnicity in Contemporary Nepal.* Delhi: Oxford University Press, 2016.

3 Cf Madeleine Biardeau, *L'hindouisme, anthropologie d'une civilisation.* Flammarion:1995. And Marc Gaborieau, "La transe rituelle dans l'Himalaya central : folie, avatar et méditation", *Purushārtha*, 2, 1975, pp. 147-172.

4 Yet *ghora* means also "terrible, awful, frightful", in Sanskrit.

5 Men also share these signs.

6 Article 31(3) of the New 2015 constitution draft still criminalizes any "act to covert another person from one religion to another" (*The Kathmandu Post*, 11 August 2015).

7 Maheshraj Maharajan, "Festivals and Festival-goers of the Kathmandu Valley," unpublished M.A. dissertation, Patan Multiple Campus, Tribhuvan University, 2008.

8 Alexander W. Macdonald, "La sorcellerie dans le code népalais de 1853", *L'Homme*, 1968, 8 (1), pp. 62-69.

9 Jules Michelet, *The Sorceress; a Study in Middle Age Superstition.* 1939 (English translation by A.R. Allinson): Citadell Press.

10 Cases reported by S. Shakya. See Shova Shakya, "*Boksīko bāta*", *Annapurna Post*, May 2, 2013.

CHAPTER 5

Shifting Patterns of Culture

The shift from a closed society to an open, globalized social space, marked by growing interaction with the outside world, takes myriad forms. As this volume seeks to demonstrate, contemporary Nepal is undergoing extensive societal and cultural changes, contrary to those who argue that, basically, nothing has changed in the country. In this chapter, I focus on a limited number of cases upon which I have personally carried out research: the attitude towards animal sacrifice, astrology, travel abroad, vernacular and globalized forms of art, new concern for the preservation of cultural heritage.

But first of all, let me situate these phenomena in a broader perspective. How is modernity, *ādhunikatā*, to be defined in Nepal's contemporary context? I will restrict the discussion here to socio-cultural issues, leaving economic aspects for a later chapter [chapter **13**].

The first thing to remember is that Nepal has only been widely exposed to modernity since 1951, that is a much shorter period than India, a country that was colonised from the eighteenth century onwards. There is therefore a wide gulf between the two countries in these matters. Secondly, signs of modernity must not be taken univocally. This concerns Nepal just as much as other countries. One can be dressed in a Western way, in a mini skirt or jeans, live in a modern building made of concrete with large bow windows, and still lead a very traditional way of life and be mentally turned towards the past. One can eat with a fork and spoon with friends at a restaurant, and still exclusively use one's hands in a household setting. To take another example, the same Nepali person can defend the monarchy and promote the most avant-garde, modern form of art. Conversely, an open-minded person in social matters can be extremely conservative in other fields, for instance, in the domain of aesthetics. But agency also has to be considered. The Ranas outwardly adopted a number of European signs of modernity (and power) in their uniforms and palaces. At the same time, they deliberately kept the populace away from the influence of the West. The dichotomy between conservatism and modernity must therefore be analysed from different angles.

Beyond external appearances and opposing trends within the same person, modernity, in present Nepal, refers to a wide range of behaviour and modes of thinking which are more or less synonymous with the concept of 'liberal' in the socio-political realm. One cannot be totally modern (or liberal) without being open to egalitarian ideas, defending feminist causes, rejecting the excessive segregational aspects of the caste system, welcoming criticism, and surfing on the current secularist tide. In other terms, it is difficult for a Nepali opposing the main ideas put forward by the two *āndolans* popular movements to call themselves an all-modern individual. In this respect, the concept is very similar to its equivalent in Western Europe in the late eighteenth century and in the nineteenth century. Modernity presumes a new mindset, supposedly more adapted to the new conditions of the epoch, a belief in rationality, open society, self-criticism, and political pluralism. The tendency is to totally dismiss what was done under the Ranas and the Shah monarchy and to erect an impenetrable barrier with these former periods. To take another example, in Nepal, a modern person is likely to be appalled by animal sacrifices that they deem too ostentatious [**29**].

Does this modern posture automatically bear witness to the triumph of Western instrumental rationality and the loss of religion, as argued by the sociologist Max Weber in his reflection about modernity in Europe? The answer to this question is no. As I demonstrated in Chapter 4, changes in Nepal have not eroded people's religious practices and beliefs. The persistence of astrology in all sectors of the population, even among politicians, is a good example [**31**]. But many other cases can be mentioned: the resistance of marriage and death rituals over time, even if they have been slightly modified to match current fashions, the huge attendance at festivals and pilgrimages (1.5 million pilgrims, in August 2015, for the month-long Godavari Singhastha Melā held every 12 years),[1] and so on. Religion throughout South Asia is clearly not conceived as anti-modern, as was the case during the French Revolution and as still prevails in the French republican tradition. In this sense, modernity in Nepal is not fully synonymous with Westernization. The history of modernity in South Asia cannot be equated with its history in the West.

It is precisely at this point that difficulties with the concept arise. The main problem of modernity in Nepal (and India) is that it was introduced by colonial history and/or exposure to a foreign, mainly Western, influence. There is an ongoing tendency in these two countries to identify modern ideas with Western culture and to view them as opposed to the country's own traditions. A number of groups in Nepal share a distrust of modern Western ideas, even if they have adopted some of its liberal political ideas and a large number of its commodities. This inclination is found within a large section of the population, from left to right, and not only among the poorest. In fact, the South Asian critique of modernity draws attention to the dissolution of moral values and of communitarian links in the West. In its most radical Gandhian forms, the critique extends to nearly every aspect of modern civilisation. Whether it be a machine (not self-produced), a political structure, values, or the functional specialisation of professions, the rejection of modernity is, in this case, almost total. More recently, the critique also underlined the perversions of the Euro-North American mercantile, capitalist system, the abasement of things into commodities. Yet there is nothing specific to South Asia in these ideas, which are also widely shared in Western countries.

Another difficulty with this complex notion of modernity ought to be highlighted. Though progress, development, modernity are valued mostly among Nepalis, in striking contrast, foreigners in Nepal tend to be committed to the traditional, —if not backward—, aspects of Nepali civilisation. Westerners have a predilection for the picturesque, rudimentary features unspoilt by modernity. There is therefore a noticeable inversion of dominant views that often leads to a misunderstanding.

Let us not forget that a non-negligible anti-modern posture exists in Western countries, especially in the field of art and literature. For the poet Charles Baudelaire, who is credited with coining the term 'modernité" (in French) in 1864, modernity was a sign of decadence. More precisely, Baudelaire equated modernity with a regression of spirituality, what he called the soul, and a concomitant triumph of materiality. It may be presumed that a number of Nepalis — the most educated persons living in urban enclaves — have already come to the same conclusion. How could it be otherwise when contemplating the disaster that development and modernity have brought to the Kathmandu Valley?

29. Violence and Ahimsā

Public sensibilities have gradually changed over the years. The last two Gadhimāī Melā (November 2009 and 2014) in the Tarai, provoked waves of protestation in Nepal and abroad against the sacrifice of thousands of animals for religious purposes. Contemporary society seems less and less willing to accept the mass slaughtering of animals to ensure the welfare of families, crops and the overall prosperity of the country.[2] Likewise, Dasain, the festival of goddesses, is increasingly becoming a bone of contention. A growing proportion of the middle and upper classes now look askance at these sacrifices. What is particularly controversial here is the cruelty and violence towards animals. When I gave a lecture on this subject in Milan in May 2012, my Italian audience was shocked and disgusted by the photographs I showed.

The issue needs to be addressed in a dispassionate way. The first question that has to be asked is why animal sacrifices are still performed so frequently and publicly in Nepal, a situation in stark contrast to India, where buffalo and other violent sacrifices have been more or less forbidden for a number of decades now (they are still performed in some temples and in tribal areas). Not surprisingly, due to this ban, thousands of Indians, mostly from Bihar, cross the border to attend Gadhimāī Melā. In my opinion, the direct cause of this phenomenon is the persistence until very recently of the monarchy in Nepal. Hindu values associate kingship with war, blood, and violence. Kshatriya monarchs had to fight to defend their kingdom and its inhabitants against enemies and evils. They needed to placate blood-thirsty deities to ensure the prosperity of their subjects. In our modern prosaic world, the crucial role of sacrifice in the whole Hindu theology and system has often been overlooked. It is, however, the pivotal axis upon which all society and religion are based.

The slaughter of animals has always been a central feature in Hindu Shāstric tradition. Some Indologists date these practices back to the Vedic period. But *ahimsā* (non-violence) is also rooted in Indian (and Nepali) classical culture. Buddhism and Jainism not only opposed Brahmanical ritualism but their followers also fought against violence towards animals. This notion has slowly been incorporated into mainstream Hinduism itself. Vegetarianism and a non-violent ideology, for instance, prevail in Vaishnava *sampradāyas* (sects). When I was carrying out research on the Pranāmī sectarian organization in Nepal some years back, a devotee, when asked about the downfall of royalty, addressed me: "How can we respect and worship a king who orders so many animal sacrifices during Dasain?" This statement reminded me of how diverse the beliefs within Hinduism actually are.

Animal sacrifices are totally integrated in the social and religious life of most Nepali groups. It is part of the natural order of things, a way of driving away evil spirits and of gaining the favours of deities, whether male or female. The buffalo is the symbol of evil, of *asura* and *rākshasa*. It stands in opposition to the cow, the symbol of purity, as epitomised by Brahmans. These dark beasts have to be killed periodically, even though they are reared with utmost care throughout rural Nepal. At the Gadhimāī temple, like anywhere else, those possessed drink the blood of sacrificed animals on behalf of the deities. Remarkably enough, the importance of animal sacrifice concerns not only Hindu people but also most of the *ādivāsī/janajāti* groups in Nepal, from the Magars in the West to the Kirants in the East. The theology here is different but the end result is the same. Buffaloes, goats and pigs are widely sacrificed in most districts.

In most cases, sacrifice is performed as a substitute for something else. Those reluctant to kill animals now cut up cucumbers, pumpkins, and other things instead. Yet we often forget that animal sacrifice stands for the sacrificer (the patron of sacrifice) himself. This is explicitly the case in the legend associated with Gadhimāī. As a matter of fact, in a large number of legends and myths in the Kathmandu Valley and elsewhere, the sacrifice of human beings is closely associated with animal sacrifice. Over the years, I have collected a number of stories about how a king is urged to kill his own son to prevent a *dasā* or misfortune in his kingdom. In most cases, fortunately for the prince, an alternative solution is found.

Self-sacrifice also applies to the sacrificial ideology of Maoist combatants that was common during the armed conflict. Marxist ideology provides us with little insight into understanding this matter. In fact, the old Brahmanical ideology has been reformatted here, at least metaphorically. Admittedly, the fighting tradition has been prevalent in the Nepali hills for a long time. It has been fuelled by the enrolment of men in Gurkha regiments and by the military's feats of bravery. More generally, sacrifice has always been associated with the army because it is believed to bestow strength. When going into battle, Maoist fighters no doubt combined several of these ideas to glorify their journey towards death.

Interestingly enough, the issue of killing-rituals not only concerns South Asia. In September 2012, France's Constitutional Council (High Court) refused to ban bullfighting which includes the final execution of a bull in a quasi-sacrificial way by a magnificently dressed "torero", with a red cape and a sword. These fights, which belong to traditions in the South of France, and which are a national sport in Spain, are lambasted by animal protection groups. The authorities argue that they cannot abolish vernacular traditions supported by local people. This statement is reminiscent of the declaration made by the Nepali Prime Minister in 2009 who refused to interfere in the Gadhimāī case, though requested to do so by animal rights campaigners, because such practices concerned (private) religious affairs. Sacrifices are undoubtedly deeply entrenched in people's daily life. But what can the future of these mass animal sacrifices be in a republican democratic Nepal?

30. The Politics of Animal Slaughtering

With Modi and the Hindu BJP taking over the reins of the country, new importance has been given to the issue of slaughtering cows and bulls in India. A ban on slaughtering cows has long been in application in some states but recently this has, for the most part, been tightened. Maharashtra, for instance, has extended the prohibition to bulls and bullocks. The consumption or even possession of cow meat is now subject to a fine and can land you in prison. Haryana and Jharkhand, two other BJP-led states, have followed suit and have tightened restrictions both on selling cow meat and on slaughtering. BJP activists would like to make this a nationwide ban. However, eating beef and butchering cattle are still legal in some states such as Kerala, Goa, Assam, Arunachal Pradesh, and Nagaland, sometimes only under certain conditions, in other cases unconditionally.

For an overwhelming majority of Indians, the cow is of sentimental and religious value. Its products (urine, dung, milk, curd, *ghi)* are the chief ingredients for daily purification rituals. Yet voices are being raised to advocate for more respect towards the diverse dietary habits in the country. This problem is of vital importance because Muslims, Christians, Scheduled Tribes and a number of low-caste people regularly eat cow meat. Some have also expressed concern about slaughterhouses and their tens of thousands of workers. In Maharashtra, the new ban on slaughtering cattle has put thousands of butchers, transporters, cattle traders, mostly Muslims, etc. out of work, especially at the Deonar abattoir on the outskirts of Mumbai. This measure has also negatively impacted Hindu farmers who can no longer sell their old cattle to slaughterhouses. In fact, India has the world's second-largest (after Brazil) beef-export industry which is largely geared towards buffalo meat instead of cow meat, as the former is of no positive religious value.

For some years now, if not decades, the issue of animal sacrifices, of goats and buffalo for instance, for religious purposes in temple precincts or in other places, has been critically addressed in India. In Himachal Pradesh, High Court judicial authorities recently (2014) outlawed the slaughtering of animals. The main concern is cruelty to animals rather than an eating-meat issue. Sacrificing buffalo (long since banned in some southern states) and goats is the key concern here. A number of NGOs and animal lovers backed the judges in their fight for this cause and therefore approve of these prohibitions. Their stance is based on moral and modernist Westernized values. They regard these customs as "barbaric". Yet such measures take little account of public sentiment. Devotees recall the exigencies of deities in these matters. In 2002, the extension of the ban on animal sacrifices to goats (and birds) in Tamil Nadu temples, which was imposed apparently in an effort to please Hindutva forces, led to a widespread protest, especially by Dalit people. General enforcement by law of these age-old practices that carry cultural overtones reveals a reinforcement of administrative powers to the detriment of the former plurality of customs.

Similarly, it shows greater interference of the state in matters related to religious faith.

This brief excursus about India was necessary since the significance of the cow in past and contemporary Nepal can only be understood when compared to the situation in its powerful southern neighbour. Significantly, the holy status of the cow is recognized more in Nepal than in India. Gorkha, the place from which the Shah dynasty originated and from which the word Gorkhali derives, comes from the term *gorakshak*, "protector of the cow". Since Prithivi Narayan's rule and his strict Hindu policy, this animal has become the paradigm of Nepali purity, proof of the country's sanctity and of its status as *asal hindustān,* "the holy land of Hindus". The cow is the national animal of Nepal, one of the national symbols of the country, just as the rhododendron and the Himalayan impeyan pheasant are. In these symbolic matters, Nepal remains more rigorous than India. Killing a cow used to be punishable by death. Today it carries only a 12-year prison sentence but it is still considered a grave sin.

Laws on eating cow meat are less strict, though the great majority of the population regards it as a serious offence. Regarding this issue, the law is at variance with standard practice. Hindu Dalit low castes and some ethnic groups speaking Tibeto-Burman languages, such as Tamangs, often eat the flesh of dead cattle. Tibetans, on the other hand, eat yak meat, an animal often assimilated to the cow in the old legal code, and therefore protected in the past. Eating beef is still a highly sensitive subject in Nepal (just as in India). It carries the stigma of being an offence to the gods. Recently, in April 2015, Indian Vishva Hindu Parishad and BJP leaders associated the great 2015 earthquake in Nepal with the fact that Rahul Gandhi (born of an Italian Catholic mother, Sonia) eats beef and visits holy places such as Kedarnath in the Indian Himalayas without purifying himself (*One India*, 28 April 2015). These ideas are no doubt echoed by orthodox Nepali Hindus.

In stark contrast, buffalo is commonly slaughtered, and much more so than in India. It is butchered not only for its meat but also for religious purposes. The buffalo, a symbol of *asura* devils and enemies of the gods, is one of the most valued offerings to gods, especially to Bhairava and blood-drinking goddesses. As I alluded to in the previous section **[29]**, an increasing number of voices are being raised today against these "cruel" ritual killings. Notwithstanding, the two-day Gadhīmāī festival, known among animal rights activists as the "world's largest sacrifice of animals", was performed as usual, on 28 and 29 November 2014 according to the religious calendar.

The religious festival takes place every five years in Bariyarpur village, Bara district of Nepal, about 160 kilometres from Kathmandu. An estimated 300,000 animals (from buffaloes, goats, birds to rats) were sacrificed in 2014 to Gadhīmāī, a forest deity of the Sen dynasty of Makwanpur. The Indians from Bihar and Uttar Pradesh who take part in this festival took the opportunity of offering the animal sacrifices that they are no longer allowed to offer in their own country due to the tightening of the ban on animal sacrifices. A few weeks prior to this, the India Supreme Court banned buffalo exports, though this did not apparently prevent the slaughtering of animals.

Once again, in 2014 just as in 2009, the Nepali government ignored the call for banning animal sacrifices though it did give less financial backing to the temple trust (Rs 4.5 million in 2009). It would seem that Nepali judicial functionaries are less sensitive than their Indian counterparts to the "barbaric" aspects of these events. In my opinion, Nepali judges are more sympathetic towards the expectations of common worshippers and are less open to Western modernist rhetoric opposing animal sacrifices than their Indian counterparts. Furthermore, the main temples keep written records of the number and of the sort of animals that have to be sacrificed every year. These written records stand in opposition to legal decisions. What is more, the Nepali authorities defend these sacrifices on the grounds that they belong to their authenticable culture which is different—they insist—from Western culture. Yet the position of the

Maoists differs. In these sacrifices they see an expression of the outdated, now useless royalist ideology. In 2011, they blocked state funds earmarked for the mass sacrifice of goats and buffalo during the Indra Jātrā festival. But they were obliged to step down when faced with public opposition. How indeed can this pageant be celebrated without offering blood to Bhairava? From a Hindu Nepali perspective, this is totally incongruous.

One last point must be underlined. In Nepal, the slaughtering of animals (other than cows) — pork, buffalo for instance — is not organised in the same way as in India. For consumers of meat, no proper hygienic slaughtering houses exist in the country. Traders frequently purchase dead chickens at half price and sell them to consumers (*My Republica*, July 9, 2015). The high-tech Danish slaughterhouse in Hetauda was recently shut down because the Kathmandu Valley, the main market for meat, was too far away from it.

Other unsuccessful attempts have been made in the country. Kanako Nakagawa, an anthropologist friend of mine who has worked among Newar butchers in the Kathmandu Valley, told me that two small slaughterhouses were built and operated in Kakani and Thankot in the early 2000s. Both closed within a few years. A new government-run slaughterhouse is in operation in Humat Twah, along the Vishnumati River. However, it does not meet all the criteria related to food hygiene. In fact, throughout the country, most meat still comes from traditional slaughterhouses situated close to butcher-caste areas. They are run with little concern for hygiene conditions. Despite the adoption of an Animal Slaughterhouse and Meat Inspection Act in 1999, the agencies concerned have not yet bothered to enforce the regulations.

31. Nepali Time

Astrology (*jyotish*) is traditionally all-important in Nepali life, not only in people's daily existence but also in state issues. During the Shah dynasty's rule, it was a matter of national politics. Narayan Hiti Palace had its own astrologists (*jyotishīs*), which were called upon and consulted with regards the sovereign's every move and any happening in the kingdom. The dates of key royal events, i.e. international agreements, treaties, visits to temples, the monarch's birthday celebrations, the crown prince's marriage, foreign travel, etc., were at once submitted to the appointed *jyotishī* and set according to his advice. The coronation of King Birendra (1975) took place three years after his father's death following the astrologers' recommendations. In fact, according to Hindu Dharmashāstras, astrology and astrologists were vital elements in the art of governing. A kingdom without a good astrologist was doomed to destruction. These experts in the stars and the sky ensured the monarch's success, wealth and renown.

To what extent have things changed in the self-declared secular federalist democratic state of Nepal? At local level, people consult astrologers at least as frequently as during the monarchical period. The occasions are too numerous to list them all. On the whole, the main reasons for paying a visit to an astrologist include requests for a horoscope to be drawn up at the time of a birth, choosing a bride or groom, seeking help to settle family conflicts, staving off disease or afflictions caused by a malevolent supernatural being (*dasā*), performing a ceremony, predicting events and planning a long-distance journey. The Nepali certified *pāñcāng* almanac has always been a much sought after document at the time of festivals and ceremonies. Likewise, a horoscope, malevolent *cinā*, established at the time of birth has always been just as important a document for the Nepalis as their identity card. The recent success of the bestselling book *Cinā Harayeko Mānche* ["The man who lost his horoscope"] by Hari Bansha Acharya attests to the prevalence of this topic among a popular audience.

Since the fall of the monarchy, the government no longer officially uses the services of astrologers. Nevertheless, a committee still exists; the *Nepāl Pāñcāng Nirnāyaka Samiti*, which is set up by the government and is made up of nine members, all astrologers who belong to the Parbatiyā and

Newar community. Each member is appointed for a two-year term. Every year, the Committee, which comes under the Ministry of Culture and Tourism, establishes the official lunar-solar calendar and sets the dates for auspicious (*sāit*) ceremonies. Aside from this, many other private or semi-private consultations still take place in the political sphere. It is no coincidence that 19 November 2013 (*dutīyā krishna paksha*, Māngsir in the lunar calendar)—an auspicious, *mangal* or *sāit*, day for Nepal, free of the influence of the planets Gemini and Rahu—was chosen for the 2013 Constituent Assembly elections. As I was told by an astrologer with whom I discussed this issue: "an astrologer is not difficult to find in a country like Nepal".

A lot can be said about astrology in Nepal in past and present times, all of which is of utmost importance if we are to understand the country. Let me deal with two aspects. Firstly, the Nepali *pātro* almanach is established for the whole of Nepal, from "Ilam to Dandeldhura". However, in some places in the Tarai, Indian calendars are also jointly used with Nepalese ones. In other places, the Tibetan calendar is *the* reference. In addition, some local cthnic methods of calculating time are used here and there. For instance, in the Kathmandu Valley the Newars' way of calculating the passage from one *tithi* (lunar day) to another in the middle of the night is different from the Parbatiyās'. The exact date of some festivals, particularly Tihār, can therefore differ from one group to another. These differences introduce a certain variation in the calculation of time within the country; not to mention Vikram Sambat (chosen as the official Nepali calendar by Chandra Shamsher in 1903 A.D.) that coexists with Nepāl Sambat and the Gregorian calendar.

Perhaps even more importantly, the way of calculating astrological time is different in India (for example in Varanasi, one of the most famous places for astrological science) and in Nepal. This is not the time and the place for discussing technical issues, but the differences in the method of calculation (Nepal being more traditional than India in these matters) lead to finding various dates for the same religious festival, *Makar Sankrānti* for instance. The Nepali identity itself is therefore at stake in matters of astrology and the religious calendar, even if it must be admitted that different astrological schools are referred to in India to set the dates for festive events.

One thing particularly stands out here. Paradoxical as it may sound, this obsession with "sky time" contrasts starkly with a very relaxed way of dealing with time in more down-to-earth spheres. Foreigners and urban Nepalis joke about "Nepali time" to explain the frequent delay on any fixed date for an appointment. How can a country so strict regarding some aspects of life accept such impediments in completing profane deeds? This may be because the materialistic realm is devaluated compared to the religious one. Be that as it may, time —a wholly cultural concept— has not been totally Westernized or globalized in Nepal.

This dual conception of time, both strict and relaxed depending on the given realm it applies to, dictates the present and future of the country. If everything is foreseen in the sky and the stars, what's the point in fighting against political and economic forces? Why fight against the current tide of events? What role might individual deeds and initiatives play in this cosmogonist-determined environment? Unfortunately, things sometimes happen in a haphazard, unpredictable way. In June 2001, Mangal Raj Joshi, the court astrologer, confessed to an Indian newspaper (*The Telegraph*) that the massacre of the royal family in a shower of bullets had been "unpredictable", but that to forecast it would have called for a more detailed astrological study of the persons concerned!

However opinions diverge. Some well-known astrologists or persons close to them maintain that a prediction had been made in former times. It is said, to be exact, that Radhanath Lohani, King Mahendra's astrologer, had specifically advised the king not to marry his sons to women who were sisters and related to each other. This, he thought, would bring about great misfortune. But the kings did not listen to this advice.

32. Crossing the Sea

Opening the country to the outside world in 1951 has proved a crucial step in the globalization process in Nepal. The young generation is unaware that until relatively recently, re-admittance to one's caste after travelling to foreign countries —and, consequently, after being polluted by accepting illegitimately cooked food or by having illicit sexual intercourse—required the performance of a special ritual called *pātiyā*. A certificate of rehabilitation was given to the person concerned by the highest judicial authorities of the former Hindu Himalayan kingdom. The procedure for being re-admitted to a caste is described in the old code of law, *Muluki Ain*, propounded in 1854 by Jang Bahadur. The question of the intent, whether involuntary or deliberate, and of the urgent nature of the situation was taken into consideration. This could eventually count as mitigating circumstances for the transgression of this rule. Otherwise, the traveller lost his caste and his share in the ancestral property was confiscated. He was not even allowed to enter the sanctum of major temples.

It is also worthwhile recalling here the notion of *kālā pānī,* the "black waters". As in pre-modern India, travelling overseas (*samudrayāna*) was considered to be a sin and a religious offence. The transgression of crossing the sea caused the loss of one's caste. The reason behind the ban was the inability to carry out the daily rituals and the sin of having contact with *mlecchas,* foreign Christian people. Such journeys also meant breaking family and social ties. Moreover, the fear of crossing the seas derives from the notion that it meant the end of the reincarnation cycle. We thus realize how Jang Bahadur's Belait-Yātrā to Britain and France in 1850 was a breach of tradition and very risky from a religious point of view. Jang Bahadur had to undergo special rituals in Calcutta on his return from Europe. He was the first high-ranking Nepali official (and perhaps the first among the Hindu princes of South India) to cross the "Black Seas" to visit foreign countries. On his return to Nepal, Jang

Bahadur even had to face a conspiracy on the ground that he had violated caste rules while in Europe.

How many migrants to Gulf countries, North America or Europe are still aware of these old rules? Most Nepalis, even highly educated ones, no longer know the meaning of these two words: *pātiyā* and *kālā pānī*. Rehabilitation and purification after long journeys have become a thing of the past. Indeed, it is not exactly known how many of the thousands of Nepalis fighters who served during World War I and II in Europe cared about such ideas, even though they themselves belonged to a caste. Yet an arrangement with the *rājguru*, supreme religious authority, had to be found by Chandra Shamsher in 1919, and a collective nominal *pātiyā* was granted to all these soldiers.

Similarly, Newar traders, almost all Buddhists, were forced to spend months with a Hindu priest on their return to the Kathmandu Valley from Tibet, to undergo *pātiyā*, to clean away their alleged consumption of yak meat. According to Father Ippolito Desideri, in the early eighteenth century Nepali traders back from southern districts under the Mughal rule also had to undergo purification by bathing for forty days in cow's urine, by drinking it, and occasionally by eating cow dung.[3]

Recalling these rules and regulations is far from futile. It is important to situate Nepal not only in space, in relation to other countries, but also in time, between the past and the present. It helps to put into perspective the incredible series of changes that Nepal has undergone over the last century. The fall of the Rana regime in February 1951 dramatically transformed the country. New ideas, new forces, which were relegated for an initial period of time to the precincts of Kathmandu jails or to India among Nepali political refugees, suddenly irrupted and spread rapidly among the people. From this point of view, the Panchayat system can be seen as a last (and desperate) attempt to accommodate old social rules within a new, totally different environment.

Today, restrictions on crossing boundaries are limited

mainly to some rare priests and religious officials. The caretakers of some Devī temples in the southern part of the Kathmandu Valley are, for instance, not supposed to cross the limits of their villages or of their districts. Likewise, the Lalitpur *agnihotrin* (A Rājopādhyāya Brahman) is not supposed to cross the Bagmati River. However, the new freedom to come and go, *āune-jāne*, as one likes has overthrown old regulations. Nobody really bothers about the latter today. After travelling to America, the Kumārī living goddess of Bhaktapur was first stripped of her divinity and then reinstated after a cleansing ceremony (2007).

Reports on the Nepali diaspora reflect a combination of a transgression of traditional lifestyles and of the persistence of values and traditions. It is very difficult to make any generalization regarding these matters: the situation differs from one place to another. Yet, broadly speaking, Nepalis in Europe and North America gather at the time of religious and festival events and enjoy celebrating traditions as a group. If there is a big enough community, they set up ethnic associations to defend and maintain their culture. Symptomatically, most of them tend to have a home diet that is almost the same as the one usually eaten by city-dwellers in Nepal. However, their lifestyle, dress, fashion and values have changed considerably (as in Nepal itself). In the case of marriage to a non-Nepali, there is a rapid collapse of caste rules outside and inside the household. All these changes, whether profound or superficial, have weakened caste rules as a whole. Over the last few decades, globalization and the increasing rate of migration abroad have breached old hierarchical caste rules, though not in a uniform manner, perhaps in a more drastic manner than any political transformation has ever done.

33. Behind the Masks

The cultural heritage of Nepal has many faces, both material and intangible, some of which are barely known in the country itself. Nepali traditional masks from the Tarai, the hills and mountain regions are one example. These masks have been gradually brought to light since the 1970s by private European collectors and art dealers (Chazot, Pannier, Petit, among others). They have been recognized for their aesthetic qualities and powerful imagery, just like their African, Oceanic and Polynesian counterparts, which were brought back from colonies by missionaries, dealers and ethnographers in the nineteenth century. The same process, with a similar surge of enthusiasm and passion by a handful of Western aficionados, was repeated more than a century later in much the same way. In fact, traditional masks from all these countries, including Nepal, communicate a high degree of emotional intensity.

In Western countries these Nepali artefacts are much sought after today for their brutish features and their aesthetic value, challenging the divide between nature and culture. Prices can reach 50,000 to 60,000 USD for the most outstanding ones. A number of fake masks have also sprung up here and there on the market, revealing the strong demand for these artefacts. A noteworthy exhibition took place in the prestigious museum of primal art, Quai Branly, Paris, in 2010-2011. It focused on 22 Nepali masks from a major private collection — all of which had been donated to the museum.[4] Paris is in fact one of the leading centres in the world for 'primitive art'. This exhibition was followed up by a number of other ones in various European capitals.

Local Nepali people use these masks during festivals, religious ceremonies, pantomime performances and masquerades. Although most of them were made recently, in the twentieth century, some are much older. They represent animals (tigers, deer, elephants), ancestors, demons with carved fangs or clowns with dissymmetrical features, and other profane characters. They are carved out of wood and have a deeply engrained black patina on the surface, which comes from years of exposure to smoke and soot when stored at home in the loft. Masks from the hills (Magars and Gurungs, for instance) are made of hardwood covered with a glossy patina, whereas those from the lowlands (Tharu, Dhimal, Rajbansi) are made of softer wood, pigmented with polychrome or white clay. Other groups make their masks out of tree fungus or felt and goat skin. Some include fur attachments for the beard and moustache. In the southern plains, the influence of Hinduism and Hindu Epics is clearly visible. By contrast, in the middle mountains, it is difficult to differentiate between Hindu and Buddhist elements. Tibetan Buddhism has left its mark in mountain areas.

With their staring eyes, minimalist design, roughly carved noses, round or square mouths, with the rawness of their material, the nose rings and earrings that commonly adorn them, and their simple geometric facial features, these masks are indeed fascinating. They present striking similarities with ancient masks (dating back 9,000 years) from the Near East (Cisjordany). Surprisingly, we know little about them. Besides scanty ethnographical observations, no major fieldwork has ever been carried out in this field. One thing is for sure: these masks are rooted in religious (often with theriomorphic figures) and burlesque performances acted out at fixed times of the year. To my knowledge, the old man-old woman pair *burhā / burhī*, which is often to be found among them, is a major theme throughout the country.

Save for some exceptions, these masks are looked upon with relatively little regard in Nepal and are very rarely exhibited in local museums. They belong more modestly to *lok kalā*, i.e. folk art tradition, and are associated with a somewhat rustic design. In travelling from Nepal to foreign countries, these artefacts have changed status. They have become purely aesthetic objects, totally disconnected from their original signification and use. They have entered the world of art, a concept (which differs from the notion of beauty) that until recently was (and still is) little known in the country. To be worn a few days a year for religious ceremonies (and stored in the attic the rest of the time) is one thing; to be permanently displayed on the walls of a gallery or a museum is another. This radical shift represents a major change in conception and civilization.

As previously mentioned, the process recalls the discovery of "primitive" art (which has been renamed "tribal" or "primal art" as well as "indigenous art") first in Europe and then in America, following colonial expansion throughout the world at the beginning of twentieth century. At the time, young European artists, like Matisse and Picasso, were particularly captivated by such artefacts from non-Western countries. In these artistic forms, they found possibilities for non-mimetic representations as well as a way to escape naturalistic forms. Unfortunately, this awareness and admiration for "primitive art" were somewhat biased by old colonial ideas about the nature of non-Western Others. According to these false notions, this art reveals the infancy of humankind.

So far there has been little dialogue between Nepali people and the West with regards these objects. This is a pity given that the various cultures to have produced these masks are still alive, albeit facing extinction. The appropriation by the West has not been counterbalanced by any local endeavours. The time has come to re-appropriate these old vernacular artefacts by collecting, researching, exhibiting, and teaching them at art schools, and —perhaps— by using them as models in the modern workshops of young artists. Reinvesting them in contemporary Nepali creations could establish an artistic canon in the country in the same way as "primitive art" became a reference for avant-garde Western artists.

34. Rethinking Immaterial Heritage

The destruction of a large number of historical landmarks and outstanding buildings due to the April-May 2015 earthquakes and aftershocks is a good opportunity to reflect on what today encompasses the notion of cultural heritage in a country like Nepal. To fully understand the subject, several issues have to be critically addressed: the definition of a monumental site, the questionable concept of intangible heritage, the separation between material and immaterial, and UNESCO's somewhat new parochial definition of culture.

Except for the Rana mansions and Shah palaces, most of the monuments that collapsed on those fateful dates were temples that come under the authority of the Department of Archaeology. Despite this administrative control, temples cannot be simply regarded as archaeological sites. They house divinities, statues and many other types of divine images, which are worshipped by appointed priests, and celebrated at regular intervals during collective ceremonies, sacrifices and other rituals. In other words, they are living sites, visited by ritual experts and the common people. They are also substantiated by customary values and traditions. Most of them are associated with myths that are deeply rooted in the population. The research I have conducted on religious life in the Kathmandu Valley over the last four decades strongly supports these assertions. The population does not view these monuments simply as reminders of the past and as belonging to the realm of memory. They are part of daily life.

Indeed, since 2003, UNESCO has been trying to revise its strictly archaeological approach in matters of preservation of monuments by introducing the concept of immaterial cultural heritage (ICH). This concept, which has evolved over the last fifteen years, primarily concerns non-material aspects of social life. It includes a large number of fields related to the performing arts, festive events, local knowledge, social practices, skills used to produce traditional crafts, living practitioners, oral history, voices, culinary traditions, animal husbandry, pilgrimages, songs, prayers, dancing and any other type of custom. From a scientific viewpoint, this wide variety of things seems far too extensive.

This vagueness becomes apparent when the UN cultural branch declares that ICH is: "traditional, contemporary and living at the same time". UNESCO adds that ICH is, "at the same time: *inclusive* (it contributes to social cohesion, encouraging a sense of identity and responsibility which helps individuals to feel part of one or different communities and to feel part of society at large"); *representative* (of the skills and customs passed on to the rest of the community); and *community-based* (recognized by the communities, groups or individuals)". Scholars can only puzzle over this all-inclusive definition that has been elaborated in the most conciliatory terms. Some have ironically gone as far as proposing that pizza be included in the masterpieces of intangible heritage!

In fact, such a broad categorization encompasses a vast array of things. It includes all evidence of human creativity and expression, the material aspects as well as their representations. Intangible heritage has consequently become just another ill-defined name for culture and folklore. In my opinion, a number of these topics ought to be considered from different angles: sociological, historical and anthropological. To take just one example, a ritual is very rarely both inclusive and community-based. It usually excludes some persons or some categories of persons, and it cannot be investigated without analysing it in terms of power, that is hierarchy. UNESCO's broad definition therefore needs to be both addressed critically and problematized.

The separation between material and immaterial, between things and events, and between monuments and performances, is also highly problematical. In the Nepali intellectual landscape, the first of these elements belong to Sankritised and Tibetanised high literary culture; the second to folklore, in Nepali *lok-sāhitya,* or *lok-vrātya*, which is more associated with the spirit, the "soul" of the common people. Yet Nepal, like other neighbouring Asian countries, lies at the crossroads between high literary culture and oral tradition. In these areas, tangible heritage is inextricably bound up with intangible heritage. The two are inseparable. Traditional religious dances cannot be separated from costumes and painted props or curtains that are used on stage. Music cannot be separated from musical instruments, which are kept as artefacts in ethnographic museums. Any dichotomy in this domain is questionable. In Nepal, performative expressions of customs, even shamanism, are related to artefacts, paraphernalia, houses, and occasionally to architectural sites.

Another problem with UNESCO's definition is that it basically relies on disputed notions of indigeneity and autochthony. Understandingly, UNESCO's programmes are motivated by the need to defend marginalised cultures against the threat of globalisation and to react against a Eurocentric approach to civilisation. They rightly aim to preserve the fragile and ephemeral non-material heritage of minority cultures. The defence of minority cultures is therefore a noble cause. But more often than not they convey archaic, out-dated anthropological notions about so-called indigenous people. They frequently rely on essentialist concepts of ethnic identities. Emphasis is laid on the local and on ethnic boundaries to the detriment of cultural contacts. Groups and communities are viewed as independent of each other, autonomous, isolated. The processual nature of culture, and the intense interculturalism and hybridity over the centuries have been forgotten. Living cultures are de-historicised; they are seen as compartmentalized, their practices are frozen. Culture and ethnicity are merged into one.

At the same time, the division between tangible and intangible perpetuates the ancient separation between high and oral culture, superior and inferior, so recurrent in the history of civilisations, in a rather insidious manner. It also reactivates the opposition between North and South or between East and West. Instead of being applauded, these all-too-easy divisions need to be transcended.

35. Global Art

The boom in modern and contemporary art over the last decades is a remarkable feature of Nepal's modernity. It not only generates new artistic forms and performances beyond the traditional boundaries but also a profound transformation in the field of art and in the artist's social conditions. In Nepal, the introduction of modern art is conventionally associated with the return in the early 1960s of Lain Bangdel from *École des Beaux-Arts* in Paris where the young writer and painter studied, and his nomination as Chancellor of the Nepal Academy in 1972 by King Mahendra. The upsurge in contemporary art is more recent. It dates from the 1980s, with the exhibition of artists such as Shashikala Tiwari, and the creation of the Siddharta Art Gallery in 1987. However, these new artistic forms have only become more visible and substantial since the beginning of the twenty-first century. It is worth pondering this phenomenon and its significance in artistic and sociological terms.

This is a widespread phenomenon in the Kathmandu Valley, a region which, since the Middle Ages, has reached a high level of achievement in the field of painting, sculpture, wood carving, and various other crafts. Today, the city of Patan, a centre for the arts which is known throughout the Himalayas and South Asia, houses a large number of contemporary artists, particularly Newars, who practise what they call modern art.

Stylistically, the border between modern art (*ādhunik kalā*) and contemporary art (*samasāmayik kalā*) fluctuates more than in the West. The latter combines traditional and modern art. In fact, many Nepali artists (*kalākār*) are engaged in hybrid forms of art and claim to be both modern and contemporary artists.[5] In this domain, cross-pollination between cultures is the rule. These artists have all been influenced by Western art (and modern Indian orientations) and have adopted a transnational language of forms and colours. Whether trained at Lalitakalā College or Sirjanā College of Fine Arts in Kathmandu, or in India, or in the West, they have all become global.

There is considerable diversity in the styles and worldviews these young male and female artists have adopted. Some have embraced non-representational painting and abstract art (*arūpa* or *amūrta*), others still work on figuration. Others have already opted for post-modernist forms: they specialise in installation art, musical genres, they explore the realm of pastiche or make a mockery of traditional canons, they use collages or introduce photography or video, and they organise live performances. For instance, Asha Dangol's work is characterized by a touch of derision, Shashikala Tiwari's paintings by their use of feminine forms and flowers as a symbol of sexuality, whereas Ashmina Ranjit's work is emblematic of the performing arts, and Sarita Dangol draws inspiration from nature (wild animals, rivers, trees). All these protean modern trends exist in astonishing synchronicity. Most are torn between modernity and tradition.

This emerging modern and contemporary Nepali art is clearly situated at the crossroads between many different paths. Yet all these young artists have opted for unconventional forms of art, moving away from tradition or, for some of them, reinterpreting patterns from the past. They refuse to re-produce received notions and images in order to perpetuate the existing socio-cultural order. They reject former symbolic, century-long, pre-established norms to concentrate on personal experimentations. They break up symmetrical arrangements. These *kalā-premi*, lovers of art, try to depict their subjective emotions and experiences rather than represent an objective reality. They have moved on, from imitating and conforming to past models, to innovations and to a personal quest. The focus is on the self, on autonomous personhood, on the uniqueness of the individual, its creativity and potentials. The number of women among these artists—traditionally the exclusive realm of men— is a clear indication of the profound social change imparted by it. They "consciously explore their gendered situatedness and 'express' this through art making".[6] Modern art is also a gender conquest. What is more, practitioners come from a whole range of castes, some traditionally with no connection to art.

More than anything else, these artists have taken art away from its former sanctity and dedication to the gods. There is a considerable loss of religious influence even though some artists reintroduce some sacred components, *mandala*, lotus, *caitya* and *stūpa* motives, or gods' images (Samundra Shrestha) in their artistic universe. In most cases, religious elements are re-appropriated and recycled. They are assigned a more representative function than a purely religious one. The speed at which this shift towards secularization has been made is indeed amazing; what took centuries to unfold in the West has taken place here in the space of a few decades.

The progress of modern and contemporary art has greatly benefited from the mushrooming of new galleries, such as

Sangeeta Thapa's Siddhartha Art Gallery which opened in the fashionable Babar Mahal Revisited, a cluster of upscale boutiques and restaurants in the south of Kathmandu. This gallery has rapidly become a platform for contemporary Nepali art. In 2007, Sangeeta Thapa also co-founded the Kathmandu Art Center (KAC) (Patan Museum, Mangal Bazar), which sponsors young artists and offers short-term residencies. And in 2009 she launched the first International Arts Festival in the Nepali capital. Sangeeta Thapa, who was educated in the United States, plays a pivotal role in the institutionalization and the promotion of these new art forms. These galleries, exhibitions, fairs and biennales create a market for art and legitimize artworks and their authors, despite the indifference or even the hostility of the majority of the urban population, who "do not understand" these new languages.

To attend showcases and exhibitions is one thing, but to call upon individual or joint studios is another equally worthy undertaking. In this respect, visiting KAG (Kasthamandap Art Group) in Kopundol is an unforgettable experience. It gathers together seven "visual artists" (all Newars), as they call themselves, each experimenting in their own way. The place is a vibrant testimony to the globalization of Nepalese art, though some of the artists concerned still draw inspiration from their ancient heritage. This collective studio was set up in the name of Prasant Shrestha, the inspirational leader of the group, an artist who died prematurely at the age of 31. In actual fact, some of these artists work more in keeping with modern art trends than with what is regarded as contemporary art in Euro-American countries.

Artivism, which attempts to conciliate art and activism, plays a significant role in the renewal and the transformation of the Nepali artistic scene. The alternative Lasanā art hub in Bhakundol (Lalitpur) is a case in point (*lasanā* comes from *lasatā* which, beside "happy, love", also means "art" in Newari). The interdisciplinary practitioners associated with this group consider art as a tool for social change in keeping with the political preoccupations of the day. "The end objectives of all artvities are ultimately to bring around social change and political reform".[7] These activists focus on gender issues, federalism, sexuality, or any other contemporary fractured realities. They always privilege collective expressions. For them, artworks, installation art, and performances reflect political agendas, gender issues, climate change, chaotic urban congestion, and environmental degradation. They are committed to experimentalisation.[8]

Ashmina Ranjit, born in 1967 and founder of Lasanā (in 2007), is the key figure of this contemporary vanguard. She received her higher education in art in Australia in 1999, and at the University of Columbia (New York) in 2006. She has a dynamic vision of art, mixing artwork with performance, and breaking the boundaries between various art genres.[9] She refuses to limit art to entertainment or to beautification. Performativity is her main expression; she seeks to go beyond the canvas and to redefine contemporary Nepali art practices. Her performances are treated less as artworks and more as manifestos. But she also includes in her programme specific Indian techniques, such as meditation and yoga. She attempts in a convincing manner to reconcile global and local art forms.

The rapidly expanding modern art scene is not specific to Nepal. India and China are the focus of similar trends, sometimes fusing modern and folk (*lok-kalā*) paradigms. Some of these Nepali artists, such as Kiran Manandhar (among others),[10] heavily influenced by Western modern art, have achieved international recognition. It is worth noting that such ground-breaking developments have not destroyed traditional (*paramparāgat*) forms of art, which are still flourishing, especially the art of *paubhāh*, traditional Newar religious paintings rooted in Tantric traditions. In all these fields, whether modern or traditional, the Kathmandu Valley has sustained its age-long dedication to art.

Notes

1 *The Kathmandu Post*, 1 September 2015

2 It would seem that they have been heard: in July 2015, the

main priest of the goddess Gadhimāī, in the Tarai, announced that the next celebration in honour of the goddess, in 2021, will be performed without animal sacrifices. It yet has to be seen whether this promise will be kept and whether a wild goddess associated with power can be really worshipped without animal blood.

3 Richard Burghart, "The Formation of the Concept of Nation-State in Nepal", *The Journal of Asian Studies*, 44 (1), 1984, p. 104

4 Marc Petit, *Dans le blanc des yeux. Masques primitifs du Népal*. Paris: Musée du quai Branly, 2010.

5 Cf. Dina Bangdel, "Contemporary Nepali Art: Narratives of Modernity and Visuality", in Deepak Shimkhada, *Nepal, Nostalgia and Modernity*. Marg, 63 (1), 2011, pp. 59-70.

6 Kurchi Dasgupta, « Women Artists of South Asia. Working from within and outside the Known Registers », *Depart* (Dhaka), 18, 2015, p. 82.

7 In *Redefining Kathmandu Valley through Contemporary Art*. Lasana, Kathmandu: 2012, p. 66.

8 Cf. Archana Thapa, "Breaking Boundaries in the Armed Conflict". in *Glocalisation of Art*, Kathmandu, no date, pp. 18-24.

9 On Ashima Ranjit, see Kurchi Dasgupta, "Redefining Conventions", *Asian Art News*, 51, July/August 2014, pp. 51-55.

10 Kiran Manandhar was the Vice-Chancellor of Nepal Academy of Fine Arts (NAFA) from 2010 to 2014. Ragini Upadhayay Grela, a well-know female modern artist, has succeeded him.

CHAPTER

6

Images and Imagination

Imagination is one of the three constituents of cognitive human abilities, the two others being reason and memory. It is therefore a basic element of the human brain. Few social and cultural elements can be investigated without taking into consideration the way it works. Even the perception of realities is replete with preconceived ideas and images. Yet these ideas themselves are filled with the real world. As stressed by Clive Staples Lewis (1898-1963), the well known British medievalist, literary critic and novelist: "They are not imaginations: they are summarized knowledge of the real. Always the real world is the bank on which the poet draws his cheque, and though a metaphysical lyric may be a fine and private place, all the meanings embraced within it are but passengers who come there from the public, external, objective world of reality and haste thither again".[1] This happens to be true even in the most unrealistic literature and in the most elaborate allegories. The traces of earlier texts are in most cases easily identifiable.

The following series of essays illustrate the various interactions between the material and the mental in the Nepali social and imaginative world. The main angle of approach focuses on interplays, eventually discrepancies, between aspirations and realities. I highlight the imaginative dimension enmeshed in the house [**36**], in sacred sites [**38**], and in village communities [**40**]. Two other texts discuss self-centred fancies present in cyberspace [**41**] and fictional elements at work in a recent apparently realistic Nepali novel [**39**]. Dreams are also an important theme [**37**]. They involve deep emotional commitment but, more than anything else, they can be defined as the awareness of being in an imagined word in which things happen. Intrinsically they appeal to the imagination. Nonetheless, in the interpretation process, cultural patterns prevail. The same dreamful imagery is rarely attributed the same meaning across the world.

In imagination, there is the word image. How is the unseen visualised in South Asian cultures? The representational format of mental images especially plays an extremely important role in the field of religion and of aesthetics. The last essay [**42**] in this chapter deals with the links between politics and image, an important theme in the anthropology of visual representation.

36. In the Sky

High-roof terraces (*kausi*) have gradually become a major feature of domestic architecture in the Kathmandu Valley. Former pitched roofs covered with *jhingati* tiles have given way nearly everywhere to flat roofs that occupy a greater surface area and are often built on different levels. In fact, these open spaces at the top of houses were common in neoclassical Rana mansions and palaces, not to speak of Tibetan/Thakali and Western Nepal Khas dwellings. However, since the 1960s, modern brick and concrete domestic architecture topped with roof terraces has become the norm practically everywhere among all sections of the population, whatever their ethnic group or caste. Obviously, the traditional *kahsi*, a small terrace occupying a very limited space (five to seven square metres) in the *buigal* attic-cum-kitchen of Newar houses, as well as the *bhaupvā,* lit. “cat-hole”, an opening onto the upper part of the roof for light and ventilation, cannot compare with these spacious modern terraces.

These flat rooftops serve for a number of things. People use them as an open-air laundry to dry clothes, to bask in the sun during cold winter months, to grow flowers and plants in clay pots, to look down at the street and into neighbours' houses. Children use these terraces as a playground. During the Tihār festival, they fly kites and during Holī they throw water over passers-by. In agricultural areas, people often dry rice, wheat, peppers, and vegetables here after harvesting them instead of using part of the street in front the house for this purpose. Moreover, with the prevailing scarcity of water in urban centres, part of the top terrace is used to store water in plastic (formerly metal) containers of varying capacities. Solar panels may also be installed here and Tibetans hang prayer-flags that fly in the wind.

The building of terraces engenders a privatisation of space. Instead of having a common area that is shared with neighbouring families for various activities in the street or elsewhere, the domestic unit becomes introverted, curled inwards upon itself. In addition, these open spaces provide everybody with a panoptic view of the surrounding area, which was formerly the prerogative of the elite in their palaces. The all-embracing view from the top floor has replaced the much more limited, fragmented and anonymous lookout from lattice windows. In these spaces, local people are more prone to fanciful thoughts and daydreams.

The history of the balcony (*bārdalī* in Nepali) in Nepal, —which falls within this topic— has yet to be written. More or less similar structures already existed long ago in religious architecture. But in non-religious buildings, the balcony appeared mainly during the Rana period. More often than not, it included a more or less elaborate railing and curved design. The balcony was introduced here and there in the early twentieth century in the dwellings of common people. It was based on models found in aristocratic mansions and North-Indian architecture, especially West Bengalese architecture, which was heavily influenced by Western fashions. Since then, the balcony has become very popular in modern or Rana-style houses. Unfortunately, its antiquity in rural areas outside the Kathmandu Valley has not been documented.

In his book *The Poetics of Space*, the French philosopher Gaston Bachelard (1884-1962) writes: "The house shelters day dreaming, the house protects the dreamer, the house allows one to dream in peace". This applies rather well to the rooftops of modern buildings in the Kathmandu Valley. On these terraces, members of the household can give free rein to their imagination and spend time lost in their thoughts. This propensity to fantasize increases when night falls and lights can be seen twinkling all around. The family can then enjoy magical moments while preserving their intimacy.

The whole house is in fact a source of poetic images. Bachelard goes on to write about this subject: "Verticality is ensured by the polarity of cellar and attic, the marks of which are so deep that, in a way, they open up two very different perspectives for a phenomenology of the imagination". According to him, in the Western house, the roof basically covers the house and is a symbol of stability. "Up near the roof all our thoughts are clear". The cellar, on the other hand, represents the dark side of the house, partaking of subterranean forces and of the irrational.

The configuration is rather different in Nepali vernacular architecture where, among many other things, the cellar does not exist. Among Newars, the attic and the roof are associated with purity, with the preparation of food, and with domestic deities that protect the house. A "sunstone" (Sūrya) is conventionally worshipped each morning on the small roof terrace, *kahsi*. The lowest floors are used for more mundane functions, such as storage, as a shop or for cattle breeding. They are open to outsiders whereas the upper levels are traditionally reserved for family members. The ground floor is associated with impurity. It is on this level that a person's deathbed is laid out and the toilet (in modern houses) is to be found.

However, people now live more and more in a standardised space that is common to all ethnic groups/castes; they do not use rooms as before. The lower levels are often rented out and in high-rise buildings the partitioning of the different floors into apartments has provoked profound changes in the intimate lives of residents.

What is more, the conceptual idea of the house has dramatically changed over the last decades. The decline of traditional (lattice) window designs and the transferral of the kitchen from the attic to lower floors have led to a growing loss of symbolism. The sacrality of the upper part of the house has been preserved, as testified by the prayer room, *pūjā kothā*, that is often located on the top terrace, but the overall symbolic dimension has been deeply impacted. These changes have to be taken into account when analysing the transformations of local urban centres. A house is not merely a shelter, an architectural edifice. It also corresponds, in the mind of its dwellers, to a set of ideas, and it is associated with a whole series of powerful images.

37. Meaningful Dreams

In his enigmatic play, *The Tempest* (1610-11), William Shakespeare imagines a remote island where a magician by the name of Prospero, the vanquished Duke of Milan lives. In Act IV, Scene 1, Prospero says: "We are such stuffs. As dreams are made on, and our little life. Is rounded with a sleep". These few words poetically evoke the blurred distinction between dream-cum-fantasy and reality, which is a theme of this book. Shakespeare is an unrivalled expert in shaping the dramatic representations of dreams. He used them as a supernatural device to create on-stage dream-like worlds of fantasy. In fact, the ludic plays of the famous playwright refer to a world pervaded by medieval thought patterns, occult forces, old religious pageants, 'mummings' about mythical heroes, carnivals, chivalric romances, and the like. In the transitional period between the Middle Ages and the Renaissance, beliefs about dreams, witches, spirits still prevailed, —just as they do in present-day Nepal. The boundaries between the imagination and hard facts were less circumscribed than today. A few decades later, the philosopher Descartes put an end to these enchanted worlds and confusing dreams by instituting the clear superiority of rational knowledge over fancies and the imagination. He gave priority to logical order.

When reading or listening to Nepali folk tales, we are often confronted with this enchanted pre-modern world. Let us take the example of dreams in everyday life. In a large number of tales and in the daily lives of most modern-day Nepali families, dreams (*sapanā / svapna*) are regarded as being inspired by the supernatural. A person may dream about their dead relatives. It might be a sign that these ancestors are dissatisfied and expect more attention. Their *kriyā* funerary rituals were perhaps wrongly performed and therefore, an offering, *pūjā,* needs to be performed to pacify them. Deities sometimes appear to a person sleeping and order them to build a temple, a *stūpa* and to organise a ceremony or a sacrifice. This is a compelling injunction. In most cases, dreams are assimilated to a celestial vision and to a divine message. They are viewed as a possession of the body and mind by a supernatural agent that seizes or overwhelms the sleeping person. Recurring nightmares suggest that the individual is experiencing problems in their daily life. The dreamer will therefore be inclined to consult an astrologist, *jyotishī*. The practitioner will explain to them which celestial influence is the cause of the trouble and how to put a stop to the nightmare.

In other cases, a dream heralds an omen: it foretells the future either in a positive or negative way. The science of omens (Sanskrit: *shakuna*) is particularly developed in Indic culture. Palmistry, birthmarks, the reading of marks on the soles of a new-borns' feet, astrology, numerology, divination based on the observation of animal behaviour, especially of dogs and, last but not least, the interpretation of dreams were used in the past and still are to predict the future.[2] In these treatises, interpreting dreams is a science based on a repertory of signs and their corresponding meanings. Unusual phenomena and calamities are also widely viewed as precursors of future events. The very word *sapanā* may be given as a name to a person by an astrologist based on the former's horoscope.

The whole history of Nepal as narrated in the local *vamshāvalī* chronicles is replete with dreams and omens foretelling the future. The movement of celestial asters, the barking of dogs, earthquakes, and other natural catastrophes are highly meaningful for experts in astrology who are capable of deciphering these signs. As far as the history of the Shah dynasty is concerned, Prithivi Narayan Shah's birth was first announced in a dream that his mother, Queen Kaushalyavati, had and in which she swallowed the sun. The newly crowned king of Gorkha first dreamed about his conquest of Nuwakot before actually triumphing over the stronghold. Moreover, it is a well-known fact that a prediction about the longevity of the Shah ruling dynasty (eleven generations on from the time of Prithivi Narayan) was circulating well before the 2001 Narayan Hiti slaughter. These prophecies, dreams and legends are of paramount importance in local history. In a dream that Trailokya Malla, king of Bhaktapur, had, the goddess Taleju ordered that the royal Kumārī cult be set up. Laws of the universe and of the gods are superior to an individual's will and to their personal fate. Even kings can do little to oppose them.

In Āyurvedic medicine, which is practised throughout Nepal, there are wide-ranging beliefs about dreams. Dreams may be used as an aid to diagnose a dreamer's state of health. Dreams about fire indicate an imbalance in the fire element, dreams about flying indicate an excess of water, etc. In these matters, everything depends on the three vital elements (*tridosha*): *vāta* (air and space), *pitta* (heat and fire) and *kapha* (earth and water) which control the internal and external functions and constitute the body. The dreams of those suffering from a *kapha* imbalance, for instance, conjure up scenes associated with water, ponds, rivers, the sea, etc.

It is often believed that the subtle or astral body slowly rises from the physical body during sleep. It comes out and floats like a feather in the air. It can go anywhere in the world at lightning speed and come back before the waking hours. The scenes this subtle body witnesses on these mystical journeys are sometimes remembered and appear in dreams. Tantric treatises are very rich in dream interpretations, demonological texts, nightmare aetiology and impure nocturne visions provoked by "seizers", *grahi* or *graha*, i.e. incubi and succubae hordes. Tantric practitioners may enjoin the person to construct a citadel of mantras in order to block out evil spirits at night.

Despite strong popular beliefs and the wide array of its religious schools, Buddhism theoretically considers dreams as illusory and false. These nocturnal fancies symbolize the changing and impermanent nature of all things known to the senses. They are like emptiness, *shūnyatā*. If a person recites *mantra* ten thousand times, they will see Buddhas and Bodhisattvas in their imagination, and they will dream that they are spitting out a black substance symbolizing serious karmic offences. As for Rani Maya, Buddha's mother, she saw in her dream an elephant with six tusks and a body harder than iron, whiter than silver and snow, brighter than the light of the sun and moon penetrating her womb. Astrologers deciphered the dream as depicting the birth of an extraordinary enlightened child who would be honoured as the king of all kings.

To sum up, dreams in Hinduism open a door into the transfigured and somewhat tyrannical world of deities or spirits, whereas in Buddhist speculations, they stand for the ultimately empty and selfless nature of all existence. In striking contrast, Dr Sigmund Freud, the renowned Viennese psychoanalyst at the end of the nineteenth century, interpreted dreams as being based both on sexual drive, which he considered to be the determinant force of life, and the unconscious (repressed feelings, hidden phobia, subliminal perceptions) which are released during sleep.

In drawing this parallel between Western thought and South Asian culture, one particular element stands out. According to Freud (an extremely secularized author), dreams refer to the individuated self, their history, their memory, when detached from the group. Sexuality and collective forces (embodied by the father in psychoanalysis) take the place occupied by gods in the Indic world. Once again, opposition between the self and the social group comes to the fore.

38. The Present is The Past

In his *Divya Upadesh*, Prithivi Narayan Shah depicts himself and his brothers as the five Pāndavas, i.e. the five heroes of the monumental *Mahābhārata* Sanskrit narrative. This image illustrates the relevance of the famous epic text in eighteenth-century Nepal and the political use of its foremost legendary characters to enhance the kings' image. Reference to the *Mahābhārata* was made inside the country to impress the people and outside its borders to intimidate rival kings of small neighbouring kingdoms. It was used to single out the Shah family from all other local sovereigns and to glorify its dynasty.

Indeed, the narratives of the two prestigious Hindu texts, the *Rāmāyana* and the *Mahābhārata*, have over the ages been imprinted not only on the minds of people throughout Nepal and on royal titles but also on the landscape. It is no coincidence that the pre-Himalayan range straddling the country from west to east, has been called Mahabharat. This acknowledges the all-importance of the Himalayas in the epic text. It is a well-known fact that the five Pāndavas spent a period of thirteen years in exile in a forest after having lost their kingdom at a game of dice. Some localities in Nepal boast of being the place where they were actually exiled. Modern Biratnagar, which is said to have been ruled in legendary times by the eponymous Mastya king Birata, as mentioned in the *Mahābhārata*, is one of them. These identifications lend prestige to the localities and create a legendary context to which common people proudly refer.

Furthermore, in the seventeenth and penultimate chapter of the epic, after renouncing their kingdom, the Pāndavas journey (together with Draupadī) to the pure sacred Himalayas. They ascend to heaven from Mont Meru (Kailash). Yet, only Yuddhistira, the eldest of the five brothers, survives this great journey and reaches heaven on Indra's chariot. As a matter of fact, hundreds of geographical references to the *Mahābhārata* exist in the Himalayan foothills situated within proximity of the Siwalik Hills. Some archaeologists believe that the deadly Kurukshetra battlefield lay at the foot of these hills. Thus, the space is infused with legends. The sacred texts are projected onto place names to provide them with a pan-Hindu signification. The local geography is thus placed on a transcendent plane, situating it in a broader framework.

The two epics—the *Rāmāyana* belonging to the *kāvya* poetic genre, the *Mahābhārata* to *itihās* historical literature—have also played a major role in Nepali folk-theatre and in art productions. The folk performance *Tharu Barka Nāch* is a good example of this, even if the play is hardly performed now.[3] Nepal is obviously not the home of such a big event as the *Pāndava Līlā* in Garhwal which is held every twelve years.[4] But numerous *Rām Līlās* arc performed in the southern part of the country and in the low mountains, which keep the epic tradition alive. Masks depicting heroes of the *Rāmāyana* are worn on these occasions. It is worth noting that most of these performances are based on oral versions, sometimes far removed from the original Sanskrit text. Similarly, in Nepali art, painted illustrations from the *Mahābhārata* are well known to Nepali amateur art collectors. They portray Arjuna offering water to the dying Bishma, the duel between Arjuna and Karna, and the like.

The two epics are very popular among a large majority of the Nepali population. The success of the *Mahābārata* series, which was broadcast on Nepalese television in the 2000s, is still vivid in everyone's memory. Its impact has been remarkable, exceeding all expectations. Men and women continue to identify with the main heroes of the epic. Sitā in particular is an idealised model for a number of women, with her dedication, courage, and purity (in most versions), a paragon of women's virtues, at least when seen from a traditionalist viewpoint. In addition, the translation of the *Rāmāyana* is one of the major achievements of the well-known Nepali writer Bhanubhakta (1814-1868), a Brahman from Tanahun who is regarded as a primeval poet. His work is a milestone in the development of Nepali literature.

So when Narendra Modi, on both of his visits to Nepal in 2014, expressed the desire (so far unfulfilled!) to visit Jānakī temple in Janakpur, the alleged birthplace of Sītā, the heroin of the *Rāmānaya*, he immersed himself in this legendary historical setting which has been built over the years around sacred Hindu places. He did not wish to visit a secular place of importance in Nepali history but, instead, this all-religious and meaningful site. For lack of time or no doubt for other reasons, he had to limit his visit to the nearest noteworthy temple, Pashupati, which is admittedly just as important in the Pauranic texts as Jānakī. On 4 August, he performed special *pūjā* at the temple and made sandalwood offerings (just like Nepali Shah kings used to offer at Jagannāth's temple in Orissa). Perhaps he remembered the mammoth *Ekamātā Yātrā* procession launched by BJP-VHP from Pashupatināth to Kanyā Kumārī in the 1980s at the time of L. K. Advani, which was aimed at developing a sense of unity among Hindus. Whatever the case may be, it was a good opportunity for Modi to recall India and Nepal's common cultural heritage. There is nothing innocent about these visits and public statements. What is more, Indian priests have been officiating in Pashupati temple for centuries. The Nepali authorities and people were seemingly delighted by this visit that received a great deal of media coverage.

Tīrtha yātrā campaigns across India, from the Himalayas to holy places further south, were a device favoured by Sangh Parivār and were instrumental in promoting Hinduism. These *yātrā*-based politics were geared towards obvious communal political objectives. By merging politics and religion, it powerfully captured the Hindu imagination and resuscitated the old sacral geography which is glorified in the Sanskrit tradition. It is also a well-known fact that the pro-Hindutva movement has always been keen to prove the historicity of the *Mahābhārata* by relying on local archaeology, ill-proven evidence and legendary accounts.

This trend of basing history and geography on religion is nothing new. As mentioned above, processes of Sanskritisation and of reworking past histories have been active for centuries in South Asia, including in Nepal. The word Nepal is mentioned only once in the *Mahābhārata* (V.20) but there are thousands of actual references to the text throughout the country. There is a longstanding tradition of reintegrating local lore and local geography into a broader textual-based history. By and large, the past has been continuously reassessed in the course of the centuries. The same movement persists today. The present is permeated with mythologies and local legends and is regularly immersed in the past. The boundaries between the glorification of religion/cultural heritage and its instrumentalisation have become blurred.

39. A Novel's Social Landscape

The Madan Puraskār award-winning novel, *Palpasa café,* was released in November 2014 in a French translation by Suraj Shakya. After English and Korean, this Nepali best-seller penned by Narayan Wagle has thus widened its audience and has once again crossed foreign language barriers. As French translations are concerned, the book is an addition to a handful of Nepali novels, including of course *Siris ko phūl* (*La fleur bleue de jacaranda*) written by Parijat (and translated in 1998 by Corinne Atlan), but also two books written directly in English by Samrat Upadhyay.

Most reviews of *Palpasa café* stress the author's poignant depiction of the country at the height of the Maoist insurgency. Despite being a fictionalized account, the novel refers to a number of events rooted in the political and military situation during that period. A large part of the book narrates the travels of the main character Drishya through western hill districts during the conflict. In these villages, Drishya encounters various witnesses to the civil war and some of its actors. Among them is an acquaintance from the past, Siddhartha, who has become a Maoist leader. Their positions on the civil war radically differ. What is the use of violence? Are deaths and martyrs necessary to give birth to a new world, supposedly more equal than the present one? Drishya has doubts about revolutionary ideals. The book is punctuated by deaths including that, at the end, of Palpasa, the girl the narrator has fallen in love with.

The story is overall melancholic, sad, sorrowful, just as the ten years of civil war were. *Palpasa café* has often been described as an "anti-war novel" (Kunda Dixit), stressing the atrocities of the war. Schools are blown up, villages emptied and poor peasants in the hills instrumentalized by the guerilla. The fate of the common people caught in the crossfire between the two belligerents, as in many other zones of conflict throughout the world, is eloquently expressed.

However, it is worth noting that the narration is highly fictionalized. The characters for instance do not seem to belong to any caste or to any specific community. Who is Palpasa? A first-generation American Nepali who has returned to her motherland after 9/11. Besides this, little is known about her. *Palpasā* is a Newari name, meaning "lightning";[5] but the reader remains uncertain about her specific ethnic/ caste identity. For the author, these are obviously not the central issues.

Drishya also belongs to the more globalized section of Nepali society. He is a modern painter (and incidentally a writer), an occupation that is emblematic of Kathmandu and Patan society, but unknown outside the overcrowded valley. When travelling through the hills to his native land, he remains for the most part an outside observer of the realities of the country. In addition, the dramatic structure is non-linear. The gossamer-like storyline contains a number of holes. As such, there is a marked difference between this book and more realistic Nepali novels published in the past.

I personally see the book as portraying a constant balance between tradition and modernity. The first chapter is situated in Goa, a fashionable tourist destination for the Nepali middle class and Westerners. The story then shifts to Kathmandu's modern atmosphere, especially in Thamel, the tourist hub, and then finally to the districts where peasants live in close contact with the seasons. Drishya and his friends lead westernized lives. They eat *momos* but also smoked *chicken-sizzlers*. They listen to Western music, Bob Marley, the Beatles. They meet in *cafe*s not in *chiya pasal*, teashops. Palpasa brings a bottle of French wine to her new friend's party; other guests bring flowers. We are in a typical avant-garde lifestyle, the realm of a happy few.

Drishya personifies the new importance of the individual in modern society, in stark contrast to Siddhartha who, as a Māobādī, stresses collective issues and relies on more traditional forms of belonging. This opposition is recurrent in the book. The scene of the young girl in the hills who leaves her choice —to join Maoist squadrons— in the hands of her father: "I will do what he decided", is remarkable in this regard. Even when faced with revolutionary choices, the young peasant girl is compelled to adhere to traditional relations of authority within the family.

The contrast between Christina, the Dutch visitor to Drishya's art gallery —and a prevailing character in the book from beginning to end — and Palpasa is also striking. The first speaks unrestrainedly, openly expressing her feelings in a manner that leaves the painter bewildered. Despite being superficially Westernized, Palpasa is much more reserved. She conforms more to the Nepali traditional stereotype of the unmarried young girl.

Today all Nepalis have one foot in the modern world and another in traditional life. *Palpasa café* illustrates these two opposite trends. The elusive dialogue and the silent love between the two heroes are in many ways typical of Nepali traditional models, seemingly light-years away from Western modernity with its crude exchanges between persons of the opposite sex. The dialogue between Drishya and Palpasa chiefly reflects a flirtatious relationship, with its usual entreaties and minor exasperations. Instead, the undecided couple exchange romantic love letters. Moreover, the two main characters are significantly immaterial, incorporeal. They are idealised figures, almost spectral. To express her feelings towards Drishya, Palpasa says: "You have stolen my soul". Here we are in the conventional Nepali world of possession and soul-searching.

The absence of any psychological analysis, corresponding to the customary Nepali repertoire of hidden feelings, also characterises the novel. In my view, the metaphors and the poetics of the book also reveal traditional Nepali patterns. *Palpasa café* is replete with poetic images about colours, birds, flowers, and trees. These devices pertain to a clearly defined, long national literary heritage. Blue jacaranda flowers (*siris ko phul*) are very much present here.

On the whole, *Palpasa café* illuminates a confused world that is pulled in different directions. The narration reflects current uncertainties and the conflicting situations that many Nepalis experience when torn between both modern and traditional values.

40. My Village, My Land

The representation of one's native village differs considerably depending on whether one still lives there or whether one left it to work in urban areas or abroad. In the first case, the distance is rarely sufficient to appreciate the positive sides to village life. Daily chores no doubt seem to be monotonous and can lead to dreaming about spending a less trying time elsewhere. Everywhere in the world, the attraction of cities and of their commodities hinges on similar traits. Conversely, Nepalis who have migrated to urban areas or who have out-migrated and work abroad often feel nostalgic about their native locality. When talking about their villages, they speak about their roots, their relatives and friends. People cannot simply leave these attachments behind: *one's native village is a basic marker of personal identity*. Migrants miss the congenial environment of these ancestral places and the stable social bonds they have lost. The hardship associated with farm work and the backwardness (compared to life in cities) are often forgotten and the image of the locality is romanticized. Representations of the village and towns must therefore be analysed according to these different positions in the social space.

Nepal is still a country of villages. But what sort of village are we talking about? The realities of rural settlements do not correspond to the same social structure everywhere. Broadly speaking, a distinction has to be made in this respect between *ādivāsī/janajāti* and caste groups. Among a number of (but not all) Tibeto-Burmese-language-speaking ethnic groups, the notion of *gāon*, village, is of paramount social and symbolical importance. It is structured like a matrix and encompasses various forms of communality. Among the Tamangs of northern Dhading and Nuwakot districts, where I carried out research in the 1970s, the attachment to one's natal locality (*namca* is the Tamang word for village) produces not only familial, personal ties, but also a number of social rules and commitments that are difficult to shake off. The memory of the founding ancestors, forever remembered in ritual songs, strengthens this link with the soil.

The situation plainly differs in most Parbatiyā villages. In a number of districts, Hindu castes speaking Nepali as their mother tongue do not live in compact, agglomerate settlements but in localities made up of different hamlets with their own name and forming more or less separate entities. Houses are not contiguous like among the Newars, for example. They form isolated enclaves, with their agricultural dependencies disposed around them. In these cases, caste remains the main social element. Lower castes gather together in separate clusters at some distance from upper castes and from the village's main temple. The same situation prevails among Tarai Madhesī people.

In a rather thought-provoking article, the anthropologist Philippe Ramirez (who worked in Argha Khanchi district) expressed a feeling of disorientation when working in these Parbatiyā-dominated villages.[6] Indeed, such scattered hamlets reflect a specific social architecture permeated with separateness and hierarchy. Territorial bonds are still strong but hierarchical ties weaken them. This analysis calls to mind the criticism made by Louis Dumont regarding the notion of village in caste society.[7] Of course, representations associated with these forms of settlement cannot be exactly the same as those that exist among ethnic groups.

However, among both Janajātis and Parbatiyās, the idea of native village is imbued with imaginary notions. Amongst Tamangs and Gurungs, for instance, the village forms an enclosed territory, circumscribed by symbolic borders, by religious gates sometimes adorned with Buddhist paintings, or rivers on the edge of communal land, all of which fence off the territory from the outside. Common worship of the goddesses of the soil, *bhūmi devī*, and ancestors at village ritual shrines creates lasting bonds. Among Parbatiyā castes in the middle hills of central Nepal, old forts, *kot*, that formerly belonged to Hindu petty kingdoms, and the corresponding Devī temples are still at the very heart of rituals and of social life during great ritual events like Dasain. These religious sites bind together the multicaste population. Such ideas extend to small cities that have a strong historical tradition. In Panauti, for instance, all Newar children have a clear image of their town based on the nearby rivers and religious sites. When asked to sketch their locality on a sheet of paper, these representations are expressed by geometric devices (in the case of Panauti, a triangle delimited by two converging rivers).[8] These mental maps were and are still of crucial importance.

Rural communities are therefore not only physical architectural realities. They sustain a strong sense of collective belonging and often have a distinctive relationship with the land and its environment. In Nepali, this bond with the soil is expressed by the concept *hāwā pānī*, literally "air and water", i.e. the local climate. These two words, when associated with a particular village and its land, express the whole organic relationship between local people and their environment. Villagers are proud of their good climate, pure water and fresh air. In Newari, the word *lakasa* has the same meaning. These terms convey the idea of substantive continuity between the inhabitants and their land, of intricate relations between the two. The polysemy of the Nepali/Indic word *desh*, which is widely used throughout Nepal both in the sense of "village" and "country", has to be interpreted in the same light.

The village is, however, the seat of tension; on the one hand, tension between upper and low castes in Parbatiyā localities and, on the other hand, between different factions in more or less equalitarian mono-ethnic villages. Life in the Jyāpu villages of the Kathmandu Valley, for instance, is chronically undermined by factions and antagonistic divisions. From a sociological standpoint, these inner conflicts cause a split in the homogenous discourse of local people and cracks in the romanticized image of the village. Social harmony in such small localized ancestral homelands is a myth.

These persisting divisions and quarrels need to be borne in mind if we are to consider the significant role played by the trope "village" in India's political imagination. Gandhi conceptualized an idyllic vision of rural Indian communities and built an alternative model of development out of it. He instrumentalized these notions to oppose British rule and to resist Western modernity. Nevertheless, Indian and foreign anthropologists have reported much more contentious realities in their findings.

Let me convey one last general remark. For a large number of urban dwellers, the poorest and the most recent arrivals in the city, cityscapes in South Asia are increasingly becoming symbols of *dystopia* (a concept opposed to *utopia*): they are pictured more and more as dehumanized places where people lead fearful lives and where civilization is slowly being eroded by humankind's greed and violence. The anomic, dystopic, disorderly tendencies of modern metropolitan areas are strongly condemned not only in the congested Kathmandu Valley but also in Pokhara and in other expanding Nepali towns. The loss of a quality environment in modern urban centres can be evidenced everywhere. Among the urban middle class, the fashion of eating organic vegetables and leading a lifestyle more in harmony with nature is an obvious reaction against a general degradation of the urban ecosystem. This trend will inevitably continue to nurture rose-tinted fictions about villages.

41. Cyberspace and Fantasy

The development of the Internet and of cybernetic networks has considerable bearing on private and individual spheres. The usefulness of such technologies, which provide us with access to a near infinitude of information in a minimum amount of time is widely acknowledged. Today, everybody in the modern world needs a high-speed computer: to buy a ticket, to browse through news items, to look for a hotel, to download music, films, etc., sometimes even to read a book. Cyberspace has become an extension of social life. However, attention should also be paid to the sociological impact of some specific Internet services, such as Twitter, Linkedin or Facebook. In a word: these social networks induce new forms of self-identity and social bonds. They dramatically alter the way in which individuals interact with one another.

The best example of these sites, Facebook, which is regularly used by a growing number of Nepalis (over 10 million of them now use the Internet), at least in urban areas, is doing far more than merely overcoming distances in terms of communication. The first assumption is that it dampens our interest in reading books and that it cut us off from social links which in the past played a far more crucial role. Yet Facebook is much more than that. It does not only involve direct communication, interactive instantaneity, just as when calling by phone or Skype. It has its own appealing culture, creating infinite possibilities, with its own codes ("walls") and its own languages. The site also provides a sense of enjoyment. It has a rose-coloured side to it; it creates a thrilling picture which explains its success and young people's addiction. It is a particular way of experiencing and interacting with the world, at the risk of provoking a divide between our true selfhood and our online identity.

The use of English on these websites creates in most cases a common globalized language, beyond any national and ethnic boundaries. What is more, the Facebook user surfs through a world which dispenses with caste, ethnic, geographical and even gender barriers, moving beyond traditional roles. It frees the individual from the harsh reality and daily chores. It takes just a click to be connected to somebody on the other side of the planet, and, if he or she is online, you can start a conversation or —to use a more appropriate term— "a chat". You can make friends without ever exposing your person unnecessarily, but chatting can lead to a more personal relationship by employing warm terms that you would hardly use in 'normal' life, offline. Obviously, these Internet services and connections blur the distinction between one's self and society. Sociologists who have addressed the subject speak of a distinctive feature of postmodern culture.

How authentic are cyber-relationships? Does Facebook ultimately bring us closer or further apart? Interestingly enough, this network puts forward an imaginary representation of one's self. The user projects onto the computer an image of themselves which is half authentic, half idealized. A Facebook profile and the pictures it displays are the realm of interplay between reality and imagination. The addict is encouraged to write micro-autobiographies. Some Facebook users go back to their childhood and post photographs of themselves as a child or as a teenager. This *virtual self* projects an image-driven fantasy, with a somewhat superficial content. It diverges from reality, but not completely, for virtuality is also a form of reality and has an empirical content. To quote the sociologist Erving Goffman, the individual projects a self which is not the one on display in normal daily life. There is a large part of self-creation in this cyberspace.

It goes without saying that Facebook is the reign of the individual, of the self. It is an ego-centred world. When online, people forget their daily environment, their closest relatives. They enter into another world, browsing other profiles, reacting freely with others who post and comment. It is so easy to say: 'I like it'! Everybody is a "friend" in this rosy fun-loving world; some are just favourites. Nevertheless, you do also have the possibility of "defriending" somebody by deleting the digital relationship. Here, society and traditional forms of belonging have disappeared, at least partially. A new sense of closeness emerges, sometimes with a strong emotional intensity. Certain expectations may engender disappointment, even depression and tears, and accentuate the gulf between reality and imagination. All these links are far beyond the utilitarian, purely pragmatic sphere. Here the boundaries between the self and the world become rather fuzzy. There are, however, many exceptions to these tendencies. Some users play around more easily with their multiple identities, both online and offline, and some achieve their own aims better than others.

Moreover, there is a feeling shared by various Internet users that the whole wired system relies on complex machinery of which little is known. The proposed new "friends" to be contacted, the rank and the order of these relationships within the network, all suggest that somebody, some sort of "Big Brother", is behind the screen, listening to your connections, — why not their content? —, and hence spying on you. The advent of new Internet technology also needs to be viewed from this angle. The privacy of Facebook is under the all-seeing electronic eye of a "surveillance society" which can prove dangerous if misused. The new exhilarating, online freedom and the projected virtual idealistic selves therefore need to be relativised. Individuals are just as much fashioned by these technologies as they themselves forge self-images in an open-ended way.

42. Iconoclasm and Violence

In *Representations and Contradictions* (1997), the anthropologist Jack Goody provides a comprehensive inventory of the ways in which divine images provoke fear at different times and places throughout the world. Very few civilizations are inoculated against this aversion. The opposition between polytheist and monotheist religions is somewhat irrelevant in this concern. The first, which are characterized by the coexistence of various gods in their pantheon and are theoretically more inclined towards iconophilia, have in some cases developed critiques of the use of divine images.

Monotheist religions, for their part, display a wide range of different attitudes. Just compare a Protestant and a Catholic church: the first is devoid of religious icons or reduces them to a minimum, while the second presents a wealth of statues and paintings of deities. Islam, for its part, especially Sunnism, has always shown iconoclast leanings.

The murderous terrorist attacks on 7, 8 and 9 January 2015 in Paris, altogether leaving 17 dead and many others injured, is a tragic and paroxysmal manifestation of this statement. These assassinations, which intermix religion and politics, have left France wounded and traumatised. Let us recapitulate the events. On the 7 January, two Islamic terrorists killed some of the country's sharpest cartoonists in the offices of the weekly satirical journal *Charlie Hebdo*. These illustrators and journalists were celebrated for their critique against all forms of authority, from politics and religion to the military. The next day, in close connection with the first assault, another radical Islamic fundamentalist killed a member of the police force. On 9 January, this same gunman took about 20 persons (including a small child) hostage in a Jewish kosher supermarket. He killed four of them before the special police forces launched an assault, shot him dead, and freed the hostages. At the very same time, after a lengthy manhunt, the killers (two brothers) of the cartoonists, holed up in a small printing house 30 km north of Paris, were finally killed by commandos while trying to escape.

This horrifying scenario, worthy of a thriller, has provoked a shock wave and a movement of sympathy not only in Western countries but also throughout the world. On Sunday, 11 January, a mass rally against the carnage and these crimes against free press gathered together 1.5 million people in the centre of Paris and more than two million outside the French capital. Nineteen heads of government from the European Union, including Angela Merkel from Germany and David Cameron from the UK, several other heads of state from Africa and the Middle East (President of the Palestinian Authority Mahmoud Abbas, the King of Jordan

Abdullah II, Prime Minister of Israel Benjamin Netanyahu), and a number of world leaders from other countries joined the event in Paris.

Some countries and heads of state present or represented are known for their frequent infringements of freedom of press. Yet, on the whole, this republican march against the horror and in favour of a plural democracy will go down in history. Many observers have remarked that, just as the Twin Towers of the World Trade Centre were a symbol of one aspect of American culture (its prosperity), the small weekly *Charlie Hebdo* is a symbol of free press, which is the cornerstone of democratic regimes. Despite the difference in the number of victims, there is a striking parallel between the two events.

This is the deadliest terrorist attack in France since 1961 [25 November 2015 carnage in the centre of Paris, killing 130 persons, has horribly exceeded this heavy toll]. In fact, over the last decades Jewish sites and individuals, whatever their origins, have been targeted, making a long list of victims. All these acts were committed by radical Muslim movements, for the most part, affiliated to Salafist groups. *Charlie Hebdo* is a controversial newspaper because of the cartoons it has published, disparagingly portraying the prophet Muhammad. Its offices were stormed in November 2011 after the journal published cartoons about the Prophet Muhammad that had originally appeared in a Danish newspaper, prompting a heated debate. As far as the Jewish community is concerned, the largest in Europe and well represented in the French establishment, it feels less and less safe in France and some members of it are moving away in increasingly large numbers to live in Israel (more than 3,000 departures in 2013). The phenomenon is on the rise every year (7,000 in 2014).

The *Charlie Hebdo* cartoonists were murdered in the name of religion. For fundamentalist Muslims, depicting the Prophet Muhammad in a cartoon is blasphemous. Despite this, Muslim authorities in France have strongly condemned the barbarous act. Together with a number of Arab governments, they declared that the Islam of these murderers is a ghastly usurpation of the Qur'an and is opposed to true Islamic religion. Yet, jihadi sympathisers hailed this assault as 'revenge' against those who had 'insulted' the prophet Muhammad. As a matter of fact, there is a strong tradition within Islam of having no iconic representations of Muhammad. Everyone no doubt remembers how the Taliban recently destroyed statues of the Buddha in Bamiyan, which remains a notorious example of just how intolerant Islamic extremists are of religious images.

Charlie Hebdo is the pure product of a long satirical tradition which, as far as cartoons are concerned, goes back a long way in French history (with counterparts elsewhere in Europe). Underground printed political cartoons circulated before the French Revolution of 1789, showing the clergy and nobility performing all sorts of demeaning acts. Pornographic images of Marie Antoinette, the Austrian wife of King Louis XVI, were particularly popular. In the nineteenth century, Daumier, the great caricaturist, drew images of the conservative King Louis-Philippe as a Rabelaisian giant sitting on a toilet throne or with a head in the shape of a pear.

Charlie Hebdo belongs to this deep-seated anticlerical, secular, aggressive tradition that respects nothing and no one, and makes fun of everything. It often uses scatology and obscenity. Its predecessor *Hara Kiri* was banned by the French government in 1970, after printing a mock notice of General Charles de Gaulle's death. It reappeared months later under its present name. The team of writers and illustrators are known for their left-libertarian and almost anarchical spirit. Religion is one of their favourite targets: not only Islam and their fundamentalist leaders, but also the Pope (once represented with a condom and a secret lover) and radical orthodox Jews.

I would like to make three final remarks. Obviously, this satirical wit hurts some French citizens from other cultures and immigrants who are not used to this extreme form of freedom. Followers of other religions who feel shocked by these types of images have already formulated a number of protests. Similarly, most Hindus and Buddhists would be traumatised if their deities were to be portrayed in this manner. Obviously, caricatures can turn blasphemous. Likewise, feminists from developing countries would be horrified by some of the cartoons in question. I would guess that many of the heads of governments marching in the streets of Paris on 11 January 2015 had never opened the so-consummately French *Charlie Hebdo*.

The second remark concerns the growing tension in France between Muslims and the rest of the population. Muslims represent France's second religion and 10 per cent of its population. It is the largest Muslim community in Europe. Like elsewhere in the Arab world, this community is divided between an extremely rich minority (owning most of the luxurious hotels in Paris) and a large number of people living in remote suburbs of France that have turned into ghettos, with a high rate of unemployment and criminality. It is often in these suburbs that the radicalisation of religious practices takes place. A number of young Arabs find consolation for their rejected condition in taking refuge in religious extremism and its sirens. As a reaction to this, Islamophobia is on the rise throughout the country.

The threat represented by religious extremism is everybody's concern. South Asia is not immune to this. India has suffered a number of terrorist attacks over the years and fears others to come. The *fatwa* that was proclaimed in 1989 by Iran's religious leaders against the novelist Salman Rushdie, who is of Indian origin, is far from being forgotten. His novel *The Satanic Verses*, which paints a disrespectful picture of Muhammad, sparked violence around the world. The vast united Paris demonstration of 11 January 2015 against religious fanaticism can be regarded as a remarkable mobilisation by French citizens and an exceptional moment of fraternity. Yet, the future remains uncertain.

The last remark concerns the use of the media during these assaults and other similar terrorist acts. Violence here is committed to defend the purity of Islamic radical beliefs and to oppose any derogatory representations of the Prophet. Yet there is an enormous paradox between the improper staging of these events and the iconoclast contest. In fact, these faith terrorists, who wish to return to an old pre-modern age, use the power that images have acquired in our contemporary period through the media. They consequently film the decapitation of tortured victims and send these images all over the world to shock and terrorize the international public. This is a particularly malefic misuse of religion.

Notes

1. Clive S. Lewis, *Image and Imagination: Essays and Reviews*. Cambridge: Cambridge University Press, 2013.
2. David White, "Possession, rêves et visions dans le tantrisme indien", in Maya Burger (ed.), *Rêves: visions révélatrices*. Bern: *Studia Religiosa Helvetica*, vol. 7, 2003, pp. 159-180; and, by the same author: "Predicting the Future with Dogs," in Don Lopez, (ed.), *Indian Religion in Practice*. Princeton: Princeton University Press, 1995.
3. Kurt Meyer and Pamela Deuel, *Mahabharata: The Tharu Barka Naach*. Kathmandu: Himal Books, 1988.
4. William Sax, *The Gods at Play. Lila in South Asia*. Delhi: Oxford University Press, 1995.
5. In the 1980s, the Nepali painter Kiran Manandhar[35], a Newar himself, had a gallery called *Palpasa Art Gallery*, in the centre of Kathmandu, near Ranipokhari.
6. Philippe Ramirez, "Lorsque le village n'existe pas", in J. Bourliaud et J. F. Dobremez, *Sociétés rurales des Andes et de l'Himalaya*. Grenoble: Éditions Versants, 1990, pp. 51-54
7. Louis Dumont and David Pocock, "Village Studies", *Contributions to Indian Sociology*, 1, 1957, pp. 23-41.
8. Vincent Barré, Patrick Berger, Laurence Feveile, Gérard Toffin. *Panauti, une ville au Népal*. Paris: Berger-Levrault, 1981.

CHAPTER

7

Theatre and Performances

Like India, Nepal is an exceptional repository of living customs, an ideal laboratory for observing and studying traditional forms of theatre, dance, songs and other types of performance. Whether in the plains, in the hills or in the mountains, the country has maintained a wide variety of cultural practices, which have been more or less remodelled through the ages and in some cases heavily mixed in with religious elements. It would be an exaggeration to assert that each group has his own spectacular performances, but existing vernacular expressions reflect in large part the ethnic diversity of Nepal. Tibetan and Indian culture, both literary and folk, have had a considerable impact on these manifestations. But most of these influences have been mixed and assimilated into local indigenous forms to such an extent that each performing group now asserts that it is part of their own culture.

This topic has not been the subject of an in-depth study. Nevertheless, Arnold Bake, the Dutch ethnomusicologist, documented music and dance in Nepal, India and Bangladesh from the 1920s to the 1950s, primarily in audio format and 16-mm films, but these documents, kept in the British Library, London, have not yet been fully explored. Similarly, in the 1960s, Alexander W. Macdonald and Mireille Helffer carefully investigated the oral literature of Gāine/Gandharva,[1] Carol Tingey published a book on Damāī music in 1994,[2] and, very recently, Anna Stirr submitted her PhD dissertation on the dohori tradition of improvised singing duets in western

Nepal.[3] Yet a number of folk theatrical performances, lyrics, and spectacular forms of entertainment have seldom been studied so far. For instance, much is known about masks of all sorts, but very little about their use in performances.[4] The Newar field, which will be dealt with in detail in the following texts, is also vast and has only been partially covered.

These cultural forms are not only aesthetical expressions — a fusion of colour, sounds and images — but also mindful products of imagery and imagination. They therefore lie at the heart of my subject. Theatre in particular is a fictional representation of the reality. To be more precise, it is a world where illusion blends with reality. The play relies on the ability of the viewer to believe and to disbelieve simultaneously, on ordering the imagination, and on simulacrums of truth. As soon as there is a stage, there is transposition, mimicry, and stratagem, all of them placed in a precarious balance between the real and the fictive.

The shift from ancient to modern forms of theatre plays a considerable role in contemporary Nepal [**45**]. In old religious theatrical forms, the distance between the character and the incarnated divine figure is almost blurred. Masked dancers forsake their names and are engulfed by their mythological roles. The performer is a divine embodiment, a sacred, impermanent representation, and viewers are inclined to confuse the disguised character acting on the stage for the embodied divinity. Otherwise, they would not offer lamps, rice, flowers and animal blood to the practitioner, and they would not join their hands in a gesture of respect and prayer while attending the performance. In modern theatre, the mutability of the self is less dramatic. The actor remains human.

The study of living vernacular performances which are produced locally by villagers or urban-dwellers is a vital issue today. Modern mass media, TV, modern film productions are threatening the future of these popular practices. Many sacred art or more secular oral traditions have been pushed to the brink of extinction or have lost their momentum.

They are being put under pressure to transform their codes and repertoires in order to adapt to global tourism and modern inclinations. The alternative is to "globalize" or "perish". A compromise between the past and the present has to be found.

43. Procession and Drama

During the late European medieval period, religious processions through cities often included playlets or longer plays staged in the streets. These dramas, called "mysteries", used to enact legendary accounts taken from the Bible. They often dramatized episodes of the Easter story, such as Mary Magdalene, the prostitute, entertaining a client, Christ's entry into Jerusalem or his long ascent to Golgotha. These were performed by craft guilds first in Latin then in vernacular languages. Each guild was responsible for a particular sequential piece of history that was staged in public within an open space on a piece of scaffolding. In England, each play and life tableau were performed on a decorated cart called a *pageant* that was moved around the city to allow different groups of people to watch every play. These plays have retained their religious nature but have gradually lost their strict liturgical meaning. They have little by little integrated music, dance, costume, set design and have become more and more a spectacle *per se*. Performances were watched from down in the street and from the windows of the houses next door. A competition between the different troupes was often organized and prizes were awarded. Most Western historians concur with the opinion that these enactments depict early forms of theatre that subsequently developed in a more secular way during the Renaissance period and during the seventeenth century.

Similar dramatisations of liturgical actions can be seen during the flamboyant festivals that take place every year in the Kathmandu Valley, especially during Indra Jātrā, which is performed at the end of August or in September in the streets of the capital. Dance troupes belonging to different Newar castes perform on *dabū* square stages at various places in the old town during the procession of goddess Kumārī and of the gods Bhairava and Ganesha. Each company is organised according to a local *guthi* association, which is essential in traditional Newar social life. These groups obviously bear a remarkable resemblance to European mediaeval guilds. Choreographic plays (it is almost impossible to separate drama from dance in South Asian traditions) have mainly derived from Purānic texts depicting the fight between Devas and Asuras. They are not only performed for the pleasure of the spectators amassed along the processional path or posted at windows but also to entertain the Kumārī goddess and her two accompanying living gods. Just as long ago, back in Europe during the Middle Ages, artistic competitions were organised to select the best companies. These contests have gradually become tourist attractions.

Just as in late medieval England and France, these Nepali processions which combine a playful atmosphere and acts of devotion showcase the ranks and categories of the whole social 'architecture'. They objectify the determinants of the social order. The hierarchy between the groups making up the city is made visible by allegorical representation. The king or his symbol (sword or palace) often appears (or appeared) in person, as the main performer and/or the privileged spectator at the performance.

Altogether, the parallel is striking and prompts further study. In traditional Nepal (and India) as in pre-modern European times, dramatic religious performances unfold during processions. In both types of enactments, these processions are a key component. In the Indic universe, the original Sanskrit term for festival is *yātrā*, which essentially means "procession", "travel" **[25]**. In Bengal, this term still designates a distinct theatrical genre of a ceremonial type. In medieval Europe as in Nepal/India, processions engender dramatic activities and spectatorship. Theatre becomes an index of pageant. The semiotics of processions has further implications: the march shapes the identity of a specific city and of its residents. In some ways, religious parades provoke a loss of individuality among its participants and create shared communality among those partaking in the movement.

Moreover, what is at stake in these processional performances is a gradual shift from ritual to play. Religious texts are divided into distinct staged narrations and arranged to provide an entertaining performance. The drama is expected to be viewed not only by followers and devotees but also by onlookers attending a spectacle. In Kathmandu, as in former medieval London or Paris, the performance is made up of an intricate web of religious and theatrical relationships. Determining a boundary between ritual and play becomes more difficult; this cuts across conventional dichotomies. In other words, traditional Nepali theatre that is performed during these ceremonial events is infused with religion in a manner that recalls what happened in Europe in bygone days. The persistence of religion in Nepal (and India) is of particular interest here in understanding where theatre comes from. It sheds light on the relationship between ritual and play in a way that is no longer possible in Western European countries.

Viewed from this perspective, Indra Jātrā is of special interest: the whole festival is linked to theatre and can be regarded as a dramatization of the legend of origin of theatre in classical Sanskrit India, as narrated in the seminal *Nātyashāstra* treatise. As all Indologists well know, this tale is centred on the display of Indra's banner, which normally must be rolled out at the beginning of every theatrical play to commemorate the mythical event. And indeed, what is erected on the first day of Indra's festival in front of the old Hanuman Dhoka palace is nothing other than Indra's banner, *indradhvaja*, in the form of a tall pole. The pole symbolizes Indra and the victory of gods over the demons.[5] Although the link with classical Sanskrit is clear, the antiquity of the connection thus emphasised and the extent of changes over the years remain a subject of debate. Whatever the case may be, the lively festival re-enacts primeval times and is associated with a great number of theatrical performances. Over a period of eight days, the city itself becomes a theatre.

It is worth noting that these plays, which are situated half way between theatre and ritual, do not focus on individual actors. The performers embody divine figures, not human heroes. They wear masks and there is rarely any dialogue between them. These dramatizations are first and foremost heavenly allegories. They do not convey the image of an individual grappling with difficulties in life or facing encompassing forces, as gradually became the case in post-medieval European theatre. The characters are stereotyped and not clearly defined individualistically. They are still directly related to conventions laid down in Sanskrit Indian drama. The individual is encapsulated in enduring social ensembles and even today the performers are chosen according to old social rules.

44. Malla Court Theatre, Past and Present

In ancient times, theatre and dance were primarily royal affairs. In the three Malla palaces of the *nepālmandala* — as the Kathmandu Valley was called in the Middle Ages— a courtyard was devoted to these performances. This open rectangular or square space was called Nasal Chok, from the name of the Newar god of dance, theatre and music, Nāsahdyah. Today still, performers worship this inspirational deity at the time of their apprenticeship, rehearsals and performances. In the past plays were performed before the king, his family, royal guests from neighbouring kingdoms, and high-ranking spectators. They were inspired by classical Indian theatre. The dialogues were either in Sanskrit, Maithili, Nepā Bhāshā (Newari) or Bengali. In some cases, they combined a mixture of two or three of these languages. The Maithili connection was very important in the seventeenth and eighteenth centuries, a period during which this language was chosen as the court literary language.[6] Since the reign of King Jayasthiti Malla (1382-1415), the ruler of Bhaktapur who came from this region, cultural relationships with Mithila were highly valued at the Malla court.

On occasion, the Malla kings of the Kathmandu Valley also played a role in the performances. They wrote a number of plays and composed songs that were sung during the dramas. Bhupatindra Malla of Bhaktapur, for instance, is known to have written more than twenty plays. Theatrical performances showcased the culture of the king, his talent as a poet, *kavitā-rāja*, and his ability to defend the arts. It was also a way of promoting his kingdom. Performing arts were part of the king's duty. The patronage that the sovereign used to grant to a number of village troupes, intermittently inviting them to perform at the court, was an expression of the close links that existed between arts and politics.

Local *vamshāvalī* chronicles have kept alive the memory of the circumstances in which these plays were launched. In most cases, they were created on the occasion of a prince's enthronement or marriage, on the inauguration of an ornamental stone well or the construction of a specific monument. Yet in many cases plays were originally produced for religious purposes. The *Devī pyākhã* of Panauti was thus created to appease a cannibalistic demoness who had set about devouring children in the locality. The *Kārtik pyākhã* of Laliptur was initially enacted as a substitute for human sacrifices that the local king was reluctant to offer to a divinity. Likewise, the wild dance performances staged by Nava Durgā troupes throughout the Kathmandu Valley have links with fertility and the monsoon rains.[7] Whatever the motive may be, the origin of the play is ultimately attributed to a king.

Cosmogonical aspects, linked to the creation of the universe, were prevalent in dances. They were frequently associated with the creation of cities and villages. I have shown elsewhere how the annual folk play in the village of Pyangaon (Newari: Swangu), near Chapagaon, which is performed within the community during the Indra Jātrā pageant, is based on a synopsis of a narrative about the origins of the locality.[8] Here again, kingship is all-important: the village is said to have been founded by a Malla king from Bhakpatur, following a hunting party in the region. It is difficult to ascertain the authenticity of the event. Perhaps local people mixed up some narrative elements they heard elsewhere with the history of their own origins. Whatever the case, the performance (now obsolete) was a major event in the community and the main religious festival. I was lucky to be able to attend it twice in the early 1970s before it ceased to exist in 2007.

In fact, the dramas that are still performed in remote villages located on the fringes of the Kathmandu Valley are based on ancient royal tales. This is the case of Balāmi folk theatre[9] which is enacted at fixed dates in the lunar calendar (mostly in the month of Kārtik, October-November). This theatrical tradition is based on a limited number of roughly written synopses, more often than not in the Maithili language but with a narrative that the *sūtradhāra* (storyteller) recounts in Newari. It is a theatre of conventional gestures, of masks and painted faces, and of shouts rather than words.

These plays portray royal characters, *rāja gana*, the lives they led in their palace, their hunting parties, the amorous adventures of Rāj Kumār princes, etc.[10] As in the village of Pyangaon, royal persons are mainly played by children, all of whom are male. Dance and theatre blend into one during the spectacle. These dramas are performed all night long in the open air. They may have ancient links with court theatre from Malla capitals. Alternatively, they might have had a direct relationship with former Maithili theatre traditions (Balāmis after all live along former foot-trails that lead to Mithila), though it is difficult to establish any historical links. This folk theatre also includes purely religious masked dances, typical of the Newar culture.

This old Malla court theatre with dialogue and its associated village folklore is fast disappearing today (save among Bālamis). Only historians of theatre and ethnographers still show any interest in them. Of this Newar theatrical storytelling tradition only choreographic dramas subsist; these are still performed on ritual occasions (*dyah pyākhã*) and are inseparable from a number of religious festivals, in particular Indra Jātrā.

It may be assumed that some of these productions have lost their dialogue over the ages and have gradually become pure dance events. This seems to have been the case of *Kārtik pyākhã* which is performed every year for eight consecutive nights in Patan Darbar Square in front of the former Royal Palace. In November 2013, the U.S. Embassy granted the sum of US $75,300 to the local committee in charge of this event to help the local Newar multi-caste troupe (though dominated by Shrestha and Rājopādhyāya Hindu groups) to revive the play as it was performed in the seventeenth century and to pass on this cultural tradition to a new generation. However, the small number of seasoned dancers was sorely felt and dissent soon arose within the Newar company over how the budget should be used. The troupe failed to perform for a full month as was the case in King Shrinivas Malla's time (1661-1685). Only two days of performance were added, creating a bitter sentiment among performers and organisers.[11] The revival of old theatrical plays belonging to a non-tangible cultural heritage, without adapting them to the contemporary period, is risky enterprise that predictably ends in failure. Funding from outside, especially foreign aid, is not the best solution.

45. Theatre as a Mirror of Society

Theatre is becoming increasingly popular among the Nepali urban middle class and the younger generation. Created in 1982 by Sunil Pokhrel, the *Ārohan* theatre company has opened the way in recent years to a number of new troupes (Mandala Theatre Nepal, Dabali Theatre Group, etc.) which perform here and there in the Kathmandu Valley, Itahari, Janakpur, Sindhupalchok, Dhankuta, etc. At least six proscenium theatre houses have opened in the Kathmandu Valley alone. Troupes now perform regularly in Pokhara and Biratnagar.

This modern Nepali theatre has accompanied the move towards democracy and now aims to make people aware of the national political agenda and to rally them behind social issues. It is important in this respect to mention Ashesh

Malla (born in 1954), co-founder of the *Sarvanām* group in 1981: Malla has especially developed street theatre, *sadak nātak*, which has popularized multi-party democracy. Altogether, this modern theatre reflects the present shake-up of cultural and political values. Today, these troupes perform Nepal's contemporary repertoire as well as Ibsen, Brecht, Sartre and Camus. They reflect the aspirations of a new type of audience resolutely turned towards modernity.

This trend is obviously not new. In his book on the subject, Abhi Subedi, the well-known playwright, listed a number of initiators, most of whom were already writing during the Rana period.[12] Among them, Bal Krishna Sama (1902-1981), a consummate dramatist, was one of the most prolific writers. He penned as many as eighteen full-length plays and a large number of one-act plays. He is one the main authors who, in the 1940s, brought theatre out of Rana Courts into common specialized theatre houses. He is also credited with the first use of proscenium theatre in Nepal.

I will limit the scope of this essay to the amazing differences that exist between this new living art form and classical ancient theatre which is still performed here and there. I will base my observations on traditional open-air Newar theatre that has been performed for centuries in the Kathmandu Valley at fixed dates in the calendar. This is one of the country's major long-lasting theatrical heritages. I have studied these performances for many years and have attended an incalculable number of plays performed in villages as well as in urban neighbourhoods. Three main features of these traditional plays immediately come to mind.

First of all, religion is of paramount importance. Gods and demons are represented and are sometimes incarnated through the use of masks. Performers are so closely identified with deities that some shake in a putative state of possession. During the intervals, spectators offer the latter drink, cooked and raw food, flowers and the like, just as they would do to supernatural beings. More often than not, the play is an allegory adapted from classical Sanskrit literature. It depicts the eternal fight between gods and demons. What is more: the whole play is seen as a liturgical performance that is offered up to the deities for the community's welfare and prosperity. In Nepali, these plays are often called *shāstric nātak*, stressing the link with classical Hindu literature, i.e. *Nātyashāstra* tradition, the foremost Indian treatise of theatre and dance. Religious (or spiritual) choreographies associated with theatre are also commonly referred to as *ādhyātmik nāc*.

Secondly, there is no clear separation between the audience and the performers. The actors are not professionals; they are an integral part of the local community. Performances take place in the street or at crossroads, on permanent brick and stone platforms that are slightly higher than street level and are reserved for this particular usage. A canopy is sometimes mounted over the stage. Anybody can attend free of charge. This is a vital element: these performances are characterized by a remarkable proximity between theatre and its audience. This feature notably opposes them to modern theatre, which is known for its paid seats, its proscenium and curtains that separate the stage from the spectators.

Another difference with modern theatre is the absence of women on stage. In Nepal, women are traditionally excluded from theatrical plays. As strange as it may seem to our modern eyes, such artistic activities were customarily reserved more or less for courtesans and prostitutes. Among Newars, as in other groups, women were banned from playing any role in theatre. Crossed-dressed men play women's parts. This ban goes as far as forbidding women from playing traditional musical instruments. As a matter of fact, theatre and music come under the authority (and inspiration) of a deity, Nāsahdyah, an invisible form of Natarāja Shiva; women are forbidden to have any contact with him. As can be seen everywhere today during festivals, far-reaching changes have taken place in this field over the last three decades.

Traditional theatre therefore reflects the social order, the subordinated status of women, the importance of communitarian values as well as the prevalence of religion. It reflects ancient times when kings were at the centre of society, patronizing the arts and theatre. Theatre and music were inextricably linked to religion and plays were interlaced with ceremonial events. In the Newars' sacred theatrical dance, even the roles of certain deities were handed down from one generation to another in some families or they were associated with a certain caste. The play's cast therefore expresses the traditional distribution of people among lineages, socio-religious organizations *guthi* and castes. In entertaining people and in honouring gods, theatre and music aim to reproduce society as defined by tradition.

Over recent decades, modern theatrical plays written by clearly authenticated authors have shifted from being allegories and mythological stories to portraying social realities. They have become *sāmājik,* "socially oriented". They have turned into a socially didactic theatre, fully alert to social errors and political issues. In addition, this new theatre now constitutes an autonomous field that is totally distinct from the encompassing society, keeping spectators at a certain distance from performers. This process has taken place everywhere in Asian countries where strong theatrical traditions still exist today, side by side with modern practices. An entire book on the changes that have taken place in Nepal could be written based on the social history of theatre.

The main difference is probably that this new theatre does not only reflect a changing society; it also aims at transforming it. As examples from other countries have shown, though theatre is swept up in the tide of social laws, it is able to initiate transformations and engender change in our perspective of the world. It can help us to rethink society, religion, gender, justice, etc. It is a living laboratory for further change.

46. Itinerant Performances

The old choreographic and theatrical tradition of the Kathmandu Valley constitutes a living treasure that belongs to the country's cultural heritage. Unfortunately, this body of performances dating back to the medieval ages is now threatened by modernization, today's mass media and the gradual disappearance of old gurus who have been linked to local music and theatre troupes. The preservation of this heritage thanks to tourism —for instance through special shows in luxury hotels— will unavoidably transform the traditional pattern of the performance.

In the pre-television and pre-cinema era, these old-style enactments, mostly masked and accompanied by bands playing religious music, were both a devotional expression by people when worshipping deities, and a major form of entertainment for both the young and older generations. More importantly, they were situated at the juncture of popular oral traditions and the royal court with its experts in written poetical and religious traditions. To shed light on the country's immaterial heritage, I would like to focus on two opposing aspects regarding the movement these troupes within the Kathmandu Valley.

These companies were associated with specific urban neighbourhoods and various villages. In peripheral zones, at a short distance from forests, Balāmis, former woodcutters and wood-sellers, were (and still are) specialized in such performances. They have preserved a large body of plays, sometimes accompanied by dialogue in the Maithili language. Elsewhere, the main actors were taken from a number of different Newar castes but above all from agriculturist, gardener and potter communities (Maharjan, Prajāpatī and Māli). These might be either Hindu or Buddhist.

How do these troupes circulate within the Kathmandu Valley and beyond? Although each troupe is based in a specific locality and performs there at regular religious events fixed by the lunar calendar (mostly during the main *desh jātrā*, local festival), theatre companies also use to stage their programmes in the nearby former royal city on which they were (and still are) more or less formerly dependent. This is one of their duties. The most famous troupes are called upon to enact their plays/dances regularly or only once every twelve years in a series of both urban and rural localities. Bhaktapur's Nava Durgā group, for instance, performs every winter and every spring in a number of Newar communities located in their district and in nearby Kabrepalanchok. Similarly, every twelve years, the Harisiddhi ensemble, one of the oldest in the Nepal Valley, used to tour about twenty sites, including Dolakha, about a three-day walk from there, in the eastern part of the valley to perform its classical play (*Jala pyākhã*).[13] This movement of troupes was based on old religious rules and customs, including a visit to local temples and the slaughtering of animals.

Former mediaeval urban capitals had and still have their own troupes which perform at major festivals or at the invitation of families when they wish to celebrate domestic rites of passage. What is more, in Malla times, theatrical and chorcographic troupes were regularly invited from one capital to another to perform at the marriage ceremonies of royal family members. Indeed, theatre was a royal concern and even a personal kingly activity.

Despite these movements and formal invitations, the circulation of these troupes was and still is hindered today by a ban on crossing rivers. This prohibition concerns the most religious-oriented troupes, those who are strictly bound to traditions. The religious heads of the troupes put forward the specific territory of each troupe. Two words are simultaneously mentioned in this respect: *kshetra*, the Indic world derived from Sanskrit and commonly associated with a religious or an administrative territory, and *ilākā*, the word derived from Arabic designating a territory, a dominion, a jurisdiction. In both cases, rivers delimit the territories concerned.

Outside this protected area, other deities or malevolent spirits may attack the gods of the troupe, whether in their statue/vessel form or when embodied by masked actors. Deities reign over local territories, not over the entire universe. When moving around, they are therefore on putative hostile land and can be harmed by supernatural powers that are greater than themselves. Theatre companies therefore have to follow complicated traditional itineraries to avoid crossing any rivers, or to respect specific rules when crossing a river is unavoidable. During their stay in an alien locality, their members have to be particularly cautious and reverent towards local gods.

Up until the present day, troupes have moved around on foot, following the same old itineraries as in pre-modern times, without using buses or cars. But it has become difficult to respect ancient rules when new enclosures and walls have been built across old tracts of land. I have been told about troupes forcing institutions or private landlords to open a way through a wall to allow them to pass. Space has its own rules, reflecting the cosmic order which must not be transgressed.

These two constraints: visiting and performing in a number of localities on the one hand, and ritual restrictions on their movement on the other hand, are worth pondering. They illustrate two basic opposite yet complementary characteristics of Newar society and culture. 1.) An obvious trend, beyond the ancient intra-kingdom borders of the former Nepal Valley, tying together all Newars living in this zone. 2.) A marked social introversion in small enclosed, more often than not endogamous territories, living almost in isolation from each other, and constituting separate linguistic and cultural unities.

These traditional patterns are still at work but obviously not for much longer. In some ways, peripatetic street theatre, *sadak nātak*, a component of modern Nepali theatre, is the successor to these old forms of performance and modes of circulation. Yet, when contemplating the transformations that have taken place from one form to another, one cannot fail to notice the radical changes. The current path toward modernity is not merely a shift of the socio-political framework. It is a radical change in civilization, the collapse of an old world and of ways of thinking that have been maintained without major alterations for centuries.

47. Carnivals and Masquerades

Carnivals and masked popular performances are a highly appealing subject for at least two reasons. Firstly, they are to be found nearly all over the globe, across cultures and religions, with the same quintessential characteristics everywhere: dance, dressing up, clownery, music, joyful processions, sometimes theatrical plays, the reversal of status, and other upside down features. They express a culture of entertainment, fun and laughter, which is incarnated mostly by young people. Secondly, in every particular cultural or geographical zone, these festive enactments have varied considerably over the centuries. In some places, they have been temporally banned by the authorities in power, in others they have declined for some other no doubt economic reason and have suddenly been reborn in new forms and practices. Interestingly, their histories often reflect tension between folk culture and the realm of politics.

Such comic, humorous parades occur throughout almost all of Nepal, in mountain areas, in the *Pahād* and in the Tarai. Teenage boys disguise themselves as females, as supernatural beings or as some sort of beast using plant or animal materials (grass, leaves, straw, foam, feathers, etc.). Performances make use of masks, choreography, songs and musical instruments. They embody a secular, extremely popular aspect of culture. In some cases, the influence of Tibetan (*atsara* buffoon) and Indian culture (*vidūshaka* or jester) is clearly felt. But more often than not, these elements have been mixed together and reformulated to produce autochthonous features.

Scholars have so far neglected local Nepali carnivals and masquerades because these performances supposedly belong to a popular, often scatological, street culture, far removed from highly literate, more prestigious items, which are more suitable for embodying the official culture. Yet, like the shamanistic tradition (*jhānkri*) prevalent in the country, they belong to the immaterial culture of Nepal, which is held in such high esteem nowadays by UNESCO. Some are on their way to becoming extinct or to being replaced by more modern forms. They must be documented, filmed, photographed and studied forthwith. They need to be studied through a local lens, in the search for indigenous terms and endogenous views, rather than by using external concepts. The purpose of this brief outline is to highlight some of their features through my personal experiences and observations.

Let us take for instance the Newars of the Kathmandu Valley. From Sā Pāru and Matyāh festivals up until Indra Jātrā, i.e. the full moon of Bhādau (August-September), or in some cases only until Krishna Astamī, time is generally devoted to comic, satirical plays and masquerades in urban and rural settlements. Buddhist and Hindu Newars have their own festivities, but the barrier between the two communities has fallen down over the years. More often than not, both groups now mingle in the street, parade together and follow the same brass and drum brands. Participants often dress in an extravagant way, some wear variegated masks made of plastic or cloth.[14]

According to the chronicles, the origin of the Kathmandu Gāī Jātrā festival derives from the decision of King Pratap Malla who ruled over the present capital in the seventeenth century CE. This sovereign wanted to cheer up his wife after the death of their son. He ordered all the inhabitants of the city to parade through the streets and to pass in front of the Royal Palace to expunge the queen's sorrow. He succeeded in his undertaking and, so it is said, the custom of sending several boys from each family disguised as cows dates back to that period. This tale is most probably only partly true. It is possible that Newar urban merchant and craft castes took their inspiration from Maharjan rice farmers, who disguised their youngsters as cows to pull a plough at that very time, even though the reverse process—influence from cities to rural areas—cannot be totally dismissed.

Whatever the case may be, among Newars, these comic enactments are traditionally associated with satirical plays called *khyālah*. The period of time between Gāī and Indra Jātrā is precisely the period during which all sorts of criticisms of influential persons and notabilities were traditionally made. The existing order and standards were challenged; oral and ethical inconsistencies were highlighted. It is obviously no coincidence that this "anti-structure" atmosphere prevails, according to the Hindu calendar, at a time when Vishnu sleeps at the bottom of the ocean, leaving the earth in a perilous position, subject to disorder and danger. This subversive tradition apparently dates back a long way in Newar culture. It survived more or less clandestinely during the Rana period and it has been revived today in a literate form and in increasingly sophisticated ways. Dozens of *khyālahs*, for instance, were published towards the end of the panchayat period. Some Newari journals even reserve a space in their daily or weekly issues for such subjects.

What is interesting during these pageants is the interplay between an old rural type of comic performance featuring upside down practices, tricks, gags, jokes, and a more elaborate satirical brand of humour targeting social evils as well as political excesses and failures. The first type of comedy belongs to what is called *hāsya* in Nepali; it is centred around a grotesque wit, hypertrophied figures, a parody of religious signs, a violation of official rules and regulations, the mixing of sexes, and scatological jokes. It is mainly based on an oral tradition. The second type, closer to the Nepali *byanga*, includes more elaborate parodies; it takes the form of dialogues, distancing itself in some ways from farcical and buffoon carnival elements. Its more elaborate form diverges from the social collective basis to become a more individualistic performance. Within the Kathmandu Valley, these two aspects are not mutually exclusive. Together, they characterise a culture that combines rural and urban elements.

48. Rituals of Laughing

One thing that struck me the most during my study of new religious groups in Nepal is "laughing therapy sessions". I have attended classes on self-induced collective laughter, known in Indic languages as *hāsyayoga*, alongside a number of young Nepalis of both sexes in Osho and Manokrānti religious organizations. These sessions are performed in a sitting or standing position and take place in between more orthodox yogic exercises and meditation. Forced laughter often turns into contagious, real laugh. Such a playful form of therapy, invented at the end of the twentieth century, aims at releasing internal tension within the body, at pacifying the mind and at developing a positive attitude. It also establishes a bond within the group and is said to cure depression. This practice exists not only in India and Nepal, but also in Western countries (mostly in a secular context) as part of a yoga course. As one can imagine, the recent creation of the Ministry of Yoga (AYUSH) in India, which includes *āyurveda* medicine and homeopathy, will probably go towards upholding and even developing such programmes.

In a number of religions there is a clear-cut boundary between laughter and ritual. Jesus is often called the "one who never laughs" and during the mediaeval Christian period, such forms of playfulness were associated with evil. They were seen as a threat to the condition of monkhood. Islam is openly very reactive towards any form of caricature of the Prophet [**42**]. To turn religion in derision is a form of blasphemy punishable by Sharia law. In Nepal itself, is it hard (though not totally impossible, especially in satirical plays) to imagine a Brahman being interrupted by a joke or spontaneous laughter while performing a ritual. But during Holī, like many other Hindu festivals, fun and playfulness are an integral part of the ceremony. In another related sphere loaded with religious themes, oral poetic literature sung by Dholī tailor-musicians in western Nepal (*bhārat* epic songs) features a whole range of comic figures and situations.[15] The heroes of these songs are mainly driven by gluttony and sex. On the whole, forms of religion in Asia, including Nepal, are more relaxed than in the rest of the world. In Tibetan and Mahāyāna Buddhism in particular, laughter is recognized as being a positive element, and in China and Japan the figure of the laughing Buddha is commonplace. Lamaist *'cham* masked presentations which are acted out in Tibetan monasteries often combine *atsara* clownish plays and dances performed by deities.

Interestingly enough, there are several cases in Nepal where playfulness, laughter and ritual coexist. The links between them are all too obvious in the public sphere. A number of religious festivals include clownish performances caricaturing religious or social characters. Among Janajāti groups, the figure of the Other that incarnates a different lifestyle and values, such as *sannayāsin*, *jogī* and sometimes even Brahmans, is thus ritually represented in comic form by jokers and jesters. During these events, which are performed at fixed dates in the lunar or solar calendar, men dress up as women and children disguise themselves as different sorts of animals, ranging from monkeys to dogs and bears. They dance around or parade in the streets in fancy dress. They incite laughter and generate a hilarious atmosphere.

In the Newar culture of the Kathmandu Valley, farcical theatrical performances are regularly staged [**47**]. Political and social figures are targeted in a comical way and parodies of rituals are sometimes enacted. Even religious-inspired plays are often punctuated with comic episodes. For instance, the first three days of Kārtik Nāc in Lalitpur, which is performed every year during the lunar month of Kārtik (October-November) for a period of eight days, are entirely devoted to farcical performances. They feature three heroes called *bāthah*, which means "clever", "cunning". These *bāthahs* commit amoral acts and play tricks on each other and on other persons; they are mainly motivated by a desire for food and sex. Their ruses recall the comic characters mentioned above in *bhārat* oral literature. Besides obviously entertaining spectators, these farces are also perhaps aimed at frightening and driving away evil spirits that are said to abhor sexual jokes.

The situation among Nepali shamans is more complex. I have met *jhānkri* shamanic intercessors in the hills who claim that it is forbidden to laugh when dealing with spirits. But among other groups, such as the Kham Magars of the

Dhaulagiri area, shamans frequently officiate alongside a priapic buffoon who waves about a wooden penis as a ritual device and dances around making obscene gestures.[16] This joker is said to scare evil spirits or to keep them away. Any allusions to reproduction would terrify maleficent supernatural beings because they themselves do not procreate.

Scatological humour and sexual jokes are universal features of these comedies. The usual taboos on sexual matters that are widespread in Nepali society are temporarily transgressed on these occasions, much to the public's enjoyment. Actors sometimes brandish phallic representations and mimic acts of sexual intercourse. Interestingly enough, these plays are mainly performed by men and occasionally serve to symbolically abuse young girls. They therefore include a gender dimension with a dominant male emphasis. Likewise, hilarious parodies of ploughing that are often staged during these comic events, not only by rural Newars during Gāī jātrā but also among groups of highlanders speaking Tibeto-Burmese languages, no doubt have sexual undertones.[17] They symbolize the penetration of the soil (viewed as feminine) by the male organ. This symbol of fertility, which is associated with agricultural tasks, is to be found in many other countries, including European countries.

The link between laughter and ritual is therefore a prominent enduring feature of Nepali popular religion — often called "folk-religion". It is worth noting that these fascinating grotesque elements are simultaneously *conjunctive* and *disjunctive*. They strengthen the community's social bond, uniting all the spectators and participants from the audience around the same fun and values. Yet at the same time laughter and buffoonery are used to stigmatise the stereotyped figures of Otherness that stand on the edge of the group or to incarnate certain contested values within the community. Hence, *Homo ridens*, laughing man, has far-reaching socio-political implications.

49. Powerful Satire

Thanks to some of my Nepali friends, I had the opportunity

of attending the MaHa Jodi programme at Kamaladi's Academy Hall in 2004. For three hours, Madan Krishna Shrestha and Hari Bansha Acharya, the foremost Nepali comedy duo, together with some other actors, paint a hilarious portrait of Nepali society and the current difficulties of life in the country. Although the two comedians were absent from the stage for seven years, the situation in Nepal has barely improved over that period of time. The double act describes a state where civic feelings are conspicuous by their very absence. Self-interest and egocentric attitudes prevail everywhere. Load-shedding, bribery, corruption, divorce between *netā* (politicians) and the people, procrastination in writing the much-awaited constitution are comically denounced in a very transparent way. The absence of a worthy leader for the country is sorely deplored.

The programme unequivocally brings to light various recognized forms of social identity that are at work. During the first sketch, three comics—aside from the MaHa (Madan + Hari) pair—parody problems concerning India-Nepal border issues. One of them, carrying a basket on his shoulders, wants to send over to India the Nepali Constituent Assembly (CA) members who are fans of that country and over to China all the Nepali CA admirers of the giant communist neighbour.

The second part centres on two "Bahadurs", with Madan Krishna dressed as a Bahun, and Hari Bansha as a Newar Maharjan with a red flower behind his right ear and wearing a black *topī*. This inversion of the roles allows for all sorts of jokes about the various stereotypes usually ascribed to Newars and Bahuns. The common tendency of members of these two communities to see everything through their own eyes and to forever attribute a dominant status to their respective communities is portrayed with great irony. Food habits as well as the flaws of the caste system are criticized in laughable terms. The negative aspects of dividing Nepal into ethnicity-based micro-states are also the subject of sarcastic mockery.

Another skit takes place in a photographer's studio (Madan *dāi* is depicted as a leader of the mafia) and satirizes the growing trend of providing criminal gangs with political protection. Dons have become all-powerful. A recurrent theme runs through the performance: how can people live in a country like Nepal with such constant load-shedding? It's better to go anywhere else: "first to America, second to the USA and third to the United States!" in order of preference.

The show offers a brilliant demonstration of the comic talent of the two actors, a much applauded and renowned talent that has earned them well-deserved celebrity. The MaHa complement each other in the best possible way. Hari Bansha's buffoonery and extraverted game offer a stark and amusing contrast with the more restrained performance by Madan Krishna. However, aside from this, Hari Bamsha and Madan Krishna break all the rules of the "politically correct" public discourse. They entertain the audience by lampooning the evils of today's society and its leaders, and by magnifying reality. They obviously dream of a society where caste and ethnicity have, if not disappeared, at least lost some of their respective influence. The audience, clapping and laughing at the bitter wit of the actors, apparently agrees with this vision that transcends caste, ethnicity and creed. Here humour is used as a weapon to draw attention to broader issues of society, without attacking anyone personally.

In many ways, the MaHa duo is way ahead of its time in its portrayal of current Nepali society. The actors provide keen insight into Nepal's contemporary social life. Indeed, they have the edge over social scientists who persist in interpreting in purely ethnic and caste-based terms, facts or data about a society where considerable mixing, interaction and intermarriage have taken place over the last decades. In addition, the comedians leave lots of scope for agency, for the personal dimension and for a self-critical vision, which is generally totally absent from scholarly work. The faculty of self-mockery is an often underestimated dimension of social life and is not sufficiently taken into account by sociologists, anthropologists and the like. Such a faculty often challenges the relevance of sophisticated abstract theories.

I met the two actors a couple of years ago in Kopundol while I was working on the Newar *khyālah* satirical, comic tradition [**47**]. Madan Shrestha is in fact the inheritor (as well as a reformer) of the much-developed Newar satirical heritage, which is specially enacted during Gāī jātrā and Indra Jātrā in the Kathmandu Valley. He was and still is called *khyāli juju*, the king of satire, within the Maharjan peasant caste. Interestingly, this ancient oral tradition persisted in Newar towns and villages during the Rana period in spite of strict censorship. It is still very much alive today, even though it has taken on a more literary form and makes use of more modern media channels than before.

My Nepali friends were delighted with this early-evening show. One of them joyfully remembered the well-known sketch showcased some years ago in which Madan Krishna and Hari Vamsha impersonated a couple exchanging *dohori* improvised songs. Using folklore to satirize society and to raise awareness among the people is, after all, just as effective as street theatre, *sadak nātak,* which uses more pedagogic, instrumental devices. For my part, I reflected on the capacity of artists of all genres and of all countries to generally keep ahead of society at large and to express very freely and in a comical way public evils and flaws. To seize upon these evils, to ridicule them and to entertain people in this manner is no doubt a superior form of humour. Satire, let us not forget, is the weapon of the powerless against the powerful.

Notes

1 Mireille Helffer et A.W. Macdonald, "Remarques sur le vers népali chanté", *L'Homme*, 1968, 8 (3), pp. 37-95, and *L'Homme* 1968, 8 (4), pp. 58-91.

2 Carol Tingey, *Auspicious Music in a Changing Society. The Damai Musicians of Nepal.* London: School of Oriental and African Studies.

3 Anna Stirr, PhD Dissertation, 2009: *Exchanges of Song: Migration, Gender and Nation in Nepali dohori Performance.* Columbia University, 2009.

4 The recent book by Pascale Dollfus and Gisèle Krauskopff, *Mascarades en Himalaya. Les vertus du rire.* Paris: Findakly, 2014, gives some information on Himalayan masquerades, including Nepalese ones but, unfortunately, it is not fully documented and is not presented in a scholarly way. Many other publications, including my book on the Newars, deal with theatre and spectacular performances. This short note is not meant to be exhaustive.

5 Cf. A. Bake, "Quelques éléments religieux dans le théâtre indien", in J. Jacquot (ed.), *Les théâtres d'Asie.* Paris: Éditions du CNRS, 1978. Et G. Toffin, *La fête-spectacle. Théâtre et rite au Népal.* Paris: Éditions de la Maison des Sciences de l'Homme, 2010.

6 Cf. Kamal P. Malla, *Classical Newari Literature. A Sketch.* Kathmandu: Educational Enterprise Pvt. 1982.

7 Gérard Toffin, "Jeu théâtral et acte rituel chez les Néwar du Népal. Une introduction au théâtre néwar". In Ève Feuillebois-Pierunek (ed.), *Théâtres d'Asie et d'Orient. Traditions, rencontres, métissages.* Paris: Peter Lang, 2014, pp. 141-164.

8 Gérard Toffin, "L'Indra jâtrâ à Pyangaon; essai sur une fête néwar de la vallée de Kathmandou", *L'Ethnographie,* 1978, 76 (1), pp. 109-137.

9 Bālamis are a Newar group of former woodcutters living near forests on the western and southern edges of the Kathmandu Valley. Cf. Gérard Toffin, *Newar Society. City, Village and Periphery.* Kathmandu: Himal Books/Social Science Baha, 2009.

10 Gérard Toffin, "An Ancient Nātak in Nepal: the Balāmi *Kāttī pyākhan* (Kārtik Nāc) of Pharping", in *Sangeet Natak Akademi Journal*, Delhi, XLV (1), 2012, pp. 3-18.

11 In 2014, the troupe performed for twelve nights.

12 Abhi Subedi, *Nepali theatre as I see it.* Kathmandu: Arohan/Gurukul, 2006.

13 Cf. Linda Iltis, "Seeing the Unseen. The Dance of Harasiddhi Gods", in *Dabu Souvenir*, Harasiddhi, 2011, pp. 29-52.

14 Gérard Toffin, "Chemins du rire et des morts; carnavals, burlesque et satire au Népal", in N. Gauthard (ed.), *Fêtes, mascarades et carnavals.* Montpellier: Éditions l'Entretemps, 2014, pp. 105-131.

15 Cf. Rémi Bordes, *Héros, bouffons et affligés. Anthroplogie d'une poésie orale himalayenne. Doti, Extrême-Ouest du Népal* (unpublished thesis). 2 vol. Bordeaux.

16 Anne de Sales, "Chamanes et bouffons (Népal et Sibérie)", in *Études mongoles et sibériennes: variations chamaniques, 2*, Nanterre, Laboratoire d'Ethnologie et de Sociologie comparative, 1995, pp. 17-39.

17 Pascale Dollfus and Gisèle Krauskopff, *Mascarades en Himalaya. Les vertus du rire*. Paris: Findakly, 2014.

CHAPTER

8

Social Whirl

When depicting a country and its people, a social scientist can hardly compete with a photographer. Photography breathes life into the representation of reality. It becomes an art when what the eye sees blends in an aesthetic dimension to highlight some aspects that had so far gone unnoticed. Snapshots sometimes give the illusion of being more real than reality itself. From this vantage point, photography is a more suitable media for capturing the passage of time, the changes in everyday life among urban and rural people, the contingent aspects of things. A good picture catches the spectacle of modern and traditional life in an incomparable way, at the boundary between emotional vision and sharp reportage. For the French poet Charles Baudelaire (1821-67), a staunch admirer of old engravings and paintings, photography was an allegory of modernity. It was therefore entirely condemnable [Ch. **5**].

The scholarly approach intends to go beyond the photographic print; its aim is to surpass the brute living reality. In contrast to the photography, the social sciences aspire to put hard facts in perspective by comparison with other regions and by situating a phenomenon or a fact in relation to the past. Otherwise, there is no science, merely a mechanical documentary process and the love of alluring images. In other words, the academic (whether a sociologist or an anthropologist) charges the reality with contextual information and provides the fullest possible understanding.

My perspective is enriched by my having been in Nepal more or less continuously over a period of more than forty years, between regular trips back and forth. I have observed changes by myself and can date at least approximately the emergence of such and such a transformation. The Nepal I discovered in 1970 has little to do with the country today, at least in urban centres. It would have been difficult during King Mahendra's time to attend a "secular marriage" performed without any rituals or priest. And Tundikhel, the open space in the centre of the capital, was better known (is indeed still known) for its military parades than for yoga sessions supervised by an Indian guru, attracting thousands of Nepalis. These are two examples of the changes I ponder in the subsequent texts. Moreover, unlike today, it would have been impossible to attend a Gay Parade during the Gāī Jātrā festival. Many are the themes that need to be studied. I have made my selection here.

50. Uncle and Auntie

The two English terms *uncle* (Nepali *ankal)* and *auntie* (Nepali *āntī*) are used more and more in cities of Nepal, especially among young people belonging to the middle class, to address the elderly in everyday conversation or interaction. Interestingly enough, these terms are not only used to address foreigners, as observed some years ago by the linguist Mark Turin,[1] but also among Nepalis themselves. These two borrowed words, which are derived from the nineteenth-century Anglo-Indian language, express a close, familiar as well as respectful relationship with somebody older, and generally much older, than oneself. They are used inside and outside the family and may refer both to kin and to non-kin. 'Uncle' is sometimes even extended to other domains. For example, a policeman or a tiger can also be addressed as "uncle" or by the corresponding local term.

This new usage is worth noting and deserves some comment. Let us first of all recall that such a practice is widespread in South and South East Asia where, whether in English or in the local language, the local lexical item "uncle" denotes a respectful person who deserves to be referred to by this term and is therefore included in a quasi-familial relationship. "Uncle Ho" (Ho Chi Minh), "Uncle (U) Thant" (U Thant) are well-known expressions that have been applied to former prominent Vietnamese and Burmese leaders respectively. In Nepal, in a number of communities and castes, local words for "maternal uncle" are used colloquially in this sense to address a wide range of elderly persons. Frequently, in an urban setting, unrelated persons are not called "sir" (*sar*) or "madam" but are addressed by these closer, more familiar words.

In all these cases, the term "uncle" is used instead of "father", which implies a more authoritarian relationship. The two collaterals of the immediate ascendant generation are thus clearly identified. As a matter of fact, relationships with uncles are much more affectionate and more easy-going than filial relationships.

Here English terms are bent to fit in with local kinship usage. Extending kinship terms to older non-relatives is in itself a highly significant phenomenon. This realm of "fictive" kinship reveals a '*familization*' of society which is very different from the more impersonal Western view and usage.

What is even more interesting is that such loanwords from English blur the essential distinction in most of Nepal's kinship terminologies between *kākā* and *māmā*, that is between the father's brother and the mother's brother, two types of uncles that are not recognised in most European kinship systems. This distinction is related to the eminent position held by the maternal uncle. The *māmā* is a very close relative. He plays a vital role when his nephew performs his rites of passage, to an incommensurably greater degree than *kākā*. Yet differences exist between the groups. In contrast to Newars and other Nepali groups, the sister's son, *bhānij*, is for instance considered to be an honoured guest, almost of divine status, among high Hindu Parbatiyā castes. Uncle has to bow down before him. In these castes, a nephew's visit to his maternal uncle is so relaxed and enjoyable for the guest that *māmā ko ghar*, the "maternal uncle's house", is often referred to satirically as "prison" in Nepali, a place where you simply have to wait for food to be prepared for you!

Such a disparity between Nepali kinship words and English ones is just one of many others. People in Nepali address all their male cousins (as well as a number of non-kin persons) as "brother", *dāju* for older and *bhāi* for younger, according to one's age, as well as "sister", *didi/bahini,* for the same. What is more, *dāju/bhāi* are also used as reference terms in Nepal for cousin, in contrast to European terminologies, where cousin and brother, who belong to the same generation, are referred to by different terms.

Nevertheless, here again, dissimilarity prevails among communities. In a number of Tibeto-Burmese languages, such as Tamang, cross cousins (descendants from parents' opposite-sex siblings) are distinguished from parallel cousins (descendants from parents' same-sex siblings), who are referred to by the same terms as siblings (own brothers and sisters), in accordance with cross-cousin preferential marriage that is in usage in these groups.

By and large, in the two examples given above, Nepali kinship terminology is alternatively more precise (descriptive) than European terminology regarding the father's generation upwards by distinguishing between different kinds of uncles and aunties, and more classificatory in the Ego sideways generation, by merging different sorts of kin.

These semantic differences between kinship terms are not merely pedantic distinctions reserved for experts. They are of great import in social life. They have a direct impact on the construction of social relations and they denote a specific way of interacting with others and of classifying unrelated persons. In addition, they echo a society based on kinship, patrilineal clans and lineages that is slowly adapting to the new globalized social fabric of the planet. When reflecting on the unity and diversity of Nepal, as well as on issues related to citizenship, all these features need to be borne in mind. Marxism and economic liberalism, which are both exogenous systems to Nepal, as well as foreign experts, often fail to understand these basic features of Nepali society.

51. Contested Globalization

According to many points of view, the multifaceted aspects of ongoing globalization —encompassing cultural, psychological, economic, demographic fields—have led to a gradual homogenization of ideas, artefacts, values, and institutions. In the political sphere, the worldwide trend towards human rights, civil liberties, pluralism, the separation of power, the rule of law, the empowerment of minorities, etc., demonstrates unparalleled standardisation of the ideal democratic political regime. Article 1 of the UN's Universal Declaration of Human Rights: 'all human beings are born free and equal in dignity and rights' applies to a greater degree today. It reveals the triumph of values (equality, individual freedom) which initially emerged in eighteenth-century Europe and North America. Their universality currently opposes all forms of dictatorship. For most nations, democracy has thus become the new *mantra*, the epitome and destiny of modern societies. Even the Māobādīs (at least their main party) in Nepal have joined the democratic process and now take part in elections.

Many other examples of globalization (in Nepali the word is translated by *bishvabyāpikaran*) may be mentioned in this respect. The multiplication of high-speed means of communication across boundaries has contributed to the massive displacement of populations. All sorts of migrants from poor countries now venture to richer countries and developed regions, especially to the West or to the Gulf. Vernacular traditional cultures are therefore exposed to broader values. Similarly, the development of the Internet and of electronic networks has created a common transnational language and a sense of belonging to a larger world than before. These phenomena have imposed new types of links and behaviour.

These all-powerful forces have led to a gradual integration of economic, political and cultural systems across the globe.

Some analysts foresee a world where a growing range of social activities will take place irrespective of the geographical location of participants. Key notions of 'connectivity', 'network' and 'interdependence' are said to undermine disciplines, such as social anthropology which was formerly devoted to the study of small bounded and self-contained communities. How is one to conduct empirical research on a forest-dwelling group or on a remote Himalayan village where half the population has migrated to the Gulf and the other half use mobile phones? Here a fundamental disjuncture emerges between place and culture.

When seen from South Asia, these views must nevertheless be addressed critically. In the first place, the pattern of globalization cannot be reduced to a one-sided encompassing process. A phenomenon of 'Asiafication' also needs to be taken into consideration. Let us not forget that the success of several Asian countries, including India, in the business sector has brought a halt to the industrialization of other developed countries. In scientific fields, the presence of a number of brilliant scientists of South Asian origin in Western universities indicates that the situation is even more complex. Moreover, South East Asia has exported a number of cultural patterns including Japanese animated films which have had a tremendous impact worldwide, especially on North American, European and Middle Eastern markets, as exemplified by the influence of Manga comics on cartoon strips. What about the new Hindu or Buddhist spiritualistic movements, focusing on happiness, meditation, release from stress, etc., which originated in India and have expanded to Western countries over the last decades? These processes counterbalance the Western-induced view of globalization and the Euro-centricity of much of its literature.

But there is more to it than that. We are far from the idyllic vision of a global village in which everyone is closely connected. More often than not homogenization remains superficial. Macro-studies which tend to produce such sweeping statements pay insufficient attention to ethnographic particularities or to changes and continuities that exist below global level, on a local, regional or national scale. A number of local cultures, whether they belong to an oral tradition or to a high literate non-Western canonical civilization, have succeeded in resisting globalization and Westernization. This trend in some ways relativizes the universalistic dimension of human rights, which are based on the individual and are widely promoted by the UN. In other words, globalization is often used as a non-historical descriptive rather than an analytical concept. Its forces are in most cases translated and integrated in vernacular entities.

Such resistance sometimes leads to 'deglobalization' and 're-territorialization" processes, which are characterised by collective closure. The widespread series of discourses on entrenched communalism and ethnicity, occasionally supported by the UN, may be mentioned in this respect. Ethnic revivalism has become a permanent element in political communication, discouraging other unitary or more citizen-oriented initiatives. In India and Nepal, ethno-separatist movements have been increasingly vocal in making their claims. The airing of ethnic voices and the surge in autochthonous movements in South Asia have been one of the major phenomena over the last decades and an important aspect of change in local contemporary societies. Autochthony, i.e. a special link with one's native soil, has become a primordial quality.

The ethnicity idiom, based on unfashionable ethnographic concepts and ideologies dating from the nineteenth century, tends to portray each ethnic group as a *collective self*, with its own territory, its own language, its own culture, and so on. These ethnic communities supposedly highlight mutuality, relations of reciprocity within the group, common history, a sense of equality, autochthony as well as indigeneity. In reality, violent discourses on ethnicity embody a new quest for belonging in reaction to current streams of globalization and the broad encompassing changes affecting most areas of Asia. The proposal, which was finally abandoned, to divide the Federal Republic of Nepal into regions along ethnic lines, has to be viewed from this context.

52. Passion for Equality

In 1948, Balkrishna Shamsher Jang Bahadur Rana (1903-1981), a member of the ruling family in Nepal, changed his name to Sama, which means "equal", after spending several months in prison for associating with political forces against his family's undemocratic regime. It is by this pseudonym that the great Nepal playwright is still known today. Opposition to autarkic Rana rule notoriously fuelled egalitarian and democratic conceptions in the country. The use of the adjective, *samā,* and its corresponding noun *samānatā*, "equality", in the political sphere dates back mainly to this period.

The introduction of equality paradigms ran counter to orthodox Brahmanism and untouchability. As a matter of fact, the 1854 Nepali Legal Code of Jang Bahadur was entirely based on caste hierarchy principles. Everybody's position in the social order depended on their alleged permanent degree of purity or impurity. All Nepali people, even those situated the farthest away from the world of castes, were ranked according to these rules derived from old Sanskrit texts. In matters of law, punishment was proportional to a person's hierarchical position. The lower your status, the more severe your sentence.

Opposition to caste hierarchy and to the predominance of Brahmans emerged a long time ago in India, especially, among the Buddhist current, which has been anti-Brahmanical since its inception. Similarly, reformist Hindu movements later opposed Brahman exclusivist ideas. A number of religious organizations, mostly among Vaishnava *sampradāyas*, disseminated equalitarian ideas that ran counter to the privileges of Brahmans and to caste rigidity. Throughout South Asia, the ideology of equality stemmed from religion before becoming a political discourse.

These ideas slowly spread through Nepal. From the end of the eighteenth century onwards, Pranāmī, Josmanī, Kabīr *sant* devotional movements, to name just a few, had already gained ground in the Himalayas. In Nepal they spread either in a subterranean manner, like the Pranāmī sect, or openly like the Josmanī cult in both urban centres and rural areas. At the end of the nineteenth century, Ārya Samāj, a movement that had long been forbidden in the Himalayan kingdom, emerged in the country. This organization, which rejected Hindu polytheism in favour of a belief in a single supreme being, condemned the caste system. All these movements spread a more universalistic message accessible to everyone, including low castes. They contested the principle of untouchability and the relegation of women to the status of second-class citizens. In most cases, Ranas and high-ranking Brahmans tracked down these social reformists who threatened their dominant position. Yet Josmanīs penetrated so deep within the royal court that Rana Bahadur Shah, Prithivi Narayan Shah's grandson, underwent an initiation ceremony within this *sant* religious order.

The introduction of a Western democratic creed through colonial India also played a major role. Oppositional politics in Nepal, mainly Nepali Congress and Nepali communist parties, were heavily influenced by these conceptions, even if most of their leaders belonged to the Brahman caste. In recent times, Nepali Maoists have radicalized this quest for equality. In the regions under their control, Māobādīs took drastic measures to establish equality between men and women, tenants and landlords, between different social groups, notably castes, and even between religions. Their experiments did not meet with the same success everywhere. They are, however, of great symbolic importance. Today, the utopian belief of a totally egalitarian society is widespread in large sections of society.

The social realm of Ādivāsī/Janajāti is often opposed to the caste hierarchy. It is true that Magars, Gurungs, Newars, Rais, Limbus, and Tharus have long had their own social rules and ethos which contrast in many ways with Hindu values promoted by Nepali-speaking upper-castes. They are much more egalitarian within their own community. In Pyangaon, a uni-caste Newar village where I lived in the 1970s, all agriculturist villagers used the same non-honorific forms when addressing each other and they shared meals on some occasions (*desh bhoj*) to express the equality of the inhabitants. Yet despite this, the language of caste emerges as soon as village boundaries are crossed. Service castes that Pyangaon people call upon in their daily lives are viewed from a Hindu hierarchical perspective. Similarly, Tamangs, who live among themselves on a very communal basis, treat Kāmi blacksmiths (who make agricultural tools for them) as low-caste people, that is inferiors who are liable to pollute them. They enforce the same bans as Hindus in relation to so-called "untouchables".

Caste disparities and inequalities are less prevalent among these ethnic groups. Nevertheless, they have not totally disappeared. Janajāti cannot therefore be considered as proponents of equality in all meanings of the term. To see forms of *ādim sāmyabād*, primitive communism in their social organization, as Marxists claim, is totally misleading. The Janajāti hierarchical system is not based on caste but on gender inequality (even if it is sometimes less strict than among high-caste Hindus), on junior versus senior, and on the principle of first occupancy of the territory. This is the reason why so many clans that arrived first have pre-eminence over others at ground level in political and religious concerns. The segmentary clan/lineage system is egalitarian in comparison with multi-caste society, but it is still unequal in many respects.

The genesis of equality-related idioms would not be complete without mentioning the influence, over the last decades, of various religious movements advocating the equality of all human beings. This is especially the case of Christianity and Theravāda Buddhism. After being banned for centuries by Shah/Rana kings and their Bāhun *purohits/gurus* (though authorized by late Malla kings), the number of converts to Christianity suddenly rocketed in post-1990 Nepal after the return of democracy and the implementation of a more pluralistic religious policy. The number of converts is still low compared to India, but it has risen in an exponential manner over the last two decades. The groups with the greatest number of converts are from particularly subjugated and downtrodden communities (Maharjan, Tamang, Chepang, Bādi, etc.). Similarly, Theravāda monastic Buddhism has spread through different ethnic groups, such as the Newars, Tharus, Magars.

The religious component of egalitarian (and revolutionary) ideas cannot be ignored. Indeed, some Western historians believe that the role of Protestantism and Catholic currents opposing the royal mainstream played a major role in the outcome of the 1789 French revolution. The genealogy of revolts and uprisings is obviously more complex than postulated in the Marxist theory of antagonistic social classes. The equalization of status as posited by democracy has been fuelled by a whole chain of ideas, some of them religious.

53. The Rise of a Peasant Caste

Since 1951, Maharjan (Jyāpu or Dangol), the traditional agricultural caste of Newars and numerically the largest group in this community, has experienced a fascinating rise in its standard of living. In the sixties and the seventies, most Newar farmers in the old villages and cities of the Kathmandu Valley were barely educated and their lifestyle was devoid of any modern aspects. Admittedly, their general situation was much better than that of hill peasants (among Maharjans the staple diet had long consisted of rice, but often of inferior quality) and it varied from one place to another. In urban centres, especially in Kathmandu, Jyāpus led a more arduous existence than those in rural areas. In cities, they mainly tilled other people's land and were subservient to higher Hindu and Buddhist castes, whereas in villages they privately owned a large part of the land and often enjoyed the role of dominant caste. However, on the whole, Jyāpus were economically and socially backwards. Their living conditions were wretched. Even their name carried negative connotations and was sometimes used as an insult. Politically, here and there, the poorer sections secretly backed the Communist Party.

Having spent time living in Jyāpu villages in the 1970s, I remember peasants walking barefoot in ragged clothes, leading a rustic life totally given over to agricultural work. Wristwatches (exclusively for men) were a rare sight, money was hardly ever used, and houses were often unhealthy places that one shared with animals. By and large, over the last decades, food, clothing, housing, people's general tastes and their standard of education have improved. Farmers have embraced the modern world; they have bought televisions and electronic devices. They eat more meat than before (like many other groups in the country). The gap between them and higher-status groups has dwindled. Jyāpus have gradually moved over to non-agricultural work in various white-collar sectors very far removed from farm work. Upper-ranking and wealthier families have even started to join the urban middle class. Some have married Shākya and Shrestha girls who belong to their former landlord castes whom they used to serve. They now wield authority over others. A number of them are still pro-UML, but a growing number have joined Congress In regard to these *rājnītik* (political) issues, sweeping generalisations must be avoided. As people say: "even within a family, sons and daughters can vote differently from their parents and even from one another".

This remarkable success is due to several factors, five of which are particularly noteworthy. Firstly, since the fall of the Ranas, Jyāpus have benefited from the 1960s and 1970s land reforms. Tenants have obtained greater security of tenure, and some of them working on *guthi* land have registered land in their own name, thus becoming outright owners. Secondly, production has increased in a spectacular fashion over the years due to the introduction of chemical manure and improved selected seeds imported from abroad. Thirdly, the price of land has increased tremendously and farmers, who were formerly reluctant to offer their land for sale, have started to sell some of their fields, suddenly becoming just as rich and even more so than high-status Newar and Parbatiyā castes. Fourthly, this money has been invested in the education of their children who have obtained university degrees and have slowly started to compete with students from traditionally richer groups. Finally, Jyāpus have greatly benefited from their location within the Kathmandu Valley and from the proximity of good schools. They are not yet totally *bhāju*, an honorific term for high-status, respectable castes, but they are not far off. The higher-ranking Jyāpu "creamy layer" has clearly undergone a gentrification process.

These economic achievements have gone hand in hand with the loosening of caste regulations to which Newar farmers were formerly subjected. Nowadays, Jyāpus, who in the past were used as servants and messengers by landlords and high Newar castes, especially during rites of passage, increasingly refuse to fulfil these tasks, regarding them as derogatory.

More amazing still is the fact that Jyāpus have succeeded in placing themselves at the centre of Newar society thanks partly to the growing popularity of the indigenous *ādivāsī* discourse. Today, they picture themselves as the most genuine Newars, the epitome of their society and culture. Through their community organisations, Mahāguthi and Samāj, they increasingly speak on behalf of all Newars. They now have their own museum and their own festive day, Jyāpu Diwas, celebrated on the full moon of Māngsir (November-December) and during which Miss Jyāpu is elected. These developments have made them proud to be Jyāpus. Today they openly claim that they belong to this community. Here again, they have clearly won the battle: nowadays during ceremonies even upper-caste Newar women wear the traditional Jyāpuni black skirt decorated with a red border at the bottom to assert their "Newarness". Similarly, women from lower groups, like Khadgī (butchers), have adopted the farmer woman's style of dress. In the past, Jyāpus were able to climb the social ladder by becoming Suwāl, Singh and, more often than not, Shrestha. Today, they are striving for their status to be fully recognised by preserving their identity and by priding themselves on it.

Of course, this is far from being a total transformation. Caste barriers still exist and stereotypes about peasants as opposed to urbanites are hard to shake off. A number of inequalities persist in the prevailing pyramidal social structure. Maharjans have not yet reached high-ranking positions in political spheres for instance. In addition, by selling their land, they have jeopardised their income and financial resources. This material success is indeed a slippery path.

The overall improvement of their situation cannot be contested. Money and a higher status have helped farmers to overcome their social handicap. Remarkably enough, this upward shift is not due to government policies (save the land reform) or to certain affirmative action measures. Jyāpus, who might be classified as an OBC caste in India (though they regard themselves as Ādivāsī in Nepal), have climbed the social ladder on their own thanks to their skills, their investment and their enterprising spirit. What Dalits need is perhaps not necessary the case for all OBC-like castes. This is just one lesson of this success story.

54. Climbing the Social Ladder

In his play *George Dandin, or the confounded husband,* which premiered in Versailles in 1668, Molière, the great seventeenth-century French comic author, presents a rich peasant, Dandin, and the aristocratic wife he has secured thanks to his wealth. Though wedded to her, his *sasurālis* (in-laws) of a much higher social status and even his spouse still regard him as a vulgar commoner. Angelica, his wife, does not hesitate to flirt with a young unmarried marquis, cheating on Dandin in front of practically everybody. At the time it was created, the story was interpreted as a farce, mainly because such a hypogamous union was almost unimaginable, scandalous and could only end in disaster. The commoner was immediately identified as a usurper. By contrast, the reverse situation, of hypergamous marriage (a female commoner marrying an aristocrat), was a much more readily acknowledged possibility. Molière's great talent, beyond the wonderful humorous text, was to imagine an inconceivable framework that became increasingly common in nineteenth-century European countries.[2]

The difference between the two types of marriage had already been established in ancient classical India and judged in a similar way as in seventeenth-century France. Hypergamic marriage (union with a wife of lower status), known in Sanskrit as *anuloma vivāha*, was an acceptable type of marriage whereas hypogamous marriage (*pratiloma* in Sanskrit) was severely condemned.

Traditionally, the situation in Nepal more or pess follows this pattern. Since the eighteenth century and perhaps even earlier, Chetri men in the central western region have often taken their wives from among Magars (though the members of this group are considered to be Matwāli, who drink alcohol, therefore indicating a lower status). Hamilton even reports that some Thakuri ruling clans from former Chaubisī kingdoms are of Magar origin. Their descendants have been raised to Rajput status. Likewise, it is not unusual for a Upādhyāya Brahman to seal a formal wedding agreement with a Chetri girl, especially as far as a second marriage is concerned. Today the number of Brahman clan names among Chetri family names is a clear indication of such unions. Remarkably, with their father's help, offspring may gradually obtain the right to wear the sacred thread. Upward mobility is therefore a reality, though a disputed one.

Even within one caste, for instance among Chetris, marriage between a man of higher status and a woman of lower status is commonplace. After all, it is the rule in many parts of North India, to the point of now being a normative principle. The superior status of bride-takers over wife-givers is a distinctive feature among a number of high-caste Parbatiyā families (though not everywhere). It is a well-known fact that the Shah family's claim about descending from a Thakur(i) caste that fled Mewar and Chittorgarh is subject to caution. It may be a legendary construction to upgrade their status. Upward mobility has proved successful here.

Whilst hypergamy largely prevails, hypogamy is less commonplace. In the old Nepali Code, hypogamy was even considered to be a punishable act.[3] For a man, punishment for committing this offense was imprisonment and a fine. As for the woman, she lost her natal caste status and was reduced to the caste of the man who had seduced her. As in seventeenth-century France, there is therefore a considerable difference in the types of inter-status marriage. Climbing the social ladder depends very much on the wife's status. The question is too technical to be dealt with here fully, but the main trend is clear: hypergamy was traditionally one possible path towards social ascension (for a woman), whereas hypogamy was a rather more difficult avenue (for a man). Yet cases of extreme hypergamy (between a Bāhun man and a Dalit woman for instance) were also widely condemned and severely punished.

Interestingly, the ban on hypogamous marriage has always been less strict among Newars than among high Parbatiyā castes. This feature has largely gone unnoticed by most anthropologists and sociologists. Though the ideal marriage among Newars (as is theoretically the case among Parbatiyās) is between persons of the same status, a union with a wife of a higher status is not entirely inconceivable. It has long been recognized as a (difficult) path towards a higher social ranking. Marriage between a man from the Jyāpu farmer caste and a girl from the Shrestha shopkeeper and merchant castes, for instance, is not completely new.

The subsequent status of the wife in a hypogamous inter-caste union is a complex and rather confusing issue. Today, this is still not totally clear. It mostly depends on the families concerned. In some cases, the wife retains her caste name; in other situations, she is referred to by her husband's caste name or she adds her husband's caste name to her father's caste name. As far as their children are concerned, they normally join their father's *guthi* association and are therefore integrated into their father's caste. Whatever the case, the marriage of a Jyāpu man to a Shrestha girl (i.e. of higher status) does not preclude the possibility for the husband of remaining a member of his *guthi* and caste. And a change in name (Shrestha instead of Jyāpu) is still a possibility. Now, in the event of a hypergamous union, if a Jyāpu boy marries a girl belonging to a lower caste, he will only be able to retain his caste if he does not eat the rice cooked by his wife. Marriage is possible but commensality is highly contested.

Whether hypogamous or hypergamous, the number of inter-caste and inter-ethnic marriages has increased considerably in the young Nepalese republic, especially in urban areas. Among Newars in particular, marriage between a man of (slightly) lower caste and a girl of (slightly) higher caste, for instance between a Jyāpu and a Shrestha girl, is on the rise. Even marriage between a Jyāpu man and a Bāhun girl (which obviously corresponds to a wider gap) is on the increase. As there are no longer any legal codes to refer to in these matters, the social acceptance of these inter-caste marriages varies according to the families, which may be more or less liberal. If staged today in the Kathmandu Valley, Molière's *George Dandin* would therefore be identified as a likely story, not as an absurdity. Does social ascent automatically mean marked improvement in one's financial situation? The question has yet to be documented. As far as I know, in Nepal today ritual status still differs from economic status.

55. The Crucible of Civil Society

The rise of civil society — a concept usually translated in Nepali by *nāgarik samāj*, or *nijāmati samāj* as proposed by the late Saubhagya Shah—[4] has been a highly significant phenomenon in Nepal over the last two decades. Since 1990, the country has seen an efflorescence of countless movements and organizations associated with social change, at local, regional and national level. Among these, NGOs (more than 40,000 in the country) have been at the forefront of all sectors of change and social work (*samāj sevā*). Similarly, the media today represent a potent counter-power to challenge political institutions. These non-state entities have various functions: they promote human rights and the freedom of expression, they encourage local entrepreneurs and better inclusion of women, *dalit*, *janajāti*, and so forth, they fight against corruption, they encourage socially deprived groups to claim their rights and to challenge social inequalities. Some of them monitor elections and include voter mobilisation activities. Their importance in educational undertakings and philanthropic activities is also worth noting. By and large, these associations experiment with new approaches to solving social problems, to implementing democracy and to assisting deprived sections of the population. They are one of the main pillars of modern Nepali society.

The boom in these non-government organizations has been the result of a two-tiered movement. They are directly linked on the one hand to the reestablishment of a democracy in 1990 (*prajātantra*). Their number at the time amounted to only about 220! Suddenly, after decades of absolute royal power, individuals re-appropriated their formerly confiscated initiatives and speech. They became active agents of their future and expressed their opinion through these new channels. On the other hand, such a proliferation of NGOs has been prompted by the blatant inefficiency of government structures, by the country's ungovernableness and by the weakness of the state since Āndolan 1. These autonomous associations have gradually assumed a prominent role and have become a key element in the functioning and reshaping of Nepali society.

Alexis de Tocqueville, the nineteenth-century French sociologist, clearly showed the positive role civil associations played in democratic countries like the United States and Western countries during his lifetime.[5] In fact, in most countries, these groups have so far had a beneficial effect on establishing horizontal links that cut across the vertical ties of kinship, caste and patronage. They enforce democratic norms— deliberative procedures for decision-making, equality, autonomy, freedom of entry and exit— and create a sense of participatory citizenship. Civil society is thus a living arena for combating authoritarian tendencies and the power of the state. It is crucial for the consolidation of a democracy. In fact, the two go hand in hand. It is interesting to note that the main reasons these groups have mushroomed over the last years are the growing tendency towards individualism and the horizontal forms of mobilization in the absence of a charismatic leader. Sociologically, it exemplifies a gradual shift from the collective to the individual.

Nonetheless, the overall picture is not entirely rosy. To limit ourselves to Nepal, some negative elements need to be highlighted. For instance, in many but not all cases, these groups are funded by foreign aid. Their English-speaking elite is mostly based in the Kathmandu Valley although it includes a number of persons living in the hills as well as in the Tarai. This elite, which belongs to the more privileged ruling class, naturally tends to reproduce its advantages or to defend its achieved positions rather than to transfer services, goods and money to remote districts. This segment of the population is not totally isolated from more global and political issues. More often than not, it is pervaded by Western definitions of proper governance designed by international agencies such as the United Nations or IMF. These external agents, ideologically charged with a liberalist economic culture, dictate their own norms that may not fit in with local realities and ethical values. Ulterior political motives (to ensure control over the population, to discourage revolutionary tendencies, for instance) and other Western biases are sometimes clearly evident.

Sociologists usually define these very diverse groups by situating them some way between familial and state structures. They are, so it is said, 'in between' and do not depend on the state apparatus. Another alleged feature of these organizations is that they are set up on a voluntary basis. They thus stand theoretically apart from customary forms of belonging. There is some truth in these assertions. NGOs, for instance, are often characterized by an anti-state connotation. Yet from my own experience, their boundaries with the state and, more than anything else, with kin networks are much more blurred that is commonly asserted.

In fact, traditional forms of identity deeply entrenched in Nepali society tend to interfere in the functioning of civil society (just as in the state structure). These organizations do not consequently escape from what the late Ernest Gellner called in other contexts 'the tyranny of the cousins' and what in Nepali is termed *nātābād-kripābād*, familism and favouritism. They are still hampered, to a certain degree, by clientelism, familial influences and vertical hierarchical ties. Hence civil society mirrors existing global society. It is not an independent sphere and, more importantly, it does not have to be equated automatically with democracy.

It therefore comes as no surprise if the politics of ethnicity (and of religion) based on primordial bonds also play an all-important role in this emerging civil society. Such communal (*sampradāyik*) ties reflect the persisting strength of the community over individual forces. They compete with the autonomous ethics of civil society and are more often than not an obstacle to open democratic membership-participation. In sum, civil society must be regarded as an arena of conflict between internal rival forces rather than a secluded realm of peaceful interaction.

56. Secularizing Society

During a recent trip to Nepal, I attended what is locally termed a "political wedding" or a "people wedding", *janatāntrik bibāha or janabādi bibāha* (sometimes also *pragatishīl*, progressive, or *krāntikārī*, revolutionary, *bibāha)*. The venue was a restaurant in Naya Baneshwar, Kathmandu, on the top floor of a modern building. The bride, the groom, and their families, all belong to the UML Communist Party (Emāle), and, incidentally, to the Brahman Parbatiyā community. The couple's parents had agreed to the marriage. There was no ritual, no ceremony, no priest, no *kanyā dāna*, neither before nor after. At this sort of wedding the bride and groom simply exchange garlands of marigold flowers (*saipatri-ko mālā*), or they shake hands. They sat on a large sofa, as is customary at wedding receptions, to welcome friends and relatives, and to receive gifts. Coincidentally, the day chosen to celebrate the event was Prajātantra Diwas, Democratic Day (19 February 2015).

More and more UML communist and Maoist activists celebrate their marriage in this simple non-religious manner. It is part of their secularist posture. In fact, leftwing and communist politicians express growing indifference towards religious matters, and, in some cases, display a more aggressive non-religious stance. They have replaced ritual practices with a marked interest in economic, secular and social aspects (and in counting votes!). Their aim is to make Nepal a secular society, totally free of what they call "superstitions". As a rule, such a wedding party is generally followed by a civil marriage, *dartā bihā*, which merely consists in signing legal documents before the CDO (Chief District Officer). This type of marriage, which is recognised by the state, is greatly encouraged by feminist associations. It helps when having to file a divorce.

Non-religious marriage creates a deliberate rupture with the past and with ritual traditions. The sacrality of marriage vows is no longer sanctioned by the gods but by the will of the couple and by their parents. Marriage is becoming a social event rather than a religious sacrament. It is being desacralized. The buffet that is served on such occasions highlights the social get-together. In fact, in the wedding above, politics seemed to have become a substitute for religion (even if there was no hint of politics at the wedding). This trend seems to be widespread among the urban middle classes and to extend beyond a person's political sense of belonging. Young people are increasingly becoming secular in their outlook, rejecting old religious prohibitions.

Such secularized wedding ceremonies correspond to the spread of interconnected ideas related to democracy, science, freedom and equality. The increasing number of Nepalis benefiting from a Western education, disconnected from religious rules, also encourages a different attitude towards personal problems and civil life. In addition, the constraints of modern life, such as mixing with other people in public transport, working together and sharing tiffin at lunch-time, sitting side by side at the same table with different people, do not make it easy to respect rules of purity and impurity. In some families, the spread of liberal ideas about codes of conduct has considerably Westernized people's way of life. At home, even the kitchen is secularized. The hegemonic rule of traditional religion is clearly being challenged.

Earlier in this book, I wrote about the tenacity of religion in contemporary Nepal, specifically at a collective level [**22**]. As far as India is concerned, some studies have even shown that rather than lessening the influence of religiosity,[6] modernity has globally reinforced it through new forms of faith and practices. Let us not over-generalises about this topic. The trajectories of religion and secularism in modern South Asian societies are anything but simple. Schematic statements found in the media need to be dusted off and critically questioned. When addressing these topics, whether at a micro or macro level, the relevant social space must, above all, be clearly defined. We can safely say that Nepal is still a predominantly traditional, rural country which is deeply committed to religion. But on a smaller familial scale, religious rules and ceremonies carried out in urban centres in the Kathmandu Valley (and more particularly in the capital) are on the decline, except in some religious orthodox groups (among Bāhuns or Shākyas for instance). The young urban generation professes a desire for secular ceremonies. If *pūjā* is performed during life-cycle rituals, it tends to be done in a simpler way than before (*chotkari bibāha,* in the case of marriage). Here we are not facing a privatisation of religion, but its decline, if not its partial disappearance, at least from certain ceremonies.

The saffron *hindutva* nationalist movement is fighting against this growing process of secularisation and Westernisation. In Nepal, as in India, Hindu nationalists are determined to defend the Hindu creed in all sectors of life and to endorse the supposedly ancient traditional rules governing their lifestyle. They intend to rouse the whole Hindu nation and to restructure their respective nation in

Hindu religious terms. In both the aforementioned countries, this project is a critique of the state's official commitment to secularism. In India, where *hindutva* represents a powerful force, some leaders among Narendra Modi's BJP majority would like, for instance, to withdraw the word "secular" from the constitution. The Nepali branch of Vishva Hindu Parishad, for its part, is demanding a national referendum on the issue of the secular state. Their members are planning a return to royalty and to Hindu kingship. However, this current is far weaker in Nepal than in India, save in some parts of the Tarai. In the 2013 second Constituent Assembly elections, the main political representative of the Rashtriya Prajatantra Party Nepal (royalists) only came fourth after Congress, UML, and the Maoists, with only 23 seats out of a total of 575.

The spread of the secular ethos in society and the decline of religion in the private family sphere in urban milieus clearly take on a political dimension here. In India, the admission of saffron-clad individuals into the Indian parliament has politicised religion. In Nepal, tension is less acute. Secular viewpoints are expressed in vague political terms, as in the example given above. Yet generally speaking, any opposition lies between two different visions of society: a traditionalist view that is attached to its caste rules and old forms of hierarchy, and a liberal standpoint more open to a Western influence and to the modern world. It would be interesting to distinguish in this domain between what is advocated publicly and what is done in private. But, by and large, this dichotomy cuts across political parties. Traditionalists oppose the use of secularism as an instrument of national integration and stress the sacred character of their country, *pitribhūmi* or *punyabhūmi*. They are likely to be suspicious, for instance, of Muslims and of the recent progress of Christianity in their country. By introducing the ambiguous Hindu concept of *sanātana dharma* in the 2015 Constitution, these traditionalists have largely achieved their goal. They mitigated secularism.

Notes

1 Mark Turin, "Call me Uncle: An Outsider Experience in Nepali Kinship", *Contributions to Nepalese Studies*, 28 (2), 2001, pp. 277-83.

2 In fact, Molière was a brilliant satirist of all forms of mobility. In *Le Bourgeois Gentilhomme*, he develops the hypogamous situation presented in *George Dandin*. Monsieur Jourdain, a bourgeois commoner (of a higher status than a peasant), and the ridiculous hero of the play, courts the daughter of an aristocrat.

3 Prayag Raj Sharma, *The State and Society in Nepal. Historical Foundations and Contemporary Trends*. Kathmandu: Himal Books, 2004.

4 Saubhagya Shah, *Civil Society in Uncivil Places: Soft State and Regime Change in Nepal*. Washington, D.C., East West Center, 2008.

5 Alexis de Tocqueville. *Democracy in America*. London: Penguin Classics, 2003.

6 K.N. Panikkar, "Religion Dominates State", *The Hindu*, February 21, 2011.

CHAPTER

9

Social Ties, Exclusion and the Self

One of the most striking features of contemporary Nepali society is without a doubt the resilience of the strong social bonds and forms of cooperation among the people at various local levels. Indeed, the 2015 earthquake exemplifies these links: in the absence of any intervention or, in some cases, in respond to the late intervention of state emergency rescue services, private individuals automatically lent assistance to each other, taking charge of the seriously injured and lending a hand to rebuild neighbours' damaged houses.

These social networks are also active in everyday life. Farm work, building, the exchange of high-altitude produce for rice from the lower plains, all this is organised and achieved today just as before on a collaborative, reciprocal basis. Lineages, clans, the customary obligations between takers and givers of wives (especially in ethnic groups) still play a dominant role in daily life. They provide a form of security for peasants living in a hostile, dangerous environment subject to natural disasters (floods, landslides, earthquakes, etc.). This is their social strategy for survival. Just as in the past, farmers still rely on the *padma* collective system of mutual help, working in each other's fields on a rota basis. Salaried work and daily waged labourers play a growing role in agriculture, but mostly to complement old forms of dense cooperative systems.

The situation has changed more significantly in urban centres, especially within the middle class. Children from these families are more exposed to modernity and undertake longer studies in schools and universities. They are far more Westernized with regards their dwellings and dress. It is in this sociological milieu that the rise in individualistic behaviour is more tangible. Individuals broaden their horizons by choosing to follow norms that are different from their parents' and do not hesitate to break certain rules. Intercaste marriage, for instance, is much more common in cities than in the countryside. Likewise, the growing impact of a utilitarian economy and of consumerism tends to create new optional interpersonal links. However, in cities just as in rural areas, the population is faced with the same hollow state and the same bungling administration. People therefore have to organize themselves. Here again, as in rural areas, kinship ties are the rule; there is close cooperation within lineage and caste subgroups. Anomic tendencies and forms of isolation do exist [**60, 63**], but so far they have, for the most part, been closely circumscribed.

57. Trust Networks

Trust is a crucial component in building a democracy. A democratic state cannot work without a certain amount of trust between its citizens and their elected representatives. Robert Putnam and Charles Tilly, two American political scientists/sociologists, have convincingly argued that there is a close connection between mistrust and authoritarian regimes all over the world.[1] Mistrust threatens and weakens democracy.

These theoretical issues directly apply to Nepal. The country's current situation reveals the public's increasing mistrust of the political elite, and, even more importantly, of all state-controlled bodies and organisations. Political parties are accused of only being concerned about their own interests, of serving themselves first, and of not worrying about the welfare of citizens, or only in a rhetorical manner. How different from the euphoria and expectations of the demonstrators during Andolan 1 and Andolan 2! Over the last decades, the political realm has been discredited in the

eyes of the general public and most state-sponsored institutions in the country are now regarded as more or less corrupt.

Such mistrust leads people to rely more and more on their own devices and to conduct their affairs independently. Regular visitors to Nepal are surprised at the vitality of civil society and at the energy harnessed by people in initiating development projects or in managing local trust institutions. The success of flourishing cooperatives at local level, of micro-finance saving systems, of *samiti* (committees) for all sorts of cultural, financial or economic matters may be mentioned in this respect [**85**]. Similarly, people involved in the booming NGO sector backed by foreign countries or simply supported by a local budget, display a sense of responsibility, of collective commitment, which is in stark contrast to what can bc read about politics in daily newspapers. Not to mention the diverse charitable organizations that provide free medical care, create bonds and ensure forms of solidarity. The political microcosm seems to be increasingly disconnected from the living forces of the country.

A good example of this general mistrust in the capacity of state-funded institutions to resolve the daily problems that individuals face is water management in urban areas of the Kathmandu Valley. In Lalitpur, for instance, some neighbourhoods (still a limited number), often based on old Buddhist monastic (*bāhāh*) ties, have created their own organisations to tackle difficulties regarding water supplies. Local bodies are clearly suspicious of KUKL (Kathmandu Upatyaka Khanepani Limited), the public utility in charge of such problems. These local organisations buy extra water on the market; they stock it and distribute it among their members. These parallel systems of pooled water rely on local ties and are based on a mutual help system. People seem satisfied with such organisations which are run by people they themselves know or whom they can easily control. Mutual aid groups make up for state deficiencies. Trust networks are dissociated from political institutions.

There is nothing new in these local collaborative systems and self-sustained projects. Plural Nepali society has long been managed primarily by local institutions at grass-roots level, caste by caste or ethnic group by ethnic group, as far as its internal administration and local justice are concerned. Such a fragmented mosaic applies to the situation prior to the unification of the country at the end of the eighteenth century. Yet it has survived since then in spite of the gradual extension of state control during the Rana and Panchayat periods. When I was working in North Dhading district in the seventies, in remote Tamang villages at the foot of the Ganesh Himal range, the state was practically absent. Schoolteachers, doctors, nurses and forestry officials, all representatives of the state and originally from low-altitude areas, stayed in these faraway villages for a minimum length of time, with the feeling that they were in a foreign environment. Moreover, there was traditional hostility towards the central state and its representatives, even if some local headmen did benefit from the Rana dynasty to launch their own business enterprises. The success of the Maoist insurgency in many parts of the country can be explained, at least in part, by this rebellious tradition.

The resilience, and sometimes the revival, of these self-managing forces based on kin and locality networks is a remarkable sociological phenomenon in Nepal. The state has not yet established a relationship of trust with the people. It is still widely separate from civil society. The country can be depicted as a divided society where the different groups harbour deeply rooted grudges against each other and are unable to reach a consensus on issues of vital importance. A greater sense of citizenship and a certain form of nationalism seem to have emerged in recent years. Yet locally, at district level, forces other than central ones are predominantly at work. The state seems to stay almost on the margins of what is taking place in society. I contend that a causal link exists between these centrifugal tendencies and the difficulties public politics face today. To borrow terms used by Joel Migdal, in Nepal the state is *weak*, but society is *strong*.

The reinforcement of ramified clientele links, which is a main feature of traditional Nepali society, as described by the late Dor Bahadur Bista, is another aspect of this situation. For many people, the best way of obtaining something from the state is to cultivate interpersonal relationships with persons in high places. Instead of placing one's trust in government bodies supposedly working for the state and the nation, people tend to rely on a series of obedience- and opportunity-based hierarchical links with so-called powerful persons and intermediate bodies which may ensure them benefits and protection. Bribery and nepotism are a direct outcome of such situations. These paradigms exist throughout the world. Yet, when they persist as the principal way of interacting with the state, it can be said that democracy has failed to take root in society.

58. Spirit of the Gift

Economists and developers working in Nepal, whether foreigners or nationals, often underestimate the role of non-market forms of distribution based on religion, kinship or traditional forms of power and prestige. In fact, a huge volume of services, products, and money are dispersed, exchanged or spent at grass-roots level (*dāna, koseli, samarpan, upahār,* etc.) during ceremonies, rituals, and through other non-utilitarian channels. To take just a few examples, Dasain, Tihār, as well as many other local festivals, all involve distributing, exchanging, and even destroying a great deal of wealth in the case of animal sacrifices, either to fulfil obligations between categories of different relatives, to enhance one's prestige, to make the receiver indebted, to placate divinities or simply to respect local customs. Similarly, marriage often entails enormous expense, sometimes crippling families with debt. This happens not only in rural areas, but also in cities. Such a continuous, repeated flow of money and commodities that escapes the market economy has a tremendous impact on social relations and on cohesion within society itself.

Gifts and donations play a central role in social economics, whether within or outside capitalist formations: they pervade the entire domestic Nepali economy including the remittances sent from migrants abroad. In this respect, three distinct types of gift can be identified. The first one is offered up to the gods and their representatives on earth. It not only includes offerings made at temples or in households during religious ceremonies but also gifts presented to priests in exchange for their services. In some cases, priests are given presents primarily because they embody religious authority, such as in the case of *go-dān*, the gift of a cow, or because the presents are meant to free the giver of individual sins or dangerous substances by passing them on to a worthy recipient (*kātto khuvāune*).

The second type concerns the exchange of products and services, which are not quantified in strictly economic terms, between relatives, and sometimes between friends. Every ceremony that accompanies an individual's life cycle includes these types of provisions (clothing, money, food, even land in some cases). Exchanges are carried out between in-laws, wife-takers and wife-givers, as well as between parents and children, and vice-versa. Throughout Nepal, the constant flow of goods between relatives also marks the time of the year. It sustains contact between kin, friends, neighbours, and co-workers at all levels of society.

The third type, perhaps the most important for the global economy, includes donations made to religious bodies and philanthropic or social organizations. In a religious society like Nepal, these contributions are of utmost import. I myself only realized how central this flux actually is when carrying out research on new religious—mainly Hindu but also Buddhist—organisations that are currently spreading throughout urban areas. Most of these non-profit-making bodies work on a private, voluntary and donation basis. Charity and alms-giving also belong to this category of services.

This sphere of exchange and redistribution is qualitatively different from the market economy. Gifts and donations not only pertain to goods and money, but they also encompass values, ethics, honour, a person's self-image and transcendent concerns. They involve immaterial things and establish a qualitative relationship between the transactors, which is totally foreign to market exchange. In giving, the donor passes on more than a mere sum of money. He gives part of himself, some of his own substance. He creates a personal relationship. Reciprocation of the gift, if indeed this is expected, takes the form of merit, *punya*, or some other future reward. Be that as it may, the social dimension prevails. Interestingly, in charitable donations, individuals sometimes seem to derive more benefit from the very act of giving than from the benefit their gift confers on others. The emphasis is on receiving public recognition.

Nepal belongs to the group of countries where the economy is still partly or dominantly controlled by these moral values and altruistic aims. Coins are commonly used during ceremonies and are mounted onto jewellery in some social groups. Money, as well as gold and silver, are worth much more than their market value. Indeed, their symbolic value far exceeds their exchange value; they are often turned into objects of prestige or into items of aesthetic value.

In other words, the monetarization of social relations is far from being fully achieved. It would be more fitting to speak of a mercantile exchange sector that coexists with the realm of gifts and other redistributive patterns in a number of contexts. For instance, the Newar economy which has long been familiar with the market economy and transactions is replete with private gifts and donations. Newar Buddhism would not have achieved its magnificent artistic expression over the course of history without its wealthy lay donators. Noticeably, the spirit of the gift is far from having disappeared from the advanced Western world.

The role of this distributive economy is of considerable importance in strengthening links between people and in creating trust and confidence. It places ethics above profit. From a more general viewpoint, striving exclusively for profit and benefit has never constituted a society per se; it has a corrupting effect. Throughout the world, the history of capitalism illustrates the shortcomings of accumulating capital, its flaws and negative impact if left uncontrolled by superior values, whether the latter are embodied in the state as a regulating body or in transcendent notions exemplified by morals and religion. Maximum profit-making creates a gaping divide between small minorities that handle vast amounts of money and the majority of poor people. It contributes to social differentiation and threatens former communal relationships and mutual reciprocity within the group. More than anything else, the practice of offering gifts binds individuals together.

59. Images of the Self

Glass mirrors have long been part of Nepali life. Everything goes to suggest that they appeared at least during the Mughal era. At that time such items were widely used in North Indian courts to decorate the inner walls and ceilings of palaces, especially in Rajasthan. Ladies looking at themselves in a mirror abound in Indian paintings of this period. Good-quality miniature mirrors presumably crossed into Nepal from India. In the nineteenth and early twentieth century, gilt glass mirrors were one of the items that were greatly sought after by Ranas to beautify their palaces. They were imported from Europe, from Venice and Belgium, or directly from India, along with other types of Western interior designs. In the Kathmandu Valley, medium-size mirrors were introduced into affluent families at nearly the same time. They were sometimes offered to women as *dāijo* (gifts to a woman from her family). During the nineteenth century, small-size glass mirrors were brought into the hills by *lāhure* [Nepali soldiers recruited outside Nepal] and migrants returning home. Moreover, in accordance with the Indian *shīsā* style, Tharu women had no doubt been using sparkling mirror embroidery for their blouses for a long time. In the 1970s and probably well before then, small round mirrors which came with a plastic comb and were aimed at small girls were to be found on market stalls practically everywhere.

As far as metal mirrors (in Sanskrit the common term for mirror is *darpan*) are concerned, they have been documented on the subcontinent since ancient Hindu and Buddhist times. They were also used in Nepal before the unification of the country, at least in the ritual sphere. Here mention can be made of the Newar ritual bronze mirror (set), *jvalā-nhāykā̃*, which is a symbol of the goddess Lakshmī/ Vasudhārā, i.e. auspiciousness and emptiness, depending on the follower's religion (Hindu or Buddhist). In the Indic world, a mirror is an attribute of the goddess and an element of the eight auspicious, *astamangal* objects. Mirrors were obviously first used for ritual and decorative purposes, and only afterwords to look at one's appearance.

So much for history. I hasten to add that in premodern times mirrors were of little use to admire one's own beauty. They were not part of household implements and were rarely used when washing or bathing. A person was more familiar with their simple reflection in water. I remember that in the early 1970s local village people, especially men, rarely used mirrors. These objects aroused much interest and curiosity when shown. They were not commonplace. Mirrors fixed to the outer walls of temples (for religious purposes) were (and still are) often used to have a quick glimpse of oneself when offering *pūjā*. At about the same time, Nepalis were amazed when travelling abroad to see large glass mirrors in the bathrooms of five-star hotels or in luxurious Western houses. What is now becoming a more widespread item was then still something new.

I argue that the scarcity of mirrors in premodern times and the growing use of them over the last four or five decades in urban areas have had a relatively significant sociological and psychological impact. Based on observations made in Western countries, psychologists and psychoanalysts have shown the importance of the so-called 'mirror stage", i.e. the moment young children discover their image in a mirror. Babies between the ages of 6 and 18 months become capable of recognizing their own mirror image. It fills them with great joy and helps them to understand themselves as separate individuals. This discovery is linked to the development of one's sense of individuality. These first images induce incalculable transformations in one's personal psyche and in relationships with other people.

Parallel to this, one might assert that in a society devoid of any mirrors, the self is still largely perceived through the eyes of other persons, and is consequently not totally isolated from the group. Some historians claim that the concept of individualism that emerged during the Italian Renaissance period is linked to the spread of high-quality mirrors at this very period. This may be one factor among several others. Whatever the case may be, mirrors play a role in the genesis of individuation. Their frequent use in daily life helps individuals to develop a consciousness of their selfhood. It induces an amplification of personal values.

The recent interest in photography in South Asia, at least as far as the general public is concerned, has had similar consequences. It is a means of looking at one's own appearance in a way that differs from the way one is seen through the eyes of others. During my fieldwork in various villages, I noted the importance people attached to being photographed when well-dressed and surrounded by all their family or alone. Other anthropologists and Western social workers have had similar experiences. Thanks to photographs, relatives and co-caste members are no longer the only mirror they have of themselves. New opportunities have opened up to them. Selfhood is less encompassed by the group than before.

Nepal is still very far from a society made up of self-contained, autonomous persons. Social groups still play a major role and hinder the full development of free individuals in many sectors of life. Divergences between Western and Asian societies persist in this field of self-systems. In Euro-American zones, societies are characterized by an independent construal of the self, based on a relatively bounded sense of one's personhood that is subjectively distinct from others. Even though excessive generalizations and typifications need to be avoided, Nepali culture (as in most Asian cultures, including Japanese) is based, in striking contrast, on an interdependent construal of the self. The individual is fundamentally connected to others. He is encapsulated in wider groups. Reliance on religion, hierarchy, tradition still predominates.

Yet more individualistic leanings and an autonomous construction of the self are in the making. In my opinion, these major changes are enhanced by devices such as mirrors and photographs. These tools, which I suggest calling "technologies of the self", have a profound impact on human cognition (connectivity, interpersonal knowledge) as well as on social links which may possibly be weakened by individualistic momentum. The "selfie", a self-portrait taken by a hand-held digital camera phone, is not exclusive to the West: it has also become a fashion among young Nepalis. It nurtures narcissist tendencies. By and large, we are prompted to pay closer attention to the various images of the self in society and to their sociological role. This undertaking will enrich our understanding of the changes that occur in present-day Nepal. A new "Culture of the Self" combining individualistic and relational holistic features is clearly emerging in the country.

60. Experiences of Solitude

It is often assumed that in a country like Nepal, as in other traditional South Asian contexts, society prevails over the individual. Such an assumption is based on theories that were formulated long ago by Western sociologists and anthropologists (Tönnies, Durkheim, Dumont, among others). It applies not only to pre-modern Asian societies but also to pre-capitalist, pre-industrial European countries. It is taken for granted that individualism first emerged in Europe at a period that fell, according to the authors, between the thirteenth and eighteenth centuries. Christianity, the development of capitalist forces, the philosophy of freedom and social criticism are cited as being among the main reasons for this evolution. According to this view, large sections of the rural population in India and Nepal are still subject to a somewhat tyrannical communal rule. It is believed that confrontation with the modern world will gradually strengthen individualities.

I myself experienced this iron law when I lived in a Newar village in Lalitpur district during the period 1971-72. It was the first time that the members of this remote community welcomed a Westerner (I was referred to as *deshi* foreigner)[2] among them. Though the inhabitants maintained religious and economic relations with their neighbours, they thought of themselves as different, unique. Traditionally, they intermarried exclusively within the village and over the ages even developed their own Newari (Nepā Bhāsā) dialect. They were not economically self-reliant but socially and mentally introverted. Such introversion ('confinement' would perhaps be a better word) was associated with strong organic unity in the community, strict marriage rules and the undisputed authority of the eldest over the youngest. The "I" of the individual could not claim to rule the world.

In such a situation—where family, lineage and local religion are practically everything—, a solitary individual who abandons his family, friends and culture to settle in a totally different place is immediately an object of suspicion. Though I had been accepted, it was not as a solitary individual; in fact, I was assigned friends and putative hosts who were in some way responsible for me.

I have never experienced such an uncompromising denial of personal autonomy in any other Nepali village or town. In subsequent studies, I nevertheless discovered that nearly everywhere lineages, clans, castes, sub-castes, local ties, ethnicities are pivotal social parameters that impose a number of constraints on individuals. These elementary groups offer few opportunities for the individual to escape social regulations. The strength of communal bonds provides substantial support to individuals in the event of disease, natural disasters or ill-fated situations, but it compromises any private aspirations. Yet people readily accept exceptions to the rule, and admit a need for privacy and for being alone.

Paradigms of individuality and isolation are clearly recognized in Indian and Nepali traditional society. *Sannyāsi* renouncers, hermits living in caves, in pits or alone in the forest, imprisoned in their silence, have existed for a long time in the Himalayan and Indian social landscape. They are accepted and highly valued, even though they have severed links with their family and regard all human beings as their relatives. They are believed to have acquired extraordinary powers thanks to an extremely long and strictly observed isolation. The transgression of common social rules and isolation from society may therefore have a positive effect. Yet solitary mystical renouncers are rare. Most *sannyāsi*s, *jogi*s in fact live in communities of their own, in *āshram*s, *math*s (monasteries) and so forth. A number of them have even married and nevertheless retain their renunciatory status.

Modern life and growing globalization engender new claims for self-autonomy and create more occasions for being alone than before. Hedonist demands and the rejection of ancient moral codes are on the rise, sometimes creating conflicts within families. In extreme cases *disaffiliation* and an intensification of the relationship with the self may lead to drug addiction, depression or severe mental illness, all processes marked by a rapid depersonalisation.

Yet altogether, when compared to the West, family ties still prevail. The high rate of individuals, whether male or female, who live alone in modern European cities after a divorce, for instance, has no equivalent in Nepal. Economic difficulties often cause people to join forces; a deep sense of solidarity between generations still prevails. Contrary to Western society, grandparents are cared for at home, and in many cases the custom of brothers leaving the family home and going their own separate way at a late age persists. Nepali individuals still live at the crossroads of a multiple set of social relations, whether elective or inherited from parents. Organising regular festivals, such as Dasain and

Tihār, have so far maintained these close familial and social ties.

Trajectories of pure solitude are rare. Even the new wave of modern artists, mostly painters, that has flourished over the last decades in the Kathmandu Valley [**35**] has more often than not been sustained by a communalisation of their workplace—if their workshop has been set up outside the family home. Expanding individualism does not therefore automatically rhyme with isolation and a loss of identity. Individual itineraries have hardly led to solipsism; they are still regarded in collective terms.

While bearing these matters in mind, it is important to differentiate between loneliness that is imposed against one's own freewill and freely chosen isolation. Historically, they both exist in Nepali families, the first making life a misery, the second being more compatible with luminous horizons. To give just one example, single women, whether divorced or widowed, have often endured an arduous life within their family. Social integration may conceal loneliness, mental isolation and personal anguish. Sexual minorities that deviate from standard law may also be mentioned in this respect. If rejected, their members may face dereliction.

What about the experiences of migrants abroad? Interestingly enough, new associations and mutual aid groups are often set up in foreign countries, providing fellow Nepali migrants with a new social life. In the same way as Gurkha regiments were formed on the basis of ethnicity or caste in the nineteenth and twentieth centuries, Nepali labour migrants in the Gulf who are buffeted by the winds of history recreate their own social links. Nepali expatriates in the West, for their part, form their own ethnic cultural associations, maintaining social bonds and a firm sense of identity. There is therefore a lesser sense of suffering and of total uprooting. Old social ties are reformulated but are preserved.

61. Unseen Violence

Reading the newspapers these days is terribly daunting. Every day, at least three cases of violence committed against women are reported. Women being raped by their boyfriend, a boy goading his friend to rape his girlfriend, gang bangs, a father raping his daughter, 5-to-6 year-old baby girls being raped, old women raped by a boy who sheltered for the night at their house, domestic workers raped by their master or his son. Or else we hear about dumb or disabled young girls being raped by their neighbour or by relatives, a husband burning his wife's intimate parts or violently beating her, a father or other family members burning a daughter, in-laws burning their daughter-in-law, a wife killed by her husband because she didn't come with gifts from her *māiti*, etc. All these crimes are ignominious. While the "Occupy Baluwatar" movement is forever demanding 'to stop violence against women', the number of such extremely violent actions is on the rise from one day to the next.

Unfortunately, this is only the tip of the iceberg. Unseen day-to-day violence and everyday discriminations against women are still not reported in the media. I would like to address this issue by considering the case of single women in male-dominated Nepali society. Single women are in fact the most vulnerable to physical violence and represent an alienated social group. Indeed, unmarried women are not considered to be totally accomplished adults. They cannot perform death rituals for their parents. For a couple, marriage is still considered a major social and religious achievement. And it is meritorious for parents to give their daughter as a gift, *kanyādān*. As a Newar saying goes: "Neither a woman who has never borne the pain of childbirth or a man with no experience of building a house can understand what suffering, *dukha*, is." An international conference was held in Kathmandu at the beginning of February 2013, mainly to discuss widowhood and widows' rights. In Hindu society, widows are frequently held responsible for the death of their husbands. There are blamed for their own condition. Yet other categories of single women exist: unmarried, abandoned and divorced. These women are particularly prone to aggression and exploitation.

In the course of research sponsored by SIRF (Social Inclusion Research Fund) that was recently carried out on single women in the town of Laliptur, Shova Shakya recorded a number of life stories documenting the subject.[3] The cases analyzed include an unmarried woman whose life is totally taken up by household chores—taking care of her ailing old mother, of her sick nephew, cooking, doing the laundry, cleaning the house, fetching water, etc. From early morning to late evening she is so busy that she has no time to rest. During her childhood she had to support father and mother, and to look after her brothers and sisters. Thus, there was no possibility for her of benefiting from any schooling. Although she is very keen to save money, she never has a single *paisā* in her purse. She works all day without being paid and has become an all-too-reliable domestic slave for her brothers and sister-in-laws. Even though this person is a member of a family, she still has no property share. To leave the house she even needs to ask permission from her family members. She is trapped within her own family with no individual rights.

Another unmarried woman describes her extremely distressing situation. "It's like strict *tapasyā*", she said. "Men are always bothering me, they are forever finding an excuse to touch my body, they show improper attention and only offer help with ulterior motives in mind. It is very difficult for me to dodge such colleagues at work. Married men are the most dangerous; they just want to be near me. They even telephone at any time of the day for no reason, just to flatter me. I always have to be careful with this kind of man. I am fed up of this life". Such cases of harassment are common in interviews.

One respondent actually got married without even seeing the groom beforehand. She simply trusted her mother and brother with preparations for her wedding. Yet when she arrived at her husband's house, she realized that the groom was ugly and old. She was totally appalled. "It is impossible for me to live with this man!" So she decided to leave him. The very next morning, she moved back to her *māiti*. She never dared to return to her husband's house again. Time passed and her mother got older. Her brothers drifted away from the family. At present, she is the only one looking after her mother who is becoming increasingly sick and needs medicine. She has no financial support from her husband. Furthermore, her brothers have not even given her her property share because she is married. "How can I provide the medicine my mother needs? I can't even go out of the house and look for for full-time employment. How will I care for my mother in the meantime?" Her life is full of trials and tribulations.

These voices, mixed in with tears when recorded, convey profound *dukha*, pain. Admittedly, some single women have succeeded in securing their own independence and in leading rewarding lives. However, in most cases, they remain extremely dependent on their family, they are sexually harassed, and discriminated against socially and religiously. Beside, 98 per cent of respondents were unaware of their legal rights. Although the weight of cultural traditions plays a prominent role in all these matters, it would be interesting to investigate the difference in how single women are treated according to their ethnic group or caste. Whatever the case may be, the number of unmarried women in Newar society seems to have always been relatively high compared to other communities. Generally speaking, access to higher education and modern living conditions have led to a significant increase in the number of single women, without actually putting an end to the misery faced by these abused citizens. It is now time to break the silence.

62. Born Sinful

The *Multidimensional Social Inclusion Index* published in 2014 by Tribhuvan University's Central Department of Sociology/Anthropology lists seven Madhesī (Tarai) Dalit castes —Dalit being the new word for "untouchable castes"— among the 10 lowest-ranking marginalized Nepalese population groups. In ascending order (of their degree of exclusion) starting from the bottom are the Musahars, Doms, Khatwes, Tatmas, Dusadhs (Paswan or Pasi), Halkhors, Camārs (Harijan or Ram). Madhesī Dalits who all together include 9 to 10 castes are therefore not only the poorest among the poor. They are among the most segregated populations in Nepal and are relegated to the very bottom of the hierarchy. Their situation is worse than their hill Dalit counterparts.

This project, funded by the Social Inclusion Research Fund, which is now closed, also published a series of *Ethnographic Profiles* on the 42 most historically excluded caste and ethnic groups based on data collected by L. Bennett and D. Parajuli for the World Bank.[4] Field research was carried out by young Nepali researchers, mostly MA students. These monographs provide interesting ethnographic data on population groups that have so far been overlooked and—for some of them—are totally unknown. I myself took part in the project as a reviewer and met most of the authors at various internal seminars.

Having reviewed work on Dalit groups, especially those from the Tarai, I focus here on Madhesī Dalit monographs, four of which have already been published. An *Atlas* containing data from the 2011 Census completes the opus and provides valuable spatial information on each of these groups. Halkhors (4,000 individuals) are concentrated mainly in the Janakpur area. Doms (13,000) are confined to the eastern Tarai (Saptari, Dhanusa, Sunsari and Parsa. Camārs (336,000) are scattered over various districts situated in the eastern Tarai. As far as Musahars (234,000), Tatmas (105,000) and Khatwes (101,000) are concerned, they are also mainly located in eastern Tarai districts, though some small groups may live here and there in other parts of Nepal. Dusadhs (209,000) and Dhobis (109,000) can be found all over the Tarai, but mainly in the eastern and central part. Bantars (or Sardars) (55,000) are located in Morang, Sunsari and Saptari. Depending on the region where they live, these people speak Maithili, Bhojpuri and Awadhi (and, as far as Doms are concerned, a specific language called Parasi).

All together, the Madhesī Dalit population amounts to 1,167, 000, i.e. 4.4 per cent of Nepal's population, compared to 2,151,000 hill Dalits (8.12 per cent of the whole population). They live mainly in rural areas, save Halkhors (or Mestars) and Musahars who are mostly urban castes and often squatters. In Chitwan and Jhapa, Chidimars (1,254 individuals), who specialize in using nets to catch birds which they then sell or eventually eat, are listed by Rashtriya Dalit Ayog [National Dalit Commission] among the ten Tarai Dalit castes. Yet the profile written on them challenges such a label: they belong in fact to Janajāti groups and are not "untouchables".

These downtrodden castes cultivate fields and earn their living through several other additional activities. Yet, within the caste system, what marks them out are the ritual services they have to provide for the middle and upper pure castes in the region. These services cannot be provided by pure castes out of fear of being defiled. Dalit castes are therefore permanently in contact with impure substances (working with leather, raising pigs, washing dirty linen, disposing of garbage, cleaning toilets, eating rats, etc.). This contact with polluting agents explains their impure status. However, some of them (Camārs for instance) play music at collective events, like Damāīs in the hills, bringing a touch of auspiciousness during festivities and marriages. Women from among the same Camārs are also well-known midwives. It is worth noting that Khatwes and Dushads mainly do farm work and do not have to perform ritual services for pure castes. It would seem that some of these so-called "untouchable" castes were ethnic groups in the past and that they became Dalits at a later date. This is particularly the case of Musahars.

It is still difficult to break down caste barriers and even more so here than in the hills. Madhesī Dalits suffer various forms of discrimination. They live in separate hamlets at some distance from pure castes and their access to schools or to public wells is limited. They cannot sit or remain seated while speaking to people of a higher caste and their children are turned out of houses. As one informant put it, segregation and low status are regarded as *pāp*, a (inherited) sin that accompanies them through life. This engenders intense self-depreciation regarding one's status. More often than not, there is a sense of shame in disclosing one's caste identity to others who belong to "pure" castes. Yet this situation varies from one region to another, and a number of bans have recently been lifted. Over the last decade, easier access to education and a higher standard of literacy among these castes have, for instance, paved the way for improvements in their situation. The standard of modern amenities is also on the rise: among Camārs, 78 per cent of families have a mobile phone.

Besides speaking the same languages that are spoken on the other side of the Indian border, these castes are in permanent contact with India and regularly cross the border. They often marry an Indian of the same caste and regularly visit temples in Uttar Pradesh or Bihar. What is more, a number of these castes originally came from India and only settled in Nepal recently. Interestingly enough, some of them practise cross-cousin marriage.

Economically speaking, Tarai Dalits are bound to their pure-caste clients and to the landlords in whose fields they work. The system of bondage, called *haruwā-charwā* in the eastern and central part of the Tarai, is very similar to *kamaiyā* among Tharus and *riti-bhāgya* (patron-client) in the western hills. It leaves tenants little freedom and epitomizes their dependence. Control over the land is obviously one of the means by which these groups are linked to higher castes. The hierarchical ritual system on which the caste system is based here (like elsewhere in Nepal) has deep-seated economic roots. These two aspects are inseparable.

Little is known of the type of Hinduism practised by Madhesī Dalits. In these matters, Tribhuvan University's Ethnographic Profiles provide a wealth of detailed observations. Despite being excluded from most high-caste temples and not being allowed to light incense for deities, Dalits themselves declare overwhelmingly that they are Hindu.

They worship their own deities, gods and goddesses (Sansārī Māī for Camārs, for instance), and in most cases they have their own temples. The cult of earth-deities predominates. Death is highly polluting and each group has its own rituals of purification which are performed a few days after cremation. Most Hindu festivals are celebrated. From the published monographs it is difficult to assert that a Dalit's religion is essentially pragmatic (making offerings to gods mainly in exchange for favours) as is frequently said to be the case in India.

One lesson to be drawn from these ethnographic accounts is that Madhesī Dalits contest their own position in the caste system more than the system itself. They consider themselves to rank higher than hill Dalits because, as they say, the latter eat beef. In fact, relations between Dalit castes replicate the overall caste hierarchy. Each caste claims to be superior to the others and does not accept rice cooked by other "untouchable" castes. Moreover, when possible, Dalits use Brahmans of lower status to celebrate their domestic rites and *Satya Nārāyan pūjā*. In their origin myths, they often see themselves as failed Brahmans because some of their ancestors committed ritual errors.

The TU Ethnographic Profiles published in Nepal by Nepali scholars are a step towards a better understanding of these excluded groups. It is hoped that this undertaking will also contribute to creating a new school of professional Nepali anthropologists. In these times of rhetorical policies about cultural diversity, this is indeed a real necessity.

63. Suicide and Society

Suicide (*ātmahatyā*) is no new phenomenon in Nepal. *Satī prathā*, the religious-connoted custom according to which a recently widowed woman throws herself on her husband's funeral pyre, was banned in Nepal in 1920 (the British abolished it in India in 1829). A local chronicle reports that altogether nine women offered themselves up as a sacrifice on Prithivi Narayan Shah's pyre in 1775, though this does seem to have been a rare occurrence, especially among commoners. People killed themselves in other contexts. The Ranipokahari pond in Kathmandu, situated in front of Durbar High School, was traditionally a favourite place for drowning oneself in an act of despair. Trisuli, Kosi and Mahakali Rivers were (and still are) also popular sites for committing such acts.

According to popular tradition, Jogmaya Neupane, the rebel reformer and elderly female ascetic, committed suicide in the early 1940s by throwing herself into the River Arun (Bhojpur district). Sixty-seven acolytes allegedly followed suit. This mass suicide is commonly interpreted nowadays as a protest against the Ranas' failure to establish a *dharmarājya*, a religious state, in Nepal. More recently, while I was working in Jyāpu villages in Lalitpur district in the 1970s, I occasionally heard of cases of suicide—mostly by hanging. These desperate acts were attributed either to a mental disorder or to tragic inter-caste love affairs. Yet, altogether, these self-inflicted deaths seemed to be a rare occurrence. In Pyangaon locality, during the period 1980 to 2010 there were five suicides (three women and two men).

What are today's figures for suicide? Statistical data on this subject are poor and should be interpreted with caution. The national death registration system itself is not totally accurate. Moreover, it is a well-known fact that cases of suicide are often hidden or rarely reported locally due to the social stigma attached to them. Hence it is difficult to draw any valid conclusion. We are unable, for instance, to evaluate the impact of the People's War on suicide.

According to WHO, the World Health Organization, the leading international organization in this field, the annual suicide rate in Nepal is over 20 for 100.000 persons. In 2012, it reached 24.9 (for 100,000 persons). However, these figures are contested by other sources. Based on different sources of data, the *Nepali Times* (6-12 February 2015) publishes a rate of 14.1 in 2014 for the whole of country. According to the Nepali police, between 4,000 and 4,300 persons commit suicide every year in the country (*The Kathmandu Post*, 12 September 2015). This corresponds to a suicide rate slightly inferior to the one recorded in France (16.5 for 100,000 persons). The area of Nepal with the highest number of people who kill themselves is the mid-western development region (19.4). For the sake of comparison, the annual rate in India is 21.1 (WHO), though the government (Crime Reports Bureau, Ministry of Home Affairs) reports only 11.2. All these figures must be interpreted with caution.

Whatever the case may be, the country has undeniably seen a sharp rise in suicides over the last decades. The overall rate was about 3.5 in the 1980s and 7 in 2004. In its 22 November 2008 issue, *The Kathmandu Post* writes that: "the number of suicides reported by police rose by 40% in the past four years. Official statistics showed 2,789 suicides in 2007, up from 1,992 in 2004." According to the newspaper, 659 cases were reported during the first three months of 2008, which is equivalent to a record total for the whole of 2007. Other sources assert that Nepal's suicide rate has nearly doubled in the past four years, and that this is to be blamed mostly on the growing number of cases of depression among young people.

The number of suicides is particularly high among the younger generation (15 to 29 years old), especially in relatively prosperous districts. Youngsters are more exposed to radical societal changes and economic difficulties. They clearly emerge as a high-risk group. It is worth noting in this respect the link between migration and suicide. The lives of poor young Nepali workers in the Gulf or in Malaysia are particularly trying and these migrants have difficulty reimbursing the loans taken out to pay for the journey there and to find a job.

Recent reports (2010-2014) also highlight a high suicide rate among young Nepali women aged 15-49, i.e. of reproductive age (Ukaid). Gender-orientated NGOs have studied this trend and have reported a notable increase in recent decades. Today, suicide is the first cause of death among this category of people. The underlying factors seem to be related to the extremely subordinated status of women, the fragile position of the bride in her in-laws' family and gender-based violence. The custom of *chaupādya* (or *chaupādi)*, i.e. seclusion of menstruated and parturient women in cowsheds, which is practised in far western Nepal (Jumla-Kalikot for instance), has often been pointed out. This causes great distress, loneliness and a feeling of humiliation in women [90].

Causes of suicide are extremely diverse. It may be provoked by mental illness, depression, alcohol abuse and drug dependency, failure to pass school exams, a broken heart, bankruptcy, poverty, copycat suicides and so forth. Among these causes, inter-caste marriage is obviously a significant one. Rejected by relatives, often driven away from their village, ostracised by everybody, the unfortunate couple suffers enormous psychological stress and endures a de-socialization process that may eventually drive them to commit suicide.

Suicidal behaviour is abnormally high among many young rural women. Nevertheless, it would be hazardous to assert that, on the scale of the whole country, the suicide rate among women today exceeds that of men, as some gender activists claim. In most countries, except for China, the reverse is true. As far as the means of suicide are concerned, the use of pesticides—which are readily available in most farmhouses nowadays and extremely lethal (more so than sleeping pills)—seems to be the commonest method. People also frequently kill themselves by hanging themselves or by drowning in a river.

Durkheimian sociologists are at odds to explain suicide in a country like Nepal. In his foundational text (*Le Suicide*, 1897), Émile Durkheim tried to correlate suicide with the social state of society. This famous French sociologist regards suicide merely as a lack of social integration, which rises in periods of *anomie*, i.e. the weakness of integrative social norms and the fragmentation of social relationships. There is obviously some truth in this approach. High suicide rates reveal a crisis in collective values and a general dilution of social bonds. They are, in significant ways, socially patterned.

Yet this sociological method fails to consider the cultural factors, such as the low status of women in South Asian societies. This approach does not throw light on whether marriage in these countries amounts to the traumatic uprooting of young girls from their family and how this can lead to a tragic end. Similarly, it does not take into account the psychological/psychiatric dimension of suicidal deaths or failed suicide attempts, the personal motives that lead to such a violent death, and especially the mental health problems. The high suicide rate in barely industrialized areas, where self-support is supposedly stronger than in modern urban societies, strongly refutes the Durkheimian theory. Here, marriage is not a protective measure; it may have disastrous effects.

The problem of a high suicide rate needs to be addressed by implementing an adequate prevention policy. However, the intellectual framework adopted in the overall analysis is crucial in itself. One of my conclusions in this concern is that suicide cannot be explained by a single cause. It reveals a break in a person's link to society as well as an individual psychological crisis. The two factors cannot be dissociated. Suicide is the result of a combination of motives rather than just one driving force. To understand it fully, we need to add more layers of complexity.

Notes

1 Robert Putnam, *Making Democracy Work. Civic Traditions in Modern Italy*. Princeton: Princeton University Press, 1993. Charles Tilly, *Trust and Rule*. Cambridge, Cambridge University Press, 2005.

2 In Newari, *deshi* (or alternatively *bhuyū* , *bhuyūcā* lit. "white") means foreigner. In Nepali, foreigners are called *bidesi*, or, colloquially, *gorā* and *kuire*. In the Tarai plains, the word *deshi* applies mostly to Madhesī/Indian people.

3 Laxmi Shova Shakya, *An Assessment of Socio-Economic Condition of Newar Single Women of Patan City*. Patan, SIRF, 2013.

4 L. Bennett and D. Parajuli, *The Nepal Multidimensional Exclusion Index*. Kathmandu: Himal Books, 2013.

CHAPTER

10

Revolutions

Since 1990 the Left has dominated political life in Nepal. Left-wing parties were excluded from the government only during King Gyanendra's short direct rule (Feb. 2005-Apr. 2006). Despite their defeat in the November 2013 elections, Maoists are still capable of mobilising people in the street in a spectacular way. CPN-UML (the reformist communist party), for its part, is a pillar of the establishment and competes with Nepal Congress for first place. Since 1990, its leaders have played an almost continuous part in government administration. Since 2008, they have been ruling the country in association first with the Maoists, then with Congress; and they have already occupied the office of prime minister three times. Nepali Congress is also theoretically a socialist party, affiliated to the Socialist International. This affiliation is ignored by those (Māobādīs, for instance) who regard Kāngresis (members of Congress) as retrogrades and reactionaries. Moreover, the Nepali political landscape is marked by the weakness of right-wing parties, which are mostly royalist or related in some way or other to the former kingship rule. In Nepal, there is no equivalent of the all-powerful Indian BJP.[1]

The level of underdevelopment and the ongoing social inequalities that characterize Nepal explain the prevalence of the Left. Indeed, communism and socialism are regarded as avenues that lead to progress. During the Panchayat period, Parijat and Bhupi Sherchan, two brilliant Nepali writers and rebel personalities at the time, displayed a radical left-wing stance. It comes as no surprise therefore that Marxist terminology prevails in political rhetoric. Let us take, for instance, the terms *tānāshaha*, dictatorship, and *sāmantabād*, feudalism. These two words are widely used in reference to the former *panchāyatī* and royalist rule. The first term belongs mainly to Maoism, but the second, a crucial concept in Marxist ideology, has become synonymous with ancient Nepal, and is used in any context to describe a backward-looking person. In communist journals, the words *dāsa prathā* (or *dāsatā*) for slavery are also frequently used in reference to the corresponding ancient mode of production which supposedly existed in pre-democratic times. Even the word "patriarchal", *pitrisattātmak*,—which mainly comes from the work of Friedrich Engels, Marx's colleague—is commonly used among all feminists and Nepali experts on social gender,[2] irrespective of their political affiliation. Similarly, it is not rare to note in Janajāti leaders' speeches some of Engel's old ideas about primitive communism.

Most of these concepts make reference to the Marxist materialist theory of change, and of class warfare in particular. By and large, this conception hinges on the belief that history necessarily develops according to certain principles or rules towards a determinate end. For Marx and Engels, the different societies in the world have to undergo five main historical phases — tribal (primitive communism), slavery, feudalism, capitalism and communism—, each characterised by a social mode of production and a specific regime of inequalities. These clear-cut stages of evolution are encompassed within a historicist vision of the past and future of societies. Moreover, these socio-economic laws are supposed to apply to all parts of the world, regardless of their own cultural traditions. What happened in Europe or in the West must inevitably happen in the rest of the world. In its most dogmatic form, this amounts to saying that India (as well as Nepal) has to endure pain in order to create its own London and Manchester.[3]

Such assumptions are pure fancy and have to be questioned. Empirical studies of historic Western and Eastern societies have proved that the thesis predicating inescapable universal stages is contradicted by the facts. Nepal clearly cannot follow the same lines of development as the US or the UK. In reality, it is difficult to know what the future holds. Unforeseeable actions undertaken by individuals have to be taken into account.

The seven essays compiled here critically address the Marxist perspective on social change and revolution, in keeping with empirical Nepali facts. They aim to frame a new analytical vision of recent revolutionary events. The shift from monarchy to republic in this Himalayan country is just as much the result of contingents trends (2001 royal palace slaughter and the temperament of the new king) as the resolution of an immutable conflict between reactionary forces and new emerging educated classes eager for freedom, change and equality.

64. The Patan Commune

The Patan uprising in March-April 1990 represents one of the most vibrant and significant pages in the history of Andolan I, i.e. the popular movement which compelled King Birendra to reinstate a multi-party (*bahudal*) parliamentary system and democratic rights in the country on 8 April 1990, after almost thirty years of the panchayat autocratic partyless system. For a whole eight days, the inhabitants barricaded the city and declared their town a “liberated zone”, *mukta kshetra*.

This episode has been dealt with in more or less detail in both reports and books (T. Louise Brown, G. Katsiaficas, M. Paudel)[4]. Yet a in-depth local history and an ethnographical account of the revolutionary movements are sorely lacking. What actually happened and what were the motives behind the mobilization? I recently investigated this topic assisted by some of those who took part in these events. The inhabitants of Chyasal Tol, in Patan, were the first to help me to understand how the uprising broke out and developed.

The story started on Friday 30 March 1990 (17 Caitra, 2046 BS). On that day, two Patan residents were shot by the security forces around and within the city. Meanwhile policemen entered private houses in pursuit of activists. The local people's reaction was immediate. The next day, 31 March (18 Caitra), fearing for their safety, the inhabitants erected barricades at the main points of access to the old city trapping 128 policemen in the process. A public statement was made declaring Patan a "liberated zone". The people of Chyasal, to the south of Mangal Bazar, inhabited mainly by Vyañjankārs (Newari: Tepay), were at the forefront of events. Vyañjankārs, a Newar farmer caste specialised in the cultivation of vegetables, are among the descendants of the first settlers of the city and claim Kirant ascendency. Other urban dwellers, especially Jyāpus and Shākyas, joined their ranks spontaneously.

The insurgents held the city for a week. Trenches were dug and barricades built to protect the city against further attacks from the police. The first barriers were erected in Bal Kumari. Conflicts between male Communists and Kāngressis (Congress) broke out on various occasions (the former reproaching the latter for being too timid and not sufficiently proactive), especially when the Communists suggested taking over the administration of Patan themselves. Nevertheless, on the whole, a common front was maintained. People armed with farm tools, iron rods and sticks were ready to defend their city around the clock. Every neighbourhood had its own security force. Women from farmer castes noticeably played an important role in the blockade. After a week, the government finally sent in the army to take possession of Patan. Rather than fighting a suicidal struggle, the inhabitants let in the soldiers.

Vyañjankārs, Jyāpus, and other Newar activists were not alone in the battle. Newar farmer castes had long been hiding in their houses communist leaders who mostly belonged to Parbatiyā Hindu upper castes. These underground activists who were sheltered by Newars played a major role in the revolutionary process. Indeed, the Patan insurgency can be analyzed as being the conjunction of these radical, largely exogenous, communist elements and even older endogenous

Newar ethnic antagonism towards successive post-Rana governments. Newars could not recognize themselves in the panchayat regime whose hegemonic Hindu non-Newar caste officials often looked down at them with contempt.

The Patan commune alone was not enough to overthrow the panchayat regime. In fact, the unrest began on 18 February (Phāgun 7) with a counter-demonstration against the Royal Palace's celebration of Democracy Day. The clashes between the two camps were followed by the usual strikes, *bandh*. Commerce and transport sectors were shut down. Effigies of *pancāyatīs* were burned and communist protestors brandished black flags, *kālo jhandā*, in the streets. Likewise, an open revolt started in Bhaktapur, a Newar city which, like Patan, had long been a communist stronghold opposed to supporters of the panchayat regime. What is more, the Patan insurgency was followed by huge street demonstrations (*birodh ko julus*) and rallies in Kathmandu, which were tragically (dozens of deaths on 6 April) decisive in the fall of the royal family. Nevertheless, by and large, the Patan commune largely contributed to the whole process.

My analysis is inspired by the *microhistory* academic school which the Italian historian Carlo Ginzburg, among others, developed. Despite its very local scope, such a *microhistory* approach may raise more general issues. Three remarks immediately come to mind. Firstly, the Patan uprising underlines the basically urban character of Āndolan I and the decisive role the Newars played in the movement. Āndolan II was characterized by widespread mobilization throughout the country which went well beyond the urban middle class. Secondly, this local rebellion testifies to Patan's communal bonds, its deep sense of separateness, as opposed even to Kathmandu, its sister city situated only three kilometres away. Examples of this distinctive phenomenon can be found in many other domains. The third remark pertains to the erroneous "reading" of Newar historical towns exclusively in religious terms. Admittedly, the spatial organization and the rituals performed stress a close interrelationship between the cosmos and the human plane. But this religious interpretation conceals the political context and the antagonistic relations with the encompassing political power. Newar religious cities can indeed turn into insurgent cities very rapidly. The way Newars organise their colourful pageants proves their capacity to coordinate collective enterprises, albeit in a rather explosive way, and their communal spirit.

These riotous events have so far been remembered and commemorated vividly each 18th Caitra, especially among Vyañjankārs. Communists see in this event a decisive victory against what they called: "bureaucracy", *nokarshāhī*,[5] "dictatorship", *tānāshāha* and "feudalism", *sāmantabād*. For them, the Patan commune also heightened the meaning of sacrificing one's life, *balidān*, which is performed for the sake of collective political liberation. Whatever the case may be, this civil insurgency has been a source of inspiration to the whole country and has provided Patan citizens with a sense of pride.

Yet, despite the success of the democratic movement in 1990, a note of dissent has tarnished this year's twenty-fifth anniversary of Patan *mukta kshetra*. In my interviews, a number of Newar activists and local intellectuals expressed their dissatisfaction. They feel that upper-caste Parbatiyā leaders and their political parties have instrumentalized them. They believe that the current reluctance of mainstream parties to grant them federal rights and autonomy is a blatant betrayal of their common struggle in the past. Ethnic and caste tensions still weigh heavily on the country's political debate.

65. *Talking about Revolutions*

The French Revolution of 1789 was often referred to during the 1996-2006 armed conflict in Nepal and is still very present in today's post-Shah politics. For a number of Marxist-Leninists worldwide, including those in Nepal, this event is considered as something of a model or at least a reference. Friedrich Engels admired the French Revolution and Karl Marx theorized about it while conceptualizing what he called the 'proletarian dictatorship". It soon became the paradigm of all subsequent revolutions. However, any comparison between the 1990 and 2006 Nepali *Jana Āndolan*s and the French Revolution needs to be treated with caution. The label "revolution" to describe the downfall of the Nepali monarchy is itself highly questionable.

The French Revolution reinforced the pre-existent centralised state, in stark contrast to the current move towards a federal structure in Nepal. French revolutionaries opposed the former "provinces" of the Old (royalist) Regime. They regarded this ancient regional architecture based on parochial cultural traditions and local privileges as reactionary and as an instrument in the hands of the aristocracy. They were reluctant to grant communal rights; they privileged the individual citizen and the unity of the nation. In addition, French revolutionary leaders defended a unilingual state, giving priority to French, the national language, to the detriment of minority languages, which were considered to be in keeping with the old hierarchical and regional structure. There are therefore considerable differences with Nepal's present official multilingual and multiethnic agenda. Last but not least, French republicans openly opposed religion, priests, churches, especially the Catholic Church—an official organ of the former royalist regime—, and they persecuted religious institutions. Nothing like this has happened in Nepal since the downfall of royalty. The declaration according to which Nepal is recognized as a secular state has introduced few changes in comparison with the previous period. The President of the Republic endorses most of the religious roles held by the former monarch and Maoist leaders often attend religious ceremonies.

Despite these blatant differences, some similar points may be highlighted. The resentment towards royal absolutism; the cult of the heroes of the revolution and the so-called martyrs, *shahid* (an Arabic word); the theme of a more or less imaginary counter-revolutionary plot, instigated by royalists, with the aim of implementing a more radical policy against their opponents; fervent nationalism (in the Nepali case, Maoists harbouring an anti-Indian feeling); a messianic belief in a totally new era, together with the creation of new festivals to commemorate the advent of the republic. Rightist and conservative movements in the two countries even explain the fall of the monarchy in similar terms, advocating a simple combination of circumstances. They raise the question: was the collapse of royalty a historical necessity or a totally unpredictable event? Had the slaughter of a large part of the Nepalese Shah royal family in Narayan Hiti Palace in June 2001 not taken place, would the monarchy have collapsed a few years later? There are inevitably some doubts about this.

It is interesting to note that French historians' interpretation of the 1789-1793 Revolution has fluctuated over the decades. Until recently, the legacy of the French Revolution was viewed from an entirely positive angle. Historians celebrated the overthrow of the abominated royalists and of oppressive feudalism by a republican regime. The Declaration of the Rights of Man and of the Citizen (1789), which is of lasting importance and based on popular sovereignty, was glorified. In addition, the reign of tyrannical Terror (1793-94), a period during which thousands of representatives of the old social system were persecuted and beheaded after summary judgements, was regarded as a necessity in order to defend the Revolution's achievements. During the 1989 bicentenary anniversary of the Revolution, French state authorities held the same discourse celebrating the revolutionary upheaval "as a whole", ignoring its authoritarian and bloody moments. They commemorated the triumph of rationality over superstitions and inequality. The French Revolution and the subsequent Republican regime have thus been gloriously mythicized, occulting all its negative aspects in matters of democracy and human rights.

The Marxist approach to revolutionary movements has been criticized in a more fundamental way. The primacy of what the Marxists call the economic infrastructure over social phenomena and changes does not fully apply to the French revolutionary turmoil (or to the Nepali *āndolans*).

Otherwise, how does one explain that the French Revolution engendered three different political systems within a short period of time: a republic, the authoritarian Napoleonist monarchy, and, few years later, a constitutional monarchy? Political structures cannot obviously be considered as being determined solely by the economy and by the "social relations of production". In his book, *Interpreting the French Revolution*, which was published in 1978, the French historian François Furet attacks the "revolutionary catechism" that Marxist historians preach. He stresses the continuity between the first revolutionary period and the totalitarian episode, culminating in the Terror. Furet furthermore blames Marxist historians for interpreting the French Revolution as the result of a social and class conflict, and for underestimating the role of politics and ideology. Other historians have even suggested religious causes (the role of Christianity) to explain the expansion of democratic ideals in Europe. They have also stressed the role the shift between Catholicism and Protestantism played in the outbreak of the French Revolution.

One of the most fascinating findings of this series of historical and sociological research is the persistence within the new republican state of old features pertaining to the "Ancient Régime". In France, the first scholar to carry out this long-term structural analysis is unquestionably Alexis de Tocqueville who, in 1856, wrote a key work on the French Revolution, *The Old Regime and the Revolution*. This brilliant intellectual particularly emphasized the continuity between monarchical and republican regimes despite the ideological revolutionary slogans. This approach is still valid when applied to the present period: the typical monarchical manner of exercising French presidential power, for instance, has been highlighted. As for Nepal, a great deal could be written (some works have already been published) about how the Maoists re-appropriated the monarchical structure [**67**].[6] Is "Nayā Nepal" really "New Nepal"? The historiography of the French Revolution may help to answer this question. The matter is of direct concern for political leaders and social scientists working on Nepali contemporary history. It is a crucial issue in these times of a growing divide between politics and civil society.

66. The Maobadi Thermidor

In June 2012, the spilt between the left wing of the Maoist movement and its mainstream historical party, the Unified Communist Party of Nepal (Maoist), UCPN (M), currently headed by Prachanda [and Baburam Bhattarai till 2015], is no exception in communist and socialist world history. The poll-boycotting, hardliner party known as the Communist Party of Nepal (CPN-M), and its leader Mohan Vaidya (alias Kiran), a big figure in Nepali Maoism, have a number of historical antecedents in chronicles of revolutionary movements. In the Soviet Union, just as in Asia, Europe and Latin America, Marxist-Leninist movements are replete with dissent and internecine conflicts between compromising and more radical streams. This has led to internal clashes, assassinations and armed combat.

This reformist and realistic moment is known to historians as Thermidor, following on from the episode in the French Revolution after the fall of Robespierre and of the Jacobins (1794). After a period of massive executions of so-called counter-revolutionaries and of vehement verbal violence, the Revolution suddenly took a more tolerant path, it rejected violence and compromised with other parties. Thermidor is thus seen as a reaction to revolutionary excesses. For post-Trotskyite Marxists, the word Thermidor has retained a derogative meaning. It is the moment in the rise of a revolution when the masses begin to withdraw from active intervention in history and the original leadership of the revolution is replaced by a conservative bureaucracy. In the communist vocabulary, it is a rejection of fundamental Marxist premises, a form of revisionism.

In his book, *Anatomy of Revolution*, which was published in 1939 and is a classic in political science, Crane Briton writes about Thermidorian reactions in all four major political revolutions: the English (1640), the American (end of the eighteenth century), the French (1789-1794), and the 1917

Russian revolution. The author outlines common patterns in these four periods of political turmoil. Behind these different Thermidors, he stresses the restoration of many pre-revolutionary practices and a return to more conservative ideas about social issues. Yet, according to Briton, save the American Revolution, all the others end in political forms akin to dictatorship (Cromwell, Napoléon, Stalin) and in the replacement of a "missionary spirit" to spread revolution by an aggressive form of nationalism.

A number of differences exist between these four revolutions, but the same process has essentially been repeated in Nepal. The struggle between two opposing Maoist factions, the reformist and the extremist, traversed the entire history of the *jan yuddha* (People's War). The major bone of contention concerned the decision by Maoist leaders to join the political pluralistic mainstream in 2005. Kiran was in prison in India at that time, but he was quick to express his reservations. He subsequently condemned the policy Prachanda and Bhattarai had implemented after 2008 in collaboration with the "feudal" and "capitalist" parliamentary establishment. Vaidya's followers deemed particularly degrading the manner in which former Maoist combatants, "the Army of liberation", were integrated in the Nepalese Army. They considered Prachanda and Bhattarai's entire policy a blatant failure and a betrayal of revolutionary ideals. They brandished the threat of a second People's War to promote the rights of the exploited. It will be difficult to reconcile the two rivals, even tactically, after the debacle of UCPN (M) in the November 2013 elections.

It is worth noting that Vaidya denounces the role of the Indian government and encourages a sense of Nepali nationalism to which royalist supporters are sensitive. Let us not forget in this respect that the shift from revolution to social peace has been bitterly criticized by the international communist movement and labelled as opportunistic and counter-revolutionary. It has especially created tension with the neighbouring Communist Party of India (Maoist), CPI (M).

The arguments brought forward by Bhattarai and Prachanda to defend their choice of substituting a military rebellion with a political fight are twofold: the unfeasibility of overcoming the loyalist state armed forces in urban centres and Nepal's geopolitical environment. After ten years of insurgency, the two Maoist leaders, Prachanda and Bhattarai, both concluded that Nepal cannot survive behind a closed boundary to the south, and with no foreign aid or NGOs on its territory. However, this decision must have been difficult to take [cf. also epilogue **88**]. To abandon revolutionary objectives at a time when most of Nepal's rural areas were practically under their control is rather puzzling. The agreement seems to be purely tactical: conciliation between the two previously opposed leaders to the expense of the left wing.

Whatever the case may be, the Thermidorian reintroduction of UCPN (M) in mainstream politics has led former revolutionaries to accept a "bourgeois" order and to compromise their ideals in a somewhat risky manner. They have succeeded in establishing a republic but their years of unproductive rule have altered their image. Marxist activists from UCPN (M) have recently been nicknamed "Cash" in view of the supposedly large amounts of money they have amassed, as opposed to the "Dash" hardliner CPN-M because, unlike most of the other communist parties that use brackets in their name, Vaidya's party uses a dash: Communist Party of Nepal-Maoist.

Interestingly enough, Prachanda's supporters are still called Māobādīs/Maoists. This persistent usage seems to be nothing but political amnesia. After all, UCPN (M) has renounced its armed rebellion and put an end to the revolution. Its members still revere Stalin and Mao Zedong, two of the greatest tyrants of the twentieth century, but they have abandoned the project to conquer the "bourgeois" or "feudal" state with the use of arms. Any new tactical change will be problematical and incomprehensible to most people. What is more, the conclusion of the 1996-2006 civil war blatantly contradicts one of Mao Zedong's strategies about seizing power by encircling the cities with armed peasants. Such a tactic dramatically failed in the hills and the mountains of Nepal.[7]

67. Fervent Revolution

Along the road from Kathmandu to Lalitpur, red lettering on a wall close to a local university campus reads: "'Revolution'; our religion; 'Work', our faith; 'Change', our culture". The slogan is signed ANNISU (R), an ultra-left student organization which aligns itself with the Unified CPN-Maoist. The religious connotation of such a striking declaration reminds us that revolutions —in particular the French and the later communist ones— have not totally severed links with the sacred.

Karl Marx contrasted his scientific approach to reality with the idealistic illusions of religion, which he called 'the opium of the people'. In fact, these connections are still going strong. The ultimate values lying behind the ANNISU (R) slogan evoke a transcendent plane, a supreme reality which has its roots beyond the human realm. The visionary belief in year 0, in a radical shift from the past, has something messianic about it and runs parallel to utopian religions that aim to remake society and start afresh. The very language of rebels is animated by an all-powerful force. And it has religious overtones. During Māobādī public rallies in Nepal, the portraits of Marx, Lenin, Stalin and Mao Zedong are paraded around like divine images. And participants even sometimes look like believers.

It is not uncommon to hear that all modern revolutions are essentially religious in origin, even if they profess to be atheist. In the Western world, the revolutionary spirit has often been compared to the rebellious nature of the early Christian sect, with its emphasis on equality for all before God and its promise of a Kingdom of Heaven. The French writer André Malraux once noticed that the revolution came to play "the role which once was played by eternal life: it saves those that make it" (in *Man's Fate*, 1933). Almost all modern revolutions no doubt aim to liberate individuals from old-religious-based customs governing people's lives. Yet, to fill the room left by religion in the social realm is not an easy undertaking and requires a sound substitute. The path towards secularization is therefore paved with difficulties.

The policy the Māobādīs implemented during the *jan yuddha* armed conflict (1996-2006) in districts under their control was overtly anti-religious. People were forced to forfeit the celebration of the Dasain festival and other Hindu rituals just because the latter are performed by Brahmans or are labelled 'superstitious'. Cultural programmes were introduced instead. Blood sacrifices, which were denounced as 'backward', were also banned. A small number of Hindu temples were vandalized and desacralized. Similarly, some private Christian schools were ransacked and church funds were extorted. This policy nevertheless met with resistance on the ground. Let us not forget that a number of guerrillas were recruited from Janajāti ethnic groups which were used to warding off malevolent spirits and to honouring local gods who are often associated with their territory or land.

Even during this chaotic period, religious symbols prevailed. Pushpa Dahal was often portrayed in the Party's propaganda with kingly features, regally enshrouded, with a divine halo over his head, as if he, in his own way, upholded the Shah dynasty with its deified kings. The cult of martyrs of the revolution, though not entirely new in Nepal's political imagination, also has a sacrificial religious dimension (7,000 Maoists were declared martyrs by Pushpa Dahal's government in 2009), which is common in religions of salvation. The word *mukti* (which in Sanskrit also means liberation, release)[8] was also frequently used in the propaganda.

After the proclamation of the republic, Maoist-led governments adopted a very cautious approach to religious affairs. No frontal attack on the freedom of cults has actually taken place. Successive Prime Ministers, Dahal and Bhattarai, continue to appear at official religious ceremonies, such as Indra Jātrā, or to visit temples. For a while Pushpa Dahal himself was the chairperson of a committee, Extensive Lumbini Development Project, (backed by China) which was set up to develop the Lumbini Buddhist site and to manage its preservation. Admittedly, Maoist state authorities tried to appoint Nepali (Newar) priests to Pashupatināth temple instead of traditional South-Indian Bhattas, but after much protest, they were obliged to abandon the idea.

The 2008-2013 official policy exemplifies a more pluralist vision of religions. Local festivals have been more readily acknowledged than before. Some Maoist leaders have even shown an interest in new Hindu or Buddhist cults stressing the importance of happiness, meditation, and yoga practices, probably in the hope of retaining, among other things, ideological control of this important sector of Nepali society. So far, the secularizing policy has not prevented the state from financing Hindu religious institutions. In short, dialectical materialism has proved to be highly compatible with religious so-called 'idealism'.

The contrast with the French Revolution in these matters is striking. French revolutionaries of the eighteenth century implemented much more radical solutions than in Nepal. Churches were burned, priests pursued and guillotined. A new calendar was adopted, at least for a short period of time, replacing the old Christian one. The year of the execution of the king and the proclamation of the republic was counted as year one. Yet the need for gods in the republic soon re-emerged. The leaders of the revolution strove to found an entirely new cult, the Cult of the Supreme Being, dedicated to reason and ideas inherited from the Enlightenment period. But the introduction of such a secular religion failed and was abandoned some years later. The Chinese Cultural Revolution (1966-1976) also led to violent attacks on traditional religion and its followers. A number of priests were imprisoned. Yet, after these dramatic events, the communist policy adopted a considerably more mellow tone. At present, the Chinese government sees Buddhism and Taoism as integral parts of Chinese culture and guarantees the freedom of cult for everybody (except, it must be added, in Tibet and Sinkiang).

The Nepali Maoist Revolution did not presuppose the total abolition of religious beliefs but its overall loss of relevance to political and social realms. However, the 1996-2006 Māobādī insurrectionary movement was in some ways a 'religious revolution', *dhārmik krānti*, or at least a substitute for it.

68. The Revolutionary Myth

Across the globe, the word 'revolution' is charged with emotion. In France, the 'great' 1789 Revolution has so far been a cornerstone of modern political ideology. The republican regime which was established that year and the Declaration of the Rights of Man and of the Citizen have been raised to the status of a foundational charter of French social values. Similarly, the term is still regarded as sacred in China and Cuba and continues to be a mandatory reference in the official jargon —in spite of the changes and the gradual accommodation of these regimes since their inaugural era. In these models of 'celebratory history', the loss of human lives, summary executions and blind violence that have often accompanied these events are frequently underestimated. Likewise, the link between 'revolution' and totalitarian regime is forgotten.

It therefore comes as no surprise if, in a country where revolution has provoked a major break with a former weakened regime, disagreement over a particular revolutionary sequence (blind violence, for instance) or the alteration of the whole self-glorified process engenders aggressive reactions. Accusations of disseminating a false revisionist history are rife. To the utter despair of historians and social scientists, revolution has become a myth, a legendary story with its heroes and its epic victories, which leaves no room for criticism. Revolutionary creeds rapidly turn to passionate tirades and sometimes blend together with religious beliefs.

The Māobādī People's War was fertile ground for epic constructions and mythologies. In their songs, films, posters and cultural performances, revolutionaries resorted to rudimentary caricatures and over-simplified figures. Feudal landlords, *sāmantī*, were (and still are) portrayed as leeches sucking the blood of the common people. The Congress Party, identified by its four stars, was also stigmatized as one of the main political rival propagating erroneous ideas. By the same token, India has been demonized as the treacherous enemy (*dushman*). This country—so it is said—merely wants to meddle in Nepal's affairs and to 'swallow' it up whole.[9] On the other hand, sympathy for the toiling masses (*garikhāne,* those who have to work to eat) and the pain, *dukha*, of the poor were omnipresent themes. The political target was twofold: to win the hearts of the people by brandishing images and slogans that meant something to them, and to shift the conflict gradually from a traditional caste/ethnic realm to the vision of a class war.

These stereotypes enabled the Maoist Party to stir up patriotic and warlike feelings. The time had come for the people to fight and to support the guerrillas to the best of their capability. Danger was everywhere, not only with the army and police. Reactionary forces were allegedly plotting against the masses and conspiring against the peasantry. This real or imaginary threat has been utilized in a number of revolutions in order to mobilize people and to precipitate the transfer of power to the communists. In this respect, the 'catechism of revolution' (an expression used by the French historian François Furet) and revolutionary propaganda are surprisingly similar from one country to another. In Nepal, an implausible 'Prachanda path' was promulgated with no clear ideological references, yet effectively enough—it was assumed—to rally people's support for the final elimination of the class enemies. The religious content is sometimes explicit: some Māobādī revolutionary songs are called *muktiyuddhaka git,*[10] thus playing on the religious significance of the word *mukti*, "liberation".

The Marxist representation conveyed by these images and performances erase local differences and pre-modern forms of social stratification. It portrays a dichotomous picture of social realities, which oversimplifies much more complex situations. As a matter of fact, the analysis of Nepal's rural hinterlands in terms of a single peasant class undermines the differences that exist from one district to another and even within the same district. Nor is this consistent with the local social morphology that is made up of fragmented social spaces. On a village scale, a study in terms of class tends to overlook client relationships that permeate society. It ignores the traditional sources of power and the role of the "big men", *thulo mānche*. Undoubtedly, the concept of peasant class masks a number of internal conflicting interests.

Criticism of nineteenth-century Marxist theories may be extended to other domains. What is, for instance, the validity of the 'feudal mode of production' concept in a country like Nepal ('feudal' being a notion originally applied to medieval European origin that is less and less used by historians)? It is indeed a reliable notion in parts of the Tarai plains where there is clearly an exploitative land-owning class opposed to tenants and poor labourers. Yet it is inappropriate in most hill regions for, despite the prevalence of Dalit landless families, such a mode of production does not encompass all members of hill society. Local situations show some interplay between powerful pre-capitalist economic formations and capitalistic production relations without establishing any clear dominance of one system over another. The diversity of geographical situations needs to be taken into consideration. Besides, up until very recently, the Nepali state was barely present in many remote mountain or hill districts. Hence any interpretation that stresses state domination over the communal nature of landholding according to the famous 'oriental despotism' model is debatable.

From a more general standpoint, another major difficulty of communism, as Marx, Lenin, Trotsky and Stalin theorized, needs to be mentioned. In his writings, Pierre-Joseph Proudhon (1809-1865), a French thinker and a contemporary of Marx, has emphasised the importance of the local associative level in villages, factories and urban centres. According to him, the requisite for socialism lies in these mutual bonds, this cooperative style of association and organization which provide help and support to individuals. The infra-communal level must be privileged and never sacrificed for the sake of other supra-interests. Otherwise a dictatorship may develop. Proudhon, as such, criticized the authoritarian socialists of his time.

Communists, who stressed what they call "democratic centralism" and the necessity to build a communist state by establishing at its head a proletariat dictatorship, categorically rejected these ideas which are the roots of anarchism. The problem is that these communal bonds, somewhat idealized by Proudhon, already largely exist in a country like Nepal at the infra level despite hierarchical structures. In villages populated by Janajātis, Māobādīs had little to offer to peasants. On the contrary, they themselves had a lot to learn from them in matters of mutuality and togetherness. And, as Proudhon feared, any attempt to construct a communist state in an organic, centralized manner, inevitably leads to despotism, autocracy and alienation, if not the destruction of, precisely, these formal mutual associations. The history of communist states in the twentieth century largely corroborates this statement.

The works of Marx (who violently opposed Proudhon in his works) should not be burned but be rethought and his exegesis should be updated in the light of globalization and modern developments. Similarly, the revolutionary dynamic needs to be revisited. More often than not, the mythology of revolution is a political instrument used to legitimize the power of the ruling communist 'nomenklatura' or to rally the working class to seize state power. One major lesson is to be learnt from this all-too-brief sketch: an unbiased account of events that have unleashed so much passion and where so many political interests are at stake is a perilous yet necessary task.

69. Permanent Revolution

The future of the Maoist movement is currently a popular topic of discussion in Nepal. The defeat of UCPN (M) in the

November 2013 general election and the persisting feud between its two main leaders are likely to marginalise this party for a long time to come or even for good. The sweeping victory of BJP and Modi in India will probably accelerate this movement even if unforeseen secret alliances are not to be ruled out. Moreover, the exclusive Vaidya faction has so far not been able to convince a large number of followers. Their members spurned the last elections in 2013, but they are on their way to becoming part of mainstream politics. There is little chance that the Maoists will take up arms in the near future.

Does this mean that the revolutionary repertoire of the Māobādīs has come to an end? To answer this question, let us recall that, in Marxist-Leninist thought, a revolution is not to be regarded merely as an insurrection, a single battle against official representatives or authoritarian powers that have become an object of hatred and contempt among their own citizens. Revolution is viewed in the long term as a chain of events, a succession of socially forward and backward ("reactionary") phases depending on the fluctuating desires of the social classes and of the respective forces. A revolt or a war of liberation goes through various stages, oscillating between disorder and order, feverish activity and institutional stability. It has its own life cycle, engendering both reversible and irreversible effects.

In Russia, the events of 1905 were a first insurrectionary stage which was quelled by the Tsarist army. It is still seen in Marxist historiography as a failed rehearsal of what finally took place in 1917. That year, the moderate success of the Mensheviks in February was followed by a radical overturn by the Bolsheviks in October. What is more, recent history has shown us that insurrection can also be directed towards communist parties that have betrayed the revolution and have turned it into a corrupt bureaucracy or a dictatorship. The Hungarian and Czech rebellions in 1956 and 1968 respectively, the 1988-1989 Polish Solidarnosc revolution, and finally the fall of communism throughout the Eastern Block countries in 1989 were all movements that sought to overthrow old fossilized Stalinist Marxist-Leninist parties and to re-establish people's freedom that had long been confiscated.

Events never exactly repeat themselves. In Nepal, a large part of the urban middle class joined the Maoists at the time of the 2008 election. In 2013, the same electorate switched to other political parties. The situation, Māobādīs claim, can be reversed once again. In 2007, UCPN (M) secured an agreement from other contesting parties to establish a Republic. It sacrificed its red army of liberation for that cause. Their leaders now have to clarify their next target.

Indeed, according to Marxist-Leninists, revolution never really totally ends. In Communist textbooks, the 1830 and 1848 insurrections as well as the 1871 Paris Commune were the immediate consequences of the glorious 1789 French Revolution. These movements were merely trying to achieve the unfulfilled aspirations from back in 1789. They erupted onto the paved streets of Paris more or less spontaneously on the initiative of local workers, various categories of craftsmen, the 'petite bourgeoisie' and unemployed poor people.

Trotsky, the Russian revolutionary leader, conceptualized the notion of permanent revolution. In his view, revolution must not stop until it meets all its objectives. It has to go on without making a compromise with the national bourgeoisie. 'Capitalist' forces will never address the real social issues that are so fundamental for the workers. In short, 'permanent revolution' is one 'that makes no compromise with any single form of class rule, which does not stop at the democratic stage, which goes beyond socialist measures'. Revolution will 'end only in the complete liquidation of class society'. The whole system has to be eradicated.

Such a warlike and extremist discourse —more in phase with Mohan Vaidya theories than with Pushpa Dahal and Baburam Bhattarai's policies— is not held by all Marxist-Leninists. Some former political leaders, like Stalin, defended a more gradual, step-by-step development of the revolutionary movement, which was more attentive to nationalist issues. The situation is not always 'ripe' for the most disadvantaged popular layers of society to seize state power. The limitations offered by political conjunctures ('concrete understanding of the concrete situation') must be acknowledged. Yet the persistence of riots and revolutionary events that arise in so many developing and poor countries has to be taken into account. These explosions reoccur episodically, progressively losing their impetus, then suddenly reappear. The metaphor of a stream or a flowing torrent, just as much as a thunderstorm, is still used by rebels.

The Māobādī revolution ended a first time in 2006 when its leaders decided on a general cease-fire and joined the democratic stream. It ended a second time in November 2013, with their electoral defeat.[11] Both episodes have to be regarded as society taking revenge over the illusion of messianic politics. They also marked the victory of representative legitimacy over revolutionary legitimacy. However, Marxist-Leninist movements are not about to disappear from the political landscape. Their influence in Nepal dates back a long time and inequalities are still deeply entrenched throughout the country.

70. Violence and Revolution

It is still difficult to carry out a full, balanced appraisal of the ten years of the chaotic People's War that was waged by the Māobādīs from 1996 until 2006. Humanly and economically, it was a total disaster. The loss of lives, the injury, the missing persons, the displacement of populations, the delay in development programmes, the destruction of common infrastructures, the rise in the rate of migration, the negative impact on Nepal's image abroad, and so forth: it is the bloodiest and most tragic episode in the country's recent history. Today, the trauma is still in everybody's mind. Politically however, *jan yuddha* (the People's War) revolutionaries can boast about putting an end to the monarchy and about replacing it with a republic. To boot, they urgently addressed a number of social issues and developed a sense of equality. Are such achievements worth the price that has been paid? To what extent are Maoists responsible for the present divisiveness in the country? This is a hot issue. Clearly, the Maoists' role in post-monarchy politics has proved non-constructive and rather negative.

Violence as a political means is nothing new in Nepal. In the course of the eighteenth and nineteenth centuries, the country was unified by military action and by the conquest of territories. A number of communities lost their autonomy and their resources in this process. The stigma attached to these military annexations still exists today. Likewise, during the turbulent nineteenth century, plots, conspiracies, assassinations were common in the political sphere. In districts, demonstrations of ethnic resistance, messianic uprisings and agrarian revolts took place at regular intervals. In the 1950s, in the aftermath of *bhūmi-sudhār*, the land reform, ethnic violence against upper Hindu caste landlords erupted. The opposing political parties, mostly Congress, also resorted to an armed insurrection to oppose the Shah dynasty in 1950-1951 and in 1961. At that time they used revolutionary rhetoric. In the 1970s, a group of radical communists (known as Jhāpālis, from the name of the district of Jhapa), inspired by the Indian Naxalite movement, launched an armed insurgency in the eastern Tarai. They were forcibly repressed by the Nepali army in 1993. On the whole, violent political actions prevailed over the non-violent Gandhian tradition of *satyāgraha* resistance borrowed from India and concomitantly used to oppose royal autocracy. After 2008, non-violent actions (*dharnā* sit-in protests and hunger strikes, for instance) were frequently undertaken in reaction to the immobilism of successive governments.

The Māobādī People's War differs from these earlier violent movements in its length and in its wide expansion through the country. Guerrillas and armed squads were inspired by dialectical materialism and the glorious example of Mao Zedong's "Long March" in China. They engaged in revolutionary action, under a red banner, with a specific Marxist-Leninist ideology that had been absent from any previous insurrections (save that of Jhāpālis). *Jan yuddha* had clear ethnic and caste overtones but propaganda presented it as a class war. Following Maoist precepts, the ultimate aim was to seize political power by encircling the cities from the countryside and thereby capturing them. Today, the Indian CPI (Maoist) still follows the same line. To understand the People's War we therefore have to refer to the communist credo.

Let us not forget that Marxism is not merely a systematic economic theory, an explanation of capitalist society, and an evolutionist account of history. It is also a theory of revolution based on a vision of class struggle through the ages. To create a new society driven by social justice and ruled by former oppressed classes, a radical break with tradition is needed. The ruling bourgeois or feudal classes have to be fought and eliminated. Engel and Marx saw "force (violence) as the midwife of every old society pregnant with a new one". Violence is necessary if a new society is to be brought forth. Mao Zedong's famous slogan 'Power comes out of the barrel of a gun" is a suggestive addition to this active rhetoric. You cannot make a revolution without killing men just as, so it is said, you cannot make an omelette without breaking eggs. Only then will violence die out and Man will be reconciled with himself, with his fellow men, and with nature. Communist political leaders are thus engaged in a glorification of action. For Marx, revolutions were the "locomotives", the driving forces of history. The romantic fascination with revolution has attracted a large number of people over the last decades; it stems from this violent and messianic message.

Combatants are transfigured through the exaltation of revolutionary deeds and exploits. As expressed by the Māobādī slogan: "One year of *jan yuddha* equals thirty years of a democratic system". By fighting so-called "class enemies", its armies and its police, guerrillas understand the real function of the bourgeois state and the essence of politics. "Only in those violent periods does history show its true face and dispel the fog of mere ideological, hypocritical talk"

(Hannah Arendt, *Between Past and Future,* 1961). Violent revolution is therefore the main aim of the proletarian and peasant revolution. All tactical and momentary alliances, whether with Dalits or Ādivāsīs, are subordinate to this end, though they can be used to accentuate the inner contradictions of the social system and to sharpen polarities at some particular moment in the struggle. By the same token, violence is not merely justified by counter-revolutionary acts and the need to fight them. Armed rebellion is the core of the communist political doctrine.

This vision of a society divided into antagonistic classes is in complete opposition to the realties of Nepali society, its deeply grounded customs, its hierarchical rules, its fragmented social space, its patron-client links running from top to bottom, the importance of religion, the everlasting pre-modern features in rural areas. Recent studies have revealed how, from east to west, Maoist fighters were never understood by most of the Nepali population.[12] The traditional village doxa is based on different rules. Communist leaders therefore had either to accommodate local mentalities once and for all or to institute a dictatorship in order to overcome resistance and to achieve their 'glorious' vision of society. There were no other alternatives.

Notes

1 Gérard Toffin, "Religion et politique au Népal (1951-2010)", in C. Jaffrelot et A. Mohammad-Arif (eds.), *Politique et religions en Asie du Sud. Le sécularisme dans tous ses états?* Paris, Éditions de l'EHESS, collection Purusharta, 2012, pp. 117-135.

2 For instance: Seira Tamang, "Legalizing State Patriarchy in Nepal", *Sinhas,* 5, (1), 2000, pp. 127-156.

3 Admittedly, one can find in Karl Marx's early (1850s) writings references to a specific so-called "Asiatic mode of production" which tried to accommodate India and China's own particular agrarian features in his grandiose world history. Yet the data (mostly excerpts from British colonial reports) on which this notion rests are themselves highly debatable. Similarly, the Chinese Maoist revolution challenged the necessity to undergo a capitalist stage before reaching communism. Nevertheless, the communist vision of history is still structured round a

progressive framework and defends the idea of ineluctable laws of social progress.

4 T. Louise Brown, *The Challenge to Democracy in Nepal*. London: Routledge, 1995. G. Katsiaficas, *Asia's Unknown Uprisings*. vol. II. Oakland: PM Press, 2012. Madhav Paudel, "Patan Mukta Kshetrako Ghoshanā", in *Nawayug* (in Nepali), March 2014, pp. 57-58.

5 The proper Nepali word for bureaucracy is *karmacārītantra*.

6 Cf. for instance, M. Lecomte-Tilouine, "Regicide and Maoist Revolutionary Warfare in Nepal: Modern Incarnations of a Warrior Kingdom", *Anthropology Today*, 2004, 20 (1), pp. 13-19.

7 On Nepali Maoism, the book by Michael Hutt (ed.), *Himalayan People's War: Nepal's Maoist Rebellion*. Bloomington, Indiana University Press, 2004, is worth quoting. In this volume, the chapter by Philippe Ramirez, "Maoism in Nepal; Towards a Comparative Perspective", pp. 225-242, is important. See also Deepak Thapa & Bandita Sijapati, *Kingdom under Siege: Nepal's Maoist Insurgency*. Kathmandu, Zed Books, 2004, and Judith Pettigrew, *Maoists at the Earth, Everyday Life in Nepal's Civil War*. Philadelphia, University of Pennsylvania Press, 2013. This list is not exhaustive.

8 One of the several connotations of *mukti* in the Indian philosophical context refers to "liberation from religion".

9 The 'unofficial blockade' imposed by Delhi against Nepal after the promulgation of the constitution in 2015 supported this argument. Some members of BJP Hindu nationalist party still dream of an Akhand Bhārat, "Intact India" (or undivided India) covering Bangladesh, Pakistan and Nepal.

10 Anne de Sales, "Remarks on Revolutionary Songs and Iconography", *EBHR*, 2003, 24, pp. 5-24.

11 The recent departure of Baburam Bhattarai from UCPN (M) to form his own party is another important moment in the breakdown of the Nepali Maoist movement in the post *jan yuddha* war.

12 For instance, Pustak Ghimire, "The Maoists in Eastern Nepal: the Example of Khotang, in M. Lecomte-Tilouine (ed.), *Revolution in Nepal. An Anthropological and Historical Approach to the People's War*. Oxford: Oxford University Press, 2013.

CHAPTER

11

Predicament of Democracy

In the past two decades Nepal has undergone sweeping political changes. Contrary to a commonly held belief, the fall of the monarchy and the advent of a republic have not been the main detonator. The monarchy self-destroyed on 11 June 2001 during the Narayan Hiti slaughter. Ten members of the royal family, including the king and his two sons, were killed during this familial tragedy that was fomented within the palace itself and perpetrated by the Crown Prince Dipendra. This assassination considerably weakened the monarchic institution. In May 2006, a popular movement, Āndolan II, directed against an over-confident royal successor, simply completed the work and ousted the Shah royal family from the political game. The decisive moment had in fact occurred ten or more years earlier, in April-May 1990, at the end of the first national movement, Āndolan I, which forced King Birendra to restore a multi-party policy and freedom of expression, both of which had been confiscated in 1960 by his father, King Mahendra.

The sudden advent of democracy in 1990 and its consolidation in 2006 have drastically changed the political landscape and the faces of the country. All of a sudden, different sectors of society became mobilized.[1] In Nepal the common people who had been silenced during the thirty years of an oppressive regime started to speak up, to express their grievances and expectations. Dozens of newspapers were launched, associated with all types of political current, but predominantly with the left and the extreme left wing.

They were sometimes short-lived but they boosted a sudden and decisive freedom of speech. The variety and the number of media exploded. About 350 FM radio stations started broadcasting all over Nepal, even from the Tarai, and sometimes in local languages. More than ten TV channels, most of them private, were set up. A new generation of journalists was born.

After so many years of enduring a monolithic cultural policy favouring Hinduism, the Nepali national language, the unity of the country under the iron rule of the Shah Parbatiyā dynasty, the voices of the myriad ethnic groups, castes, and cultures of the country suddenly resonate everywhere, in all directions, sometimes in an autistic way. Freed of all their authoritarian bonds, women are claiming their rights, Dalits are expressing their subjugated dramatic conditions, and Janajāti are asserting their identity and demanding proper recognition in the country. Madhesī have taken longer to lay claim to their rights but since 2006 they have taken central stage. This freedom of expression and the mobilisation of people that has accompanied this emancipation have been the most transformative features of the last two decades.

Government policies and local and international NGOs have suddenly become all-inclusive, backing marginalized people and striving to empower them. Inclusiveness, guaranteeing proportional representation of the different categories of people at all levels of authority and administration, is now the new political mantra. This motto has captured people's imagination in an incredible manner. Following the path that India has long since taken, the first measures in favour of affirmative action were adopted in Nepal. At present there is an air of egalitarianism in the country. To be fair to the Maoist movement, one must acknowledge the part the slogans and actions of its activists played in accelerating the implementation of this policy in the period after 2006. Nevertheless, international movements and human rights groups have also largely disseminated these ideas. These associations have exerted their influence through the continuous foreign aid and assistance they provide to Nepal.

The results were not long in coming. To take the 2008 elections, which were won by the Maoists, one third of the 601 members of the Constituent Assembly were elected from Janajāti groups, another third from Madhesīs. Forty-nine Dalits were elected (a little less than their share of the population) and women amounted to 33 per cent of the total number of parliamentary seats.[2] It has so far been the most inclusive House in Nepal's history. These three groups obtained slightly lower yet honourable scores in 2013. Both these Houses stand in stark contrast to the less representative parliaments elected during the 1990-1999 period which enhanced the over-representation of men and upper Hindu castes. For instance, only one Dalit was elected in 1991 and none in 1994 or 1999.[3]

Though the 1990 movement operated major positive change in the country, the process went rapidly off the rails. Within a few years, Nepali politics was hijacked by intra-party battles — which were incomprehensible to the public— by shady agreements between leaders, by the clientele system within parties, and by the general paralysis of public action. It was a time of despair, upheaval and regression. Violent communalist and separatist movements threatened the unity of the country. Within the parties, traditional hierarchies, patronage links, intestine conflicts were jeopardising the democratic trend. Pseudo-political arguments only served as a cover for personal rivalries. The Nepali people felt that they had gone back to the pre-democratic period. Leaders and their dependents behaved no differently from the royals and their clique. Civil society sought to disentangle itself from politics and to find its way on its own.

National elections took place in 1991, 1994, 1999, 2008 and 2013. However, it bears noting that no local election has been held since 1997. This discrepancy is highly significant. The gulf between central government in Kathmandu and the realities of the provinces far from the capital is a key impediment to the country's development

[83] and a major obstacle that the young Nepali democracy has to overcome. Sujeev Shakya, an economic expert, asserts: "Kathmandu has been Nepal's political and economic center, leading to a disconnect with the population outside the valley".[4] How is a federal constitution to be built in these conditions?

It is this failure that is the focus of this chapter. The political fiasco has led to a gradual atomisation of society between rival and exclusionary groups. Communalism, as stirred up by Maoists, and what I call partocracy (not oligarchy) seem to me to be the two main causes of this general collapse. The country has also suffered from the absence of responsible, broad-minded, trustworthy leaders, like Nehru or Ambedkar in India.

The essays included here are rather unconventional. They go far beyond the day-after-day chronicle of political events and statistical data on which political scientists usually rely. They address more fundamental issues about equality, republicanism, secularism, and have more to do with the philosophy of politics than with empirical political science. However, the last four pieces try to capture more closely and more directly Nepali political realities. They put forward some reflections on the course of the events and on the decisions that have recently been taken. For further information about the Māobādīs and Madhesī rebellions, the reader is invited to proceed to the epilogue [91] for an overview of the events.

71. Freedom and Equality

In her fascinating and particularly sharp account, *On Revolution* (1963), Hannah Arendt opposes two distinct trends in revolutionary uprisings and events. The first one that focuses on freedom is directed against tyrannical and authoritarian power. The second, mainly concerned with equality among men, aspires to address social questions and to completely change society. The first trend, typified by the American Revolution, strives to divest repressive governments of legitimacy and to overthrow governments that no longer satisfy the people's wishes.

The second trend, more characteristic of the French Revolution, rests on an abstract notion of general sovereignty and intense compassion towards the poor and deprived categories of people. Although some form of violence is justified in both cases, terror and excessive passion are more likely to burst forth from the second. Arendt quotes the words of Francis Bacon: "The rebellions of the belly are the worst". Resentment, greed and vengeance ultimately lead to the misuse of power. According to the author, total egalitarianism leads to single-party dictatorship and terror. It "devours its own children".

It is tempting to apply this dualistic model to the post-1990 political landscape in Nepal. The upheavals during Āndolan I and II were mainly directed against authoritarian royal power which appeared to be more and more of an oddity in the new international democratic environment and no longer corresponded to the aspirations of the masses, mainly urban educated people. The Maoist *jan yuddha*, however, intended to proceed with a more radical transformation of society and to experiment its ideas in areas directly under its control and administration. Māobādī revolutionaries sought to go beyond the structure of the political realm; they wished to intervene in the private sphere and to inculcate new principles in people's minds. The changes they imposed in religious matters illustrate these concepts. Māobādīs were attempting to bring about the birth of a new world dominated by the impoverished masses. Yet their reticence towards the freedom of press and pluralism within their own party testifies to an inner conflict, which is intrinsic to their doctrine, between freedom and equality.

If one accepts these two opposite extremes, then the endless discussions between leaders of political parties, their incoherent conclusions and the delays in writing a Constitution are easier to understand. Behind each specific political issue lies deep confrontation between two different visions of Nepali society. For Māobādis, the establishment of a republic was a first step towards a total reformation of Nepali society. For the other political forces, such an institutional shift was an ultimate concession to an old, outdated social structure that needed to be reformed to fully satisfy modern requirements in terms of environmental issues and social justice. These reformist political forces, more pluralist than the first, focus on defending the freedom of individuals. Two different, mutually exclusive visions of the future therefore clash with each other on the country's political scene. The predicament of Nepal's current political situation derives from this confrontation.

The situation is of course more complex. The opposition between freedom and equality is not as marked as affirmed by Arendt. Twentieth-century revolutionary movements cannot be reduced exclusively to fighting for equality. The upheavals that overthrew communist regimes in Eastern Europe were clearly a combination of the two. Similarly, the current transnational notions of human rights derive in many ways from egalitarian notions. In Nepal, non-revolutionary leftist activists have accepted the pluralist viewpoint of a democratic regime and have become openly reformist parties without forsaking their concern for the poorest and the downtrodden.

Hannah Arendt's book has been the object of attacks by Marxists and has been denounced as having a politically pro-Western bias. According to communists, freedom is a 'bourgeois' notion that is less important than overthrowing the capitalist upper classes and replacing them by the poor masses. Like all pure Marxist-Leninist communists, Nepali Māobādīs have difficulty in admitting democracy, i.e. majority rule. They basically view such a regime as a 'bourgeois' individualistic institution. Freedom comes second in their revolutionary objectives. Yet the actual history of the course that revolution has taken clearly gives credit to Arendt's account. It is attested to by the tangible realities in diverse countries. In China, the Soviet Union, and in Cuba, political transformations have led to a single-party communist dictatorship, a ban on democratic freedom, and censorship.

The antinomy between individual rights and the takeover of power by a Marxist political party that identifies itself with the masses is all too significant in Nepal. The problem is that the eighteenth-century American Revolution, which is seen as exemplary (up to a certain point) by Arendt, occurred in a freshly populated state living in relative prosperity, with few old, established inequalities and no deep class divide. It even initially led to a restoration of the monarchy. The upheavals and rebellions in Nepal, much like the French Revolution in 1789, erupted in a country with a long-established tradition of inequality and hierarchical order, whether feudal or monarchical. The opposition between the monarchy and the republic therefore became the major line of battle.

Now that the kings have been dethroned, a long path still has to be travelled before totally riding of the old entrenched structures of subordination and dependency. In its actual political sense, equality itself is a new notion in South Asia, and is even more recent in Nepal than in India. I argue that today the most dangerous option Nepal could choose would be *tabula rasa politics*, with the intention of rebuilding the country from scratch. Experience from elsewhere has taught us that this always paves the way to major disaster.

72. The Lost Treasure of Republicanism

In the wake of a massive popular uprising against royal autocracy and the surge in new political forces (namely Māobādī), Nepal was declared a Republic (*ganatantra, ganatantrātmak*) in May 2008. For the nation, this event which was celebrated throughout the country primarily signified the fall of the monarchy and the start of a new era in the history of Nepal. Yet the word "republic" is a rather broad, vague concept that calls for reflection and clarification. It is worth noting first of all that most states (136 out of 193) in the world lay claim to this appellation. Among Nepal's immediate neighbours within the Himalayan range, India, Pakistan, Bangladesh and China are officially referred to as Republics. Pakistan is an Islamic Republic just as Iran is, with both countries applying Sharia religious law; what is more, the latter is governed by a clerical figure. Today "Republic" does not therefore necessarily rhyme with secularism and does not inevitably entail a separation of religion from the political realm. Paradoxical as it may sound, it may even be synonymous with enduring religious sanctions in all sectors of life.

Furthermore, "Republic" does not necessary imply freedom of press, uncensored Internet, the separation of law from political power, and egalitarianism. The People's Republic of China and the Socialist Republic of Vietnam, neither of which are regarded as fully democratic regimes, may be mentioned in this respect. A republic, which theoretically implies *the appropriation of the power by citizens*, can even exist alongside a single-party system and the rule of a minority. A republic can therefore become a dictatorship. And lastly, democracy and kingship are not mutually exclusive. The United Kingdom is a vivid example of a parliamentary kingdom, which is well known for its deep-seated democratic political tradition.

Consequently, the term "republic" means little on its own today. It is an "empty word", shifting in definition according to each state's history and its particular political physiognomy. There are as many republics as so-called republican countries. What is more, republicanism is not *ipso facto* synonymous with good governance. It does not preclude excess power on the part of one party or social class and the use of state power for the exclusive benefit of politicians. In other words, *Homo republicanus* has become a mythical creature.

Nevertheless, the term prevails and is constantly referred to in an almost sacred manner in France ("Freedom, Equality, Fraternity" is the French Republic's motto) as well as in the United States of America. The massive rally on 11 January 2015 in Paris after the terrorist attacks was commented on by several observers as being a vivid effusion of a grass-rooted republican spirit beyond any class, religion, or other forms of belonging [**42**]. As far as Nepal is concerned, the authorities have more importantly decided to associate this term with the adjective "democratic", *lokatantra*. This has changed everything, paving the way for a particular type of outward-looking republic associated with freedom and a balance of power. The path is therefore open to a constructive and inclusive political regime.

Two main types of historical model stand out. The ancient Roman pattern at work for centuries immediately before and after CE is said to be the original system. The word "republic" itself comes from the Latin *res publica*: "public matter" that is, common interest. It used to designate a non-monarchical regime where political leaders were not chosen by hereditary rule but through recurring election. The emphasis was on civic virtue and public concern. It was in fact an oligarchy controlled by the main patrician families of the Roman state. As in the ancient Greek democracy, women and slaves were not allowed to vote. The French Republic, which was proclaimed in 1789 after the Revolution, was plainly inspired by this Roman model but in a different democratic, egalitarian, secular manner. Yet it took some time before a total opposition between republic and monarchy (or empire) was enforced. In 1804, Napoleon Bonaparte declared himself the Emperor of the French Republic.

The second lesser-known model flourished in the tumultuous mediaeval cities of northern and central Italy (Sienna, Florence, etc.) from the twelfth century onwards. This was based on the communal autonomous power of small cities that wielded authority over the surrounding countryside. Power lay mainly in the hands of aristocratic families, priests and *populo grasso*, affluent traders, who gathered together in advisory councils and assemblies. This system was based on township and was greatly opposed to the seigniorial system that was synonymous with autocracy. Though based on royalty, the small medieval Malla kingdoms of the Kathmandu Valley (especially Lalitpur with its Pradhan king-makers) are reminiscent of this system. Aside from the king's authority, they devolved some powers to the local people. In 1871, the revolutionary commune of Paris resuscitated this ancient ethos of self-governing bodies in a much more radical and populist form. In her writings on politics, the philosopher Hannah Arendt emphasizes this grass-roots system based on deliberating councils as well as on the people's almost full and direct participation. For her, such a paradigm of non-dominance and freedom is a precondition of democracy and the lost paradigm of republicanism.

What about the word *ganatantra*? It refers to an ancient South Asian institution that is documented mainly in Buddhist and Jaina sources and which is said to have existed before CE in ancient India, mainly in the Gangetic plains, in the form of non-monarchical sovereign bodies. There are divergent interpretations of such a system, which are unfortunately often permeated with current political motives. There is even some contestation as to what the word *gana* refers to exactly. Most historians, however, suggest that the term has nothing to do with European Republican models. Whatever the case, such a system has always been marginal in comparison with kingship.

In my opinion, the choice of the world "republic" in Nepal in 2008 pertains mainly to the symbolic sphere. As emphasised at the time in some newspapers, it makes (dubious) reference to the French Revolution and to the subsequent creation of the French Republic. It was defined primarily in opposition to the monarchy. Urgency lay in removing an unpopular king and in restoring a parliament at the heart of governance. The rest —i.e. the devolution of power to the people, the core of republicanism— is still rather vague. The creation of a new regime represented a violent rupture in the terminology. Two daily newspapers, (one in English, the other in Nepali), *Republica* and *Nagarik*, even took their names from the republican repertoire. The problem is that the code of rights and duties, which is vital for a Republic, has not yet been adopted within the political sphere. Furthermore, parliament has so far remained an extremely weak institution that is unable to lay down the law of the land. "Words, words, words", as Shakespeare says (*Hamlet*, 2,2). It is not that easy to give substance to the terms used. The building of a "Democratic Republic", *Loktāntrik Ganatantrātmak,* still has a long way to go.

73. What is a Secular Nation?

In a book published in 1865, *When one travels*, the French novelist and litterateur, Théophile Gautier (1811-1872), speaks of his surprise at seeing a procession headed by a Catholic priest walking under a red canopy, a ciborium in his hands, followed by assistant priests, a church boy ringing a bell, with armed soldiers in tow. All along the procession route, people knelt down and recited prayers. This religious march was staged to deliver the last sacraments to a dying person. T. Gautier saw this ceremonial display in the streets of Caen, a town in Normandy, and he expressed his astonishment: in the mid-nineteenth century, such a spectacle, he remarked, was already a rare sight in the streets of the capital. He wrote: "In Paris, religion does not take the risk of leaving sanctuaries or churches. We have long been unaccustomed to seeing such external manifestations of ritual life."

This remark throws light on the rapid (yet also chaotic) process of secularization in the capital in nineteenth-century France, almost sixty years after the Revolution, and on the persistent hostility of French Republican forces towards the Catholic religion. However, the comparison with Nepal is even more illuminating! Throughout Hindu and Buddhist Nepal, public space, whether urban or rural, has so far been widely used for religious processions. Cohorts of Nepalis march in ceremonial order, in line or in corteges, in the streets during funerals, weddings, *bratabandha*, various *vrata*s, and on so many other similar occasions. At festive times, people take part in a ritual march or watch a divine parade in public space which is usually devoted to secular activities.

Interestingly, what can still be seen in Nepali cities (and in most Indian towns as well), was common in pre-revolutionary times in Catholic-dominated France and during the whole of the nineteenth century in its provinces and rural areas. These collective, processional performances in the public space have slowly declined in Europe over the ages. They have almost totally disappeared today, except in some Southern-European Catholic countries (Italy, Spain, Portugal), which are more resistant to the process of secularization, and on some rare and special occasions such as official visits by the Pope. Protestants in northern and central Europe were the first to put an end to these practices and to turn to an interiorized form of religion.

The process I would like to stress here is precisely the *privatisation* of religion. In North America and Western Europe, this phenomenon is recognised by sociologists as a central process to the development of modernity. In a word, religion in these countries has increasingly become a matter of individual choice rather than of social obligations. The situation is radically different in South Asia. In Nepal, religion is still a public act performed in public. Rituals and ceremonies are performed in view of everybody and of the gods whose abodes are scattered throughout the public space. Rituals are put on display; they are not only part of the family but of society at large. There is no distinction between private and public affairs in these matters. In the whole of South Asia, including Nepal, religion is in fact still a holistic subject. Personal faith is still encompassed by widely shared communal values regarding morals and social status.

Making religion a private domain implies the separation of the transcendental realm from other spheres related to the life of a country, including its politics. The streets belong to the citizens and their representative organizations, not to devotees and followers of a particular religion. The same logic has recently led French authorities to ban ostensible religious signs expressing a person's sense of belonging to a specific faith, such as the hijab, the Islamic scarf (but also the Christian cross) in schools. In sociological terms, this privatisation of religion is closely associated with both *secularization*, i.e. the process by which religious values are losing ground in society, and with modernisation. However, the term secularization insists more on the decline of religious beliefs and practices, whereas privatisation refers more to a change in the way one expresses one's beliefs and practices.

Secularism, a term coined in England in the nineteenth century, has yet another meaning. It involves two basic prescriptions. The first is the strict separation of the state from religious institutions (very few countries have achieved this goal). The second is that people of different religions and beliefs are equal before the law. Secularism is therefore more a political concept, such as democracy (to which it is closely related), and is related to the proper governance of a country. In Nepal today, it is associated more or less with minority rights. In contrast, secularisation is more a sociological word, focusing on the position of religion in society. All these terms need to be set apart to avoid confusion in debates and any misunderstandings.

Unfortunately, the common meanings of these words are not totally distinct. The connotation of the word secularism sometimes overlaps with what is meant by secularization. Both terms ultimately lead to the withdrawal of religion from public life even when seen through a South Asian lens. In Westerners' eyes, Nepal is everything but a secular country. It is difficult to understand how a country where religion is still all-pervading and where the political realm is so overloaded with religious symbols can be called "secular". Similarly, how secular can a country be where most offices remain closed for weeks during two major Hindu festivals, Dasain and Tihār, a period during which most people are busy making offerings to the gods. All in all, the proclamation of Nepal as a "secular state" in 2006 has so far had no visible effect, save the abolition of kingship, and some changes in festive calendars as well as in some judicial matters. Religion, the opium of the masses according to orthodox Marxists, remains a crucial element of Nepali self identity and social life.

74. The Reign of Brahmans

The fall of the Ranas in 1951 brought about a significant reshuffle of the political elite. Hill Brahmans (Bāhuns) in particular, who in former decades mostly played a secondary role or were limited to religious positions, suddenly extended their influence throughout the political centre and became the main competitors for leading functions. The factual work of Joshi and Rose, *Democratic Innovations in Nepal* (1966), readily attests to this. Over the years, Ranas progressively disappeared from government cabinets. Bāhuns formed the overwhelming majority of ministers and Prime Ministers during the post-democratic period, 1951-1960. They were at the forefront of the political scene, in full control of the state. The reestablishment of royal authority in December 1960 opened a long thirty-year interval during which, as in ancient times, Kshatriyas/Thakuris kings and their co-caste affiliates returned to power. Yet, once more, the instauration of a democratic regime in April 1990 was accompanied by the arrival of Bāhun leaders in the political arena and the persisting influence of a limited number of Kshatriya families. The same phenomenon occurred after 2006 in the wake of the abolition of the monarchy. This situation still prevails. The time of Ranarchy is over, but we have entered the reign of Bāhuncracy.

This is not an epiphenomenon but a solid piece of evidence. During the three parliamentary elections held during the period 1990-1999, the representation of hill Brahmans was proportionally three times greater than their share of the population.[5] In fact, Bāhuns are not only the leaders of most of the leading political parties, from Nepali Congress to Communist CPN-UML, not to mention the Maoists, but they exert a form of monopoly on entire pivotal sectors of public life, at key posts, such as in justice and journalism. They dominate political, judicial and media sectors. Only the army lies outside their sphere of influence. Although they constitute a mere 12.2 per cent of the population (2011), they control a large part of the state structure and only share their power with Chetris, Newars, and, increasingly, with Tarai political leaders. They dominate all factions even within important political parties. This fact is well-known among Nepalis and has provoked a violent reaction, especially within Ādivāsīs/Janajāti ethnic groups. The fight against what they call in Nepali *bāhunvād*, the reign of the Bāhuns, has become one of their slogans. From 1990 onwards, this recrimination became one of the bitterest leitmotifs in the political sphere. The notorious book by Dor Bahadur Bista, a Kshatriya himself, *Fatalism and Development*, published in 1991, and its accusation regarding Brahmanism, must be viewed in this context.

These are indeed considerable changes when we bear in mind the previous Rana and Shah period. In Nepal, power was traditionally held by the Kshatriya Hindu *varna* and its highest subgroup: the Thakuris. In the western and central hills, the heads of the various kingdoms were all Kshatriyas and belonged to different royal dynasties. In the Kathmandu Valley, royal power was the monopoly of a Malla lineage, which originally derived from Jayasthiti Malla in the fourteenth century. During its first phase, the post-unification period was characterised by violent internal fights between different Chetri clans, especially Thapa and Pande, under the arbitration of the Shah Thakuri family from Gorkha. From 1846 onwards, a lower-ranking Kshatriya family, the Ranas, seized power and became the *de facto* rulers of Nepal till 1951. During the entire post-unification period, the nobility, *bhārādārs*, belonged to Kshatriya families and their allies. Locally, power has long been in the hands of heirs to royal dynasties. In many places, the situation still persists, at least symbolically. The ten-day long annual celebration of the pan-Nepali Dasain festival in autumn is a testimony to this resilience.

The political predominance of Kshatriyas was in keeping with ancient Hindu Dharmashastra texts which reserve army posts and sovereignty for members of this *varna*, whereas religious authority, teaching, the function of domestic priest and servants to the gods, are set aside for the Brahman *varna*. In the classical Indian system, the latter is superior to the former. If a king were to kill or imprison a Brahman, he would be committing a grave sin. Louis Dumont, the French sociologist, a pioneering figure in the anthropology of caste, underlined this hierarchical dichotomy. In his terms, the disjunction between ritual *status* and political and economic *power* is one of the main features of the overall caste system. Power is subordinate to status and the ranking of caste is religious in nature. Though this disjunction has been critically addressed by a number of authors, it remains a useful concept when analysing the caste system at a theoretical level.

The replacement of the Thakuri/Kshatriya elite by Brahman leaders after 1951 is of paramount importance and worthwhile discussing. It blurs the traditional dichotomy: Brahmans still hold the highest religious functions but they have combined this ancient occupation with political power. Admittedly, the same families do not hold both functions and in some cases (Maoist, UML) Bāhun leaders refer to themselves as atheists or agnostics, and are very liberal in religious matters. Despite this, they both come from the same caste. These situations sometimes occurred in ancient India (Brahman rulers are not unknown) but the political landscape of contemporary Nepal is marked by a change in scale; the appropriation of power by Bāhuns is rather systematic. The departure of the Ranas and Shahs has created a vacuum that has been filled by Brahmans.

From a sociological standpoint, Brahmans exercise both their traditional religious *authority* according to the old religious pattern and political *power* from which they were excluded in the past. Whether they seized power by force or whether they were naturally inclined to usurp Kshatriyas because of their high-ranking position, superior standard of education, ability to debate and to command people, is a subject of debate. Whatever the case may be, the new configuration deviates from old patterns. It is a conjunction between old collective structures of authority and more individual forms of power, which is achieved thanks to personal charisma. The Brahmans have thereby accumulated ancient schemes of hierarchy and modern forms of power.

This growing concentration of political power and ministerial functions is obviously prejudicial to democracy. It implies a perpetuation of caste discrimination and unequal access to power. The public debate is therefore limited to a small elite that is rooted in traditional hierarchical structures. The rest of the population, discriminated groups and various ethnic groups are kept away from the main centres of power. They merely play a tactical role of light reinforcements, as was the rule during the Panchayat period under the aegis of the Shahs. A tiny privileged elite has confiscated the power.

This portrayal would be incomplete without mentioning the emergence of a new class of highly educated persons in a vast array of different, mostly non-government (engineers, professors, doctors, lawyers, etc.) fields. Many have been educated at top private schools in Nepal and have obtained their degrees in Europe, the USA or Australia. They often already have a working experience in these countries and have developed a global mindset which enables them to analyse situations from multiple perspectives. They come from various social horizons, including Janajāti groups (Newars, Gurungs, Magars, Rais, Limbus, etc.) and today they form a cluster of excellence which is eager to play a growing role in the young Nepali republic. For some time now they have represented an alternative to the reign of Hindu upper castes and they will no doubt challenge the traditional political elite. The problem is that the boom in higher education is still driven by the younger generation's desire to leave Nepal and to aspire to a better life in other parts of the world. Most students who go abroad to pursue their university education never come back to Nepal.[6]

75. Monarchy and Communism

At first glance, monarchy and communism are diametrically opposed. The first is basically hierarchical, the second—at least theoretically—is the ultimate form of egalitarianism.

In the first system, a person or a hereditary family rules over the state, while in the second, political power supposedly lies in the hands of the people. However, this is only true on paper. In practice, as the twentieth century has clearly shown, these two forms of government often converge. Stalin's regime was much more authoritarian than many monarchies in the world have ever been, and North Korean communist leaders have often been referred to as communist monarchs. Who can seriously say that Mao Zedong ruled for the good of the people? The Communist Party dictatorship has proved to be the oppression of the nation by a political elite. Communist leaders enforce stricter censorship and a tighter ban on all forms of opposition than any other form of government has ever done.

Nepal, which has been a stronghold of both political systems over the last decades, is a fascinating laboratory for studying the relationship between the two. The Communist Party of Nepal (CPN), which was created in Calcutta in 1949, was originally set up to fight against the autocratic Rana dynasty. In the early democratic years, 1951-60, the Party split into different factions. One of them (Keshar Jung Rayamajhi) officially supported the Shah monarchy and even the 1960 royal coup. For them, India was the Nepali people's principal enemy, and they preferred a "feudal" despotic monarch to any collaboration with democratic political parties which they referred to as "India's brokers". This line (as opposed to Pushpa Lal, another Communist leader) engendered further splits, some pro-Russian, others pro-Chinese, etc. Despite a fight by more radical political lines, stressing the necessity for mass movements against the king, the Panchayat period witnessed a number of confluences and links between Communists and King Mahendra's regime.[7] This was particularly the case during the "Back to Village" Gaon Pharka policy that was launched in 1967. The Communist Party played a large part in this and through it considerably extended its influence. Indeed, the campaign's motto calls to mind Mao Zedong's little red book. In many cases, Nepali communists retained a more anti-Congress position than an anti-royalist stance.

Another period of considerable interest with regards our topic is the beginning of the People's War that was launched by the Maoists in 1996. The rebellion had recourse to Janavādī Krānti (a People's Revolution) to overthrow the monarchy and to establish a "People's Republic". [8] But when examined more closely, the situation seems to be much more complex. At first, Maoist insurgents appeared to be just as keen to eliminate their rivals, the activists of democratic parties (in particularly CPN-UML communists who had agreed to take part in the parliamentary system in 1990), as they were to fight State security forces. As a matter of fact, before 2001, the Māobādīs maintained a theoretical form of opposition to the monarch but refrained from any direct attack on the institution.[9]

The royal authorities' delay in reacting to the Māobādīs insurgency at its outset has been discussed by many a scholar. The royal Nepali government was loathed to employ legitimate force to contain the armed rebellion. There has been some conjecture, whether real or imaginary, about secret links in the upper spheres between the royal palace and the Māobādīs during this period. King Birendra might have seen in these insurgents a means of counterbalancing his democratic opponents—Congress and CPN Communists—in the parliamentary system. At any rate, some form of convergence was clearly worked out.

After the Narayan Hiti slaughter in June 2001, the picture totally changed. The Maoists portrayed King Birendra as a patriotic figure who had been assassinated by American and Indian intelligence agencies. They accused the Gyanendra-Girija clique of being part of a larger conspiracy. They claimed to be the only nationalist forces left from the illustrious patriotic lineage of Prithivi Narayan, Mahendra and Birendra. On their posters and in other forms of propaganda, they portrayed themselves as the rightful inheritors of the dead king's patrimony and legitimacy. As Prachanda assumed a kingly posture, emphasis was given to the cult of personality. Maoists became more openly committed to abolishing the monarchy and to establishing a Republic.

In 2006, the Maoists joined the political mainstream and became a competitive political party [**68**]. Two years later, the monarchy was abolished. The Maoists, filling the vacuum created by the fall of the monarchy, won the first general elections. Naya Nepal, "New Nepal" was one of their slogans with, as its cornerstone, a secular regime instead of the previously enforced Hindu theocracy. Yet, just as during the Shah monarchical regime, the Māobādīs frequently attacked free press as well as other fundamental liberties in the judicial realm; for instance, to prevent any cases of war crimes from being filed against their leaders [**16**].

The last case of conflation dates back to the period immediately preceding the 2013 Constituent Assembly II elections. Surprisingly enough, a tacit agreement was reached at the time between the royalist parties, *rājavādis*, (Kamal Thapa, for instance) and the hard-line Maoist wing led by Mohan Vaidya. Both adopted fierce anti-Indian and extreme nationalist positions. They vehemently accused mainstream political parties of incompetence and corruption. However, Mohan Vaidya's party joined the coalition of small parties which called for a boycott of the elections, whereas the royalists took part in them.

Having seized power, communists and royalists generally express similar reluctance towards the non-official press and oppositional politics. More broadly speaking, they lay emphasis on collective forces and on holistic forms of social bonds rather than on the individual. Interestingly, the Panchayati political structure was based on a supposedly harmonious system of "social classes", *varga,* (women, workers, peasants, the young generation, former soldiers, etc.) which its leaders created as a substitute for the forbidden political parties. These *varga* were abolished in 1990 when the Panchayat system collapsed. In striking contrast, Marxists imagine classes as being in permanent mutual conflict (for the most part, workers opposing the bourgeoisie). Yet, in both cases, whether among royalists or communists, the emphasis is on social groupings. The Loktantrik democratic regime is clearly more individualistically orientated.

76. The Peril of Partocracy

The re-establishment of a democracy in 1990 in the wake of the Āndolan I people's movement drastically transformed the political structure. The shift from a partyless regime to a multi-party system disrupted the political landscape and the internal mechanisms of power. Instead of a single political centre, such as the Royal Palace and its Secretariat during the royalist authoritarian Panchayat administration, two dominant elected forces emerged: Nepali Congress and the Communist Party of Nepal (UML). This was a major turning point. All of a sudden, the political arena turned into a licensed field for open confrontation. Power could be seized by the most widely elected party, thanks to the tactical complement provided by smaller parties, including former *panchāyati* royalists.

What has been the result? May 1990 was the beginning of a decade of political instability, marked by improbable opportunistic alliances (for instance, between royalists and communists) and an incapacity to reform society. One government rapidly succeeded another. The leaders' main objective was their own survival rather than anything else. Political parties did not fight for the common people but appropriated power and state resources. Internal feuds and dissensions within each party became the rule and this jeopardised the creation of a stable majority. Within the Nepali Congress, leaders such as Girija Prasad Koirala, Sher Bahadur Deuba, Krishna Prasad Bhattarai, and Ganesh Man Singh competed with each other. Down in the streets, recurrent violent acts perpetrated by leftist groups, *bandh* (strikes) and *chakkā jām* (traffic blockade), periodically paralysed the national economy and the daily lives of ordinary citizens. Economically, foreign aid proved to be more and more vital to the national economy and a hidden source of additional revenue for political parties. The number of cases of corruption and bribery rose considerably compared to the time of the panchayat system. Indeed, this period calls to mind the hectic 1951-1960 post-Rana decade with the never-ending conflict between democratic forces and the emerging royal power. However, the post-panchayat democratic period has proved much worst in matters of narrow-mindedness, state paralysis, and petty politics.

The shift from a monarchy to a republic in 2008 did not actually change the system which had so far been grounded in fruitless rivalry between parties and in intraparty factionalism. The situation further worsened with the arrival of the Māobādīs and, a little later, of the Madhesī Tarai forces. There were no longer two but four major players competing against each other, most of whom were busy looking after their own interests. Scores of tiny parties arose on the fringes, struggling for a piece of the cake. Constant changes in the government and the self-centred interests of the ruling parties prevented any real development policy from being implemented. This led to poor governance and to a total absence of any vision of the future. Short-term rent-seeking was favoured instead of entrepreneurship and long-term investment. Besides, once in power, egocentric politicians forget the mandate for which they were elected. Despite the elections, the whole system of representation has proved a failure. Election procedures (such as the possibility to stand in two or three constituencies to win a seat) contributed to perverting the system.

The incapacity to address the country's main problems, to reduce inequalities and to better the lot of marginalised groups has engendered considerable disillusion among the population. The success of the Maoist insurgency is rooted in this blatant failure and disillusionment. Yet the inclusion of Maoist leaders in the political mainstream has prompted UCPN-Maoist to become involved in petty politics and in corruption practices in a similar way to other parties. During the four years or so they were in power, the Maoists were incapable of putting an end to the tax havens in the Kathmandu Valley and of transferring power to the districts. They became a constituent part of the overall political game, merely defending their own privileges. Up to now no party or leader has enjoyed a really positive image in the eyes of the public. The political class finds itself distanced from ordinary citizens. Hence the huge trust deficit.

It is not the multi-party system *per se* that has created such a chaotic and undemocratic situation. Political parties are one of the pillars of a democratic regime. They are crucial components in the public debate. It is the misuse of parties that is to be blamed, the prioritization of power over public services, the corruption of political ideals by self-centred motives and personal gain. The future of the country has become continuously overshadowed by the struggle for power and stratagems of political parties. The chosen solutions are those that suit individual interests rather than those that suit the nation.

These impediments are linked to the persistence of a clientalist structure, which is still the basis for distributing power. Only members of patronage networks protected by party leaders can receive state benefits or enjoy opportunities in the various State-regulated sectors. A large portion of the population remains outside these patronage links. Kamal Prakash Malla categorically asserts: "The state of Nepal has always been the stronghold of a few family elites, the so-called *thar-ghar*, and this has not changed".[10] Politics consequently evolve around individuals rather than specific platforms or programmes. The accumulation of these obstacles to democracy generates opposition to change. In many sectors, bureaucrats openly drag their heels over reforming society.

The term *partocracy*, government not for the people but for the parties themselves, seems better suited than *oligarchy* (*alpatantrīya shāsana* in Nepali) to designate the ills of this type of regime. Oligarchy pertains mainly to a non-elected regime with few democratic mechanisms. The current political system has little to do, for instance, with the Rana oligarchy (*Rānā shāsana*), which relied on collusion between a small hereditary political elite and the religious *pandit/purohit*, even if there are some obvious outward similarities are evident.

One of the greatest weaknesses of the current Nepali partocracy is the politicisation of the overall state machinery. The main contentious points in the 2015 Constitution have been almost entirely discussed and settled by the four dominant parties, not by the Constituent Assembly, thereby undermining the sovereignty of the House. In fact, the whole of society and the entire economy are pervaded by political parties. All important government positions are distributed according to party quotas (*bhāgbandā* in Nepali). Civil services therefore enjoy very little independence from political parties. Let us take the Ministry of Foreign Affairs and its representatives on missions abroad. For a long time, a large number of diplomatic posts did not appoint ambassadors because political parties had difficulty in reaching an agreement. In fact, within this Ministry, a non-written rule stipulates that 60 per cent of assignments are political and only 40 per cent professional. And this is no isolated case. Clearly, the Nepali road to a substantive democracy is a long and winding one.

Similarly, the collusion between businessmen and political leaders for their mutual benefit is a major impediment to economic development. Sujeev Shakya, an expert, writes: "More often than not, political bickering gets in the way of project development and unnecessarily prolongs implementation. Media and society at large thus tend to pay more attention to the political reactions to a project than to the economic benefits it may bring".[11] The over-politicization of issues is a major obstacle to the expansion of democracy in Nepal

77. Democracy and Caste

There is a common understanding that caste is antagonistic to democracy. Indeed, the hierarchical universe of the caste system is theoretically at odds with the egalitarian requirements of substantive democracy. It is rather difficult to achieve and even to envisage Article 1 of the French *Declaration of the Rights of Man and of the Citizen*, dating back to August 1789: "Men *are born* and *remain* free and equal in rights", in a country like Nepal where 81 per cent of the population is Hindu and divided into unequal castes based, among other hierarchical values, on the language of purity and impurity. *Homo hierarchicus* appears to be fundamentally opposed to *Homo aequalis*.

This inconsistency between caste and democracy is frequently voiced in Nepal by intellectuals, activists and politicians. In his book, *Fatalism and Development*, Dor Bahadur Bista, an anthropologist, explains the failure of the country in various sectors, its incapacity to turn around its economy and society owing to the prevalence of Hindu values and to the high-ranking position of Brahmans in the hierarchical order. In examining alternative models, Bista points to the egalitarian spirit that prevails among Tibeto-Burman-speaking ethnic groups. In other words, the caste system is seen as *the* evil of Hindu countries, the cause of its weakness, its fateful flaws.

Despite a lack of infrastructure and huge disparities between geographical regions and sectors of the economy, India has succeeded, however, in raising the standard of living of a large part of its citizens and in competing with Western capitalist countries in a number of economic sectors, including even the most sophisticated ones. It is presently emerging as an economic superpower. The largest caste society in the world has successfully transformed itself, though all the while following its own models and upholding its cultural traditions. India has proved that high-growth-rate development is not incompatible with caste, despite the tenacity of the latter in society.

In fact, the Indian democracy has adapted well to the caste system. Thanks to affirmative action policies that have been implemented on the subcontinent since the end of the nineteenth century, Dalits and low castes have benefited from numerous quotas and are much more integrated today in the mainstream social structure. Reservations have conferred social privileges on Dalits and OBCs who have thereby reached a high position in the political sphere, including within the federal state structure. Narendra Modi himself, the new Prime Minister, comes from an OBC caste.

Obviously, positive discrimination has induced a complete change of the political elite, especially in the northern Hindu belt. Low- and middle-caste associations have become extremely powerful and play an important role at regional state level, especially in the North. In other words, caste appears to be a positive instrument for democratising India.

Anthropologists, for their part, have shown that in the absence of a strong (or sound) state, the caste system provides local communities with a form of cohesion. The system counteracts the atomization of society; it links together groups even if it is based on unequal bonding; it introduces commonality and mutuality, especially at a very local, village level. In many rural parts of India and Nepal, traditional Muslims for instance are integrated in the Hindu caste system and they take part in performing rites de passage. They share rituals and beliefs, even if they do not mix. Caste protects them in many ways from further exclusion and stigmatization. It may even be asserted that the weakening of caste links in cities and the strengthening of a religious consciousness have exacerbated the Muslim situation. More often than not, fundamentalist religious identities are more of a threat to democracy today on the subcontinent than caste. In addition, studies by social scientists have demonstrated that the separation of status and power, politics and religion, has helped to establish secularism, and that Hindu traditional notions of *sevā* (service) have positively impregnated the political milieu.

There are, however, some obvious limits to these explanations. First, caste has not entirely changed. It is still an instrument of domination and exclusion in both India and Nepal. Despite the politics of quotas, Indian upper castes remain over-represented in assemblies. In fact, affirmative action has failed to address many forms of inequality in education, health and employment opportunities. In Nepal, affirmative action is still in its initial stages and the situation of the Dalits and the Tarai 'low' castes is worst than in India. The patronage system still prevails in local assemblies and prevents people from freely participating in civic life. Moreover, politics is not the only area where caste prevails; it exerts its influence in daily secular and sacred domains, often invisible to the external observer, and it is much more exclusionary.

As a number of Indian sociologists have warned, discriminatory rights have also proved to be a danger to democracy if they are established once and for all. They transform castes into competitive, corporate, substantialized bodies to the detriment of former linkages in the past. Likewise, reservation legitimizes caste; it strengthens social barriers and inhibits the emergence of trans-boundary forms of belonging. Politics in these affairs is grounded in extremely parochial concerns. In order to cumulate advantages, groups can even compete for backwardness, which is obviously not the essence of democracy.

Be that as it may, it must be remembered that even if caste has changed over time, it has its roots in ancient India, whereas democracy is a new concept in South Asia. The encounter of the two notions and social orders has to be seen as a historical process consisting of the accommodation of two sets of opposed values. Democracy has been vernacularized and integrated in the caste language. At the same time, caste has been transformed into a corporate affirmative group to adapt to the new political game. The relationship between caste and democracy has to be scrutinized at the junction of these two processes.

Notes

1 On the period, the book edited by Sebastian von Einsiedel, David Malone & Suman Pradhan, *Nepal in Transition, From People's War to Fragile Peace*. Cambridge, Cambridge University Press, 2012, is a useful introduction. A more personal and insider account can be found in Manjushree Thapa, *Forget Kathmandu. An Elegy for Democracy*. Delhi: Penguin Book, 2005.

2 Cf Prashant Jha, *Battles for the New Republic*. Delhi, 2014, p. 296.

3 Cf Mahendra Lawoti, "Elections and Under-representation in Democratizing Nepal: Electoral laws, Party System, and Weak Mobilization of marginalized groups.", paper presented to the Fourth Annual Kathmandu Conference on Nepal and the Himalayas, 2015.

4 Sujeev Shakya, "Enleashing Nepal's Economic Potential: A Business Perspective", in Sebastian von Einsiedel, David Malone & Suman Pradhan, *Nepal in Transition, From People's War to Fragile Peace.* Cambridge: Cambridge University Press, 2012, p. 123.

5 Mahendra Lawoti, "Elections and under-representation in democratizing Nepal: Electoral laws, Party system and Patronage, and weak mobilization of marginalized groups", paper presented at the 4th International Conference or Social Science Baha, Kathmandu, 2015. Bāhuns played the most significant role in high-ranking positions in the CPN-UML communist party, four times more than in Nepali Congress (*idem*).

6 Tsering Dolker, "Losing our young", *Nepali Times*, 17-23 July 2015.

7 During the Panchayat period, Nepali Congress often saw communists as Palace agents, *darbārias* (Prashant Jha, *Battles for the New Republic.* Delhi: Aleph Book Company, 2014, p. 15).

8 Krishna Hachhethu, 2008-09 "The Communist Party of Nepal: from insurgency group to a competitive political party", *European Bulletin of Himalayan Research,* 33-44, pp. 39-74.

9 Saubhagya Shah, "A Himalaya Red Herring? Maoist Revolution in the Shadow of the Legacy Raj", in M. Hutt, (ed.), *Himalayan People's War.* Bloomington: Indiana University Press, 2004, p. 208.

10 Kamal Prakash Malla, *From Literature to Culture*. Kathmandu: Himal Books/Social Science Baha. 2015, p. 461.

11 Sujeev Shakya, "Enleashing Nepal's Economic Potential: A Business Perspective", in Sebastian von Einsiedel, David Malone & Suman Pradhan, *Nepal in transition, From People's War to Fragile Peace.* Cambridge: Cambridge University Press, 2012, p. 126.

CHAPTER

12

Nature in Translation

For more than four decades now I have been a member of a team of CNRS researchers who focus mainly on relationships between Man and his environment in the Himalayas. I myself have worked on these subjects in the Kathmandu Valley, in rural as well as in urban zones, in Gulmi and Argha Khanchi districts, in northern Dhading and Nuwakot districts, among others. In addition to this, I have followed the work of other colleagues, geographers, ecologists, climatologists, agronomists, and botanists, who have carried out research on irrigated rice cultivation, natural disasters, glacier melting and other topics. The members of this CNRS research unit do not only investigate the system of production, the rural economy, the use of will edible plants for food, animal husbandry at high altitude, and so forth. The team also strives to understand the way nature is tamed and conceptualized by peasants. Ecological concerns, representations of the nature and environment policies have therefore, ever since my early years in Nepal, been one of my main concerns, and, indeed, one of my areas of expertise.

What are my conclusions? Jack Ives and Bruno Messerli challenged the role Man plays in the degradation of the Himalayan ecosystem.[1] These authors noted that environmental deterioration and the depletion of forest resources are age-old phenomena in the Himalayas. According to these scholars, the climatologic and geological processes at work in these mountains are several times more powerful than any human activity. Some deforested areas have recently been re-colonized by forests, and therefore the effects of numerous landsides are no longer noticeable after several years.

However, today Nepal is threatened by rapid degradation of its ecosystem, both in rural and urban milieus. This assessment is indisputable and is widely shared by the local people themselves. The main determinants of the worsening situation are: climate changes, *jalvāyu parivartan* in Nepali, demographic growth (though this has progressively swung the other way over the last decades) caused by the introduction of modern health care, uncontrolled urbanization, and, here and there, the intensification of modes of production. Deforestation (compensated by the expansion of forests in some areas thanks to community forest user groups) and the decline in crop diversity for the profit of commercial and cash crops also represent a danger for sustainable livelihood systems. However, some areas are more affected than others. My own research in rural areas of the Kathmandu Valley shows that the overuse of chemical fertilisers over the past decades has damaged the soil. These factors have a serious negative impact on ecosystems.

The extreme dependency of most Nepali rural societies on environmental resources and the high risk of naturals disasters (landslides, floods, earthquake, glacier lake outburst floods) are major feature which need to be stressed. Not only do these small-scale societies live in close contact with forest, fields, domestic and wild animals; they also depend on all these elements for their livelihood. A simple disruption, a simple disturbance in this relationship can threat their existence.[2]

Religious representations and related imageries of the environment illustrate this extreme dependency and the dangers posed by the non-pacified environing world. Two opposing logics are at work here. The first one conceptualizes the continuity between wild animals, the forest and human beings. A number of Nepali myths and rituals stressed this continuum; they portray villages and the wild world as sharing an alliance relationship. The metaphor of the villager (mainly the male shaman) and his female forest supernatural partner is sometime used.[3] Here the village is directly connected to the uninhabited world. In a number of ethnic hill groups, relations with earth spirits, *bhūmi deutā / devī,* are thus prevalent. They determine a harmonious life, peace, and prosperity.

The second logic highlights the never-ending conflict with the natural world and the dangers it personifies. Here wild spirits of the forest incarnate predating, aggressive forces that roam around at night threatening human beings. These ghostly creatures need to be pacified by performing blood sacrifices. Such duality is crucial to understanding the interrelationship between Man and nature. Even earthquakes are seen as expression of the anger of wild supernatural forces.

The chapter starts with a text illustrating an aspect — landslides— of the present ecological crisis. It questions the responsibility of the liberal capitalist economic model in matters of environmental deterioration. The second text focuses on a traditional craft, using bamboo to make measuring boxes, and its difficulties in embracing the modern world. Most traditional artisans in contemporary Nepal have to cope with the same problematical situation. Then come two essays on traditional architecture and the changes it is undergoing in the Himalayas, a theme on which nearly three decades ago (1991) I published an edited book: *Man and his house in the Himalayas,* Delhi, Sterling Publishers. The last essay deals with the changes in the relationships between Sherpa climbers and international mountaineering expeditions.

78. Ecology and Democracy

The Himalayas, one of the world's richest biodiversity zones, constitute a particularly threatened ecosystem. As the massive landslide in Sindhupalchok district on the Sunkoshi river in August 2014 reminds us, the Nepali Himalayas are, geologically speaking, young and fragile. What is more, this entire mountainous zone is vulnerable to the slightest change in the climatic system. Although Nepal produces low levels of greenhouse gases, temperatures have increased here faster (almost three times more) than in any other part of the globe. This warming has a direct impact on wildlife, the growing pattern of plants and glacier melting. A number of glaciers have retreated at the rate of 2-100 m per year. A joint study led by the International Centre for Integrated Mountain Development (ICIMOD), shows that Himalayan glaciers have retreated by approximately one kilometre since the Little Ice Age [from 1350 to 1900] and those in Nepal have shrunk by 21 per cent over the last 30 years.[4] This situation is likely to cause major geohazards, glacier-lake outburst floods for instance.

Similarly, the rapid deforestation of the country, in the Tarai as elsewhere, engenders floods, soil erosion, a decrease in groundwater reserves, and stagnating agricultural yields. It makes the mountain slopes fragile and seriously affects individual livelihoods. Today forests cover less than 25 per cent of Nepal's total surface area (45 per cent in 1964) (FAO figures). As far as the Kathmandu Valley is concerned, the gases emitted by all sorts of vehicles have caused massive air pollution, which compromises the health of the population. In fact, the number of cars is spiralling out of control. If nothing is done soon to address these issues, the pessimist forecasts circulating among experts about the habitability of whole regions of the southern Himalayan slopes, as well as of others parts of South Asia may prove to be true.

The dangers have become more acute over the two last decades with the expansion of economic globalization. Despite this alarming state of affairs, eco-politics at national level is still in its infancy. Major political party programmes touch upon the environment only superficially. Since 1951, Nepal has been striving to meet the essential social objectives of eradicating poverty, inequality, malnutrition, and other socio-economic deprivations, often to the detriment of ecological issues. Environmental issues have been acknowledged and addressed but inchoately and with mitigated success. During Panchayat Raj, King Mahendra's slogan *Hariyo Ban Nepāloko*

Dhan (green forests are Nepal's wealth) was lampooned by some as *Hariyo Mahendra Sarkārko Dhan* (green forests are King Mahendra's wealth), though in a rather unconvincing manner. In addition, it is a well-known fact that policies concerning National Parks are highly contested by local populations. Contrary to Europe, there is no major political party at national level that is fully devoted to these causes and to sustainable ecology. The Green Nepal Party (Hariyali Nepal Party) obtained 241 votes at the last elections in 2013 (out of over 9.4 million votes)!

In a country like Nepal, ecology has so far mainly been dealt with either by scientific experts from specialized institutions, such as ICIMOD, FAO, or by local initiatives, informal volunteer groups and NGOs at grassroots level. The State itself is often absent from the debate. This is unfortunate because local projects in the country's remote districts have met with some success. Yet they can hardly combat smuggling and bribes within a corrupt 'forestcracy' which for instance allows wood to be cut illegally and to be sold to India (the demand for timber has soared on the other side of the border). At the same time, sustainable development is gradually becoming a major issue. It is no longer a mere luxury for a poor country to worry about the environment, but a *sine qua non*. Uncontrolled liberal development causes a drop in yields, the depletion of resources and growing rate of pollution. My long-term study of the Kathmandu Valley clearly shows this degradation.

I am pleasantly surprised to see that in various places in Nepal a new awareness among different groups of citizens has emerged. Local associations have won battles against destructive development projects and the misuse of chemical fertilisers.[5] Despite some difficulties, they are setting up organic farms and striving to protect the environment. Similarly, over the last thirty years, the community forest movement (a quarter of all forests in Nepal is under the control of these local bodies) has engendered an increase in woodlands in some districts. In Nepal there is huge potential regarding these issues at grassroots level. Yet at state level, a more committed form of political governance prioritising an ecologically and culturally defined landscape is required. Environmental problems must be actively addressed and a sustainable relationship with nature restored. Ecological concerns have to be formulated and programme objectives achieved in a structured manner. Indeed the rights of citizens over consumer preferences have to be protected.

The relationship between democracy and ecology is notoriously difficult all over the planet. Tensions exist between the necessary development of a country and the preservation of its environment. But there is also a real danger of a day-to-day type of democracy with no concern for the future. Political decisions have to take into account the long term regarding the economic benefits for the country. Ecotourism, for instance, can generate new sources of income and could eventually supplant conventional forms of tourism which sometimes damage the environment. In addition, measures in favour of a more inclusive society, with fewer inequalities, will fail dismally and never be achieved if a greener political agenda respecting the natural world is not adopted forthwith. New modes of governance, less top-down and more decentralized, need to be tested. Of course, it is a global and regional fight (India is the world's third biggest emitter of CO_2 after China and the United States), but national environmental polices are still crucial. Excluding NGOs and grassroots forces from decisions about the environment is not the solution. It is time to restore an economy that is more in tune with nature. With its rich biodiversity and vast areas of wilderness, Nepal could indeed be a model for South Asia.

79. Bamboo as a Paradigm

All over the world, the monetisation of the economy and the development of exchanges have dealt a fatal blow to artisanal products. Just like elsewhere in South Asia, handicrafts and various wares made locally using natural indigenous resources — wood, earth, grass, wild fibres, and plants, etc.— are on the decline in Nepal. For a long time

Nepali handicrafts were protected from Indian imports by Shah kings and the Ranas, but today's free market is jeopardising their future. New materials are gradually invading people's material existence and replacing old handmade items. Plastic receptacles inexorably serve as a substitute for brass bowls, earthenware jars and wooden pots. As far as buildings are concerned, metal parts and corrugated iron roofs are now replacing wooden shingles and thatch, which are considered to be more liable to rot. Moreover, fishermen increasingly use nylon nets instead of string nets made from natural fibres. The law of economics that has been in application over the last centuries is unbending: manufactured products bought in the market strongly compete with handmade artefacts.

The economic imperative of purchasing and marketing crafts, and even of exporting them as in the case of the carpet industry, is strongly felt everywhere in Nepal. Even in rural areas, more and more people buy their fabric or cloth at the nearest bazaars instead of weaving their cloth themselves out of cotton or wild fibrous plants. Except for blacksmiths who are still called upon to make agricultural tools and jewellers who are hard to replace, craftsmen are becoming a thing of the past, especially in rural areas. Government support for the cottage industry and for regular handicraft (*hastakalā* or *hastashilpa*) fairs at urban markets to promote local products have so far given inconclusive results. India, whose handicraft sector dwindled under British rule, today seems to have managed to preserve its handicrafts more effectively than Nepal.

Traditionally, products made of bamboo and cane— non-timber forest resources— were (and to a great extent still are today) of prime importance throughout the country. These plants are traditionally used to make baskets for carrying goods, boxes, sieves, rounded plates, combs, ropes and a wide range of other objects. They have played a vital role nationwide, and even more so in the Limbu/Rai culture owing to the profusion of bamboo in those areas. In western Nepal, a section of the Kāmi population traditionally specialized in basketry. In the Kathmandu Valley itself, where handicrafts were in great demand on urban markets, the Pahari ethnic group, heavily influenced by the Newar culture, specialized in bamboo crafts and sustained their livelihood by making bamboo products. Members of this community used to barter their crafts for grain all over the Kathmandu Valley.

The Newar people of Pyangaon village, in Lalitpur district, near Chapagaon, belonged to this bamboo craft tradition. In the past they used to make bamboo boxes for measuring grain (rice, wheat, etc.) and for storing food products (oil, spices) as well as some other items (lamp wicks, cotton, tobacco). Some villagers also used to make traditional brooms (*tuphi*) out of *Thysanolaena maxima* grasses (in Nepali: *amriso)*. In bygone days, villagers spent almost a month each winter (from the full moon of Māgh till the full moon of Phāgun, i.e. from mid-December to mid-February) further south in the forest covering the southern slopes of the Mahabharat range (Makwanpur and Chitwan districts). There, men would cut old wild bamboo and select the inner layer of the bark (*hāpā*) for their craftwork. The knife, *cupi*, used for this job was worshipped as Bhimsen and was offered a roaster at the beginning and at the end of this period. The layers of bamboo were flattened over a source of heat, and then soaked in water to tighten them. A stick (*katusi*) was used to curve the bamboo sheets. During these forestry expeditions, men wore special shoes made of rice straw suitable for their work in the jungle. Cutting bamboo was not allowed on Tuesdays and Sundays.

The name of Pyangaon village itself comes from the term used to refer to these boxes in Nepali: *pyāng*. This activity was central to the identity of the village. Local people used to make *mānā* half a litre capacity (or 0.450 kg), 2, 4 and 6 *mānā* as well as round *pāthi* containers (to hold 8 *mānā*, i.e. about 3.6 kg of rice), which corresponds to the ancient legally recognized system of grain measures. Much bigger containers called *dilpvā* were also made for carrying the lunch-time meal to the fields. Likewise, smaller (1/2 and 1/

4 *mānā*) boxes, round or oval, were made to hold salt and spices. This bamboo production was bartered in winter throughout the Kathmandu Valley for grain and potatoes. Some items were designed with lids and divided into several inside compartments. In Nepā Bhāshā, these boxes and containers are known by various names: *dyāncā*, *pvācā*, *hāpā*. They are said to be insect-proof.

The craft has been on the decline since 1960 when government authorities banned the cutting of bamboo in these forests. It has also suffered from the gradual shift from the old *mānā/pāthi* system to the Western metric system of measures and from the advent of plastic products. It is now on the verge of becoming extinct. In 2010, only one man (Purna Bahadur) was still capable of making these measuring boxes and few other elders had the relevant skills. In 2009, an agreement was signed with the Nepal Tourism Board to develop Pyangaon as a model craft village for ecotourism. And last year (2013 AD), VDC Chapagaon municipality decided to organise and finance a training course in Pyangaon for all craftsmen interested in reviving these ancient skills. Twenty young individuals, both men and women, were taught over a one-month period. Today the craft is slowly being revived mainly to sell the products on the Asian market, especially in Japan, which has a long tradition of bamboo craftwork. But any attempts to regenerate this craft are a delicate undertaking owing to the fragile economic situation. The low price that craftsmen can ask when selling these products is disproportionate to the amount of work required and the continuously rising cost of living.

Pyāng boxes are still widely used in traditional Newar kitchens to measure rice before cooking. But they are said to be not as strong as they used to be. Smaller bamboo containers are also required for some domestic rituals, especially those marking men and women's entry into old age (*jāku*). This craft clearly belongs to Nepal's cultural heritage. It is a testimony to a lifestyle that was much more closely linked to nature than the artificial one that now prevails.

80. Fragile Vernacular Architecture

The massive earthquakes (*mahā bhūkampa*) that hit central and eastern Nepal on 25 April and 12 May 2015 caused considerable damage to traditional homes and historic monuments, ranging from dangerous cracks to total destruction. According to the UN, it has destroyed or badly damaged more than 900,000 homes. Some villages, especially in the worst affected districts like Gorkha, Nuwakot and Sindhupalchok, had been totally razed to the ground. The Kathmandu Valley has been badly affected but the hills have also greatly suffered, for instance in Tamang, Gurung, Ghale, Kirant and Parbatiyā areas, mainly among poor families who lived in old precarious houses. Despite some controversy among engineers, clay-mortar houses (brick-and-mud constructions) have proved to be less resistant than those using cement-mortar or those reinforced by cement. The use of traditional building techniques and of standard local materials has thus been seriously questioned. Rebuilding projects will have to take into account this architectural fragility in a zone that is so prone to seismic activity. These projects are in demand for quake-resilient materials and structures. Some NGOs are suggesting that houses made exclusively of bamboo are the solution but other materials like corrugated zinc roofing, *jastā*, and concrete seem to be what the local population prefers. The text below is a scholarly presentation of traditional building techniques in the Nepal Himalayas and some of the current changes affecting them. It was written in association with Joëlle Smadja.

Ranging from an altitude of 100 to more than 8,000 metres, stretching over a distance of 2,500 km and watered by a humid tropical monsoon flow that decreases from East to West and is blocked by the high range in the North, the Himalayas cover a vast array of environments. The contrasting ecosystems provide varied renewable natural resources widely used by populations in their domestic architecture. At an altitude belt situated between 3,500 and 1,800 m, tree species such as *Abies spectabilis*, *Quercus glauca, Pinus excelsia* and *roxburghii* among others in the central and eastern

Himalayas, *Cedrus deodara* in the western Himalayas, as well as various sorts of bamboo, play a particularly important role in building materials. At a lower elevation (Tarai and Bhabar areas), in the foothills, *Shorea robusta*, *sāl* in the local language, as well as various Graminae and reeds are also of paramount importance in making buildings.

Up to an elevation of about 4,500 metres, the region is home to numerous kinds of dwellings that are determined by the availability of natural resources and by climate conditions. Let us consider a transect in the central Himalayas, from the top to the lower belt. In high-altitude Tibet and Tibetanized arid areas, characterized by a mineral landscape, stone or/and rammed-earth houses organized around a courtyard, with few openings to protect the occupants from the cold, and with terraced roofs suitable for drying grain and combustible materials, are the dominant feature. The walls are thick (0.45 m). In the Nepalese middle mountains, the wooden façades of Tamang houses, for instance, with a shingle roof weighed down with stones, differ markedly from the wattle and daub walls and thatch roofs of the houses inhabited by the multi-caste and multi-ethnic hill populations. In some cases (Gurung ethnic group, Bāhun caste) houses are not of a rectangular shape but have an elliptical or round form (warmer and stronger, so it is said) and are covered by conical thatched roofs.

Newar houses in the Kathmandu Valley, for their part, have heavy sloping roofs made of tiles and highly decorated overhanging eaves. In the eastern middle hills (Arun valley) and the Tarai (Jhapa), houses are often built on piles and their walls are woven out of bamboo and reeds. In addition, all over the Nepalese mountains, roofing stone or shingles cover fixed shelters for herdsmen. At lower altitudes, mobile shelters for shepherds (Nepali: *goth*) with mat-top covers are a ubiquitous sight. These temporary structures characterise an economy in which livestock roams all year over the fields, fertilizing them. In the western Tarai plains, the walls of Tharu houses are made of ochre-coloured mud and clay (wattle and daub) and are covered by a large sloping thatched roof which is supported by several rows of wooden poles. The roof extends out over the low outer walls. The house is very dark because there are only a few small openings to protect the household from the heat.

Despite the numerous contacts between groups over the course of history, the vast ethnic diversity of the Himalayas is still reflected in its architecture and spatial patterns. Social and cultural elements play a crucial role in most geographical regions and among most populations. For instance, from the western to the eastern part of the Himalayas, Tibetan and Tibetanized houses present common architectural features. They normally comprise at least a ground floor for keeping animals and for food storage (salt) and a first floor that is used as a kitchen-cum-living room, oratory and grain store. In the most affluent families, dwellings have an additional storey and servant quarters. In most cases, the tripartite religious structure of the world, divided between the gods of the upper regions, the deities of the intermediate realm, and the *klu* spirits of the underground world is often applied to the house. This provides a cosmological dimension to the dwelling and reinforces its vertical dimension.

The tent of the Tibetan nomadic herder wandering over the Tibetan plateau is also worth mentioning. It is made of good-quality yak overhair which is taken from the sides of the animal in the month of June. The tent is of a rectangular shape and consists of two halves; the right side is masculine, the left side feminine. It covers a hexagonal area ranging between 12 and 28m^2.

The houses of the Newars, inhabitants of the Kathmandu Valley and who have settled in many small towns throughout Nepal, display their own compartmentalization of vertical space, their own structure reflecting their social patterns. The polarity between pure and impure is a central feature. Their houses are tall, from two to three storeys high. Each storey has its own function. The ground floor is used as a stable or shop, the first floor as a bedroom and granary, the second floor is traditionally a large open living room with no dividing partitions, and the third one (attic) is used as a kitchen and oratory for the household deities. These houses used to be famous for their carved wooden windows that are now on the verge of extinction. In the early twentieth century the most opulent ones were highly influenced by the Rana style. Their facade incorporates neoclassical Western decorative elements such as: pilaster, stucco figurations, volutes, meander designs, Rocaille décor, capitals with angels, caryatides, mascaron with foliage faces, painted stucco plaques. By and large, the Newar house of the Kathmandu Valley constitutes a unique piece of traditional architecture.

In the western Tarai plains (Dang-Deukhuri District), Tharu villages are mostly oriented along a north-south axis. The houses are built side by side in two rectilinear rows facing each other. Dwellings are built on a level piece of ground that forms the floor. Tharus live in large joint-family households, some of which can include eighty or ninety people. The inner rooms, occupied by nuclear families, are separated by partitions that consist of large grain storage containers. The kitchen and the deities room are the innermost part of houses. The outer walls (in some cases the inside walls as well) are decorated with moulding in relief, flower designs, paintings, animal figures, engravings.

In all cases, houses are built without architects. Yet, craft-specialists from outside the village are sometimes called upon. From a religious viewpoint, the main post and the fireplace are of great sacred significance in most of this vernacular architecture. They are often associated with the household's ancestors and prosperity. Whatever the case, the threshold between the inner and the outer part of the house is always clearly marked and is the place where important rituals are performed.

Since the 1970-1980s, significant socio-economic transformations due to the opening of this region onto the outside world, to forest protection and to restricted access to resources have led to several architectural changes. There has been an individualisation of housing due to children leaving their large family house and to changes in building materials, especially roofing materials. In the hills, straw used for roofs now competes with the need to use it as fodder for cattle, while in the middle mountains fir trees for making shingle now have to be purchased. Today roofs of these types are often replaced by slate, corrugated iron or even flattened tin cans. In the Kathmandu Valley, traditional bricks that are moulded using local earth are being replaced more and more by concrete. In this region as in other urbanized areas, the traditional architectural heritage is on the decline. By and large, throughout the range, Westernized modern houses tend to be built in a chaotic fashion, with no organic relation to the land or to each other.

81. The Backdrop to House Construction in the Kathmandu Valley

When visiting Paris (and some Mediterranean capitals), Nepalis are generally impressed by the distinctive stone architecture of ancient monuments and houses. There is indeed a marked difference with the Kathmandu Valley, where for nearly two millennia the traditional building material has been fired or sun-dried bricks. In this valley few monuments are made of stone, even though some do exist. Lets us not forget that Nepali Rana palaces and mansions in the nineteenth and twentieth century were made of brick that was then covered in plaster and stucco. There is a striking contrast in this respect with the local cream-grey limestone of Paris. What visitors often ignore is that the materials used for buildings in the French capital were extracted from below the city itself and from the surrounding region (south of the Oise *département*). The Paris underground is riddled with limestone quarries, especially below the left bank of the River Seine. These quarries were in operation during the Middle Ages and up until the eighteenth century. Like Newar cities and villages, the buildings in the French capital are therefore the expression of its local underground resources. This intimate link is a feature of vernacular rural and urban architecture throughout the world. Paris is built on a calcareous geological formation, whereas the cities and villages of the Kathmandu Valley are built almost entirely on clay soil.

A recent book penned by Viggo Brun prompts us to revisit and reflect on the close relationship between the types of building and the immediate environment.[6] This work presents first-hand documentation on brick-making in the Kathmandu Valley. The author provides a wealth of detail about the technical process of making bricks, from the traditional field clamp and walled clamp used for local production (often limited to one house) to the more recent industrial fixed-chimney BTK ("Bull's trench kiln") introduced in the 1980s, while mentioning in passing the highly polluting movable-chimney BTK which was abandoned in the early 2000s because of the environmental damage it caused. There are at present 113 kilns in the Kathmandu Valley, which are located in former rural zones. BTKs, which had been in existence in neighbouring India for a hundred years before they were introduced into this valley, can produce far more bricks and at a much faster rate than the old clamps. Their production capacity is about 27 times greater. Unlike intermittent clamps, they can fire bricks continuously.

Two other types of modern brick kiln operate at present in the region. *(a)*- The forced-draught kiln, known as the Habla kiln, from the name of its German inventor. It is the most fuel-efficient machine that makes the best use of heat and is the cheapest to build. Its kiln is square rather than oval. It requires a constant supply of electricity and therefore needs a backup generator in case of a power outage. The first one of its type was built in 2003 in Chapagaon. *(b)*- The Hoffman kiln, which is the most mechanised and produces high-quality bricks, has been used to build prominent buildings such as Tribhuvan International Airport.

Due to climatic constraints and to the rice cultivation calendar, production from all these kinds of kiln, whether traditional clamp or more advanced ones, is seasonal. It lasts from the beginning of December to the end of May; that is during the cold dry season. In 2011, there were only two walled clamps still in existence in the Valley. The others have been replaced by more modern kilns. Wood was formerly used to fire the bricks. Today it has been replaced by coal, mainly from Assam.

Brick production is a highly fragmented process. It is made up of different steps that are undertaken by separate teams or groups of persons. First the clay has to be prepared: using a mattock, the hard soil is hacked into small enough clumps for it to crumble easily, and then arranged into a heap. This heap is soaked in water, and kneaded with bare feet. The earth is then moulded into bricks, left to dry in the sun, stacked, and carried from the brick-fields to the kiln. Nepali porters carry their load of bricks in the local way, on their backs, hanging from a tumpline that is wrapped around the forehead, whereas Indians carry bricks on the top of their heads. In the kiln itself, work is divided among setters (who set batches of bricks), dust-men, coal-men, firing-men, roof-openers, red-brick porters (to load the trucks), to mention only the main operations.

The main value of Brun's book lies in the many interviews the author conducted with workers, contractors and entrepreneurs from this economic sector, and the description of the various manufacturing processes. On average, BTKs employ 300 persons in factories (as well as 20 animals, horses or donkeys —mostly from Nepalgunj— for transportation), but some kilns are said to be operated by twice this number of people (p. 5). Except for owners and office-workers, almost all kiln workers are seasonal migrants. Brick-moulders are often poor farmers from neighbouring districts such as Kabre and Sindhuli. Those who carry green bricks from the fields are often young people from the hills, while all those who work inside the kilns (coal-men, firing-men, dust-men) are recruited from Bihar in India (p. 5). Middlemen and contractors hire this workforce well in advance. Most workers belong to marginalized ethnic groups or castes from India or Nepal. The hardest and most tiresome tasks (which are sometimes done at night) are carried out by Indians. By and large, work in brick kilns is not looked upon favourably. It is regarded as unskilled labour.

Living conditions are rudimentary, to say the least. Workers live in small dwellings made of brick walls and covered with a corrugated iron roof. Each hut houses four or five people. Drinking water and sanitation facilities are very limited or non-existent. Workers inhale dust and smoke all day long and are exposed to highly polluted air. They suffer from respiratory problems, eye infections and skin rashes. In December-January, as soon as the sun sets, the temperature falls to about 5-10 °C. It is therefore bitterly cold in the small huts and many children working in the factories suffer from a permanent running nose.

In fact, child-labour is one characteristic of the kiln workforce. A number of children under the age of 16 work in kilns and several are even younger than 14, the legal working age in Nepal (p. 6). Children mould and carry bricks in and out of the kilns, and then drive the herd of donkeys. Child brick-moulders usually come with their parents and work with them as part of a team. Child employment has had negative consequences in matters of education. Despite attempts to set up temporary schools, hardly any children of migrant workers benefit from any schooling while they live at a kiln.

According to employees, these harsh conditions do not differ much from other sectors of the economy (p. 6). With regards their salary, most persons interviewed asserted that they were well paid and that they could make good money, especially if several family members worked together in the kilns. Children are paid the same rate as adults. If workers avoid falling into the trap of asking the contractor for an advance on the following year, and consequently of becoming perpetually indebted, the money a family can make from this seasonal work is said to constitute a substantial amount. Yet a worker's individual salary is very low: 5,000 rupees per month, plus a bonus for the persons in charge of the firing process. This type of worker is normally able to take home about 20,000 rupees at the end of the brick season, which is not a large sum. As one employee points out (p. 83), Indians like coming to Nepal instead of taking a job in India, because the wages for working in kilns are paid at the end of the season, therefore enabling them to save more money. By and large, labourers are used to working in similar difficult conditions with comparable wages in other sectors of the economy. They have little therefore to complain about.

Traditionally, kilns in the Valley were operated according to a domestic or semi-domestic pattern, —more often than not by an enlarged family along with some friends all of whom worked on a reciprocal work basis, *bvalā jyā* in Nepā Bhāshā (personal data). In such cases, house-builders were their own brick-makers. Such was the case at least in Jyāpu agriculturist villages. In other situations, people called on the services of some Newar castes, such as Āvāle masons and Prajāpatī potters (who also used to live in towns) specialized in baking clay objects. Thus, there was a division of labour—especially for city-dwellers who were not involved in agricultural work—in accordance with the caste system and its distribution of ritual work and duties. Seen from this perspective, the appearance of modern kilns that produce a large number of manufactured bricks has led to a major radical transformation in production techniques and in the associated social relations.

Today, there is a shift from a traditional, pre-modern society to an industrial social organization based on capitalist methods, principles and practices. These processes run parallel to those that emerged in eighteenth-century Europe and North America. However, the transformation is not yet complete. Contrary to eighteenth-century British factories that flourished in Manchester and elsewhere, the Nepali brick industry has so far only been a seasonal activity and operates alongside agricultural activities during the rainy season. Labourers sometimes even work as craftsmen in the carpentry and masonry sectors for the remaining months of the year. The prevailing role of caste or ethnic divisions among the working class is also worth noting. Even if they are subjected to more or less the same living conditions, labourers gather together at their work place according to their caste or ethnic group and do not mix unless strictly necessary (p. 88). Yadavs live together in one hut, Rams in another, Sadais in yet another, and so on. At one kiln, Bihari Muslims live in their own hut, well away from Hindus. Traditional rules forbid inter-caste commensality. These exclusive patterns, typical of Indo-Nepali culture, have resisted the standardization of working conditions as well as the industrialisation process.

Besides, labour is still only partially mechanised, except at the most modern Habla kilns. Most of the work is still done by hand, using rudimentary tools that sometimes belong to the workers themselves (mattocks, for instance). Bricks are moulded by hand one by one using wooden moulds. Altogether, the number of machines is very small. Trade unions, for their part, do not appear to play a significant role in this sector of work. Entrepreneurs fear and thus avoid them. However, their influence (especially those affiliated to CPN (UML)) over some issues is growing, for instance regarding child-labour and illiteracy.

The exponential increase in housing projects in the Kathmandu Valley has therefore induced a major transformation in the social mode of production and a *proletarisation* of labour forces. According to my calculations based on Brun's data, the number of persons employed in the Kathmandu Valley's brick industry has reached at least 35,000. These workers often switch from one factory to another depending on the contractors they happen to meet. The large majority of them would like to settle permanently in the Kathmandu Valley. Even if the sector has retained some traditional economic features, the development of kilns has entailed a surge in capitalistic economic enterprises. In other words, the current transformation of the Kathmandu Valley into a vast, highly populated, urbanized zone is accompanied by the emergence of a class society that is organised in a different way from traditional caste social architecture.

The future of brick production in the region concerned looks very bleak. At present, this industry is facing a rapid depletion of suitable soil to run its factories and to produce bricks. Many kilns will soon lack the right soil and are already having to transport more and more suitable earth from elsewhere. Brun's book also highlights the persisting negative impact of kilns in terms of pollution. Smoke-belching brick factories in this cauldron-like high valley which is surrounded on all sides by mountains are having a disastrous effect on the health of its inhabitants. Moreover, the rental of farmland for brick production is posing more and more problems due to the drop in soil fertility after the setting up of brick factories on this land. In the future farm production will see a drop in its yield, even if farmers use fertilisers. In addition, heavy trucks from the kilns are damaging the roads. In the long run these factors will obviously increase production costs and limit the massive use of fired bricks in buildings.

What is more, the use of non-baked bricks made of compressed waste material and cement, —processed without using heat from coal-fires—, is now on the rise and offers an attractive alternative. For the moment, the general public prefers red-coloured baked bricks, which are nicer to look at and allegedly of better quality. Yet recent high-rise constructions in the region are not built using fired bricks. A drastic change is likely to take place in the years to come, which may lead to new types of factories. Like everywhere else, here modernity implies an unprecedented split between human beings and their natural environment. Inhabitants find themselves disconnected from the natural world. A new relationship, dysfunctional in many ways, is being established with the ecosystem.

82. Fight Over the Mountains

Traditionally, Tibetan and Tibetanized people tend to circumambulate mountains rather to climb them. This is in keeping with their ancient beliefs and traditional ways of worshipping snow-capped mountains. Himalayan summits are the abode of the gods, not of human beings. The gradual transformation of Sherpas (150,000 in the 2011 Nepal Census) living in Solukhumbu into mountain climbers carrying loads is a later development in their history and a result of their early encounter with Western Himalayists in search of assistants, high-altitude porters and guides to lead them to the roof of the world.[7]

The first attempts to ascend Nepalese Himalayan peaks date back to the early 1920s. In 1922, a British expedition reached an altitude of over 8,000 metres on the Everest slopes but failed to reach the summit; seven Sherpas died in an avalanche below the northern pass. As far as Mount Everest is concerned, several expeditions followed from the northern Tibetan side, a number of them undertaken with the help of the Sherpa Tenzing Norgay. It was only on 29th May 1953 that the New-Zealander Edmund Hillary and the same Tenzing Norgay reached the summit of Everest (with the support of 102 Sherpas who were members of the expedition). In 1965, Nawang Gomby Sherpa became the first Sherpa to succeed in climbing Mount Everest twice. And in May 2011, Apa Sherpa ascended Mount Everest for the 21st time, a record that still stands. It is worth noting that the most experienced Sherpas have climbed many other Himalayan peaks, in Nepal, Sikkim and Pakistan. In the same way, the word Sherpa has become to be used by foreigners for any Nepali working in the mountaineering sector, whatever the ethnic group they belong to (Sherpa, Tamang, Gurung or Rai).

The transformation of Sherpas into early explorers of the high range of Himalayan mountains and into professional climbers is mainly due to the proximity of their native land, the Solukhumbu district, with Everest and other eight-thousanders, such as Makalu. Another reason for this is the genetic adaptation of these men to high altitude since their permanent settlements are to be found at over 3,700 metres. Towards the west, in the Annapurna or Manaslu range, Gurungs have played a similar role, but in a much less marked manner. Gurung villages are in fact situated at a much lower attitude than Sherpa villages. Their inhabitants have very rarely had the possibility of competing with the Sherpa elite in higher-altitude zones. Similarly, Tamangs, who have played a massive role in Himalayan expeditions as low-altitude porters (one of their traditional occupations in many other contexts), are not —save some exceptions—referred to as climbers.

Working as a Sherpa for the benefit of paying clients can be a lucrative (2,600 euros per season) yet highly dangerous business. During expeditions, these Nepali mountaineers are responsible for the groundwork, for carrying heavy equipment from one camp to another and for fixing ropes and ladders on paths for future fee-paying clients to ascend. In high-risk corridors and icefalls, they are exposed to the worst types of danger. They have indeed paid a high price over the years. According to a reliable Himalayan database which keeps track of the number of victims, 174 Sherpa climbers have died while working in the mountains of Nepal (99 on the Everest slopes), with 15 in the past decade alone. Many others have been left disabled by rockfall, frostbite and altitude-related illnesses such as cerebral vascular accidents and oedema. Climate change and melting ice obviously increase the risk of having an accident. On 18th April 2014, a serac collapsed above the Khumbu icefall, causing an avalanche of massive chunks of ice and snow which killed 16 Nepalese guides, mostly Sherpas (plus a Tamang, a Khatri from Taplejung and a Gurung from Laprak). The following year, on 25th April 2015, an avalanche triggered by the mega earthquake ravaged the Everest Base Camp and then part of the Khumbu icefall. It killed 19 climbers including 10 Nepali Sherpas. Routes over the icefall toward Everest were closed for the rest of the season.

Over the years mountaineering has become a major source of income for Sherpas and the Nepali state. In 2014 alone, 39 expeditions (27 in 2013) to Everest were scheduled and these brought in a considerable amount of income. At the same time, the development of tourism and trekking in Solukhumbu has totally transformed the livelihood and the economy of this population which in the past subsisted on herding, agriculture and trade. Over the years Everest has become a tourist attraction, the cornerstone of a trekking and mountaineering industry. The creation of Sagarmatha Park in 1974, which covers the Sherpas' traditional habitat, has accelerated the changes in the social life of Sherpas. Countless lodges have sprung up to accommodate trekkers around Pangboche and the entire life of the local people is now geared towards this lucrative industry. Crowds of tourists come to this part of the world every year on sightseeing tours and to walk along mountain trails.

Perusing recent accounts written by mountaineers about the ascent of Nepali peaks proves to be highly instructive.[8] One is particularly struck by the uncontrolled, unstructured, somewhat anarchic world of mountaineering from Kathmandu to the Everest Base Camp. The plethora of mountaineering agencies which are mostly run by foreigners and the private helicopter rescue companies that compete with each other make up a discordant picture. The presence of foreign guides (New Zealanders, French, Italian, German, etc.) working alongside Sherpas and escorting their private clients up the mountain, complicate the situation, just as individual foreign mountaineers do when they climb solo, with no assistance, but nevertheless using the groundwork laid down beforehand by Sherpas. In Nepal, there is no equivalent to the "Compagnie des guides" in Chamonix in the French Alps. This private guild has a form of monopoly on mountaineering expeditions, with new jobs rotating between the registered guides. The Nepal National Mountain Guide Association which was registered in 2005 and has been recognized by international alpine companies is not run along the same lines. This association consists of only 37 professional guides, all of whom have obtained a high-level of specialization and a fully recognised diploma. Most Sherpas do not belong to this association. This overall picture, which is also pervaded by politics, echoes the country's global situation and mirrors Nepal's confused and anarchic state. The inertia and inefficacity of the state's rescue plans in April 2014 are reminiscent of the late response of the government during the 2015 earthquake.

Moreover, despite strong community ties, Sherpa porters and climbers are a loosely structured community. The varying levels of experience and technical skills, from porters to highly experienced mountain professionals, have not been fully recognized. Likewise, those who follow a mountaineering apprenticeship and who obtain a diploma abroad, mostly in the French or Swiss Alps, are underestimated and sometimes even cause jealousy among other Nepali guides. As in other sectors, the Nepali state has failed to properly coordinate the mountaineering industry and rescue work. Sherpas are demanding more security and more financial compensation, but these requests have met with little success. The state is mainly interested in the extremely high fees the Ministry of Tourism pocketed for each expedition. The authorities fix the amount of the insurance claim to be paid in the event of an accident, yet the rate is not always respected. In 2014, in addition to a maximum mandatory insurance policy claim of US $ 10,000 for the families of guides, the Nepalese government paid compensation (after numerous demands made by Sherpas) that amounted to 500,000 Nepalese rupees to the victims' next of kin.

This disorganised and tense situation may explain the unprecedented altercation that occurred on 4th May 2013. That day, three highly experienced Western climbers (a Swiss, an Italian and a Briton) came face to face with an angry mob of 100 Sherpas at Everest Base Camp II because the three alpinists had crossed ropes that the Sherpas had just set up. The fight was widely reported and came as a shock to everybody. All expeditions were stopped for a year. The conflict can be largely explained by the growing number of younger Sherpas in the mountaineering business, who do not have the same relationship with clients as before and who contest their own subaltern position. They no longer want to be treated as colonized people on their own land. Interestingly, most local trekking/mountaineering agencies and indeed the most profitable ones in Kathmandu are owned by foreigners. Only one-third is owned by Sherpas.[9] Moreover, these mountain workers are exasperated by repeated ascensions by Westerners without their help. Nevertheless, these are not the only causes. The overcrowding of the mountains and the uncoordinated state of mountaineering activities no doubt also contributed to this headline fight.

Notes

1 Cf. J. Ives and B. Messerli, *The Himalayan Dilemma: Reconciling Development and Conservation*. New York: Routledge, 1989; J. Ives, *Himalayan Perceptions: Environmental Change and the Well Being of Mountain Peoples*. London: Routledge, 2004. The arguments developed in these two books have not met a consensus among experts and environmentalists.

2 The two main books in this regard are: J. Smadja, (ed.), *Reading Himalayan Landscapes over Time. Environmental Perception, Knowledge and Practice in Nepal and Ladakh*. Pondichéry: Institut français de Pondichéry, 2009; and B. Campbell, *Living Between Juniper and Palm. Nature, Culture, and Power in the Himalayas.* Delhi: OUP, 2013. The first of these books (to which I contributed) falls within J. Ives and B. Messerli approach, but rightly shows that the diversity of situations has to be taken more into account in studying the degradation of the environment.

3 Anne de Sales, *Je suis né de vos jeux de tambours. La religion chamanique des Magar du Nord*. Nanterre: Société d'ethnologie, 1991.

4 Richard Armstrong, *The Glaciers of the Hindu Kush-Himalayan Region*. Kathmandu: Icimod/Usaid 2010.

5 To prevent soil deterioration, organic liquid pesticides (mixed with Artemisia *tite pāti*) are increasingly used in rural areas of the Kathmandu Valley.

6 Brun Viggo. *Fired Earth. Bricks, Kilns and Workers in Kathmandu Valley*. Kathmandu: Himal Books, 2013. This study [81] has already been published in a longer form in *Studies in Nepali History and Society*, 2013, 18(1), pp. 179-185.

7 On changes among Sherpas, see James Fisher, *Sherpas: Reflections on Change in Himalayan Nepal*. Berkeley: University of California Press, 1990.

8 See for instance, Patricia Jolly & Laurence Shakya, *Sherpas, fils de l'Everest*. Paris: Le Monde/Arthaud, 2015.

9 Vincanne Adams, *Tigers of the Snow and Other Virtual Sherpas*. Princeton: Princeton University Press, 1996, p. 215.

CHAPTER

13

Economy and Development

Nepal is one of the world's least developed countries. Over the last decades the country has made some notable achievements in various socio-economic domains (life expectancy, infant mortality, reduction in the number of poor people, road construction, increased literacy rate), but aggregate data hide large variations across geographical regions, gender and ethnicity **[83]**.[1] In fact, successive development plans over the last 50 years have not succeeded in significantly improving the situation. Nepal has not raised its economic status compared to other South Asian states.

The overall situation has all the hallmarks of a failure scenario. The privatization of the economy and the implementation of market-oriented policies in industry and trade, for instance, have not boosted the private sector or investments. The export-orientated carpet and textile industry has virtually collapsed. Moreover regular transport and labour strikes are not likely to be an incentive for foreign investment in the country.

By and large, the overall picture is grim.[2] The 1996-2006 Maoist insurgency greatly weakened the country's economy and infrastructure. Power cuts in the Kathmandu Valley are routine and make life difficult. Despite an enormous hydropower potential (estimated at 42,000 MW),[3] water resource development is poor, especially in urban areas. In 2014, the economic growth rate was 4.6 per cent but the forecast for 2015 is much lower due to the consequences of the earthquakes. Inflation for 2014 reached 7.7 per cent. The unemployment rate is also extremely high: 42 per cent.[4] All this creates a sense of hopelessness in rural and urban Nepal. In addition, since 2008, the task of restructuring the state has distracted leaders from focusing on development projects. A reversal of the failed development paradigm will necessitate drastic changes in social and political structures. There has so far been a rampant misuse of resources.

Concomitantly, Nepal is one of the poorest countries in the world in terms of per capita income, with about one quarter of its population living below the poverty line. It ranks twelfth among the poorest countries in the world and it is the poorest state in South Asia. These classifications mean little when confronted with people's real lives. Notwithstanding, poverty persists and national production is not enough for people to live on. An increasing number of Nepalis are leaving the country to find employment abroad. In fact, Nepal is one of the world's largest recipients of remittances, which amount to some USD 5.1 billion (2012). The remittances of Nepali workers abroad have boosted growth and have significantly enhanced the purchasing power of rural households. Their income now accounts for over half of the country's GDP (World Bank, 2015).

Social and geographical inequalities persist and are sometimes even reinforced. In rural hill areas, household food insecurity and poor nutrition are major concerns. Most rural households have little access to basic health care, safe drinking water, sanitation and other basic necessities. Poor families are often obliged to send their children to work instead of sending them to school, perpetuating the cycle of poverty. Government projects and foreign aid (which exists since 1951) do not seem to reach the poorest or to substantially improve their situation.

In the face of this blatant failure, foreign aid which amounts to more than 25 per cent of the state budget—and much more if development expenses are taken into account—is under debate. A number of Nepali experts view it as an obstacle to sustainable development and as a major source of corruption among the elite. More often than not the money is simply not spent. This debate is not specific to Nepal but is worldwide. Countries regularly benefiting from foreign aid underline the constraints associated with development programmes decided on by donors and the interference that outside help causes in domestic politics. These constraints and interference, they complain, may not be in keeping with their countries' own interests and those of their inhabitants. These questions have recently led to rather heated debates in Nepal. One thing is clear: in this Himalayan state, recent progress in alleviating poverty appears to have been made mainly thanks to remittances from migrant labourers, not to foreign aid.

About 80 per cent of Nepal's population live in rural areas. Agriculture remains the country's principal economic activity, employing 70 per cent of the population and providing 33 per cent of the GDP. Yet only the lowland Tarai region (housing 50.1 per cent of the country's total population) produces a farm surplus. Hilly regions are food-deficient. The underperformance of the rudimentary, monsoon-dependent agricultural sector in these regions is a major factor that has contributed to the failure to develop the country.[5]

Out-migration of unskilled labour for manual work has negatively affected peasant farming. In the hills, the amount of fallow land has increased, transforming villages from spaces of production into space of consumption. People residing in villages are mostly women, children, and elders. Consequently, women today constitute more than 60 per cent of the agricultural labour force.[6] Furthermore, farming is no longer an attractive occupation for young people. The new generation is looking for other opportunities (*bidesh jāne*: to go abroad) and prefer jobs where they "keep their hands clean". Peasants are regarded as backward. The agricultural sector, especially the subsistence rural economy, is on the verge of collapse. In actual fact, the entire macroeconomic scenario is undergoing changes: the contribution of the agricultural sector to the GDP has dropped from 61 per cent in 1981 to 33 per cent, while its contribution to the service sector has increased from 27 per cent to 48 per cent over the same period.[7]

83. Uneven Development

To view Nepal solely through the lens of the Kathmandu Valley is totally misleading. The urbanized Kathmandu Valley and the rest of the country, especially rural areas, are worlds apart. The contrast is obvious to anyone who travels round the country for several months. The disparity between villages and urban areas is a recurrent feature throughout the world but the difficulties associated with the mountainous relief and the over-centralisation of the Nepali state in Patan, Kathmandu and other towns in political, cultural and economic matters have greatly heightened the divide over the last decades. The benefits the Kathmandu Valley has reaped are disproportionate to its size. Given the easier access to education and to health services, this central region has become the prime destination for internal migration. However, politically and socially the capital is only loosely connected to the rest of the country. “Kathmandu lives in a bubble. Rulers here tend not to notice, or underestimate the anger outside” (Kunda Dixit) [8]. The gap between the two has a lot to teach us about Nepal’s flaws and structural deficiencies.

This calls to mind the fieldwork I did during the 1970s, in northern Dhading District, a four-day walk from Trisuli Bazar. These high-altitude areas, dominated by the Ganesh Himal range and its snow-capped peaks, with no roads, no market places and no electricity, were worlds away from Kathmandu city. There were practically no development projects, no health post, and no state representative in these villages (Barang, Sertung, Timling). Elementary schools were run with the means available, mainly by local Tamang teachers. This upper valley was almost exclusively populated by Tamangs, with some Kāmi blacksmiths who spoke Tamang and a few Gurungs. The only non-rural site was the Lari zinc mine situated at high altitude (4,110m) and operated by Indians; access to it was difficult and the mine only employed a handful of people. Since then it has closed. At that time, when I came back to Kathmandu periodically after a three-month interval, I travelled not only in space but also in time, between radically different worlds.

Despite the construction of numerous roads, the implementation of a large number of educational, agricultural, medical projects, and sustained foreign aid over the last decades, the gulf between the Kathmandu Valley and the hinterland has remained the same. The hills, where agriculture is the main economic resource, are still a food-deficient area. Farmers only produce between six and ten months of their annual food requirements. Men are forced to migrate to sustain their families.[9]

To tell the truth, some areas around secondary urban centres have made economic progress over the last years. Yet in many places the gulf between them and the country's capital has widened. This is especially the case of remote areas that have few proper links with headquarters and provincial cities. These disparities generate great socio-economic inequalities. Poverty is ten times greater in the hinterland and the chance of growing up to be a literate adult is about three times lower than in the area surrounding the capital.[10] Local hill people are all in favour of development yet no substantial improvement has been made to their lives. On most trails, porterage with *doko* (basket carried on the back) still prevails.

The hills in far western Nepal are clearly the poorest and the most backward areas in the country. In these zones, poverty affects 45-46 per cent of the population, which is much higher than the average 25 per cent for the whole of Nepal. The eastern hills have always been slightly richer and more economically and educationally advanced. The proximity of Darjeeling and Kalimpong in western Bengal—both famous for their high schools since the nineteenth century—partly explains this difference. Eastern districts also receive more rain (approximately 2,500 millimetres of rain per annum) than the western part of the country (about 1,000 millimetres), which is a considerable advantage as far as agriculture is concerned. In most western districts, it is difficult to cultivate anything on the poor soil. This difference may explain the slow but continuous west-east movement of populations over the centuries.

Yet, by and large, national and international funds, company headquarters, ministries and institutes of higher education tend to stay in Kathmandu despite the growing pollution and overpopulation. Most families that manage to climb the social ladder in terms of power and money strive to own their own house in the Kathmandu Valley. They are bent on sending their children to the best schools, to seize the best opportunities in terms of employment and to be those nearest to the centre of political decisions. This trend became more marked during the decade-long Māobādī insurgency. A great number of Nepali hill people escaped the armed conflict and the Maoist coercion/extortion by moving to the Kathmandu Valley. The destruction by the PLA (People's Liberation Army) of a large number of infrastructures (airports, official buildings, etc.) in remote districts seriously curbed local development.

In February 2015, I was able to witness this deep-seated divide for myself in the course of a short trip I made to Palpa and Gulmi Districts. I conducted research in the same area in the late 1980s as a member of an interdisciplinary team made up of CNRS researchers. My feelings are perhaps somewhat impressionistic, but thirty years on, the agricultural landscape, the living conditions of people (mainly Parbatiyās and Magars), agricultural techniques, and domestic architecture looked relatively unchanged to me, even if gendered roles are slowly changing due to the exodus of migrants abroad. By contrast, the Kathmandu Valley has been dramatically remodelled. Māobād (Maoism) has done nothing to reduce the gap, even in places that were its bastions, such as Rukum. On the whole, the last three decades has seen some economic success stories but many more stories of failures. A development process that leaves people on the wayside, constantly alienated from the rest of the country, is perilous: it can lead to long-term unrest.

The earthquakes that hit the country in April and May 2015 heightened this wide gap. Except for some localities and a number of monument sites, the Kathmandu Valley came out relatively unscathed. It did not take very long for the capital to return to normality. In comparison, just only a short distance away, the hill districts of Gorkha, Dhading, Rasuwa, Nuwakot, and further east as well, faced a calamitous situation. Devastation is an understatement. Villages in these zones, mostly Ghale and Tamang, have been totally or largely destroyed. Traditional buildings made of stone and wood, especially those with two storeys, did not withstand the earthquake and the subsequent tremors. Lives were lost, homes destroyed, infrastructures obliterated. Rescue teams and international aid took much longer to reach these devastated areas, first by helicopter, and then by road. A large part of the local population spent months living in tents and under tarpaulins (*tipod*). A number of them, desperately needy, (from Salme village, Nuwakot District, for instance) are still housed in refugee camps in Trisuli Bazar, unaware of what the future holds for them.[11] The Red Cross very rarely comes to visit them. Refugees do not expect anything from the government *(sarkār)*, which is too far away, too inefficient. Aid arrives through private channels. The fault line cutting across Nepali society is not only underground, in the earth; it is visible every day in the appalling dissimilarity between regions that are geographically not far from each other.

84. Morals and Economics

In the course of a recent visit (February 2015) to Shri Shri Ravi Shankar Ashram in Bangalore, I attended a seminar organised by the Art of Living organization. The theme of the gathering was "Moral and Economics". A number of economists, bankers, accountants, entrepreneurs, and company directors attended the event alongside the heads of the religious movement which is in fact based at this huge Ashram centre. They all stressed the need to find a new path some way between liberal economics with its dire effects and a centrally driven top-to-bottom socialist economy with its own flaws. If left uncontrolled, the first path leads to the over-exploitation of the environment and growing social inequalities. The second path, for its part, breaks the will of the people and replaces it with the unidirectional decision of a small number of top-ranking persons, thereby confiscating individual initiatives and liberties. Strikingly, the compassionate, inclusivist values highlighted in the various papers given at the seminar were all associated with a search for maximum economic efficacy and growth of the gross domestic product. What on earth was this place?

This argument finds an echo among Indians. It reiterates Mahatma Gandhi's fight for a moralised, redistributive economy, his determination to serve the poor and to improve the quality of life for Dalits. Let us not forget that in 1932 Gandhi set up the Harijan Sewak Sangh for Harijan, a social welfare organisation run by people to eradicate untouchability from Indian society. He drafted the Sangh constitution himself and gave a large space to this constellation of ideas. The organisation still exists today and pledges for the same objectives as when it was created. Furthermore, to limit my scope here to contemporary India, this missionary ideology corresponds not only to certain aspects of the Indian Congress Party's old socialist heritage but also to some preoccupations of the Bhāratiya Janatā Party of the current Prime Minister Modi in its search through old Indian vocabulary and values to match modern realities and to provide solutions to today's difficulties. It is the South Asian version of social Catholicism that sprang up in certain Catholic Western European countries in the nineteenth century or of 'moral economy', a term coined by E.P. Thompson, a British social historian, which emerged at about the same period.

The papers presented at the Art of Living conference laid emphasis on a sustainable economy and on carrying out social work among the poorest. They drew attention to the fact that harmonious development can only be achieved if it respects social and moral norms. By and large, a common model emerged from the papers: a model adapted to Indian cultural values, combining a liberal economy with social commitments and defending harmonious relationships between people and their environment. The discourse held by all the speakers was far-removed from the Marxist revolutionary ideology based on class conflict. Interestingly enough, this half religious, half economic paradigm, pervaded with ethical norms, is quite influent today. And I must say, more so in India than in Nepal. The Art of Living is one organization among many others which promote such an original hybrid template.

I argue, however, that a similar paradigm,—combining yoga, voluntary work, social work, *sevā*, joy and happiness—, animates a number of social movements in Nepal. This is particularly evident in civil society and crosses religious boundaries, especially between Hindu and Buddhists, who share common values in these matters. The sheer number of Nepali people devoting their time and energy to charities and to community work without any financial reward is remarkable. It is particularly noteworthy among young and middle-aged people, not just among women. Since the earthquake in 2015, social work among Nepalis, for instance, has become a noticeable feature of voluntary work to help damaged Tamang villages in the Kathmandu Valley area.

The notion of *sevā*, service, is central to these conceptions and commitments. This concept was obviously developed and widely spread by Hindu reformists such as Vivekananda and Ramakrishna in India in the nineteenth century and at the beginning of the twentieth century.[12] It may have been influenced by Christian ideas of charity.[13] Yet *sevā* goes back a long way in Hindu culture which antedates the later Christian influence. Vallabhacharya, the twelfth-century Vaishnavȧ saint, prescribed it as an act of devotion and surrender to the divine lord as opposed to traditional practices of fasting and asceticism. Today, the prism of *sevā* is still part of this old religious background and is somewhat related to piety and morals. It is clearly a complex hybrid notion, around which a number of ideas from different horizons have agglomerated over the centuries. However, its elements of sympathy and charity towards oppressed people and minorities bear some resemblance to compassion and charitable works that are common in non-Hindu or non-Buddhist countries.

This alternative route, some way between uncontrolled liberalism and an administered socialist economy, has the ambition to mitigate a utilitarian economy, to temper its negative aspects. It represents a form of marriage somewhere between ethics and capitalism. Is this option viable? Marxists consider these ideas as a hidden form of capitalism. According to them, such an economy would cater to the same private interests of the privileged ruling class just as any capitalist enterprise would do. But the realities are much more complex. Religion, morals, politics and economics are intrinsically interconnected. In Indian BJP pro-Hindu circles, notions of service and cooperation are more or less related to the theme of unified brotherhood (a notion introduced by Vinayak Damodar Savarkar, one of the main ideologues of the Hindutva nationalist movement). However, in India as in the Nepali Himalayas, ideas of service, assistance and sharing have a broader humanitarian scope. They are deeply rooted in social relations and are far-removed from any political ideologies. More importantly, in Nepal as in India, this paradigm provides ethical grounds and social constraints for sustaining the logic of development. It imposes a language of duty instead of a language of rights in a way that differs from the welfare state inspired by Western socialist ideologies.

85. From Guthi-Groups to Cooperatives

In the preceding sections, I have already touched upon the role of self-governing cooperatives and other types of associations based on reciprocity and assistance [**57** and **72**]. These communal groups, which are theoretically motivated by the notion of service rather than by profits, are of great import in defining the encompassing society and economy. I would like to come back to this issue and to focus on the recent boom in cooperatives, *sahakārī*, which practise microfinance in Nepali urban and rural settlements.

To begin with, a short review of their historical background is necessary. In Nepal, cooperatives date back a long way. The Sājhā Prakāshan partnership, an "association" that publishes and supplies books, was created as early as 1913 under Dev Shamsher Rana's reformist rule. However, the main cooperative movement only dates back to the 1950s and to the Panyachat era. A Department of Cooperatives was created in 1953 under the Ministry of Agriculture to promote and to assist the development of these organizations. The very first microfinance cooperatives date from the early 1960s (to provide flood victims with access to financial services in Rapti Valley, Chitwan District).

In the early 1960s Sājhā Swāstha, for the health sector, and Sājhā Yātāyāt, for public bus transportation, were set up to provide efficient and affordable services. At roughly the same time, a number of cooperatives for agricultural development, for the purchase of farm supplies, especially fertilizers, seeds, livestock feed, and for marketing agricultural products, were created in rural zones. These organisations still exist today, even if they have suffered institutional upheavals and have undergone significant changes over the years. Sājhā buses, for instance, resumed their regular services in 2013 after being suspended for twelve years. However, today it is no longer a state-owned company.

In fact, up until 1990, the government controlled most of these cooperatives. At state level, a key figure in this respect is Bishwa Bandhu Thapa, the half-brother of B.P Koirala. He is considered to be the father of *sājhā-sahakārīs* in Nepal. It was only in 1992, after the restoration of multiparty democracy, that an act (Cooperative, *Sājhā sahakārī*, Act) was passed to grant farmers and all other citizens the freedom to set up and run cooperatives as they liked. In 2004, there were 2,978 multipurpose cooperatives in Nepal. This figure rose to 27,000 in 2014, most of which are autonomous, administratively independent structures. Today, more than 410,000 people are directly engaged in this sector and some 3 million persons are so far affiliated to these associations. The government recently (2013) declared cooperatives one of the three pillars of the Nepali economy. The term *sahakārī* has little by little suplanted the older term *sājhā*.

The number of financial microfinance cooperatives has grown exponentially over recent decades (since 1990) and this phenomenon is particularly striking in urban areas. Today nearly every Newar Bahah Buddhist community in Lalitpur has its own cooperative which parallels and complements the more ancient, traditional *guthi* organisations in charge of festivals, rituals and religious music. This is a remarkable feature of contemporary life in Nepal. These associations are also prominent in rural areas (in some villages there are more than three cooperatives) but in these cases *sahakārī* hold a lower level of deposit capital compared to cooperatives in cities, and they are mainly limited to small projects.

This expansion is part of a wider development of micro-credit that started in Bangladesh in the 1990s and spread throughout South Asia over a short space of time. However, current Nepali urban *sahakārī*s have been somewhat diverted from their initial microfinance objectives of alleviating poverty, stimulating sustainable economic growth, closing the gender gap, and winning the fight against moneylenders. In the Kathmandu Valley, they have become purely financial enterprises used by the urban middle class who lives well above the poverty line. Their members use them as a way of obtaining easy credit without having to go through all the usual formalities. In fact, it is a more communal and profitable way of handling financial matters than using the services of a bank. *Sahakārī* are indeed in direct competition with private and public banks, even though a link does exist between the two sectors (cooperative capital, for instance, is often placed in banks).

In 2014, I carried out a study on these financial cooperatives in Lalitpur and Kathmandu districts, mostly in urban areas, but also in some rural communities. The cases I chose to study concerned both Newars and Parbatiyās. Let me quote some figures to illustrate the extent of the phenomenon. In 2014, in the district of Lalitpur [total population: 468,132] there were altogether 1,071 cooperatives. Whereas credit cooperatives represent more than 50 per cent of these, agricultural cooperatives constitute only 10 per cent of them. Cooperatives exist in each and every one of the 41 VDCs (Village Development Committees) in the district. These data were obtained from a government body based in Lalitpur which oversees and monitors these societies. Out of these 1,071 cooperatives, only four per cent are facing financial difficulties. The others have continued to run a successful business. Yet most of the persons concerned reported difficulties in paying back the loans.

In the seven urban *sahakārī*s studied, the number of members ranges between 330 and 1,800. The interest rate can be as much as 14 per cent for long-term deposits (5 years) and seven per cent in other cases, with few variations here and there. It can sometimes reach 15 per cent, which is much more than banks offer. Most members subscribe to a voluntary savings (*bacat*) scheme on a monthly basis but some retailers place money on a day-to-day basis or on a weekly basis to maximise their gains. It is possible to save money in more than one *sahakārī*. Yet as soon as a loan has been taken out, this option no longer exists; the borrower is under the obligation to limit his membership to one cooperative.

In the cooperatives I have studied, loans (*udhāro*) can reach NPR one to ten *lākh*s (one *lākh*: 100,000), though the sum of money borrowed is usually much less. The interest rate (*byāj*) stands at about 18 per cent, with some differences depending on the purpose of the loan (if for education costs, this may be subjected to a lower rate) and the expected credit. The rules differ from one organization to another. Loans are never given for a long period of time. A land mortgage can be taken out as a security deposit in coordination with the Malpot (Land Revenue) Office. In most cases, people are ready to pay a little more interest at cooperatives than at banks. Values such as mutuality, trustfulness, and cooperation are crucial not only in rural zones but also in cities.

A cooperative's capital amounts to 2 to 24 crores *(karod)* (one *karod*: 10,000,000 Nepali rupees). Each cooperative is presided over by a Board of Directors made up of seven, nine, or eleven persons, among whom a chairman is elected. Its most active members meet at an annual general assembly. A festive event (banquet or reception) is generally organised on this occasion. The seats on the committee are regularly put up for election and there is therefore a large turnover. The sector in which each *sahakārī* operates is limited to a restricted territory (generally two to four VDCs or urban wards). As soon as members become shareholders, they are allowed to take part in internal elections. Most of these organizations do not invest their assets in outside business enterprises; notorious cases of bankruptcy have emerged over the last few years among cooperatives that have been too ambitious and have taken too many risks. Private communal cooperatives are under the obligation to pay taxes to the state (10 to 25 % of their profits).

Membership to these *sahakārīs* is only partly based on caste, ethnic and local bonds. Sociologically, one of their main features is their multi-caste and multi-ethnic makeup. Similarly, they are not attached to one locality alone. Cooperatives have therefore succeeded in breaking away from traditional kin and localised groups. As a matter of fact, cooperatives are mainly economic enterprises; they compete with each other to attract new members.

Let us consider, for instance, the *Hardik Bahu Uddeshya* (Mulitpurpose) *Sahakari,* one of the three cooperatives used by villagers in Pyangaon, a Newar village in Lalitpur District which I have been studying for some years now. This cooperative was set up in 2009. It has a capital of 16 *lākh*s and comprises 280 members who belong to Parbatiyā, Newar and Tamang groups. Its board of directors comprises Bāhuns, Chetris, Newars and Tamangs. Similarly, this cooperative does not have exclusive links with a single locality (25 members are inhabitants of Pyangaon). Loans are granted at a 14 to 19 per cent interest rate, mainly for small agricultural activities (rearing goats and buffalo, *tarkāri* vegetable cultivation, poultry farming) but also to develop small businesses.

This is not an exceptional case and may be regarded as representative of the 72 cooperatives that exist in the Chapagon area.[14] According to most people, cooperatives, wherever they are, have considerably raised villagers' standard of living. They have commercialized agriculture and opened new avenues to non-agricultural activities.[15]

There is a strong belief in official circles and among experts that cooperatives do not have any bearing on Dalits (ex-untouchables) and only marginally involve women. This is only partly true. During my study, I came across two cases of women's cooperatives run by low caste groups. The first one is located in Kumbheshvar, Lalitpur city, mainly among the Khadgīs (Newar butcher caste) community that lives in the locality. Of the 170 women members, 70 belong to the butcher caste, while the others come from the Deulā (Pode), another Newar ex-untouchable caste, and the Shrestha and Jyāpu community. All board members are Khadgīs. Loans are mainly taken out for marriage ceremonies, to build a house, for children's education, and for small business enterprises (shop-keeping, for instance). The organization also finances training courses for its members in various fields of activity.

The second women's cooperative is situated in Godamcaur a rural area in the south of the Kathmandu Valley mainly in habited by Parbatiyā castes. It is called *Godamchaur Dalit Mahila Krishi Sahakari* and has been run exclusively by local Sārki (cobblers, a Dalit caste) women since 2012. In 2014, two years after it was created, it boasted 50 members. Its capital amounted to NPR 172,000. The cooperative grants loans at an interest rate of 13 per cent. Savings, which are are remunerated at 8 per cent, have mainly been used to build a water-tank (costing NPR 600,000) and to supply irrigation on *bāri* (non-irrigated) land (Sārkis in this area do not have *khet* irrigated land). They have also served to cultivate tomatoes, cucumbers, pumpkins, and other vegetables in the dry season and to buy the relevant fertiliser (potassium). When sold in winter, these products can be sold at a higher price on the market and thus bring in more income. The raised tank was completed in 2014. Sārki women complain that their husbands look at this enterprise with suspicion and try to control it indirectly.

Private voluntary community-based cooperatives have met with enormous success among Newars who have long been used to dealing with money and to carrying out financial transactions. They have not replaced *guthis*, which still exist (in a more or less moribund state) for religious and other formal social purposes, though they do compete with them.[16] This expansion has in many ways secularized Newar society. It has to be noted that in Newar urban wards and Buddhist *bāhāls*, informal saving groups also exist (often called *samūha*) parallel to microfinance cooperatives. These self-help groups are not registered by the government.

More general remarks might be made about how this situation has impacted Nepali society. All over Nepal, the somewhat uncontrolled development of savings and credit cooperatives has weakened old social rules. It has created new networks based on purely contractual, optional bonds and prompted an autonomisation of the economy in other sectors of life.

These mutual aid associations, which are extremely diversified, reinforce grass-roots social bonds and intermutual trends in society and the economy. Moreover, such a communalization of economic services underpins the weakness of the state at local level even though the government is currently trying to retain control over this sector and to impose new regulations (*The Himalayan Times*, 17 May 2014). Note that financial cooperatives differ considerably from *dhukuti*, a lottery system that is used among groups of friends. Despite being outlawed by the government, *dhukuti* goups still exist here and there. According to Nepal Rashtra Bank, in 2012-13 transactions worth NPR 5 billion were made under this hazardous scheme.

86. Culture as a Resource

Since the 1990s, UNESCO has repeatedly warned successive Nepali governments about a growing loss of authenticity and integrity in the seven Kathmandu Valley "Monument zones" which feature on the prestigious World Heritage List (WHL). Experts from the international organization have pointed a finger at uncontrolled urbanisation and the erosion of heritage-related values in the Valley. They highlight a strong tendency to demolish traditional houses and to build new ones using more hybrid forms and materials. The rivers, streets, squares, chowks and other constructions do obviously need to be protected from pollution and degradation. Official reports also deplore the fact that privately owned ancient monuments are not being protected. Consequently, in 2003, the cultural branch of the UN decided to inscribe the seven outstanding sites on the "World Heritage in Danger" list. It strongly recommended that the state government redefine the core and buffer zones of these sites. In addition, it urged the authorities to put a stop to illegal activities and to ensure adequate conservation measures to protect the temples.

This decision generated great unease among the Nepali authorities. Tourism is one of Nepal's key industries, making up four per cent of the country's GDP. It brings in the second biggest foreign income after the remittances that Nepali citizens working abroad send back home. The seven famous architectural complexes were inscribed on the WHL in 1979. Together with Lumbini, Sagarmatha and Chitwan National Park, they constitute a major attraction for tourists from all over the world. Featuring on UNESCO's World Heritage list naturally leads to an increase in the number of visitors to the country and in its revenue.

It is difficult to foresee UNESCO's future policy after the dramatic 2015 earthquake which destroyed a number of historical monuments in the Kathmandu Valley. According to an estimation carried out by UNESCO, about 60 per cent of the seven World Heritage sites in the Kathmandu

Valley collapsed. It is likely that priority will be given to the rebuilding of temples rather than to anything else.

Over the last four decades the institutionalisation of the notion of cultural heritage through UNESCO's programmes has made possible the safeguard and restoration of thousands of monuments and sites of major importance throughout the world. However, recognition of a cultural site or of an item of intangible culture implies inventorying, labelling, reviving and managing it. At present, these World Heritage monuments and National Parks are the very cornerstone of an industry.[17] These assets and associated activities — including those from specific sectors such as the visual arts, music and film— are more and more important for local communities, and for the nation's export potential.

Let us focus here on cultural aspects. The policy of recognising a site or an item has transformed culture into a politicised issue that comes with high financial stakes. In Nepal, the Ministry of Culture and Tourism, UNESCO, revivalist indigenous groups, universities, and local municipalities are the pillars of this debate. Yet the World Bank, the Asian Development Bank and other inter-state agencies are also key actors in determining the economic viability and sustainability of these programmes. For more or less acceptable reasons, the government has been trying to keep the upper hand and to maintain its prerogatives.

The creation of the World Heritage List has led to open competition between various projects. The different actors jostle for a particular heritage site or practice to be valued above all others and to be ultimately selected. Within the Kathmandu Valley and its surrounding area, Panauti, Khokana, Sankhu, Kirtipur compete with each other to feature on the list. Outside the Valley, several projects, — Muktinath, Gorkha, Lo Manthang, and so forth — have also already been included on the Tentative List. These projects represent an important marker of identity. Their initiators have consequently started intense politicking to secure subsidies. Heritage protocols in particular are subject to lobbying and intrigues.

Remarkably enough, the country's growing cultural preoccupations are not limited to the government, officials and bureaucrats. They also find expression at grassroots level, mobilising a number of NGOs and local associations. The example of Lok Sahitya Folk Society in Patan, presided by Satya Mohan Joshi, the well-known folklorist, may be mentioned. The Nepali Folklore Society (NFS), created more recently by Abhi Subedi and Tulasi Diwas, is another example. Since 2010, NFS has been organising an annual international Folklore Congress at the Nepal Academy, Kamaladi. This meeting has become a vibrant arena for discussion among young Nepali scholars and international academics [Ch. **7**].

A number of other local groups: *Hāmro Panauti*, *Hāmro Panga*, which focus mostly on specific localities, have emerged, mainly among young people. They strive to revive and to galvanize traditions in their village/township, very often in the hope of securing economic advantages in return. These activities testify to the existence of a widespread movement for the preservation of local heritage, both tangible and intangible. In most cases, the programme established by these groups consists of purposeful preservation, sustainable use, and development. By and large, the increasing role tourism plays in the national economy is affecting the course that strategies to develop heritage tourism are taking.

The emerging cultural-heritage-related industry and rising cultural concerns among the population are of prime importance. Monuments are not the only cultural items to lose their authenticity. Popular intangible heritage is also concerned. There is a great risk that this cultural heritage will be dissociated from its living tradition. Indeed, in becoming more and more a means of asserting one's identity or an economic resource, culture tends to be dispossessed of its vitality.

Critical attention must be given to the growing role of tourism in these matters. Tourism promoted by local and state bodies creates an economic setting in which cultural forms often come ready packaged as market commodities. In fact, tourism tends to merchandize culture and to commoditize — i.e. reduce to a mere commodity— its items or activities. It has a propensity to subsume culture under the category of a mercantile necessity. Numerous examples from Nepal can be given, from traditional dance performances in hotels to tourist artefacts sold on markets. In most of these cases, cultural elements become meaningless for their primary users. The original meaning is replaced by global consumerist culture. Culture is no longer a shared bond, a source of belonging; it is transformed into a marketable item. Local customs have become mere tourist attractions to generate revenue.

87. The Politics of Earthquakes

In matters of foreign aid, a love/hate relationship exists between the Nepali government and outside help. Historical records on the recent post-Rana period readily substantiate this assessment. To put it bluntly, foreign money is always welcome but local authorities strive to maintain direct control over it and to negotiate strict partnerships with the governments and agencies concerned. Expatriate developers living in Nepal frequently criticize such a position that puts them in a somewhat awkward situation. They blame opaque management in channelling financial aid. Yet the local population often reproaches these experts and administrators for making big earnings on their backs. Foreign expatriates are often described as "fat cats" who are totally indifferent to accountability, transparency and good management.

Moreover, there is a widespread belief among Nepali citizens that this aid simply makes Nepali *netāharu* politicians even richer than they are now and that it never benefits ordinary people. These ideas are deeply ingrained and sometimes prove to be true. Misunderstandings arising from these conflicting views are common. This is certainly an acute and extremely sensitive issue in a country where foreign aid represents a fourth of the government's annual budget. Three quarters of the annual budget for health, education and infrastructures come from overseas development assistance.

The 2015 earthquake bears out once more this lesson. The massive foreign aid that arrived from developed countries across the globe at the tiny Tribhuvan International Airport was accepted. Compared to Myanmar's response in the aftermath of Cyclone Nargis in 2008, when the country refused any outside help despite evidence of its enormous needs which the government was unable to meet, this ready acceptance of international assistance by Nepali authorities is remarkable. But foreign rescue teams were rapidly invited to leave the country and were given a strict deadline. Some of them could not complete their mission for this reason. Firm guidelines were drawn up whereby international aid from non-government organisations (NGOs) had to go through the Prime Minister Sushil Koirala's Disaster Relief Fund and to meet the standards set by the government. Any direct assistance with no authorisation was prohibited.

As far as foreign military assistance was concerned, three Royal Air Force Chinook helicopters were denied entry into Nepal and the United States Air Force aircrafts were firmly invited to return home as soon as possible. K.P. Oli, the leader of the powerful communist UML Party, and the new prime Minister, openly disapproved of foreign countries' show-off attitude in the name of assistance: "Foreign dogs ate foods worth Rs. 100, 000 daily and also digested equal amount of allowance. But they did nothing more than sniffing some holes" *(Kantipur*, May 2015). His insistence on playing down the role of foreign aid was apparently shared by various circles.

In Nepali leaders' eyes, these issues are a matter of sovereignty and of national pride. Western-born ideologies of forced intervention all over the globe in the name of citizen rights and humanitarian causes encounter local resistance. These goodwill ideologies beyond national boundaries in matters of justice, medical assistance, economic reconstruction, emergency architecture and so forth, particularly in times of crisis, are not looked upon favourably.

Viewed from a local perspective, the notion of global citizen seems to be definitively abstract, and full of infringements. International agencies are more often than not regarded with suspicion. They are often accused of imposing external norms that are ill-adapted to Nepali realities and of not listening to the people first. They are also sometimes blamed for having fuelled ethnic and caste divisions by supporting an inclusion agenda.

Foreign interference in an emergency situation therefore questions the country's political independence. Chinese and Indian intrusion on Nepali territory, especially near the southern and northern borders in the aftermath of the earthquake was, for instance, a serious concern for the Nepali Army. After all, India never accepts foreign assistance in the case of natural disasters on their territory (2001 Gujarat earthquake or 2004 massive tsunami). The Indian authorities claim that they are capable of providing their own rescue services. The problem is that Nepal does not have the same economic resources and infrastructure as India: it is one of the poorest states on the planet. The 2015 losses were too overwhelming for Nepal to manage alone. During the international donor conference held in Kathmandu on 25 June 2015 to collect aid for post-quake reconstruction, the Nepali authorities sought to collect about USD 6.6 billion in aid.

Another problem is that Nepali bureaucrats and politicians are not known for their efficiency in matters of national development and of responding to the needs of their citizens. Nepal, it must be remembered, ranks high in the global corruption index. The fear of the misuse of foreign aid is foremost in everybody's mind. The unilateral decisions of Nepal's government in the wake of the earthquake therefore engendered tension and clashes with foreign donors and international agencies, such as the UN. The relationship of trust between the two parties rapidly deteriorated.

These difficulties need to be viewed in the long-term. What happened after the January 1934 earthquake? Nepal was cut off from the rest of the world at that time. Maharaja

Juddha Shamsher Rana allowed no foreign aid to enter the country, whether direct or indirect. He announced an "earthquake victim relief organization" and an accompanying fund but he refused to accept donations from British, Indian and Japanese governments. He only accepted donations from foreign organisations and individuals. This determination to remain self-reliant has always been rooted in Nepali policy. It is still defended by the Nepal Army (Sam Cowan, *The Record*, 10 June 2015) as well as by a number of civil servants and personalities across political party boundaries.

However, in this period of suffering, death and destruction, government enforcement regarding foreign aid appears somewhat derisory when compared with the extraordinary community spirit, volunteerism and social consciousness that the earthquake engendered throughout the country. A great number of initiatives came from below, especially from the younger generation, by ignoring political and caste lines, simply with the aim of rebuilding the country. Taking responsibility for their own fate, they distributed tents, food, and clothing to the more disadvantaged sections of the population. These volunteers collaborated with villagers to build earthquake-resistant houses using locally sourced materials. A number of teams made up of the young sons and daughters of the urban middle classes went spontaneously to destroyed Tamang villages in the surrounding area to help distribute relief supplies in an egalitarian manner. In a number of districts, these endeavours proved very effective and, in some cases, they even served as a substitute to local official bodies. This is not to say that official security forces remained inactive. Everybody knows that they did their job in an admirable, selfless manner.

To conclude, I would say that, though the 2015 earthquake revealed a nationalist spirit and sometimes xenophobic feelings among high-ranking government officials, it has more than anything else brought to light serious disparities and dysfunctions between the people and the highest spheres of the state. Nepal needs a new political elite, a redistribution of income by implementing a sound system of taxation and, last but not least, mechanisms to empower the people. Otherwise the foreign aid budget for relief will have simply served to strengthen the existing oligarchic political system.

Notes

1 Cf. Devendra R. Pandey, "The Legacy of Nepal's Failed Development", in Sebastian von Einsiedel, David Malone & Suman Pradhan, *Nepal in Transition, From People's War to Fragile Peace*. Cambridge: Cambridge University Press, 2012, pp. 79-99.

2 For more optimistic views, see Sujeev Shakya, *Unleashing Nepal. Past, Present and Future of the Economy*. Delhi: Penguin Books, 2009.

3 Sujeev Shakya, "Enleashing Nepal's Economic Potential: A Business Perspective", in Sebastian von Einsiedel, David Malone & Suman Pradhan, *Nepal in Transition, From People's War to Fragile Peace*. Cambridge: Cambridge University Press, 2012, pp. 114-128.

4 Great caution should be taken with regards these figures since there is a considerable informal sector.

5 D. Pandey, *idem*, p. 85.

6 Ramesh Suman & Keshab Goutam, "Agrarian future(s) in rural Nepal: revitalizing peasant agriculture", *Himalaya*, vol. 35 (1), pp. 65-90. Cf. also Olivia Aubriot and Tristan Bruslé, "Agriculture paysanne népalaise et phénomènes migratoires: de la complémentarité à la rupture des liens", *Autrepart*, 2012/3 (62) pp. 141-158.

7 *Cf. Central Bureau of Statistics, Population Monograph of Nepal, 3 vols.* Kathmandu, 2014, vol.2, p.7.

8 Kunda Dixit, "Votebank and Constitution", *Nepali Times*, 24 August 2015.

9 For a presentation of the rural economy of Tamang villages in a hill/mountain region of North Dhading in the early 1980s, cf. Gérard Toffin, "Système agro-pastoral et société dans une zone montagneuse à grands versants du Népal central", *Techniques et Culture*, 7, 1986, pp. 1-40.

10 John Welpton, *A History of Nepal*. Cambridge: Cambridge University Press, 2005, quoting a World Bank report. The figures date from the early 2000s.

11 Cf. Carole Mc Granaham, "The hills of Nepal are crying but why aren't we listening", *http://savageminds.org/2015/05/04*, and Philippe Ramirez, "Visite à Salme, 27-31 août 2015", internal report, CNRS, Centre for Himalayan Studies, 2015.

12 Cf. Gwylim Beckerlegge. *Swami Vivekananda's Legacy of Service: A study of the Ramakrishna Math and Mission.* Delhi: Oxford University Press, 2006, and "Seva (service to humanity): a boundary issue in the study of recent and contemporary movements", *Man in India*, 91 (1), pp. 39-56.

13 See R. Srivatsan, *Seva, Saviour and State: Caste, Politics, Tribal Welfare and Capitalist Development*. Delhi: Routledge, 2014.

14 By way of comparison, about 40 cooperatives operate in the small city of Panauti (about 10,000 inhabitants), Kabrepalanchok District.

15 To compare with India, cf. Isabelle Guérin, "Microfinance et empowerment des femmes : La révolution silencieuse des femmes aura-t-elle lieu ?", *Finance et Bien commun*, 2006 (25), pp. 76-82.

16 For the *guthi* system among Newars, cf. G. Toffin, *From Kin to Caste. The Role of guthi in Newar Society and Culture*. Kathmandu: Social Science Baha, 2009.

17 Recently, cf. Micheal Falser & Monica Juneja (eds.) *'Archeologizing Heritage?' Transcultural Entanglements between Local Social Practices and Global Virtual Realities*. Heidelberg: Springer, 2015.

Epilogue

By drawing examples from a wide array of topics, I have tried in the previous pages to portray, as faithfully and exhaustively as possible, a picture of contemporary Nepal and Nepali people. My endeavour, based on personal experience, fieldwork and readings, has not only been to draw a panoramic view of the changing faces of the country but also to provide an appropriate conceptual and theoretical framework to understand them. To achieve this objective, I have juxtaposed micro and macro studies, both past and present. My prime aim was to put into perspective socio-cultural data by introducing comparisons with other countries and with various periods of history. To take just one example, I have tried to show that the heated debate on the structure of the state cannot simply be reduced to a politician struggle between federalist forces (namely Ādivāsī/Janajāti, Māobādīs, and Madhesīs) and anti-federalists (Nepali Congress and UML)) [**11**], or between progressive and reactionary positions. The opposition lies deeper: it involves geopolitical issues and reflects different conceptions of democracy/state that cannot be caricatured as being either utterly bad or good.

The reader must have realized by now that, rather than a pompous and forever-disputable global theory, my inclination is towards a multifaceted picture in keeping with the complexities of reality. It is no coincidence that I quote Karl Popper, an empiricist, at the beginning of this book. Empiricism is tenable when its predisposition to fragmentation is compensated by general ideas. I am not in favour of theories that claim to systematically grasp the whole reality within one philosophical system or from one central vantage point, as Marxism for instance did [cf. Chap. **10**]. These tyrannical globalizing discourses should be rejected and substituted with more pluralist and multi-focus types of analyses, as I have illustrated in this book. As far as my own line of thought is concerned, I fall in with Michel Foucault. It is a well-known fact that this philosopher taught us the inhibiting effect of global, totalitarian theories. He rejected single analytical frameworks. He preferred to study the emergence of modern society and the constitution of the modern subject from the perspective of different disciplines and optics. The plural nature of phenomena must always be privileged. However, contrary to the postmodernist school, I contend that the researcher should identify structures and intelligibility in the endless flux of meaning. He must strive to seize forms of regularities, relations, and continuities that do actually exist. Similarly, macro-forces, whether pertaining to the economic or the demographic domain, cannot be neglected.

To bring this book to a close, I propose a series of five additional texts which broaden the perspectives addressed so far and illustrate the two interlinked themes that I have developed throughout the volume: relationships between change and continuity on the one hand, and between imagination and realities on the other. The first text is a review of the recent book by Prashant Jha, *Battles of the New Republic,* which traces recent political events in Nepal, especially the Maoist episode. I take this opportunity to clarify, as far as possible, my position in the current political debate. The second piece is a critical view of the opposition between tradition and modernity in the light of Joseph R. Gusfield's article dated 1967. I demonstrate why the opposition "open versus closed" society, which is outlined at the beginning of the book, is far more appropriate than the highly disputable paired opposites, "tradition versus modernity". The third text addresses feminist issues, which are a major source of change and discussion in contemporary Nepali society. The fourth essay deals with imagination in the religious realm through the theme of power. It is mainly limited to a traditional context. The final essay turns to more contemporary forms of the work of imagination in Nepali society, and beyond.

88. The Demise of the Red People

While in Kathmandu in July 2015 to attend the Fourth Annual Conference on Nepal and the Himalayas organised by Social Science Baha three months after the earthquake, I took the opportunity to read Prashant Jha's *Battles of the New Republic* which was published in India in 2014.[1] The book, penned by a journalist who worked for a long time for the *Nepali Times* and *Himal*, is an account of the recent historical period from 1990 to 2013, especially of the troubled years of the Maoist insurgency (1996-2006). It is a well-documented work, written in a colourful journalistic way. It provides a coherent narrative of the chaotic political events of the period and throws light on certain controversial and undocumented issues. The author, a committed journalist born in the eastern Tarai, had personal contact with most of the leaders at the time. He covered key events, including Nepali dignitaries' official trips to India and semiprivate statements made in the Indian Embassy in Kathmandu (which Nepalis commonly refer to as Dilli Darbar). Prashant Jha was able to take part in a number of closed-door meetings of politicians and to interview a wide range of persons. He does not write from the perspective of a distant observer: he gives his own views and makes known his personal disposition towards left-wing parties but without twisting the account in an exaggerated manner. *Battles of the New Republic* will no doubt become a key reference for understanding the political history of Nepal. Personally, I enjoyed it very much and learnt a lot from its detailed factual account.

My main ambition here is to focus on a series of points that the above-mentioned book clarifies and which I regard as all-important. Most of them concern the Māobādīs' endeavours during the insurgency and their attempt to seize power. First of all, what about the relationship between Baburam Bhattarai and Pushpa Kamal Dahal, alias 'Prachanda', the two historic leaders of the movement? It is widely known that each of them embodies a different school of thought among Maoists: a rather moderate, balanced path for Bhattarai, and a more radical revolutionary one for Prachanda. The rivalry and temperament of these two characters—on the one hand the intellectual theorist, a graduate from Jawaharlal Nehru University, Delhi, and on the other hand the populist hardliner, often accused of being a demagogue—sometimes jeopardised the unity of the movement, especially after 2001 when Prachanda expelled Bhattarai from the supreme authorities of the People's War. In September 2015, Baburam Bhattarai left the party for good.

What Prashant Jha effectively explains is that both were born into lower-middle-class families, at about the same period, to upper-caste Bāhun parents from the hills, and that from the very beginning they adhered to two opposite branches of the communist movement: the circumspect Masal for Bhattarai, the more radical Mashal for Prachanda (p. 15). Jha shows that, in the long run, they need each other and that a radical split between the two would mean the end of Māobādīs in Nepal. However, when propelled to the office of Prime Minister in the post-2008 period, both failed in their fight for a Marxist democracy and an inclusive "new Nepal". Neither of them was able to promulgate a constitution when they were in power. *Battles of the New Republic* also makes mention of Mohan Vaidya 'Kiran', the third historic leader who, like Prachanda, comes from Mashal. This third figure, the more radical and dogmatic of the three, rejects the democratic path [**68**]. The book recounts his arrest by the Indian authorities in 2001 in Siliguri (p. 92), a capture that does not seem to be imputed to a betrayal from his comrades. Unfortunately, the narrative does not succeed in portraying his character as fully as the first two.

The second issue is the notorious flexibility of Māobādīs to adjust to mainstream political arrangements throughout the given period. Were Maoist leaders really ideologically committed to communism or were their battles merely a power game? What were they fighting for: a change in society by replacing at the head of the state one class ("the comprador bourgeoisie", *dalāl punjīpati*)[2] with another class (the exploited people), or simply a share in state power? This is a vital question. Did Prachanda and Dahal mobilise guerrillas, putting the latter's lives at risk just to rule the country or were they really committed to changing the exploitive economic conditions of the great majority of Nepalis? The book does not explicitly answer the question but it presents strong arguments in favour of the first of these options. The Māobādīs had read more Lenin than Marx. They were committed to realpolitik calculations from the very beginning. They made use of people's dreams about a new, unleashed egalitarian society to seize power. The resistance of what Jha calls "regressive forces" — the king, Nepali Congress, the Communist Party, and India— does not fully explain their failure.

The military success of the Maoists during the first years of the insurgency was the result of a combination of various factors: the Māobādīs clearly took advantage of the mountainous topography and of the limited presence of the state, especially in the mid-western hills. Moreover, they received direct support from hill-dwelling ethnic groups that had long felt abandoned by the state and were helped by the absence of any strong reaction form government forces in the preliminary wartime period. They won important battles against the police and the army, they inflicted great casualties (but they were also defeated on other occasions) and they succeeded in taking direct control of a series of districts in the hills, especially in the west. But what precisely was their military capacity? Referring to the works of General Sam Cowan, an expert on these technical issues, Prashant Jha concludes: the Maoists simply did not have the firepower in terms of weapons and ammunition to seize state power and to overcome government military forces. The PLA (Maoist People's Liberation Army) could win combats of a guerrilla type but they did not have the capacity to progress to conventional warfare. They were therefore forced to downscale their aspirations. More than anything else, this statement explains their change of strategy in 2004-5: their Thermidorian turn and their "revisionist" acceptance of democratic competition with other political parties [**68**].

Their resources were, after all, extremely limited. This is also an important point which is underlined in the book under review. Māobādīs ("the Red People", *rāto mānche*) have never been backed by a powerful neighbouring communist country. China was in the expectative, fearful that Nepal would be thrown into a state of unrest, which would force India to interfere. The USSR, which collapsed in 1990 after the fall of the Soviet empire, was no longer in a position to help. Some Indian agencies tried to show that Māobādīs were receiving ISI Pakistan secret military aid but no proof was ever found. Up until 2001, India let the Maoists circulate more or less freely within their territory but did not supply arms to them. In fact, Maoists relied largely on extorting money, so called 'donations', and on looting banks and financial institutions. "In India, the migrant community was tapped, as were Nepalis in the rest of the world —workers in the Gulf and sympathizers in Europe" (p. 48). They armed themselves mainly after successful battles with weapons taken from government stocks.

The most captivating part of the book is perhaps when it deals with the relationship between Māobādīs and the Indian government, including its various secret agencies. Much speculation has been made about these links. Admittedly, as stated by Jha: "At no point did [the] dialogue cease [...] between any of the key stakeholders — the Maoists and [the] political parties, the Maoists and the king and the parties, during the conflict" (p. 43). And one might add: nor between the Maoists and India. A number of secret meetings were held in Delhi between Māobādī insurgents and Indian officials. One of the primary motivations of the Indian government in engaging with Nepali Maoists was to break the nexus between the Naxals (Indian Maoists) and Nepali Maoists (p. 117). "They facilitated a deal between the Nepali parties and the Nepali Maoists in Delhi to present a role model to the Naxalites" (p. 117). On the other hand, the border between India and Nepal is notoriously porous along its 1,700 kilometres and is difficult to control. "By his own admission, Prachanda spent eight out of the ten years of the insurgency in various cities and towns of India" (p. 29). Yet after 2001, everything changed: India declared that Maoists were "terrorists" (p. 49). They were actively pursued and, if captured, thrown into jail. This is not a brand new conclusion but needs to be reasserted: India is "an integral component of the political structure of Nepal" (p. 65).

By and large, India's intervention in Nepal's political troubles proved crucial at various moments during the period in question and after the Nepali Republic had been established. It is worth noting that Delhi abandoned King Gyanendra and the Shah monarchy after the 2005 royal coup and played a major role in the constitution of the Seven-Parties Alliance against the king. Jha demonstrates in a most convincing manner the determining role of India in the trial of strength between Prachanda and the Nepali Army (NA) in May 2009. The Indian Army and the Nepali Army enjoy historic fraternal links. Delhi considers in a somewhat imperious manner that, for security reasons, these issues fall directly within its jurisdiction in the event of possible Chinese interference. "NA is an extension of [the] Indian Army's security architecture" (p. 79). Delhi rightly suspected the Māobādīs of wanting to take control of the army and of subverting the institution from within. When Prachanda dismissed the Nepali Army chief General Rukmangad Katawal, the Indians consequently decided that the Māobādīs had crossed the redline. Prachanda was obliged to resign from the office of prime minister.

Battles of the New Republic is indeed a rich source of information. Book III in particular retells a breathtaking account of the 2007 Nepali Tarai rebellion (*āndolan*) after the killing of a young protestor, Ramesh Mahato, in Lahan (Siraha District). Prashant Jha, who is of Maithili origin, makes a clear-cut analysis of the cause of this second post-Maoist insurgency. The divide between plain-dwellers, Madhesīs, and the original hill-dwellers, Pahādis, appears to run hopelessly deep. And the recent period of unrest has heightened this gulf. Politically, Madhesī movements consider Māobādīs to be hill-centric, and perhaps even more so than Nepali Congress and UML because of their association with the myriad Janajāti ethnic hill groups.

However, Prashant Jha's book remains first and foremost a journalistic account (sometimes based on private unverifiable conversations). It is more a chronicle than a history in the proper sense of the term. It does not ponder the underlying causes of the two uprisings—the Maoist and the Madhesī—, and it does not analyse political phenomena in sociological or anthropological terms. No mention is made of the masses and the electors. The course of history is viewed mainly through the relationships between the parties. Many issues are overlooked. The sudden indoctrination of thousands of hill people who enrolled in PLA, for instance, is not addressed, as is the case of the Maoist administration and judicial rule in villages under Maoist control. Admittedly, Jha is better at explaining the Tarai conflict than the Māobādī insurgency, the latter mainly concerning the hills and the mountains. But even in the case of the Tarai, the author does not take all the factors into consideration. He hardly says anything about the specificity of the Tharus (the original habitants of the Tarai), about the hierarchical aspects of Tarai-caste society with its marginalised former untouchables [**62**], about the fragmentation of the Madhesī movement, and about land distribution and ownership. When he speaks about these topics, it is in a brief, almost anecdotal way.

I now come to my major note of dissent. Jha reads the political events that Nepal has faced in the contemporary period as being a conflict between the Right and the Left, the conservative, regressive (sometimes called *mahendrabādi*, from the name of the former king Mahendra) and the progressive (*pragatishil*). In my opinion, these terms are excessively simplistic. My book here, *Imagination and Realities*, shows that things are much more complex to say the least. To regard Māobādīs as progressive is a major mistake. Maoists have driven Janajāti to adopt archaic chauvinist reactionary models, very far from the internationalist stance of communism. They have used ethnic groups for their own strategic purposes, to seize power. What is more, they back secessionist, federal forces in times of war, but when in power, they behave in a more centralist way than any others.

Throughout his book, Jha expresses unbiased sympathy for the Maoist movement, without considering its foremost negative aspects and the basic anti-democratic orientation of Marxist-Leninism, notably in matters of multipartism and freedom of press. He does not take into account the democratic deficit of the Māobādī movement, the brutality (and cruelty) of their People's War [**16**], the disastrous Dahal/Bhattarai government rule in the post-monarchy period, the gradual corruption of their party and its incorporation in the traditional political game. Admittedly, Jha somewhat criticizes the Māobādīs' ongoing tendency to explain events in terms of a conspiracy (for instance, after the 2013 electoral rout), as has been the case in other failed communist revolutions across the world. And, at the end of the book, he blames them bitterly for betraying their PLA (People's Liberation Army) fighters. Nevertheless, he forever associates Māobādīs with what he calls "positive steps in transforming the country". The impartiality of the author may indeed be questioned here.

89. The Old and the New

One of the purposes of this book was to document and analyse changes in Nepal. My intention was not to trace a linear, unidirectional movement from a traditional past towards a modernized future. Such an approach would inevitably reify the realities and would be invalidated. In stark contrast to this, I focus on hybrid configurations, between the old and the new, rupture and resilience. Throughout my analysis, I constantly privilege interactions between these two opposite tendencies, which function dialogically in relation to each other. In many cases, what is commonly called persistence happens to be already reconfigured traditions. The religious field abounds in reformulations based on old schemes. Here I wish to sum up some of my findings in this field.

Sociologists have long regarded modernisation as a process that non-Western societies might adopt only by abandoning their traditional cultures. This binary opposition has rapidly proved to be simplistic and naïve. Social systems are not as homogenous and dichotomously contrasted as these theories might suggest. On the one hand, empirical studies have highlighted the persistency of traditional values all over the world in spite of economic and political changes. The cases of Japan, China, and India immediately come to mind. Nearly everywhere, tradition readily embraces modernity and accompanies it. With its nuclear power and its high-tech industry, India for instance has become a modern state. Yet, in this country, the political debate still mainly opposes traditionalists who are geared towards ancient Indian civilisation in matters of moral values and religion, and the Western-oriented liberal elite.

On the other hand, in the wake of the publication of the book *The Invention of Tradition* by E. J. Hobsbawm, and T.O. Ranger (1983), a number of historians and anthropologists have emphasized the ambiguity of the word "tradition" itself. Customs and culture have been widely used politically through the ages and have been periodically reinvented to meet a particular social need or to target a specific purpose. More fundamentally, the most outstanding philosophers, including those in Western countries, have criticized the positive values and the progressist assessment generally associated with modernity. Michel Foucault regarded the historical process that accompanied this movement from the eighteenth century onwards as being synonymous with new forms of surveillance, totalitarian power, coercive forces and oppression by the state. The history of the twentieth century largely corroborates this analysis, —even though Enlightenment had given birth to many valuable progressive and universal ideas.

In fact, as Joseph Gusfield observed in an often-quoted article dated 1967 mainly about India, so-called traditional societies have never been totally static. The Rana period (1846-1950), which is often seen as immobile, was in fact an era of considerable change in the country, not only as far as laws and politics are concerned but also in the field of art, commodities, society, and economy. The ruling family revolutionized architecture by introducing foreign styles and it imposed a new judicial code in the country. The considerable impact of Islamic civilization on India from the thirteenth century onwards is a well-established fact. Likewise, in Nepal, the conquest of Prithivi Narayan Shah, and the subsequent creation of the unified state of Nepal entailed significant changes in rural and urban areas. The migration of upper Hindu castes towards the east in particular has been accompanied by a general transformation of the rural landscape and of farming techniques. What seems to be immutable needs to be historicized.

The idea according to which pre-modern societies are characterized by a uniform body of standards and values also needs to be rethought. From 1850 until 1950, Nepal's religious authorities stood firm in the face of Hindu reformist movements in which they saw a threat to *sanātana* orthodox Hinduism and royalty. Yet Shaivaism and Vishnuism, Bhakti and Tantric cults have long existed side by side, providing the Hindu population with contrasting views and rituals. Similarly, Hinduism and Buddhism have cohabited in the Kathmandu Valley since Licchavi times and have influenced each other to a certain extent. It would thus be wrong to draw a picture of pre-democratic Nepal as being entirely uniform and controlled by Brahmans from the Royal Palace. The diversity of Nepal has been preserved and sometimes buttressed by Hinduisation. The religion of the literati elite of the Kathmandu Valley and of former *caubīsī* Hindu kingdoms in the hills does not totally fit in with local folk religion—what 1950s American sociologists called "little tradition".

New elements may cohabit more or less harmoniously

with old ones. Consider for example the plurality of medical remedies currently used by local people: modern allopathic medicine has not supplanted traditional healing techniques, Āyurvedic remedies or the use of possessed intercessors to bring back the stolen soul of the sick. All these different therapeutic systems are used concurrently. Though Western medicine has proved its own efficacy, the ritual songs of the *jhānkris* still prevail. Likewise, as I have shown, modern art has not destroyed traditional artistic forms [**39**] even if practitioners have taken different paths. The two schools have to be taken together. Modernism is not the antithesis of tradition. As demonstrated in the preceding pages, the advent of individualism as the hub of society (rather than of the community, ethnic group, or caste) has not killed off communitarian forms of belonging.

Indeed, new elements may reinforce traditional elements. The politics of quotas, widely practised in India and recently implemented in Nepal, has the pernicious effect of reinforcing the caste system and of strengthening caste associations [**77**]. In these cases, the old is preserved but is nonetheless transformed (castes have been substantialized and transformed into corporate protest groups), as a number of scholars have pointed out. The same phenomenon can be observed in the religious sphere. The success of yoga, of new *bābās* and new religious syncretistic organisations obviously meet the aspirations of new modernized sectors of society which feel disorientated by modernisation. Individuals turn to traditional elements and forms of authority to allay unfamiliar forms of tension in daily life. Yoga and meditation belong to an old Indian spiritual heritage but they have been largely reinvented and revitalized over the last decades in response to globalization and to changes in society. Modernisation does not necessarily weaken non-Western religions.

Tradition and modernity therefore have to be studied side by side. Modern ideas can be used to reinforce old elements or to invent a new tradition on the basis of fragmentary elements. In Chapter 2 [**9**], I explained for instance how the Western idea of independent national state and its concomitant nationalist expression are currently used by indigenous groups to claim autonomy and control over their natal homeland. Nationalism has engendered various forms of separatism. The revival of indigenous ethnic traditions that has taken place in Nepal since 1990 needs to be analysed in close connection with the recognition of the rights of autochthonous people by international associations. Tradition is an efficient weapon for resisting Westernization and the sudden rise of the individual.

The brief Maoist odyssey in Nepal can be seen as a hybrid social movement. It combined universalistic ideologies ("workers of the world unite!" the rallying slogan of the *Communist Manifesto*, 1848) with extremely parochial preoccupations [**91**]. This is the reason why marginalized ethnic groups from the hills, practising a mountain type of agriculture and with no knowledge of Marxism, actively supported the insurgency. They ignored the historical role Marx credited to classes as agents of social change. Instead, they fought for better recognition and for a share of power. What's more, Māobādīs greatly benefited from modern media to spread their influence. These new modes of expression reinforced their political propaganda.

The substitution of the monarchy for a republic is a substantial rupture in terms of the mode of government. Yet this radical change conceals a number of continuities. A new world has not been created *ex nihilo;* archaic structures dating from the nineteenth century still prevail in political life and society. The absence of transparency in the government debate and the supremacy of Kathmandu in all affairs are relics of the past. The de-ethnicisation of politics, as proposed in the 2015 constitution (for instance, the de facto ban on ethnic political parties), reinforces such centralistic models. Long-awaited promises proved to be pie in the sky. Furthermore, the system of patronage via leaders of political parties shows a striking resemblance to ancient pre-democratic models. Political parties have merely replaced previous, more or less institutionalized networks. Similarly, in areas controlled and administered by Maoists, changes have proved to be superficial and episodic. Māobādīs have not invented a new social world, nor have they eradicated old customs. Within the few years since the end of the guerrilla warfare, social and agrarian life has largely resumed its old pattern. Furthermore, when wielding power in the post-2008 period, Maoist leaders succumbed to the temptation of benefiting their own party and its cadres, just as other parties had done before them. They readily adopted capitalism along with all its flaws.

Modernity is therefore a much more ambiguous phenomenon than first believed. Westernization has provoked a number of reactions across the world. It has engendered counter-movements seeking a return to tradition or demanding autonomy and sometimes even socially regressive currents. Throughout Nepali society, even in a large part of the elite, the Western way of life, with its individualistic and materialistic values, has been largely rejected, especially as far as women's behaviour and sexual freedom are concerned. Moral traditionalism is still going strong.

Contrary to a dominant intellectual tradition, processes of change have to be seen as a dialectic of continuity and discontinuity rather than as a transition between tradition and modernity. They show a widespread trend to adopt external elements in keeping with local ways and to reinterpret exogenous values according to local patterns. In other words, they illustrate the marked phenomenon of "glocalization" (a portmanteau word combining globalization and localization) which has been described in the literature and in numerous sections of this book [**8**, **14**, **17**, **28**, **38**, **39**, **49**].

A historical break in tradition, like the revolutionary events that Nepal experienced in the period 1996-2006, and the subsequent adoption of a republican system may indeed arouse enthusiasm and great expectations among the people but changes inevitably come with some overlapping between the old and the new. They sometimes engender new forms of hierarchy and subordination. Quite remarkably, the introduction of the principle of universal suffrage and of general elections in the country has, for instance, not drastically challenged the monopoly of rule by a tiny minority of notables.

90. Redefining Gender

Since the 1950s, the status and the traditional role of women in Nepali society have been challenged by feminist groups (feminism is referred to as *nārībād* in Nepali) in a particularly strong manner. By and large, the gender issue has taken on growing importance over the years and has taken centre stage, as proved by the recent debate triggered by the drafting of the new republican constitution about the transmission of citizenship either by father *and* mother, or by father *or* mother. The first option clearly discriminates against *mahilā* (women) and is commonly explained by the fear of a number of Indian-Nepali or simply Indian couples being assimilated into Nepali society, notably in the Tarai plains. Most women, of course, support the second option. Nepali newspapers—whether in English or in Nepali—have given a lot of space to this controversy in their columns and tend to support women's demands. In stark contrast, the general opinion in the highest political spheres is that women activists are influenced by Western culture and that Nepali women who marry a Westerner do this simply to obtain a resident's permit. Marxist-Communist parties are the most conservative in these matters.

Today women are playing a more important role in public society. Thanks to the development of education and to girls' dedication to their studies, women now assume a number of positions in society that were inaccessible in the past. They embark on some professions that were traditionally monopolised by men, for instance in medical, business, education and legal sectors, as well as in the realm of politics. Even the police and the army have started recruiting them, as can be seen in the streets of the Nepali capital, where policewomen are left in charge of traffic control. In farming families, women's voices are gradually being heard both inside and outside the household due to the massive wave of outmigration by men. Their participation in social and community organizations has increased in the absence of their husbands.[3] What is more, some traditional domains such as art, theatre and music, formerly exclusively reserved for men, have become increasingly feminized. And thanks to provisions for proportional representation, women hold 30 per cent of the seats on the Constituent Assembly that was elected in November 2013. A number of women-related stereotypes in Hindu society have therefore been abandoned. And some religious rules, for instance the ban on women touching religious musical instruments, have been dropped.

This is the reason I started research on women's legal issues in 2010. I focused on regulations governing divorce (*pārapācuke*) and on the way matrimonial conflicts are dealt with by judges and lawyers at local tribunals. Divorce is not a new phenomenon in Nepali society—I realised this while studying rural Newar communities in the Kathmandu Valley in the 1970s. These matters were traditionally dealt with locally at village level, with the allocation of financial compensation and the return of *bihā kharca*, the cost of the wedding ceremony. The word 'divorce' was sometimes not even used. The couple separated with the consent of the respective families and of the community, with no further complications. What is indeed new is the growing rate of divorce and the rise in the percentage of remarried couples, especially in urban areas, and the fact that these matters are now dealt with in court.

Unfortunately, totally perplexed when faced with the judicial terminology and the specific legal conventions used in court, I abandoned my study after six weeks of research. To my eyes, the procedures carried out before the judges were all too far-removed from the real lives of the people and do not entirely reflect the real changes that are taking place in society. However, thanks to the brief though aborted study I had undertaken in Lalitpur Adalat, Lagan Khel, I did at least learn two things. Firstly and predictably, family conflicts are being dealt with more and more on a legal level (though not as much as in India). Women's groups are encouraging wives who want to divorce to attempt legal conciliation or to file a court case (which takes much longer) in order to benefit from the advantageous new provisions included in the Code, and in particular those in the 11th amendment (2002) to Muluki Ain.[4] This amendment has significantly improved the legal situation of women, for instance in matters of abortion.[5] Secondly, I came across the growing importance of non-government organisations in the defence of women's rights. I worked, for instance, with one particular association of lawyers, LACC (Legal Aid and Consultancy Centre), registered in 1987, whose specific aim is to facilitate women's access to justice and to introduce judicial changes by lobbying government and political bodies. More globally, its members are fighting for an equitable and just society in Nepal.[6]

I soon realised the centrality of women's associations on a wide range of subjects: economic, judicial, legal, and various other social issues (rape, harassment, trafficking of women abroad, violence, etc.). These groups, which are mostly urban, often include foreign voluntary workers or experts and may be part of more international organizations that defend the rights of women and children. But several NGOs, like LAAC, Maiti and Tewa, are exclusively Nepali. Whatever the case, Nepali women intellectuals and lawyers are predominant in all these groups. This is the case of Mila Dhungana and Sapana Malla-Pradhan, both famous and very influent figures in feminist causes in Nepal. These lawyer-activists relay ideas that diverge from the dominant contemporary norm. Sapana Malla, for instance, became involved in the controversy about the Kumārī child goddess, a topic that I have discussed elsewhere.[7] She questioned the divine role of the Kumārī and stressed the restraints and the privation of freedom in the little girl's daily life. Most of the Newar Buddhist community reacted violently against these objections. Its members saw in the PIL (Public Interest Litigation) filed at the Supreme Court against the Kumārī cult an attack on their community and its culture. It is widely known that Kumārīs are mainly chosen among Shākya and Vajrācārya Buddhist Newar castes.

This leads to the subject of menstruation, a domain where imagination and realities particularly merge. In Hindu society, the menstrual cycle is synonymous with threat and danger to male society and to holy things. The canonical tradition attributes menses to the sins of Indra, especially to Indra's Brahmanicide. One third of the guilt of this god was then transferred to women in the form of menstrual periods, the mark of sin, danger and impurity.[8] It is therefore a curse and a major source of segregation. Monthly periods subject women to isolation, seclusion and the observation of various taboos. Women are driven away from temples, offerings, *pūjā*, and they are not allowed to cook food or to bathe.

In far western Nepal, menses have engendered the *chāupadī prathā* custom according to which menstruating women are shut away for three to seven days in a cowshed set apart from the house.[9] Women stay in this shed, deprived of any form of hygiene. They are forbidden to touch cooking utensils and water taps, to eat fruit, milk, yogurt, butter made from cow and buffalo milk, for fear they will harm these animals and trees, and forever defile these goods. It is impossible for them to attend school where neither toilet facilities nor water are available. At some establishments they even have to sit on their own away from other children. After giving birth, a woman also has to stay in the cowshed. Nobody can touch her for a minimum of fifteen days. These forms of seclusion from society and normal life are a source of despair, fear, and emotional trauma, especially among young wives [**63**]. The custom was outlawed by the Supreme Court in 2005 but is still practised (even among low, formerly 'untouchable' castes). NGOs in the country are striving to stamp out this tradition.

Some time after 2010, Lasanā artivists launched a programme opposed to segregationist practises associated with the monthly cycle and, more generally, in defiance of the despicable conceptions regarding menstruation in Nepali society. In 2010, the leader of the group, Ashmina Ranjit, staged a performance in which she came on stage wearing a dress made entirely of sanitary towels. From a thin tube, she squirted blood (or a coloured liquid?) onto the towels, one at a time, folded them and deposited them in a rubbish bin. She thus created a representation of a menstruating body in public. In the meantime her husband, who was in the audience, was looking after their eight-month-old baby. The show, called "Feminine Force: Celebrating Womanhood", was performed at the *Alliance française* in Kathmandu to celebrate International Women's Day (8 March).[10] This type of action seeks to redefine the role and the image of womanhood in society. It sometimes receives a hostile reaction from the public, yet it contributes to countering menstrual hygiene taboos in Nepal and to destabilizing old religious representations.

91. Power Against Power

Last year, while discussing the state of religion across Asia, one of my Nepali friends suddenly claimed: "Whatever the case may be, your gods cannot do anything against us". This sentence made an enormous impact on me. In fact, it helps me to summarize a wide range of observations (and readings) I have made over the years about religion and the perception of the invisible world in Nepal. More than anything else, the religious landscape in this country is made up of different forces which are embodied in various gods that are mainly identified by their respective inexhaustible powers. It rapidly occurred to me that an essay on this topic should be included in the epilogue to a book principally devoted to the imagination. Such findings possibly apply to neighbouring India as well, or at least to a large part of it. However, this is not the time and place for discussing these links.

Let us consider the Hindu religion which prevails in Nepal. The gods of the Hindu pantheon are mainly defined by their powers. They have the capacity to disguise themselves, to become dwarves or giants at their guise, to perform miracles, to create a storm or a long and severe drought, to transform one object into another. If they are irked, they send down smallpox and other epidemics, they cause earthquakes, they weaken human beings and make them sick. They have control not only over nature but also over fertility. Barren women pray to them for a son. Hindu deities can kill a king in a second if they are unhappy with him or if he commits some offence towards them. And female gods are no less powerful in these domains. On the contrary, Hindu Tantrism, which is widespread in the Himalayas, bestows the most frightening and phenomenal powers on them. It is a well-known fact that *shakti*, power, is by essence associated with womanhood. Moreover, the ability of gods and goddesses to dance and to play music is in itself an expression of their power. That is why various deities are invoked at the time of learning to play drums and other types of instruments. If gods commit a sin, they may temporarily lose their strength. In that case, they have to do penance to restore their lost transcendent capacities. Interestingly, they use their powers not only against humans but also against each other. There are eloquent accounts of their perpetual fights and rivalries in mythology.

The situation is very similar in *jhānkrism*, the religion of Nepali shamans, and with other types of intercessors and healers. All these cults and practices are centred on power. Therapists and ecstatic practitioners are principally defined by their capacity to fight malevolent spirits, witches and other powerful evil spirits that harm common folk, capture their souls and make them sick. These specialists know how to control and overcome these supernatural forces using appropriate weapons and mantras. Shamanic séances frequently turn into theatrical, staged displays of their extraordinary powers (walking over glowing embers, placing burning hot iron tripods in their mouths, and so on) and of their fights to combat sources of afflictions. Without these powers that they have acquired through a long initiation period under the supervision of masters and without an innate knowledge of their enemies, exorcists and shamans would never be able to vanquish evil forces. They are assisted by all sorts of supernatural allies in these battles. They may lead a peaceful secular peasant or herder's life during the day but, when dressed ceremonially at night and playing drums, they become professional and formidable fighters, struggling against invisible forces.

What about Buddhism? The fundamentalist Theravāda vision of peaceful Buddha, filled with compassion for humanity and wholly made up of goodness, does not correspond to Himalayan and Nepali realities. Let us take the example of the Tamang *lāmā*, the Buddhist priest of this ethnic community of Nepal. He belongs to the Tibetan branch, mainly Nyingmapa, of Buddhism. Not only does he preside over death rituals for villagers and determine children's horoscopes when requested, he also wards off hailstorms in spring time, expels evil spirits and fights them, by hurling *shel* crystal rocks into the four corners of space or by firing an arrow at them. In all these rituals, he competes with the exorcising power of the two other Tamang religious specialists; the shaman, *bompo,* and the clan priest, *lambu*. Let us now consider Newar Buddhists who follow a hybrid religion of Mahāyāna and Vajrayāna based on Sanskrit Buddhist medieval texts from India. Their Tantric gods, both male and female, are characterised by their warlike attributes and supernatural powers. According to Buddhist priests, they are even more powerful than Hindu gods because of their Tantric *shakti*.

And last but not least, Nicolas Sihlé recently published a book based on data collected in a Buddhist village located near Muktinath. He highlights the violent Tantric exorcisms of evil spirits and the religious power of their non-monastic *ngakpa* Tantrist priests.[11] These specialists tame demons; their violence and power are showcased in local rituals. We are very far from the erroneous view of a Buddhism entirely based on monasticism, devotion and compassion.

In all these cases, the power of the gods is generally limited to small demarcated territories. Hindu and Buddhist deities do not reign and exercise their supremacy all over the world but over their *kshetra*, i.e., their distinct territory. The same can be said of chthonian supernatural forces, such as *bhūmi devī*, which reside in the hills of Nepal and are propitiated by various local ritual specialists. From a religious point of view, Nepal can therefore be described as a congeries of multiple confined concentric zones that are more or less controlled by a particular tutelary deity. This compartmentalisation of supernatural power prevailed in former small Hindu kingdoms or hill chiefdoms. It still exists today to a large extent. There is, of course, some overlapping since some gods are more powerful than others. Yet within their *kshetra*, local gods are fully in command and leave no room for any competition. As I explained above [**67**], when travelling, even deities from a neighbouring zone have to be careful and to avoid disturbing native divinities. Nepal is a country that is made up of scattered chthonian forces. By and large, this localism, which is specific to polytheist religions, is significantly different from monotheistic religions like Christianity where the supreme god has a more universal outlook and extends his power all over the world, beyond natural and state boundaries.

It is perhaps because of these universalistic leanings that, contrary to what my Nepali friend claimed, Christian gods are sometimes ascribed more power than Nepali gods. This is a controversial issue and I have heard divergent opinions among the persons with whom I have worked on the subject. But among Nepali converts to Catholicism or Protestantism, this is a common belief. In the Nepali context, this is sufficient reason to change from one religion to another. It may be just as important a motive for conversion as the egalitarian message of Christianity, the concept of love associated with godhood, or material commodities distributed by missionaries.

This *emic* view, from the "inside", challenges the distinction made by the sociologist Louis Dumont between status and power in the Indian world. Let us recall that, for Dumont, this separation between rank (Brahmans incarnating the higher values of *dharma*) and secular power (the lower status of Kshatriya kings) is a fundamental characteristic of Indian civilisation and of its hierarchy of values. What has just been said about pantheon and divine power contradicts this dichotomy. The supernatural realm is pervaded with power and is made up of divine powers that vie with each other. Their human servants and counterparts, priests and Brahmans, as well as their human incarnations, such as the Kumārī child goddess, cannot be considered as being deprived of *shakti*. On the contrary, they derive enormous strength and spiritual force from their service and closeness to the gods. Yogīs, who devote their lives to transcendental values, are the very locus and source of supernatural powers which are readily acknowledged and feared. The conjunction of power and status is therefore more consistent with local people's beliefs and religious practices in contemporary Hinduism than the absolute dichotomy between Brahman and Kshatriya that is established in the normative ancient scriptures of *Dharmashāstra*. I have even shown how, in present-day Nepal, it is easy for a Brahman to concretely combine status and power, caste rank and political functions [**79**], and to substitute kings.

Is it possible to deduce further implications from this analysis and to put forward some other comparisons with the secular world? The answer is of course yes, though in a more speculative way. I suggest that a parallel can be drawn between the fragmentation of the geographical space in separate divine territories, *kshetra*s, and the persisting lack of unity of the country at a socio-political level. After all, a federal state granting vast power to its regional subunits may well correspond to the nature of the fragmented conception of divine power, as was the case in the period prior to unification. Current ethno-regional movements may be seen in this light. However, it may be difficult to verify this hypothesis. The diversity of interest groups entrenched in Nepali society and the current mapping of political parties do not fit into this sacred geography. Nevertheless, it closely corresponds to local mindsets. In a culture so impregnated with cosmic conceptions and divine spirits, it is not totally unreasonable to search for religious imagery to conceptualise and to account for relationships between humans. A continuum clearly connects the otherworldly universe and the mundane world.

92. Artificial Realities

Imagination has long played a crucial role in the history of social groupings. The mental appropriation of the wilderness, of its fauna and of other floristic products and, at a later stage, of more a domesticated environment, has always been subject to conceptualisation, symbolization and well-structured logical constructions. Similarly, primal forms of art and performances, music and sculpture have long unleashed the forces of human imagination and have contributed to creating a fictional world. Since the very beginning, the material and the ideal have thus been closely interlinked. They derive their substance from each other. The universe in which humans move around is saturated with signs that can be deciphered only if the appropriate codes have been learned beforehand. This is the basic work of symbolisation. One example of this was given in the previous section [**91**].

However, each technological era produces its specific forms of imaginative patterns and imposes them on the individual mind. Human capabilities are not set in stone; they develop and adapt continuously to new circumstances. The advent of writing on the one hand, and the multiplication and the electronic reproduction of images ad infinitum on the other hand, have somewhat changed our relationship with the empirical world and have considerably increased the role and the strength of imagination in our daily lives. New modern electronic devices have introduced a series of additional mediations that were previously unknown. By and large, the realm of imagination has extended considerably. Even images of the reality, obtained by satellite imagery now need to be preformatted and constructed to represent the tangible world.

In contemporary Nepal we find mainly juxtaposed forms of imagination, partly pertaining to old symbolic forms and, as for the rest, to modernity. In this final piece, I would like to point out some of the more contemporary forms associated with the working of social imagination. Beyond the notion of symbolism, let us focus on the two other meanings of the word "imagination" which were identified at the outset of this book: *ideology* and *fiction*. They are both characteristic of our time.

Political imagination, which sustains ideological constructions, has been one of my favourite themes. In chapter 9, I explored the role of revolutionary ideas and Marxist theories on rising insurgency and guerrillas. Revolutionary rhetoric has its own language built upon a wide array of feelings, the most notable being the sense of being exploited. This conventional rhetoric, disseminated in books, images, and slogans, is used to mobilise all sorts of activists ready to fearlessly sacrifice their lives for the victory of the noble cause in which they have placed all their expectations and dreams. The desire for *tabula rasa*, for a drastic change of life, is one of the most profound and firmly anchored drives behind human acts. Innumerable examples can be found in history since the earliest times.

The repertoire of political imagination includes other topics such as: the passion for equality, the nostalgic quest of a Hindu nation or the progressive idea of a republic. Though the content of the ideas and notions mobilized vary from one extreme to the other, the mechanisms at work are almost the same. Whatever the platform adopted and the slogans chosen, the masses are more often than not manipulated (admittedly less so in democratic regimes) by the ambition of a small number of persons primarily motivated by their own personal interests. The imagery here is instrumental in animating individual thoughts and in inciting legions of followers to use violence against the established order or designated enemies.

Fiction is grounded in different imaginative processes. It nourishes our inner world in an individual and emotional way. It also presupposes the active participation of the receptor, reader or viewer. Novels, which appeared relatively late in the history of mankind, are one of its expressions. In fact, reading fiction is an indicator of modernity. In Nepal, early forms of novels (*upanyās*) and poetry (*kāvya*) emerged in the nineteenth century. They contained religious themes and were replete with ancient canonical forms. Modern novels have only been in existence since the second part of the twentieth century, at the very earliest, and were at first restricted to a small elite. During the panchayat period the production of literature was hindered by censorship.[12] The writing of fictional narratives only really took off from the democratic revolution of the 1990s onwards when there was greater freedom to publish and when the state monopoly on printed media was broken.

The spread of a middle class in urban areas played a major role in the development of fictional literature. This new social stratum has more leisure time than town-dwellers of the past and has shown a growing interest in the modern world. Traditionally, reading was mostly associated with sacred books and religion. It was a ritual act and a form of prayer. It gradually became a secular activity, a way of escaping boredom or the anxiety of everyday life, of taking pleasure in being drawn into a fictional universe. Novels written in Nepali by Nepali authors have been sold and read in wider circles.

Some of these books, such as *Siris ko Phul* or *Palpasa* café [**55**], have become commercial successes. They nourish the imagination and reveal a gradual opening of minds to fictional narratives. In fact, beyond the fascinating ethnographic details and numerous references to contemporary social life they contain, these bestsellers lend major importance to fantasy. My findings, based on a study carried out among the urban middle class over these last years, show that women, and especially young women, constitute the majority of the readership that belongs to a broad category of people ranging between the ages of 20 and 50.

However, the most striking phenomenon in contemporary life has been, in Nepal just as anywhere else, the invasion of seductive images in people's daily lives through new media.

Television has played a vital role in this domain. It has had a considerable impact, especially among children who are the biggest watchers, and has produced a mimetic effect (dress, accessories, fashion, attitudes). Indeed, new mass media have had a powerful effect on prevalent stereotypes, for instance on the way women are represented and idealized. Moreover, rosy images shown on TV make you forget all the worries and hardship of everyday life; they have anaesthetic properties.

Smartphones, the Internet, digital photographs, illustrated newspapers and wireless communication have also contributed to the all-pervading presence of images. Through daily news broadcasts, politics has also become part and parcel of the visual world and is impregnated with powerful images. Everybody in Nepal has, ironically, a mental image of the Maoist leader Prachanda with dozens of garlands of flowers, *mālā*, around his neck or of Madhesī members of parliament vandalizing the Constituent Assembly building! These images are commonly superimposed in the political debate. They find their way into the fabric of our social lives.

Through endless copies, images acquire their own reality that is never questioned. In other words, reproduction techniques have gradually absorbed the original world. Similarly, the visual representation of family rituals in photographs and videos is gaining importance. It allows family members to watch the ceremony again and again with their friends and relations. It creates a new memory of past events. The images become more real than the performed actions. We are shifting from *Homo faber* (Pyangaon farmer village, for instance) to *Homo imaginator*. The basic logical capabilities of the human mind remain the same but a number of additional mediations, screens, between the reality and its conceptualization have been added.

Postmodernist philosophers —Jean Baudrillard for instance, who is often quoted in this field of research— have highlighted an important feature: the artificial reality of images conveyed by new mass media. As a matter of fact, these images have their own generated life and autonomy.

They tend to create representations and signs with no original referent. Hence there is greater confusion between the real and the symbol that represents it. The world we live in is being replaced by a *copy*. The real is put into play. Baudrillard argues that the excessive number of signs and images in the late twentieth century has created an effacement of reality. According to him, the limitless power of image fictionalizes life and blurs the difference between truth and fiction. The true (the real) has started to be reproduced in the image of a *pseudo* (which this French author calls *the imagery*). Reality has been supplanted by an endless procession of simulacrums. The development of virtual reality shows, games and TV series tends to confirm his thesis. The real and the virtual become one and the same thing.

These observations require closer scrutiny. The perception of reality in particular has to be historicized. However, such trends clearly stress how, in our contemporary globalized social space, images have become transient, digitalized and transmittable electronically all across the globe. Indeed, there has been a considerable shift: new images are no longer physically anchored in a specific place; they transcend the locality.[13] The rapid stream of international news and instantaneous financial transactions at the press of a button, as well as the expansion of mobile phones and computers are signs of our time. The flow of people of all nationalities across the world consistently accompanies this flood of images. These phenomena are the sign of profound changes in the apprehension of the world, which has become more interconnected and global. These mutations bear heavily on contemporary Nepali society, in South Asia, and well beyond.

Notes

1 *Battles of the New Republic. A Contemporary History of Nepal*. New Delhi: Aleph Book Company, 2014.

2 In Maoist terms. *Punjīpati* means "capitalist", magnate", *dalāl* is a "broker".

3 Jagannath Adhikari & Mary Hobley, "Everyone is leaving - Who will sow our fields? The livelihood effect on women of male

migration from Khotang and Udayapur Districts, Nepal, to the Gulf Countries and Malaysia", *Himalaya,* 2015, 35 (1), pp. 19.

4 Divorced women can obtain *mānā cāmal*, compensation from her husband's family, or *ansha*, a share of his property.

5 Gérard Toffin, *Newar Society*. Kathmandu: Himal Books, 2010, pp. 385-386.

6 I have already touched upon gender issues in this book in two texts: [**27**] and [**61**].

7 Gérard Toffin, *La fête-spectacle*. Paris: Éditions de la Maison des Sciences de l'Homme, 2010, p. 156-57.

8 See Julia Leslie, *Roles and Rituals for Hindu Women*. Delhi: Motilal Banarsidass, 1992, p. 5.

9 Cf. Shova Shakya, "Chāupadī antya abhiyān" [Campaign against *chāupadī*], *Nagarik Daily*, 9 January 2015, and, about delivery and *chāupadī*: "Sutkeriko surtā" [Parturient women's anxiety], *Nagarik Daily*, 26 September 2014.

10 See Archana Thapa, "Blending the binaries", *The Kathmandu Post*, 3 April 2010.

11 Nicolas Sihlé, *Rituels bouddhiques de pouvoir et de violence. La figure du tantriste tibétain*. Brepols: Bibliothèque de l'École des Hautes Études, 152, 2013.

12 Michael Hutt, "Writers, Readers, and the Sharing of Consciousness: Five Nepali Novels", *Himalaya, the Journal of the Association for Nepal and Himalayan Studies*, 34 (2), 2014.

13 James Curran (ed.), *Media and Society*. London, Bloomsbury, 2011.

Index

A

C

H

I

J

K

L

T

U

V